# REVIEWS OF BOOKS ABOUT HISTORY & HAUNTINGS BY TROY TAYLOR

How does Troy Taylor continue to produce one quality book after another? Perhaps only the spirits know for sure! HAUNTED ILLINOIS is truly another top-notch, in-depth look at the Land of Lincoln. I highly recommend this book to anyone interested in Illinois ghost stories, as it goes to show that ghosts can be found anywhere throughout the state!
DALE KACZMAREK, author of WINDY CITY GHOSTS

Troy Taylor has done it yet again. In HAUNTED ILLINOIS, the author has hit that rare (and delightful) middle ground between fascinating paranormal research and compelling storytelling. His stories will put you on the edge of your seat and his insights into the supernatural will keep you there. A rare and delightful find and a must-read from one of the best ghost authors writing today.
MARK MARIMEN, author of HAUNTED INDIANA and SCHOOL SPIRITS

We have read all the books on Civil War haunts and SPIRITS OF THE CIVIL WAR is the best one ever! It has it all from the history to the hauntings and both familiar and little-known ones. This is a must-read for any Civil War buff and for anyone who believes the war continues on in the afterlife! We're not sure how Troy Taylor's going to top this one... but we'll be waiting!
ROB AND ANNE WLODARKSI, authors of HAUNTED ALCATRAZ and SOUTHERN FRIED SPIRITS

HAUNTED ILLINOIS is a generous introduction to the resident wraiths of one of the nation's most haunted states, from its most prolific ghost writer. This book is a must for natives, ghost hunters and aficionados of Americana and holds captive anyone with an interest in the wonderful experiences so often omitted from the "proper" historical record.
URSULA BIELSKI, author of CHICAGO HAUNTS

THE GHOST HUNTER'S GUIDEBOOK offers a wealth of modern and really valuable information regarding sophisticated detection equipment, investigation procedures and methods... should be essential reading for anyone in the field of paranormal research, whatever their level of interest or knowledge in the subject.
ANDREW GREEN, author of 500 BRITISH GHOSTS & HAUNTINGS

# GHOST BOOKS BY TROY TAYLOR

Haunted Illinois (1999 / 2001)
Spirits of the Civil War (1999)
The Ghost Hunter's Guidebook (1999)
Season of the Witch (1999)
Haunted Alton (2000)
Haunted New Orleans (2000)
Beyond the Grave (2001)

The Haunted Decatur Series
Haunted Decatur (1995)
More Haunted Decatur (1996)
Ghosts of Millikin (1996)
Where the Dead Walk (1997)
Dark Harvest (1997)
Haunted Decatur Revisited (2000)

Ghosts of Springfield (1997)
The Ghost Hunter's Handbook (1997)
Ghost Hunter's Handbook (Second Edition - 1998)
Ghosts of Little Egypt (1998)

- Ghost Tours -
Haunted Decatur Tours (1994-1998)
Haunted Decatur Tours (Guest Host - 2000)
History & Hauntings Tours of St. Charles (1999)
History & Hauntings Tours of Alton (1999 - 2001)

# NO REST FOR THE
## WICKED
### HISTORY & HAUNTINGS OF AMERICAN CRIME & UNSOLVED MYSTERIES

~ a Whitechapel Productions Press Publication ~

This book is dedicated to hard-working police officers, researchers and investigators who make it their life's work to make the world a little bit safer for all the rest of us. Many of you have shown your support for my ghostly writings over the years and this is my way of giving back a little bit of something in return.

And this book, like all the others, is also dedicated with love and affection to my wife, Amy, who continues to be the light in my life. No matter how dark it sometimes seems to get, she is always there to show me the way out of the shadows. Thanks...

## Original Cover Artwork Designed by
Michael Schwab, M & S Graphics & Troy Taylor
Visit M & S Graphics at www.msgrfx.com

## "No Rest for the Wicked" Title Suggested by
Pat Cody

## This Book is Published by
~ Whitechapel Productions Press ~
A Division of the History & Hauntings Book Co.
515 East Third Street ~ Alton, Illinois ~62002
(618) 465~1086 / 1~888~GHOSTLY
Visit us on the Internet at www.prairieghosts.com

First Printing ~ May 2001
ISBN: 1~892523~13~2

Printed in the United States of America

Most spirits or entities prefer to remain undiscovered... there are exceptions, however. Incidents of ghosts harming the living are rare, but they do occur. Happenings of horror, destruction and even death have been documented. These abominations have occurred in old English manor houses and castles on the Rhine as well as right here in the United States. Some of these eerie hauntings are the result of maledictions or curses when a spirit lingers to watch his blasphemous wish of evil take place.

**RICHARD WINER** in **HAUNTED HOUSES**

As parapsychologists and ghost hunters infer, where so much trauma, conflict and emotional upheaval have occurred residual energy remains. Alcatraz has the feel of an enormous haunted house complete with foggy, cold ambiance and replete with restless spirits of its former occupants.

**ROB & ANNE WLODARSKI** in **HAUNTED ALCATRAZ**

These six words seem written in fire on the walls of my cell....
"Nothing Can Be Worse than This"

**"MACHINE GUN" KELLY**

Most ghost enthusiasts are familiar with the stories of crime, murder and depravity that "haunt" certain locations. How often have we traveled to famous crime spots, only to find the building has been reduced to rubble, has been abandoned, or worse yet, has been turned into yet another parking lot? These spots leave an indelible mark on the area, the city or even the small town. They leave such a mark that it is human nature to try and obliterate the place where the horror occurred. But once these buildings are demolished... what happens to the ghosts who still linger in them?

**THE HAUNTING OF AMERICA**

I hope when my time comes, that I die decently in bed. I don't want to be murdered in beside the garbage cans in some Chicago alley.

**GEORGE "BUGS" MORAN**

# NO REST FOR THE WICKED
## - TABLE OF CONTENTS -

It was ascertained that the mysterious presence was a ghost of a peddler named Charles Rosna, who, for the sake of his meager possessions, had been murdered on the premises by a previous tenant.

**ROBERT SOMERLOTT** *in* **"HERE, MR. SPLITFOOT"**

And is you have any doubts as to whether or not ghosts and crime are intimately related, consider this... we would probably not be so fascinated with ghosts today if it had not been for a murder that took place in Hydesville, New York many years ago. Whether the Spiritualist movement was legitimate or not, it spawned the modern interest in the paranormal. Spiritualism, in turn, was born because of a death.

**THE HAUNTING OF AMERICA**

# - INTRODUCTION -

# "NO REST FOR THE WICKED"

Night had scarcely fallen on the small house in Hydesville, New York when the knockings began. The tapping and banging sounds, followed by what seemed to be footsteps, echoed throughout the house. The entire family was awakened and yet no source could be discovered for the strange noises. Were they simply the sounds of the house settling in cool darkness? Could they be nothing more than fevered imaginings? Perhaps, but then how to explain the accounts of the cold fingers that touched a girl's face in the night and the bedclothes that were pulled away by unseen hands? And the evidence of the brutal murder that took place years before?

The mystery that would begin the Spiritualist movement had its beginnings a number of years before the Fox family took up residence in New York. In those days, between 1843 and 1844, a couple named Bell occupied the cottage. In the last few months of their occupancy, a young local woman named Lucretia Pulver handled the household chores. She acted as a maid and carried out the cleaning and cooking duties for the Bell's.

One day, a young peddler came to the door of the house. He was a friendly young man and he brought with him a case of merchandise. These goods consisted of pots, pans and other useful items for the home. Strangely, the maid would later recall that Mrs. Bell seemed to know the young man. The peddler was greeted warmly and asked to dine with the family. In fact, Lucretia remembered that he stayed on with them for several days. The nature of he and Mrs. Bell's relationship has never been clearly established, but it seems obvious that some sort of friendship existed.

Nevertheless, Lucretia soon found herself fired from her position in the house. No explanation was ever given but apparently, there were no hard feelings about her dismissal. Mrs. Bell took the girl home in her wagon and before she left the house, Lucretia purchased a small kitchen knife from the peddler's selection. She left him instructions to deliver the item to her father's farm, but the knife never arrived.

Barely a week later, Lucretia was surprised to find that Mrs. Bell was again requesting her services. Thankful to have her job back, she reported for duty the next morning. Once again, she would have some unusual recollections later on. For one thing, she found that the peddler who had been staying with the Bell's had apparently departed. No one mentioned when he might have left and Lucretia never asked. She also found that a number of the articles that the peddler had carried in his case were now in the possession of Mrs. Bell, including her own knife. She remembered seeing these items in the case, but simply assumed that Mrs. Bell must have bought them before the young man left for parts unknown. Nothing seemed to be out of the ordinary, but that would soon change.

Shortly after returning to the house, Lucretia began to speak of an unsettling feeling that seemed to hang over the place. She also began to notice some particularly strange things had begun to occur. Unaccountable noises, like knocking and tapping, came from the room that the peddler had once occupied. On several occasions, she also heard footsteps pacing through the house and then descending the stairs to the cellar. Not surprisingly, Lucretia began to feel frightened and nervous when left alone in the house. She would often send for her brother, or a friend, to come and stay with her and usually, the strange sounds would cease. However, on one occasion, they continued for hours and scared Lucretia's brother so badly that he left the place and refused to return.

One afternoon, while in the cellar, Lucretia found herself suddenly to her knees in a patch of freshly turned dirt. Her scream brought Mr. Bell racing down the stairs and when she asked him why the cellar had been dug up the way that it had, he laughed and replied that he had been covering up "rat holes".

A short time later, the Bell's moved out and the Weekman family moved in, along with a relative, a Mrs. Lafe. The length of their residence in the house would prove to be a short one. One day, Mrs. Lafe entered the kitchen and as she closed the door behind her, she spotted the apparition of a man in a black frock coat standing across the room. She screamed in terror and the figure vanished. Soon, they all began to hear the rappings and footsteps in the house. They would come during the daylight hours, but mostly they were heard at night, bothering everyone as they tried to sleep. Finally, the odd happenings proved to be too much for them and they abandoned the place.

Then in 1848, the Fox family moved into the house. John Fox and his wife had two young daughters, Margaret and Kate, and they settled temporarily into the cottage. Fox was a farmer who had come to New York from Canada and had purchased land nearby. A home was being built on the new property and he moved his family into the cottage until the other house could be completed. Their stay would turn out to be very eventful.

Within days of moving in, the noises began. The banging and rattling sounds pounded loudly each night, disturbing them all from their sleep. At first, John Fox thought nothing of the sounds that his wife and children reported and were so frightened by. He assumed that they were merely the sounds of an unfamiliar dwelling, amplified by active imaginations. Soon however, the reports took another turn. Kate woke up screaming one night, saying that a cold hand had touched her on the face. Margaret swore that rough, invisible fists had pulled the blankets from her bed. Even Mrs. Fox swore that she had heard disembodied footsteps walking through the house and then going down the wooden steps into the dank cellar.

Fox, not a superstitious man, was perplexed. He tried walking about the house, searching for squeaks and knocks in the floorboards and along the walls. He tested the windows and doors to see if vibrations in the frames might account for the sounds. He could find no explanation for the weird noises and his daughters became convinced that the house had a ghost.

On the evening of March 31, Fox began his almost nightly ritual of investigating the house for the source of the sounds. The tapping had begun with the setting of the sun and although he searched the place, he was no closer to a solution. Then, Kate began to realize that whenever her father knocked on a wall or door frame, the same number of inexplicable knocks would come in reply. It was as if someone, or something, was trying to communicate with them.

Finding her nerve, Kate spoke up, addressing the unseen presence by the nickname that she and her sister had given it. "Here, Mr. Splitfoot," she called out, "do as I do!" She clapped her hands together two times and seconds later, two knocks came in reply, seemingly from inside of the wall. She followed this display by rapping on the table and the precise number of knocks came again from the presence. The activity caught the attention of the rest of the family and they entered the room with Kate and her father. Mrs. Fox tried asking aloud questions of fact, such as the ages of her daughters and the age of a Fox child who had earlier passed away. To her surprise, each reply eerily accurate.

Unsure of what to do, John Fox summoned several neighbors to the house to observe the phenomenon. Most of them came over very skeptical of what they were hearing from the Fox's, but were soon astounded to find their ages and various dates and years given in response to the questions they asked.

One neighbor, and a former tenant in the house, William Duesler, decided to try and communicate with the source of the sounds in a more scientific manner. He asked repeated questions and was able to create a form of alphabet using a series of knocks. He also was able to determine the number of knocks that could be interpreted as "yes" and "no". In such a manner, he was able to determine the subject of the disturbances. The answer came, not in private, but before an assembled group of witnesses, that the presence in the house was the spirit of a peddler who had been murdered and robbed years before.

As it happened, one of the neighbors who had assembled in the house was the former maid of the Bell family, Lucretia Pulver. She came forward with her story of finding the dirt that had been unearthed in the cellar. The story now took on a more sinister tone. John Fox and William Duesler went to the area that Lucretia described and began to dig. After more than an hour, they had little to show for their trouble but an empty hole and sore backs. That was until Fox noticed something odd beneath the blade of his shovel. He prodded at the object and then picked it up. It appeared to be a small piece of bone with a few strands of hair still clinging to it. Spurred on by the gruesome discovery, he and Duesler began to dig once more. They found a few scraps and tatters of clothing, but little else. They were far from disappointed though, as a local doctor determined that the bone appeared to be a piece of a human skull. They were convinced that the presence in the house was indeed the ghost of the luckless peddler!

Shortly after, the story of the Fox family took a more dramatic turn. The two daughters were both purported to have mediumistic powers and the news of the unearthly communications with the spirit quickly spread. By November 1849, they were both giving public performances of their skills and the Spiritualist movement was born. The mania to communicate with the dead swept the country and the Fox sisters became famous. Regardless, both of them were doomed to unhappy lives and despite amassing great wealth, both died penniless in the 1890's.

Some would say that they died just a few years too soon.....

Over the years, the credibility of the Fox family was often called into question. As no real evidence existed to say that any peddler was actually killed in the house, many accused the family of making up the entire story to support their claims of supernatural powers. Margaret, at the lowest point in her career, even "confessed" to having faked the early manifestations. She later retracted the confession, claiming that she had done it for the money, having been drunk at the time. But who knows? It comes as no surprise to the reader that the Spiritualist movement was riddled with fraud, but was the story of the murdered peddler merely a ruse to prove the powers of the Fox sisters?

It's possible that Margaret and Kate, had they not died broken and poor years before, would have been vindicated in 1904. By this time, their former home had been deserted for some years. A group of children were playing in the ruins one day when the east wall of the cellar collapsed, nearly killing one of them. A man who came to their aid quickly realized the reason for the wall's collapse. Apparently, it had been a false partition, hastily and poorly constructed in the past. Between the false brick wall and the genuine wall of the cellar were the crumbling bones of a man and a large box, just like the ones that had been carried by peddlers a few decades before. A portion of the man's skull was missing.

Dead men, as they say, really do tell tales.

It has often been said that the deeds of yesterday create the hauntings of today. Such a statement is especially true when it comes to ghosts and hauntings that are born of death, murder and crime. Most ghost enthusiasts would agree that perhaps the most prevalent reason for a location to become haunted is because a murder or a violent death has taken place there. And of such things are the stories in this book.

For many years I have been fascinated by not only ghosts, but also by the unsolved and the unexplained. This has included everything from mysterious creatures to unsolved crimes and mysteries. Searching through the lore of ghosts, it was not hard for me to determine that many haunted spots have violent and bloody deeds in their respective pasts. This has pretty much been a staple of ghostlore for centuries. With such dark thoughts in mind, the idea for this book was born.

My purpose with this volume is to collect a series of tales that are connected with both history and hauntings in regards to crimes, murders, strange disappearances, haunted prisons and the like. While I believe that I have placed more of these stories in one single book than any previous author has, I can assure you that I have not collected them all. Stories of bizarre deaths in now haunted houses and murdered college students who have returned to linger in their former dorm rooms are told all over the country. There are probably enough of these stories to fill several books. However, such common tales did not suit my motives here. What I attempted to do was to collect the most unusual and the most unique of these tales and, of course, attempt to chill your blood with the telling of them.

This book has not collected every tale of a haunting connected to a crime but it has collected tales both familiar and strange. Many of them, you will have undoubtedly never heard before. Some of them may be old favorites, but regardless, every single one of them has left its blood-stained mark on the haunted landscape of America. Many of them will frighten you, some will sicken you and others will undoubtedly have you looking over your shoulder as you read.

These are not tales for the faint of heart!

But can I tell you that every one of the stories in this book is true? Can I vouch for their complete authenticity? Can I tell you that there are not elements to the crimes that will never be revealed? No, I cannot do that. What I can tell you though is that each of them was documented as being the truth. The stories that are included in this book are presented as "real" stories that have been told by "real" people. The truth of each story is up to the reader to decide.

As mentioned, the history contained here is dark indeed, but what about the hauntings? In nearly every book I write, I always like to take the reader along on another short trip before beginning the journey into the heart of the book. That small trip always involves the "lore" of the ghosts themselves. What sort of hauntings can the reader expect to find in the places ahead? What are ghosts? And what is a haunting? And how do these things relate to the ghostly locations in this book?

First of all, what exactly is a haunting? It is defined as being the repeated manifestation of strange and inexplicable sensory phenomena at a certain location. There are no general patterns to hauntings, which is what makes them so hard to define. Some phenomena may manifest on occasion or even continually for periods which last from several days to centuries; others may only occur on certain anniversaries; and others may make no sense whatsoever.

The general public assumes that hauntings involve apparitions, or ghosts, of the dead, but in fact, apparitions are connected to only a minority of cases. Most hauntings involve noises like phantom footsteps; strange, unexplainable sounds; tapping; knocking sounds; strange smells; and sensations like the cold prickling of the skin, chilling breezes and even the feeling of being touched by an invisible hand. Other hauntings involve poltergeist-like activity such as furniture and solid objects being moved about; broken glass; doors which open and close by themselves; and the paranormal manipulation of lights and electrical devices.

While attempts have been made to try and categorize certain types of hauntings (as you'll soon see) many locations seem to defy this labeling and manifest a variety and a combination of different types. In fact, it has been my experience that some locations seem to act as catalyst for activity, causing visitors to manifest their own unconscious phenomena and giving rise to accounts which don't fit into any categories at all. The two different types of hauntings that seem to be most commonly reported are what we call the "intelligent haunting" and the "residual haunting", but they aren't alone. They are however, the most likely types of activity to be found at the places we will be discussing in the pages ahead.

The intelligent spirit is everyone's traditional idea of a ghost. It is a lost personality, or spirit, that for some reason did not pass over to the other side at the moment of death. It shows an intelligence and a consciousness and often interacts with people. It is the most widely accepted kind of paranormal activity because it is the easiest to understand. It "haunts" a place because of a connection to the site or to the people at the location. This ghost is the personality of a once living person who stayed behind in our world. This sometimes happens in the case of a murder, a traumatic event, or because of some unfinished business which was left undone in a person's life. At the time of death, this spirit refused to cross over to the other side because of these events. There is also a good chance that this spirit does not even realize that it has died, which could happen if the death was sudden or unexpected. Many of the stories that appear in this book seem to involve these "spirits with a purpose". When it comes to murder or violent deaths, it seems that many such confused spirits linger behind.

Another type of haunting that is often reported at crime scenes and murder sites has nothing to do with intelligent, or conscious, spirits at all. It is more common than people think and you might be surprised as to how many ghost stories that you have heard over the years just may fit into this category. This haunting is both unexplainable and fascinating..... and can be downright spooky too!

This type of haunting is called a "residual haunting" and the easiest way to explain it is to compare it to an old film loop, meaning that it is a scene which is replayed over and over again through the years. These hauntings are really just a piece of time that is stuck in place. Many haunted places experience events that may imprint themselves on the atmosphere of a place in a way that we don't yet understand. This event suddenly discharges and plays itself at various times, thus resulting in a place being labeled as haunted. These "phantom" events are not necessarily just visual either. They are often replayed as sounds and noises that cannot be explained, like footsteps that go up and down the stairs when no one is there. They can also sometimes appear as smells or other sensory events.

Often the sounds and images "recorded" are related to traumatic events that took place at the location and caused what might be called a "psychic disturbance". In other situations, they have been events or actions repeated over and over again to cause the impression. The locations where these hauntings occur act like storage batteries, saving up the impressions of sights and sounds from the past. Eventually, many of these hauntings wear down and fade away, while others continue for eternity.

It's not surprising that many researchers find evidence of residual hauntings at places where great trauma and deaths have occurred. These include both battlefields and of course, crime scenes. These are spots where lives have ended suddenly and with extreme violence. It's as though the dying moments of the victims have left a mark on the place where they breathed their last breath.

So, what do you think? There are many readers who believe that ghosts are real, who have had their own strange experiences over the years. Like many of us, they have tried to explain them away, but cannot. Many readers are not so open-minded though. Those who do not believe in ghosts say that spirits are merely the figments of our imagination. Such stories, these readers insist, are the creations of fools, drunkards and folklorists. Such a reader will most likely finish this book and still be unable to consider the idea that ghosts might exist. In that case, I can only hope to entertain this person with the history and horrific tales of crime and bloody murder.

However, I hope this person will not be too quick in assuming that he has all of the answers. There are stranger things, to paraphrase the poet, than are dreamt of in our philosophies.

Happy Hauntings!
Troy Taylor
Spring 2001

# - CHAPTER ONE -

# MURDER & MAYHEM!

## THE HISTORY & HAUNTINGS OF AMERICA'S BLOODY PAST

The history of crime in America is a history of the country itself. When the first colonists began arriving in the New World, the criminal element among them found a place with no social structure, customs or even laws. It seemed a paradise for those who could corrupt the emerging institutions. Some parts of the new land, like Georgia and New Orleans, were even populated by the refugees from European streets and jails. Needless to say, crime arrived in America with the first settlers.

In fact, one of the pilgrims who arrived on the "Mayflower" is even believed to be America's first murderer. His name was John Billington and he landed with the band of original 102 pilgrims at Plymouth Rock. Billington and his family came from London and were so rowdy that they were even reprimanded by Captain Miles Standish during the voyage from England. Standish became so incensed over Billington's "blasphemous harangues" that he had the offending man's feet and neck tied together as an example of man possessing a sinful tongue.

However, the painful punishment did little to mend Billington's ways.

He continued to be a problem for the colony at Plymouth, often starting violent arguments and fights. His most bitter enemy was a man named John Newcomen, who lived near Billington. They had an ongoing feud that lasted until 1830 and only ended in death. Billington hid behind a rock in the woods and waiting until Newcomen appeared, hunting for food. Billington then shot and killed the other man at close range. He was arrested by the pilgrims and hanged.

Thanks to occurrences like this, one of the first institutions brought to the New World was the jail, a place where those who broke the law could be held while awaiting their trial. While some offenses brought death, lesser crimes were punished by whipping, branding or public humiliation. Jails were never places that were used for punishment. Crimes were simply dealt with by whatever punishment was required and then the lawbreakers were set free. The prison would later become a purely American invention and one that would leave a lasting mark on our history. As we will see in a later chapter, the original intentions behind the penitentiary were good, but the horrific conditions inside of them would leave a bloody stain on criminal history and ghostlore alike.

As time passed, the criminal changed as America did, embodying an ideal that is often referred to as the "frontier spirit". Many of them became folk heroes and legends and are viewed today with a sense of mythical nostalgia. They entrenched themselves into the settling of the great cities, into the Civil War, the great westward movement and into the modern changes that came with last century. America has always easily identified with the criminal. Outwardly, he is condemned but secretly he is awarded the same recognition given to the pioneers. Today, the outlaws and gangsters of years past are considered heroes of a time that is looked at with awe and wonder.

Even during their heyday, many of the criminals of the past were seen as "misunderstood adventurers" who were driven to bad behavior. During the late 1800's, men like Jesse James became famous in dime novels and eastern newspapers. He was seen as an outlaw who was forced to break the law. Jesse, and his brother Frank, had fought as Confederate guerillas during the Civil War. The guerillas were constantly harassed and attacked by Union troops who patrolled the borders. The Federals didn't see the guerillas as soldiers, but merely as outlaws. Their friends and relatives in Missouri were sympathetic to south and when the war ended, offered protection to the brothers and their gang as they continued their lawless ways. Jesse always maintained that he committed robberies and murders because he was "driven to it by the Yankees".

There were many outlaw bands in the late 1800's, the Younger's, the Clanton's, the Dalton's and the James Gang among them. To many readers, Frank and Jesse James were the epitome of the fraternal outlaw band. They pitted themselves against authority as desperadoes on horseback. The fact that Jesse James was a cold-blooded killer made little difference to those who hungered for a legend and makes little difference even today.

The hunger for such legends of daring actually increased during the gangster era. The more sinister the gangsters appeared to be, the more popular their exploits became. Men like Al Capone were cheered at baseball games while Herbert Hoover, the President of the United States, was booed. The bootleggers of the 1920's were seen as public saviors, "giving the people what they wanted" and the bank robbers of the 1930's were seen as striking back against the establishment. It was difficult to find anyone with sympathy toward the banking system and the government during the Great Depression.

But while Americans seem to embrace the criminal element among us, there has always been one sort of crime that manages to strike fear into the hearts of us all.... cold-blooded murder. I once had a police officer explain to me the difference between a "killing" and a "murder". A killing, he explained to me, was usually something that occurred in the heat of the moment, such as during the course of an argument. It can involve anything from a woman to money, or even a fight over a baseball game. Most killings are committed by someone known to the victim. Most of them are quickly solved.

A murder, on the other hand, can be a very complex thing. The motives here are not so easy to detect and while the reason for the murder may be simple, it is usually much more carefully planned and carried out than a killing. Many such cases are never solved. In addition, many murders are committed by total strangers, for reasons known only to them. This is what makes the crime so terrifying, and so complex. Killers are motivated by love, greed, revenge, religion and even sexual aberration. Their methods range from the most basic to the ingenious.

Over the last century, we have also been introduced to a crime phenomenon known as the "serial killer". These horrifying murderers have always been with us, but they have never been in such numbers and have never acted with such regularity. Mass murderers also seem to be an exception unto themselves. They turn murder from a personal affair to a senseless slaughter, claiming anywhere from a handful to dozens of victims.

Murder is, without a doubt, the darkest of American crimes. Perhaps it is fitting that such a dark part of our history leaves such startling evidence behind in its ghosts.


## A VOICE FROM THE GRAVE
### The Murder of Teresita Basa

Thick smoke rolled from the fifteenth-floor windows of the apartment building at 2740 North Pine Grove in Chicago. Against the darkened evening sky, the dance of flames could be seen behind the glass as the firefighters arrived and ran into the building. They made their way upstairs to be greeted at the stairway by a heavy wall of noxious smoke. The smoke could be seen coming from under the door of an apartment that belonged to Teresita Basa, an employee of Edgewater Hospital. None of her neighbors knew if she was home or not.

The door was forced open and the firefighters entered the hazy room on hands and knees. Windows were opened to try and let some of the smoke escape, while other rescuers looked for the source of the fire. They found it in the bedroom. Flames had completely engulfed a mattress that was lying on the floor. They worked quickly to extinguish the blaze and then removed the soggy blankets and pillows. At that point, the unmistakable stench of seared human flesh filled the room.

The firefighters turned the mattress over and beneath it, found the slightly charred remains of a naked woman. Her legs had been spread apart and a butcher knife had been rammed into her chest so hard that half of the wooden handle had slipped between her ribs. The question of whether or not Teresita Basa was at home had just been answered.

Police detectives were dispatched from the 23rd district to investigate. From all indications, Teresita had been the victim of a random rape and robbery. Unfortunately, this sort of crime was not uncommon in the North Side neighborhood where she lived. Once the officers began to investigate though, they discovered that things were not as they first appeared. They found no evidence at the scene of the crime and there was no sign of a forced entry. It appeared that Teresita had known her killer and had let him into the apartment. They considered looking for a friend or a boyfriend who may have raped and killed her. Then, the coroner came back with another odd piece of information. Teresita had not been raped at all and in fact, was still a virgin. A motive for the bizarre crime had just vanished!

Detectives doggedly pursued the case, making lists of suspects and speaking with co-workers and friends of the dead woman. Every one of the suspects managed to come up with an unbreakable alibi and the investigation was stopped dead in its tracks. Days turned into weeks and then weeks into months. The detectives had stopped hoping for new leads in the case and soon, it was placed on the proverbial back-burner as new investigations demanded attention. They never thought to count on a new lead that would come from Teresita herself. And one that come from beyond the grave!

Teresita Basa was a 48-year-old respiratory therapist who worked at Chicago's Edgewater hospital. She had been born and raised on Negros Island in the Philippines and had come to the United States, where she studied classical music. She was considered a gifted musician and had also studied in Europe at the Royal Conservatory of Music in London. She was pursuing a career in music and worked at the hospital to make ends meet. She spent much of her free time working on a children's book about classical music and on her nights off, filled in as a pianist in a local jazz club. Although she was quiet and was slow to make close friends, she lived a full and active life. Although this life did not include men. She rarely dated, leaving her co-workers to ponder whether she simply hadn't found the right man or if she had a fear of them. Her lack of interaction with the opposite sex made the investigation into her death all the more perplexing.

As time passed and the inquiries into the murder faded away, Teresita became less and less a topic of conversation among her former co-workers at the hospital. She would never be forgotten, but after many months was rarely mentioned anymore. This is what made an event that took place in the spring of 1977 even more astonishing!

Remy Chua was another respiratory therapist who worked at Edgewater Hospital. Like Teresita, she had been born and raised in the Philippines and had moved to the United States. Her husband, Joe, was a doctor who worked at another local hospital. Although Remy and Teresita had never been close, they had always maintained a friendly relationship. Remy had been shocked and saddened when Teresita had been killed but the other woman was far from her thoughts that spring afternoon.

Remy was on her break that day, nearing the middle of her shift, and she went into the employee's lounge to relax for a few minutes. She sat down on the couch and leaned her head back. With her eyes closed, she could see nothing around her but she soon got the distinct feeling that someone else was in the room, watching her. She tried to ignore the feeling.

It's foolish, she told herself, if someone else had come into the lounge, I would have heard the door open and close.

Despite assuring herself that there simply couldn't be anyone else there, the sensation became stronger and she finally opened her eyes. She found that she was not alone! There was a woman standing several feet away from her, staring at her. The woman wore hospital scrubs and looked very familiar. Then Remy realized why she seemed familiar to her.... the woman was Teresita Basa! It was impossible and yet, there she was. She did not appear to be ghost-like at all but completely solid. Her face was just as Remy remembered it, but filled with sadness and pain. Without thinking, she lifted her hand to touch Teresita and then suddenly changed her mind. The sudden realization came to her again that the other woman was dead!

Remy sprang up from the couch and crashed through the door of the lounge. She tried breathlessly to scream, but no words came out. As she spun into the hallway, she collided with a male technician in the corridor. The hospital charts that he was carrying clattered the floor. He started to protest and then saw the look on Remy's face. She appeared to be terrified. He grabbed her arm and quickly asked her what was wrong. To his surprise, Remy explained that she had just seen Teresita Basa in the lounge.

"But, that's impossible!" the technician sputtered. He replied that she had been dead for months, but Remy swore that was whom she had seen. Together, the two of them opened the door of the employee lounge and peered inside. The room was empty.

In the weeks following the strange encounter, Remy's husband and friends began to notice a change in her personality. She began to act very moody and sad and one of her co-workers quietly suggested to another one that she was starting to act just like Teresita had. A nurse on staff would also later recall that Remy would sometimes stand transfixed in front of Teresita's old locker. In the cafeteria, Remy moved away from the table where she normally sat with her friends and began sitting alone in the same spot that Teresita used to occupy. Her friends also noticed that Remy would often seem to slip into a daze and would hum little snatches of songs. Co-workers remembered them as being tunes that Teresita often sang. When they mentioned this to Remy, she claimed that she had no idea what they were talking about.

Soon, Remy's personality changes began to cause her to have nightmares that she would vividly recall later. It seemed that whenever she closed her eyes to sleep, Teresita would appear. Before long, she began to show up when Remy was wide awake as well. One morning while she was waiting for a stoplight to change, she saw Teresita standing near her car. In moments, her image was replaced by that of an orderly that Remy worked with at the hospital. His name was Allan Showery and while Remy didn't know him very well, she found it strange that he would appear in her vision. She had never really thought about him before, but lately she had started to feel an intense hatred for the man. She couldn't understand it because he was virtually a stranger and yet she felt her stomach clench whenever he passed her in the hallways.

Remy realized that she had to discuss the situation with her husband. She told him that she had not been sleeping well and that she was having terrible dreams. He had also noticed her personality change and guessed that it had something to do with stress. She was obviously upset about something having to do with Teresita Basa, but what? He couldn't imagine that a ghost was haunting her dreams, but his wife was obviously disturbed. She explained to him that she continually saw the face of Teresita and also that of Allan Showery, an orderly that she barely knew. Joe Chua tried to reassure her. He was convinced that the nightmares would go away.

But they didn't go away and in fact, they became worse. The two faces would appear in her dreams, jolting her awake, and as she became conscious, she would experience the lingering smell of smoke in her bedroom. On a few nights, the smell was so strong that she actually got out of bed to be sure that the house was not on fire.

One afternoon while Remy was in bed trying to rest, Joe called his attorney on the phone. Just as the other man answered, both of them heard a deafening scream from the bedroom. Stunned, Joe dropped the phone and ran into the other room. He found his wife still in a deep sleep on the bed. Remy's parents, who were staying with them at the time, reached the bedroom just moments after Joe did. When they entered, they found the temperature in the room was a good ten or fifteen degrees colder than in the rest of the house. Remy's mother said later that her scalp began to tingle and she could feel the hair on her arms standing on end. It was as if someone had charged the room with static electricity. But it was soon to get much stranger!

Remy, still asleep, began to rise from the bed with her arms outstretched in front of her. She walked toward her husband and parents and then suddenly fell backwards, collapsing back onto the bed. Joe, assuming that she was sleepwalking, tried to relax her arms into a more comfortable position but they would not budge. They remained stiff and upright, no matter what he did. Thanks to his medical training, it reminded Joe of a corpse that he entered a state of rigor mortis.

Then, Remy began to speak. Her breath hissed out from between her lips. "I.... I am Teresita Basa", she said. Joe was surprised. He had never heard the voice before and he knew that it was not his wife's. The odd voice continued. "Nothing has been done about the man who killed me. You must help me! Go to the police! You are a doctor. They will listen to you."

"What do you want me to tell them?" Joe asked her. His voice quavered with fear.

"Tell them a man came into my apartment and choked and stabbed me!"

"What man?"

The voice from within Remy pleaded with him once more to go to the police and then warmth seemed to settle over the room. Remy's arms dropped and relaxed and her eyes flickered open. "What.. what happened?" she asked.

Joe and Remy's parents looked at one another. They were unsure of exactly how to answer her question. Joe had never seen anything like it before. He was a man of science, he didn't believe in the supernatural, but he was unable to explain what had just happened to his wife. Finally, Remy's father spoke up. He believed that his daughter had been possessed by the spirit of a dead woman named Teresita Basa.

Several days later, it happened again. Once more, Joe and Remy's parents were present. This time, the voice that came from Remy was even more upset. It demanded to know why Joe had not gone to the police with the information that he had been given. The voice never referred to him as Joe either, as his wife would have done, but instead as Dr. Chua, as if he was a stranger. Of course, to Teresita, he would be.

"I can't go to them unless you tell me who killed you," he answered.

"Allan killed me. I let him into my apartment and he killed me. You must go to the police." The voice explained that Allan was a friend from the hospital and then once again demanded that Joe go to the police. After that, Remy seemed to come out of the trance once more.

She opened her eyes and looked around the room at the faces that were staring at her. She asked for a glass of water but had no idea what Joe was talking about when he told her that if he went to the police with his story they would think he was crazy. He just didn't know what to believe, or what to think about the strange affliction that had come over his wife.

A few days passed and a priest and relatives visited with Remy. Some of them believed that she needed psychiatric treatment, while others, like her father, believed that she was possessed. In the middle of one of her eerie trances, her father had tried to convince the spirit to leave his daughter alone. Teresita (as they had started to believe the voice was) told him that she would not be driven away until her killer was brought to justice.

One evening, Remy once again slipped into a trance. She fell down and began to scream that she was burning. She wrapped her arms around her body and cried out. Joe quickly came to her aid. As he leaned over her, a hand clutched him by the shirt front. "You have not done what I asked you to, Dr. Chua," said the chilling voice.

"If I told the police about you, they'd never believe me," Joe insisted. He was scared of what was happening to his wife, but angry too. He snapped at Teresita. "Leave my wife and family alone! I want you to get the hell out of our lives!" he snapped at the entity.

Remy fell silent and her body stiffened. A chill seemed to pervade the room but the spirit did not speak for nearly a minute. Finally, the voice spoke once more, emerging loudly from Remy's throat. "They will believe you," it said. "Allan Showery, the orderly, stole my jewelry and gave it all to his girlfriend."

Joe asked how it could be proved that the jewelry was Teresita's and the ghost replied that her cousins would recognize the pieces as family heirlooms. She also went to on give Joe the telephone numbers of her cousins. If he had any doubts remaining about the reality of the supernatural, it vanished with these last words. There was no possible way that his wife could have known the names and telephone number of Teresita's family.

Then the voice continued. "Tell the police that Allan came to fix my television, and he killed me and burned me". After that, the voice was gone.

On August 8, Joe finally gathered up enough nerve to go to the police with his story about his wife being possessed by the spirit of Teresita Basa. One can only imagine what it must have taken for the respected physician to go to the authorities with a tale that he knew they would find ridiculous. At the precinct house, he was introduced to a detective named Joe Stachula, who had been assigned to the original case. The veteran investigator listened politely to Joe's story, but confessed that he had little faith in its authenticity. However, having nothing else to go on and no other leads to follow, Stachula agreed to at least check out the orderly for a past criminal record.

The detective set to work and put Allan Showery's name into the system. He soon discovered that Showery did have a record. In fact, he had been arrested several times in New York, twice for rape. Further investigation also revealed that complaints had been filed against Showery by relatives whose loved ones had passed away at Edgewater Hospital. It was alleged that Showery had removed and had stolen jewelry from the deceased. After discovering this information, Detective Stachula and his partner, Lee Epplen, brought Allan Showery in for questioning.

During the interrogation, Showery admitted to knowing Teresita and working with her at the hospital. Stachula told him that they had information that Showery was supposed to go to her apartment and fix her television on the night she was killed. Showery admitted that he was but said that he had stopped off in a neighborhood bar on the way. He lost track of time and then, since it was too late to go to Teresita's, went home instead.

Despite the suspect's quick answers, Stachula had a feeling that something was not quite right with the alibi. He pressed a little harder. "That doesn't fit with the information that we've heard," he told Showery. "It doesn't sound right."

But Showery insisted that he had never been to Teresita's apartment, even when Stachula told him that a number of people had seen him at the building. He replied that he had carried groceries for her into the lobby, but he had never been up to the apartment itself.

Finally, Stachula relented, or at least he appeared to. "All right," he said with a sigh. "We'll just take your fingerprints and compare them with the ones that we found at the scene. If they don't match up, you're free to go."

Showery balked at the prospect of having his fingerprints taken and his story changed once again. "Okay, I was in her apartment that night, but just for a minute or two. I didn't have the right tools to fix her TV, so I left. I went home and did some work around the apartment. Ask my wife, she'll tell you!"

Stachula and Epplen left Showery in lock-up and went to his apartment to talk to his wife. He advised Showery to think about his dates and times while they were gone and to see if he could get his story straight. All the while, Stachula had a funny feeling about Showery's version of the events... and about the weird story told to them by Joe Chua. He and Epplen recalled that the "spirit" had said that Showery had given the jewelry to his girlfriend, not his wife. One of the first things that he asked the woman who answered the door at Showery's apartment was about whether or not she and Showery were married.

"We're only living together now," she answered, "but we're planning to get married soon."

The detectives were happy with the answer and they quickly asked her if Showery had given her any jewelry between January and June. She replied that he had given her an antique ring around the end of February or the beginning of March. It had been a belated Christmas gift, she said. She went to the bedroom and returned with a box containing several other pieces of jewelry. Stachula and Epplen looked at one another and they asked the woman to accompany them back to the police station.

Before leaving the apartment, Stachula asked to use the telephone. He opened his notebook and looked at the list of names and telephone numbers that Joe Chua had given him. Any remaining doubts that he had about the story evaporated as one by one the people on the list answered his calls and said that they were relatives of Teresita Basa. He asked each of them to meet he and his partner at the station house.

As Showery's girlfriend waited with Epplen, Stachula met with Teresita's family. Each of them identified the jewelry that had been taken from Showery's apartment as having been Teresita's. Many of the pieces had been in her family for years.

The detective then took the jewelry into the interrogation room and showed it to Allan Showery. Even when confronted with this evidence, Showery protested his innocence. He had bought the jewelry in a pawn shop, he swore.

Stachula frowned and he tossed the suspect a notebook and a pencil. "Okay, you write down the name of the shop and when you bought the stuff," he told him. "Then, we're going to need a receipt that proves you bought it there."

Needless to say, Showery had no receipt and claimed that he was unable to remember where he bought the merchandise. His story was interrupted by a knock on the door. Detective Epplen was outside and he led Showery's girlfriend into the room. By this time, Epplen had apprised her of the situation and the look on her face when she saw Showery must have shocked the suspect in a way that the detective's interrogations had been unable to do. As soon as he saw the girl walk in, Showery confessed to having committed Teresita's murder.

On February 21, 1977, Allan Showery had gone to the apartment of Teresita Basa at approximately 5:00 in the evening. Shortly after he arrived there, he inspected her television set and told her that he did not have the necessary tools to fix it. He left and then returned at around 7:30. As soon as he was admitted to the apartment, he struck Teresita until she was unconscious and left her lying on the floor. He then proceeded to ransack the apartment, finding only $30 in cash but finding her collection of jewelry. He then drug Teresita into the bedroom, where he removed all of her clothing and spread her legs apart to make it appear that she had been raped. He was totally unaware that Teresita was a virgin. Showery then went into the kitchen and took a butcher's knife from a drawer. He plunged the knife into Teresita's chest, narrowly missing a rib. He then covered the body with a mattress and set it on fire. Showery fled the scene just before the firefighters arrived.

The orderly had confessed to the brutal and gruesome crime, but that was not the end of the story. After engaging a lawyer, Showery recanted the confession and a trial that was held two years later ended in a hung jury. He was returned to a holding cell to wait for his new trial date but before it got under way, Showery pleaded guilty to the murder. The plea came as a complete surprise to both his attorney and the prosecutor, especially in light of the fact that Showery had been claiming that he was innocent of the crime for months. He was later sentenced to fourteen years in prison.

Some have wondered if perhaps Showery didn't have a visitor in his cell one night.. a visitor who was not of this world. Who knows?

As for Teresita Basa herself, her spirit was never heard from again. She did not return to the Chua family and they were able to live out their lives in peace. They must have wondered why Teresita had chosen them to seek justice on her behalf, but that question remains unanswered. Regardless, the dead woman did find a voice and murder was finally avenged.

## THE MATE OF THE SQUANDO
*Murder and Mayhem on the Sea*

Old sailors always maintained that a woman had no place on board a sailing ship. Her presence could bring nothing but bad luck, they said. In the case of the Norwegian ship "Squando", a woman did bring bad luck and more. For one crew member, she brought a blood-soaked death and years of aimless wandering as a ghost.

Life on board the sailing ships of the late 1800's was an often hard and sometimes brutal existence. The work was often back-breaking and the pay was poor. All the sailors ever asked for was a good passage, a dry berth and enough pay at the end of the voyage to spend a few days ashore looking for wine, women and song. Most of the sailors turned up later at the same vessel or another one, with empty pockets and a sore head. They had little hope for a first mate that was not as tough as the last one or a captain with a little less steel in his heart.

Such was the life of the men who served aboard the Squando. In 1886, the ship was docked in the Norwegian port of Oslo, making final preparations to sail across the North Sea, along the Atlantic coast and around the Cape to San Francisco. Under the critical eye of the first mate, the ship was loaded and made ready. To the men aboard her, the passage looked to be the same as many others they had already worked before. There would be little to break the monotony this time around, they believed.

A short time before the ship was set to depart, a carriage appeared at the dock and halted alongside the vessel. A curse from the lips of one sailor caused the men around him to look in the direction in which he was staring. They saw, climbing down from the cab, the familiar figure of the ship's master. Then, the man turned and held out his hand to a woman. She stepped down beside him and waited next to a large pile of luggage that the driver was placing on the dock.

A ripple went through the crew of the Squando. A woman was coming aboard! It was something that was simply not done. No one knew what to make of it and the first sailor cursed once again in disbelief. His blasphemies brought a sharp rebuke from the mate.

"Get down there and fetch those things!" he snapped at the sailors. "And you'll do best to watch your tongues in front of the Old Man's wife!"

The mate watched carefully as he sent the rest of the men about their work. The captain and his wife came aboard the ship and the final preparations were finished. The lady was escorted to her cabin and then the master of the ship gave the order for them to set sail. Soon, the voyage was underway. Not surprisingly, a rumble continued to sound among the superstitious sailors. In this case, their fears would come to be justified.

Days passed and the passage proceeded normally. The mate and bosun continued to drive the men as hard as he always did and the cook continued to serve up the barely serviceable food. The crew's talk soon turned from bad luck and the captain's wife to the mate's obvious attentiveness to the woman. No one could help but notice either that the captain seemed especially hostile toward the younger man. The crew began to speculate as to what was going on in the main cabin when the master of the ship was away.

The atmosphere on the ship became more and more heated as the days passed. At first, the crew reacted with delight to see the mate being tongue-lashed by the Old Man, even though he would often take his ill humor out on them afterwards. Then, the pleasure gradually gave way to nervousness. More than once, the master and the mate had been heard to snap at one another over some detail of the ship. Once, the mate was even seen to turn his back and walk away while the captain was speaking to him. Some of the older seamen watched the antagonism between the men with nervousness. They could only hope that the passage would be smooth for if bad conditions came about and cool seamanship was needed, well, there was little to be found aboard the Squando.

Perhaps a few of the more discerning crew members realized what was going on between the mate and the captain's wife, but most didn't. However, as there was little to do for entertainment aboard the ship save for play cards and gossip, their improprieties were soon talked of constantly. Eventually, as was bound to happen in such a close environment, word of such talk reached the captain. One of the older sailors approached him fearfully but the captain heard him out and then dismissed the man back to his work.

What dark thoughts ran through the master's mind are unknown, but the men on deck later recalled that his face seemed flush with anger when he turned and looked at the mate. Without a word though, he vanished below decks and he went straightaway to his wife's cabin.

A few days later, a very relieved crew sailed the Squando into San Francisco Bay and let down the anchor. It would be another day before unloading could begin at the dock and another day before it would be finished, but the men were already starting to talk about their next voyages. Most swore that they would not work aboard the Squando again, especially with the captain's wife on her. They also imagined that the mate would be sent packing as well. They couldn't believe the captain would keep him, although the bickering had been strangely quiet over the course of the last several days.

On the morning that the ship was set to start unloading, the captain announced that he was going ashore on business. When he returned, the vessel would be docked and unloading would begin. Almost as soon as he left, the mate went directly to the main cabin. The lovely face of the captain's wife answered his sharp knock. She was already in a state of undress when she let him inside. The mate kissed her quickly but she playfully pushed him away.

"Let's have a drink," she urged him. "This may be our last time together for awhile." The two of them had already discussed their plans to meet in the city and the woman had agreed that she would leave her husband. As soon as the ship was unloaded, the mate planned to collect his final pay and disappear into San Francisco. The captain's wife would join him in a few days.

Or so he thought. He had no idea that the master already knew of the couple's plans and that, perhaps under threat of death, had enlisted his wife in taking revenge on the mate. He wouldn't realize that his invitation to the cabin had been a trap, until his limbs began to feel heavy and his eyes began to droop. He had been drugged, he thought with startling clarity.

Before he could stand or attempt to escape, the door of the cabin burst open and the captain rushed in. The mate never had a chance, for in seconds, they were upon him. The master wielded a long-bladed knife and his wife swung an iron bar. Despite the mate's great strength, the suddenness of the attack allowed them to overpower him. Even though he was slowed by the drugged wine, he still managed to kick and flail at his assailants. He screamed and tried to cover his face and head with his arms while the woman beat at him and the captain stabbed again and again with the knife. Then, the iron bar slipped past his arms and smashed down on his forehead. Blood erupted from his split scalp and sprayed the walls and ceiling of the close cabin.

Another blow landed on the mate and then another and finally the woman stepped back, shocked at the incredible blood lust that had filled her. She stared at her husband and she shuddered. The mate's blood was everywhere, covering their hands and clothing and drenching the walls, the ceiling and the floor. The thick stench of gore filled the room, which was now silent except for the quiet patter of dripping blood.

On the captain's command, the woman helped her husband to drag the mate's body up onto the table. As she did so, she shuddered again. Just days before, she had lovingly caressed this now lifeless and mutilated body. Her violence from moments before now sickened her, but the vile acts were far from over.

The mate's corpse was placed on the wooden slab and the captain fetched an ax from across the room. He raised his arm and with a mighty blow, cleaved the mate's head from his body. They planned to cut the corpse into pieces and dispose of it in the bay, but they never had a chance to continue the gruesome task. The mate's screams had been heard and some of the braver sailors had summoned the police. Footfalls sounded on the deck above as men scurried from the ship.

For several weeks, the crew had been expecting some sort of drama to take place, but no one could have imagined the depth of the master's fury. The bloodcurdling screams of the mate had suggested something far beyond the capacities of the men on board to imagine.

The master knew that the authorities had been sent for and even the small delay before they were confronted would not give them time to conceal what they had done. Quickly, the mate's body was wrapped in an old blanket and weighted with the iron bar, it was slipped over the side of the ship and into the water. Unfortunately, a quick glance around the cabin was enough to make the captain realize there was no hope of concealing the evidence that something had taken place there. It would take hours of hot water and soap to wash the grisly remains of blood from the walls, furnishings and floor and even from the hair and clothing of the captain and his wife. There was no chance that they would not be discovered. Their only hope was to flee the ship, which they did, rowing away in a small dinghy that had been tied up to the side of the vessel.

A short time later, the police arrived and upon entering the captain's cabin, they knew that the summons had been justified. After a brief search, one of the detectives discovered the bloody knife and another had the ill luck to discover the mate's head. It had been tossed into a bucket and had been secreted under the captain's bunk.

A week later, the headless body of the first mate was found floating in the San Francisco Bay. Somehow, the cadaver had managed to slip its bonds and was discovered by two fishermen bobbing in the water. One of the sailors from the Squando identified the body by a tattoo that the mate had etched on his arm. This old man shook his head sadly over the whole affair. Something like this was bound to happen, he told his friends. It didn't matter what kind of woman she had been, just having a female on board the ship made it certain that something bad was going to happen.

The search for the captain and his wife continued for some time but eventually, it was called off. The two of them were never heard from again. However, the same thing could not be said for the first mate. After the terrible event that took place on the ship, it began to be known as a "cursed" vessel.... and a haunted one. The Squando would never know peace again.

When the ship finally departed from San Francisco, it carried none of its former crew. All of them had joined with other ships, hoping to put the gruesome past behind them. It took several weeks to find a new master and crew, as the story of the first mate's demise was all the talk around the harbor, but eventually the owners managed it. Soon, the Squando was sailing southward for the Horn and then on to Norway.

After several days, grumbling began on the ship. News of it soon reached the new captain's ears and he called a meeting to try and clear the air. Most of the sailors kept silent, save for a group of four men who complained of the food and sleeping conditions on the vessel. The new captain was a reasonable man and a wise one. He knew that, thanks to the Squando's sorted past, he was lucky to have gotten men to serve on her at all. The caliber of sailors aboard was not the best and he believed that a gentle hand was the most careful way to preserve order. Rather than demanding that the men quit complaining and get back to work, as most masters would have done, he instead asked them what they thought could be done to approve conditions. Unfortunately, it turned out to be the wrong way to handle the four ruffians among the crew. Instead of recognizing reason, they mistook the captain's mildness for weakness. It could only mean trouble in the days ahead.

From that day on, as the Squando sailed along the coast of Mexico and South America, the crew began to rebel against orders, with the four men emerging as the ringleaders in the trouble. This continued for days but shortly after rounding the cape and sailing north again, the four men made their move. Initially, they attacked the first and second mates and after beating them, locked them in their cabins. Then, they began searching for the captain.

The attacks on the mates had cost the mutineers the element of surprise and they found the captain on deck with a long marlin-spike in his hands. While the rest of the crew hung back, perhaps waiting to see which side prevailed, the four men lunged at the master of the vessel. The captain fought bravely, inflicting injuries on the four men, but the odds against him were just too great. A knife to the ribs finally sent him groaning to the deck. The mutineers paused for a moment and then lunged at the man. The watching crew now began to protest at what was happening, but the protest came too late. The four ringleaders picked up the master and then heaved him over the side and into the water below.

After that, they turned on the crew, ordering the sailors to go about their duties and not cause any trouble. Later, the two mates were released and told that if they did not sail the Squando to the South American coast without trickery, they would suffer the same fate their captain had. A short time later, the four men had a boat lowered and they rowed out of sight. There was nothing for the mates to do but put back out to sea and continue the passage to Norway.

They carried with them another tale of horror about the Squando. Soon, sailors began to avoid the ship and would have nothing to do with it. The owners were unable to hire either captains or crew members and it was suggested that she should be broken up. Finally, a master, who did not believe in superstitious nonsense, was found and after offering a high rate of pay, a crew was hired as well. The ship sailed, but the captain never returned from the sea. During the passage, he cut his hand, contracted blood poisoning and died.

His replacement fared no better. One night, during rough weather, he missed a step and fell against the ship's rail. He cracked his head so violently that he later died. The Squando completed the passage under the mate's command. He took her into port about thirty miles south of New York and then abandoned her. He and the rest of the crew decided that the ship could rot for all they cared.

The stories continued to be told about the Squando. Lore of the sea had it that there was something supernatural about the deaths that had occurred aboard her. The stories stated that a mysterious presence lingered aboard the ship. Many believed that it was the ghost of the murdered first mate, now seeking revenge on all captains who came aboard his ship.

Even though the masters of the ship were the only ones who seemed to suffer from the ship's "curse", there seemed to be nothing that could convince the ordinary sailors that they were immune from it. Over the course of several months, the owners tried to hire many men to sail the Squando, but all refused. The owners began to worry. As long as the ship was moored in America, she was accumulating debt and losing business. Only one solution seemed possible. They would change the ship's name and hire a skeleton crew, no matter what the cost, and move the ship to another harbor. Here, she would be unknown and they could put her back into service again.

They began to draw up the paperwork and search for another crew. While this was being done, a watchman was hired to spend the night on the empty ship. He knew nothing about the history of the vessel, only that he was supposed to keep it safe from vandals and thieves while the preparations were made to move it to another harbor.

He reported to work in the evening hours and made straight for the most comfortable cabin on the ship, that of the captain's quarters. Here, he sat down with his lamp and pipe and listened to the sounds of the ship around him, alert for intruders. He was an experienced watchman and he was used to the sounds of water lapping at the sides of the ship, the creaking of the rigging and the soft sounds of rats as they scurried about, but here on the Squando, there were other sounds as well. From out of the darkness came what seemed to be whispers and the quiet tapping of footsteps. These odd noises would make the watchman listen intently and sometimes he would open the cabin door and peer out into the gloom. Hearing and seeing nothing, he would return to the comforting warmth of the lamp light.

Hours passed and he learned to ignore the strange sounds. There was no one else here, he assured himself, convinced that he would recognize the tread of any trespassers on board. He tried to relax but just couldn't seem to shake the fact that he was not in the room alone. He looked about him but he could see no one else but.....

Suddenly, near the doorway, a misty form began to take shape! It appeared to be a man, wearing blood-soaked clothing and bound with ropes. The figure slowly came into view and then stopped, for it had no head! The watchman jumped to his feet. He was frozen in place, both by fear and by the fact that the apparition was between himself and the door! There was no other means of escape from the cabin.

The headless figure began to move. It lurched forward, making no sound, but stumbling as if in pain. It came closer to the watchman, but it never reached him. Before the hideous figure could get closer to him, the man bolted for the cabin door and ran up the stairs to the deck. He vanished into the night, never setting foot on the Squando again.

After this story was told and re-told in shipping ports along the American coast, the plans to rename and put the ship back into business were scrapped. Not a single man could be found to work aboard her. The Squando was finally scrapped but this did not end the ship's bizarre legend. Shortly after the vessel was demolished, the ghostly outline of a ship began to be sighted off the Embarcadero, the waterfront boulevard that runs between the Oakland Bay Bridge and Fisherman's Wharf in San Francisco. The old sailors believed that this "ghost ship" was the phantom of the Squando, still sailing the route that was journeyed by the mate when he met his end. Some say this ship, and the ghostly mate, still sails off the San Francisco Bay today, content in the fact that he finally got his revenge.

## THE SAUSAGE VAT MURDER
### A Ghoulish Ghost Story from Chicago

The ghost of Louisa Luetgert still walks the now almost deserted neighborhood where her home once stood, or at least that's what the legends of northwest Chicago say. Louisa was the murdered wife of "Sausage King" Adolph Luetgert, a German meat packer who came to the city in the 1870's. Killed by her own husband in one of the most grisly ways imaginable, her ghost not only haunts the area around Hermitage Avenue but the legends say that she hounded her treacherous husband from Joliet Prison to the grave!

Carl Sandburg called Chicago the "hog butcher for the world" and the meat packing industry put the city on the map as a major business hub. Until the 1800's, cuts of beef were prepared only by local butchers. However in 1872, a man named Gustavas Swift began buying cattle from the western ranges and shipping sides of beef to the east on express trains that ran in the winter months with their doors open to preserve the meat. Later, Swift developed refrigerated rail cars and soon he and his competitor, Phillip Armour, were shipping most of the nation's beef and pork products.

The huge business boom that came from the industry attracted many meatpackers and operators to the city. One of these men was Adolph Luetgert, who soon found that there was a demand for German sausages in the city. Following some initial success, he opened a sausage plant at the southwest corner of Hermitage and Diversey Parkway in 1894. He was so taken with his own success that he also built a three-story frame house next door to the factory, which he shared with his second wife, Louisa.

Louisa Bicknese was an attractive young woman who was ten years younger than her husband was. She was a former servant from the Fox River Valley who met her new husband by chance. He was immediately taken with her, entranced by her diminutive stature and tiny frame. She was less than five feet tall and looked almost child-like next to her burly husband.

The Luetgert Sausage Works, Circa 1897

As a wedding gift, he gave her a unique, heavy gold ring. Inside of it, he had gotten her new initials inscribed, reading "L.L.". Little did he know at the time that this ring would prove to be his undoing.

According to friends and neighbors, Luetgert's fascination with his beautiful young wife did not last long. The couple was frequently heard to argue and their disagreements became so heated that Luetgert eventually moved his bedroom from the house to a small chamber inside of the factory. The fights with Louise were not the only reason for this move however. Luetgert was known for having enormous sexual appetites and it was rumored that he kept several mistresses. There was talk of women that Luetgert was seen squiring into the factory bedchamber, like Agathia Tosch, who owned a North Side tavern with her husband. Luetgert also became involved with a girl named Mary Simerling, Louisa's niece and a household servant. This new scandal also got the attention of the people in the neighborhood, who were already gossiping about the couple's marital woes.

By the early part of 1897, Luetgert's business began to slip away from him. Even though the factory turned out huge amounts of sausage, Luetgert found that he could not keep up with his supplier's costs. Instead of cutting back though, he decided to try expanding his operations instead. He closed down for ten weeks for "reorganization". All the while, the business plans took second place to his extravagant sexual antics.

By this time, Louisa had gotten wind of her husband's many affairs. She became outraged and confronted him one evening about his dalliances with her niece. Luetgert responded by grabbing his wife by the throat and choking her until she collapsed. He stopped just short of killing her. A few days later, neighbors summoned the police when Luetgert was seen chasing his wife down the street with a revolver in his hands. The officers who investigated were assured that Luetgert had merely "lost his temper" and that he would have never actually harmed his wife.

That was when Luetgert set a more devious plan into action. On March 11, he went to a wholesale drug dealer called Lor Owen & Company and ordered 378 pounds of crude potash and fifty pounds of arsenic. It was delivered to the factory the following day.

On April 24, Luetgert summoned one of his employees, Frank Odorowsky, known as "Smokehouse Frank", to his office. He instructed him to move the barrel of potash from the shipping room to the basement, where there were three huge vats that were used to boil down sausage material. Luetgert warned him to be careful with the potash because it was highly volatile. Both Frank and another employee were burned about the face and hands after chopping the potash into small pieces. They placed the material into the basement's center vat and Luetgert turned on the steam to dissolve the potash into liquid. According to his later testimony, Frank never asked Luetgert what the potash was for, even in light of the fact that the factory was temporarily closed down.

Then, on May 1, 1897, Louisa disappeared. When questioned by his sons, Luetgert told them that their mother had gone out the previous evening to visit her sister. After several days though, she did not come back.

Finally, Diedrich Bicknese, Louisa's brother, went to the police. The investigation fell on Captain Herman Schuettler, who author Richard Lindberg describes as "an honest but occasionally brutal detective". The detective and his men began to immediately search for Louisa. They questioned neighbors and relatives and soon learned of the couple's violent arguments. Schuettler was suspicious of the sausage maker from the beginning. He had been personally summoned himself after some of the man's disagreements with his wife. He called Luetgert to the station on two separate occasions and was even said to have stated that Luetgert had made a vigorous appeal to him to find a lost dog a short time before. "Why did you not report the absence of your wife?", he inquired.

"I expected her to come back," Luetgert calmly replied. "I wished to avoid any disgrace."

Schuettler allowed Luetgert to return home. Soon after, they began dragging the rivers and searching the alleys and empty lots on the North Side. Finally, on May 7, they returned to the sausage factory and began interrogating the workers. One man they spoke with was Wilhelm Fulpeck, an employee of the factory, who recalled seeing Louisa enter the factory around 10:30 in the evening on May 1. His story was confirmed by a local girl named Emma Schiemicke, who passed by the factory with her sister at about the same time. She reported that she saw Luetgert with his wife and that he was leading her up the alleyway behind the factory.

Frank Bialk, a night watchman at the plant, also confirmed this story. He also added that he saw both Luetgert and Louisa inside of the plant together. He had been on duty until Luetgert gave him a dollar and told him to go to a nearby drugstore and buy a bottle of celery compound. When the watchman returned, he found that the door leading to the main factory had been locked. Luetgert appeared and took the medicine and after sending him on another errand, gave him the rest of the night off.

Schuettler also made another disturbing and suspicious discovery. Just a short time before Louisa's disappearance, Luetgert inexplicably ordered the potash and arsenic from Lor Owen & Company. The circumstantial evidence was starting to add up and after speaking again to Frank Bialk and "Smokehouse Frank", Schuettler began to theorize about the crime.

According to the night watchman, he had found Luetgert in his office the next day and asked him if the fires should be left burning under the vat in the basement. He was told to be sure they were shut down and when he went downstairs, he found a hose running water into the middle vat. On the floor of the vat was a sticky, glue-like substance that seemed to contain pieces of bone. This was not alarming however, as Bialk knew that all sorts of meat waste was used to make sausage.

On May 3, "Smokehouse Frank" also noticed the slime on the basement floor. He couldn't decide what it was so he went to his employer to tell him about it. He apparently missed the fact that the middle vat was still half-filled with the grim substance. Frank later reported that Luetgert told him to keep silent about the mess. If he did, Luetgert said, he would insure that the other man had a job for life.

Frank and a crew of men began cleaning the brown sludge from the floor. They scraped it into a drain that led to a sewer and placed the larger chunks of waste into a barrel. Luetgert told them to scatter these pieces near the railroad tracks.

Schuettler was now convinced that Luetgert had killed his wife, boiled her in acid and then disposed of her in a factory furnace. With that in mind, he and his men started another search of the sausage plant. They narrowed the search to the basement and to the twelve-foot-long, five-foot-deep middle vat. The officers drained the remaining greasy paste from the vat using gunny sacks as filters and began poking through the residue with sticks. Here, officer Walter Dean found a small piece of a skull fragment, several other bones and two gold rings. One of them was engraved with the initials "L.L.".

On May 7, Adolph Luetgert, proclaiming his innocence, was arrested for the murder of his wife. No body was ever found, save for the pieces of bone, and there were no witnesses to the crime. However, police officers and prosecutors believed the evidence was overwhelming. Luetgert was indicted for the crime a month later and details of the murder shocked the city, especially those people in the surrounding neighborhood. Even though Luetgert was charged with burning his wife's body, local rumor had it that she had been ground into sausage instead. Needless to say, sausage sales declined substantially in 1897.

Luetgert went to trial but the proceedings ended in a hung jury on October 21 after the jurors failed to agree on a suitable punishment. Some argued for the death penalty, while others voted for life in prison. Only one of the jury members thought that Luetgert might be innocent. A second trial was held on February 9, 1898 and Luetgert's lovers turned against him. It would be their testimonies that would hammer the final nail into the coffin.

Agathia Tosch testified that she had asked Luetgert where his wife was shortly after she had disappeared and he simply smiled and said, "I don't know. I am as innocent as the southern skies." She also told the jury that Luetgert had hated his wife and that he said on more than one occasion that he could "take her and crush her."

Luetgert's favorite mistress, a German woman named Christine Feldt, also took the stand. She added to the Luetgert's motive by producing gushing love letters that he had written to her. She also testified that Luetgert had given her $4,000 for "safe-keeping" shortly before Louisa's disappearance. He had also given her a bloodstained knife on May 2. He had never explained where it had come from and during the investigation, Christine had given it to the police.

Not surprisingly, Luetgert was convicted and sentenced to life imprisonment at Joliet.

Luetgert was taken away to prison, where he became a shell of his former self. He babbled incoherently to the guards, claiming that his dead wife was haunting him, intent on having her revenge, even though he was innocent of her murder. Luetgert, possibly insane by this time, died in 1900.

And he was not the only one to suffer. His attorney, Lawrence Harmon, believed that his client was telling the truth and that he did not kill his wife. He was sure that she had simply disappeared. In fact, Harmon was so convinced of Luetgert's innocence that she spent over

$2,000 of his own money and devoted the rest of his life to finding Louisa. Eventually, he also went insane and he died in a mental institution.

As for Louisa, whether she was murdered by her husband or not, she reportedly did not rest in peace. Not long after her husband was sent to prison, her ghost began to be seen inside of the Luetgert house. Neighbors claimed to see a woman in a white dress leaning against the mantel of the fireplace. Eventually, the house was rented out but none of the tenants stayed there for long. The ghost was also reported inside of the sausage factory but this building burned down in 1902 and was never rebuilt.

Legend has it on the North Side of Chicago that Louisa Luetgert still walks. If she does, she probably no longer recognizes the neighborhood where she once lived. The sausage factory is long gone and the houses that once stood here have been replaced by empty lots and an industrial complex.

The stories say though, that if you happened to be in this area on May 1, the anniversary of Louisa's death, there is a chance that you might see her lonely specter still roaming the area where she lived and died.

## THE SMUGGLER'S DOLL
### Revenge from Beyond the Grave

Can hatred and a thirst for revenge be so strong that it can actually be enacted from the next world? Some would argue that it can and vintage crime buffs would be quick to point a case from the 1870's that spelled the end for a ring of New York smugglers. The verdict in the case would lead to imprisonment and death and many believe, something far more sinister.

Night was falling on the city of Manhattan in April 1870 when a steamship called the "Atlantic Star" sailed up the river to the pier near Desbrosses Street. The passengers lined the rail, taking in the cool evening air and watching as the vessel steamed into port. Among those on deck were a tall, distinguished-looking woman and a plump little blond girl who stood beside her. The little girl peered through a small telescope toward Staten Island. She eagerly scanned the shore and then exclaimed with delight as she saw her house near the water. The stately mansion was where the child and her guardian spent each summer. Each winter, they traveled to Paris to visit relatives.

As the girl laughed aloud, the older woman glanced down at her and smiled. Mrs. Ada Danforth had a distinctly elegant air about her. She was expensively dressed, as was her ward, in the rich fashions of Paris. Eighteen days before, they had departed the French city and now Mrs. Danforth was intent on reaching New York. Here, she and little Fanchon Moncare would open the Staten Island house for the season. They had been doing this every year since Mrs. Danforth took charge of the little girl at the tender age of six. She had explained to other passengers on board that she had been caring for the girl since her parents had died several years before. They left her quite well off, she told them, to the point that Mrs. Danforth was to administer the estate until her ward turned eighteen. Fanchon was a very lucky little girl.

Soon, passengers were milling about, preparing to leave the ship. People who recognized Mrs. Danforth and her ward smiled and bid farewell to the two of them. Fanchon spoke politely, all the while clutching a doll tightly in her arms. They walked along the deck as the Atlantic Star was tied off and the gangplank lowered. Fanchon, still holding her doll, was the first to leave the ship. Mrs. Danforth followed her very closely.

The ritual of passing through customs, which was an ordeal for many travelers, held no fear for Fanchon and Mrs. Danforth. They had been arriving from Paris for many years now and going through customs had become quite routine. They had gone out of their way to befriend the local officials, sometimes bringing wine and small presents for the men on duty. Fanchon danced up to one of the customs officials. "Hello, Mr. Smith," she smiled at him with a girlish lisp. "We're back to see you again. Would you like to give my dolly and me a kiss?"

Mr. Smith laughed at the little girl and playfully bussed her cheek and that of the doll. He quickly passed the Danforth trunks and boxes through the customs barrier. Ada Danforth graciously offered him a handsome smile, causing the man to blush furiously. As Mrs. Danforth walked on past, Fanchon skipped along beside her, holding tightly to her doll.

And it was well to hold onto it so tight. For inside of the doll was nearly $250,000 in stolen jewels. They had been lifted by Ada Danforth and her companion, "Fanchon Moncare", who in truth was named Estelle Ridley. Despite her girlish clothing and adorable lisp, she was no child either. Estelle was nearing her fortieth birthday!

Danforth and Ridley had been performing this act in New York and Paris for several years under the auspices of the Tweed Ring, a group of corrupt city officials who managed to bilk the New York treasury for as much as $200 million between 1865 and 1871. The organization managed not only the city offices, but also the district attorney, the courts and most of the newspapers. No votes were cast in the city without the approval of the Tweed Ring. William Marcy Tweed, the boss of Tammany Hall, became well known for his mass production of voters. On one occasion, with help from a corrupt judge, Tweed naturalized nearly 60,000 immigrants in twenty days. Few of these new arrivals understood the oath of citizenship or even the English language. When Election Day arrived, Tweed cohorts showed the new citizens how to vote.

The Tweed Ring also controlled the underworld of the city and forced criminals to pay a "duty" to operate in New York. Most of them were more than happy to pay. In the case of Ada Danforth and Estelle Ridley, they had brought hundreds of thousands of dollars into the country without fear of being caught. After paying the right people, they managed to maintain the Staten Island estate and to live in high style.

But the personalities of the partners could not have been different. While Danforth remained ensconced with Staten Island society, Ridley would shed her childish disguise to drink and carouse with low companions in the Bowery saloons and at the Rockaway Park racetrack. She had gained a terrible reputation over the years for her loose and wicked ways. It was a reputation that caused Ada Danforth to shiver in disgust.

It was at the racetrack where Ridley met a woman named Magda Hamilton. She was also known for her often scandalous sexual behavior but had tenuous connections to New York society and especially to henchmen of the Tweed Ring. She was an important ally and Ridley was quick to cultivate her. Soon, the two of them made plans to carry out a jewel robbery in Chicago.

When Ada Danforth heard about this new job, she was quick to try and discourage her partner from it. In the past, they had always confined their work to targets outside of the country. They had perfected the passage through customs and Ridley's "little girl" act. To attempt this proposed robbery was both dangerous and foolish, Danforth warned the other woman, and no good could of it.

Ridley dismissed the warning and she and Magda Hamilton left for Chicago. Their plan consisted of attracting the attention of an old millionaire named Rufus Twombly. He was a widower who had a large estate in Lake Forest. The women arranged to meet the man on a train bound for Chicago. Ridley again took the role of Fanchon and Hamilton became her guardian. They had learned already that Twombly had once had a daughter who had died at the age of fourteen. He had never forgotten her and with the death of his wife, had become quite lonely. He was duped into being entranced with the delightful Fanchon. Soon, both women were lived in the Lake Forest mansion.

Everything went according to plan. The servants were given the day off and Twombly was drugged into a stupor. They managed to make off with over $350,000 from the wall safe in his office and then they disappeared from Illinois. It all went smoothly until they returned to Staten Island and it came time to divide up the loot. Suddenly, the plan began to fall apart.

Ridley, who considered herself the mastermind behind the operation, announced that she only planned to give Magda Hamilton $5,000 of the money taken from Rufus Twombly. Needless to say, Hamilton was incensed with this plan and made a number of threats toward the other woman before taking the paltry sum and leaving. She slammed the door behind her and an ominous silence filled the house. As Ada Danforth had predicted, no good would come of the Chicago robbery.

A few days later, they closed the Staten Island house and made plans for their departure to France. The European theater season would soon be opening and there were many rich "chickens" to be plucked. They set sail on the steamship "Panonia" and went first to Biarritz, then to San Sebastian a few weeks later. Then one night in Marseilles, the Vicomte de Point Talliere was robbed as he was leaving the opera. Everyone knew that the old man always wore a fortune in jewels with his evening dress and carried hundreds of francs on his person. Unfortunately, the Vicomte, who was quite elderly, had been badly beaten in the robbery and had died on the way to the hospital.

The public was in an uproar over the murder! Pressure fell on the authorities to apprehend the killer, who was a man hired by Danforth and Ridley to carry out the deed. He was hastily paid off and disappeared but two women were concerned that suspicion might fall upon them. They had been seen in restaurants and at the theater with the Vicomte and the police were bound to come looking in their direction eventually. They seemed to have no other choice but to return to New York. There, under the protection of the Tweed Ring, they would be safe.

Within days, Mrs. Danforth and little Fanchon had booked passage to America. Danforth explained to their society friends that Fanchon had taken ill and needed to return home. She did not trust the French doctors, she told them, and wanted to get the girl home to their family physician.

When the ship reached New York, smiling Mrs. Danforth and the giggling Fanchon again lined up at the rail to leave the vessel. As before, Fanchon gripped her doll tightly. Even though the pair had been forced to cut their trip short, a fortune in jewels and cash was stuffed into the head of the doll. As the gangplank was lowered, they began to realize that the atmosphere at the dockside was tense. Two groups of men stood waiting at the pier and they took up position near the customs barriers as the passengers started to leave the ship.

Fanchon was halfway down the gangplank before she became aware of the eyes looking up at her. She stopped immediately, but the crush of passengers behind her shoved her along. She and Ada Danforth, who was walking next to her, were propelled into the arms of the waiting men. As Fanchon's foot touched the dock, a grim-faced police officer took her by the arm. He leaned down and spoke softly. "Miss Ridley, I arrest you in the name...." he began, but Fanchon's shriek drowned out his words. She heaved her doll into the water below and then let out a string of obscenities that certainly betrayed her disguise. She fought like a tiger and it took four men to finally subdue her.

Through it all, Ada Danforth stood quietly, calm and collected and staring at Ridley's exhibition. She allowed herself to be escorted to a police wagon that waited outside of the pier entrance. She did not speak until they reached the police station. At that point, she politely asked one of the detectives how they had found out about the doll and the smuggling operation. "It was a woman," he told her. "We have no idea who she was but she was dressed all in black and wore a heavy veil."

But Ada Danforth knew who the woman had been. She had been right, nothing good had come from her despicable partner's trip to Chicago.

The trial of Ada Danforth and Estelle Ridley made headlines and was one of the factors that brought about the end of the Tweed Ring. Danforth had no more reason to protect the men to whom they paid bribes and she began to name names and outline the details of the operation. These charges, combined with an incorruptible reform movement headed by Samuel J. Tilden and the fact that the Ring had nearly bankrupted the city, destroyed the organization once and for all.

Estelle Ridley, who was found to be 46 years old, was sentenced to life in prison. Her partner, Ada Danforth, was only charged as an accessory and she received a sentence of twenty years. Thanks to her cooperation in the trial, no effort was made to look into her bank accounts or estate. She was paroled a few years later and quietly took her place in polite New York society.

Boss Tweed was indicted for his crimes and brought to trial. The first trial ended in a hung jury and it was later found that a number of the jurors had been bribed. During the second trial, each of the jurors was watched closely by an undercover police officer to insure that they had not been tampered with. This time, Tweed was convicted and sentenced to twelve years in prison. He later appealed the sentence and was released in 1875, only to be indicted again when the state of New York sued to retrieve the money that he had stolen. Tweed managed to escape from jail and fled to Cuba and then Spain. Ironically, he was recognized because of a Thomas Nast cartoon that had been drawn about the scandal and was sent back to the United States. He died in prison in 1876.

A few weeks after the trial ended, the house on Staten Island that had been owned by Estelle Ridley was put up for sale. The buyer was a veiled woman and the deed was made out in the name of Mrs. Dartway Crawley, a widow. She took up residence in the mansion and never again used the name for which she was known in criminal circles, Magda Hamilton.

Years passed. Ada Danforth was released from prison to enjoy her ill-gotten gains and Mrs. Crawley continued to live in the house on Staten Island. Estelle Ridley had long since been forgotten, perhaps by both of the women. One night, Crawley, unable to sleep, turned restlessly in her bed. She had been plagued with horrible nightmares as of late, dreams of a little girl in a pink and white dress appearing on the staircase of the house. Once she even thought that she might have seen the girl when she was awake. That was something that she wanted to put out of her mind as she tossed and turned in the darkness.

As she lay there, looking at the ceiling, she suddenly had the strangest feeling that she was not alone. She glanced to the doorway and in moments was seized with fear. She sat up in the bed, clutching her night dress to her throat. A figure was there in the doorway and it was coming toward her. It was the little girl of her dreams, dressed in pink and white, but why did she seem so familiar? The girl came closer and then Crawley saw the malevolent gleam in the child's eyes... and she also saw the pudgy face and yellowed teeth of Estelle Ridley!

That was impossible, she thought, she was in prison....

And then Crawley had no more time to think.

Clutched in Ridley's hands was a doll with a china head. She held it like a dagger and when Crawley opened her mouth to scream, Ridley rammed the head of the doll down her throat! She plunged and pushed, choking and gagging the other woman. A death-like smile was etched on her face the entire time.

Mrs. Crawley was found by her servants the following morning. Blood was smeared all over her face and spattered on the bed linens. A medical examiner reported that she had died from strangulation and that the membrane of her throat had been torn. He determined that a heavy object had been forced into her throat with great violence, locking open her jaws. He was unable to say what this item may have been however, as the murder weapon was not found.

The detectives assigned to the case were unable to solve it. The house showed no signs of entry in the night and Mrs. Crawley was not known to have any enemies. No one thought to look for Estelle Ridley as a possible suspect, for one very good reason... Ridley had died in prison almost ten years before!

Time passed and real estate agents soon began to speak of the "jinxed" Crawley House. Many believed that it was impossible to rent out for any length of time. No one would stay in it for more than a few weeks and sometimes they stayed for only a few days. Tenants spoke of being awakened at night by a woman cursing and frightened by the appearance of a ghostly little girl who looked suspiciously like an old woman. She was seen wandering about the house, carrying a doll with a china head. None of the occupants stayed around long enough to question who this apparition might be.

In later years, New York Harbor authorities began to receive reports of a slight figure prowling about on the widow's walk on top of the old Crawley House. They say that she would watch the ships as they came in off Sandy Hook. Some say that the figure is a woman, while others insist that it is a child who holds a doll under one arm.

## THE MOST HAUNTED HOUSE IN OHIO!
### The Legend and Lore of Franklin Castle

For years, the gothic mansion known as "Franklin Castle" has been called the most haunted house in Ohio. During its long and strange history, the ghost stories have become an integral part of the lore. For years, tales have been told of doors that explode off their hinges, lights that spin on their own, electric circuits that behave erratically, the inexplicable sounds of a baby crying and even a woman in black who has been seen staring forlornly from a tiny window in the front tower room.

There are many ghosts here, the legends say. But what dark deeds caused this house to become so haunted? Are the stories of the murders committed here actually true, or the stuff of legend?

Franklin Castle is an eerie structure of dark and foreboding stone that has long been considered a spooky place by architects and the general public alike. There are over thirty rooms in the castle's four stories and the roof is designed in steep gables that give the place its gothic air. Secret passages honeycomb the house and sliding panels hide the doorways to these hidden corridors. It is said that a thirteen-year-old girl was once murdered in one of these hallways by her uncle because he believed her to be insane. In the front tower, it is told that a bloody ax murder once took place and it was here that one of the former owners found a secret cabinet that contained human bones. The Deputy coroner of Cleveland, Dr. Lester Adelson, who examined the bones shortly after they were found in January 1975, judged them to be of someone who had been dead for a very, very long time. Did they date back to the years of the original owners of the house?

It is hard to separate fact from fiction at Franklin Castle but we do know that a German immigrant named Hannes Tiedemann built the mansion in 1865. Tiedemann was a former barrel-maker and wholesale grocer who had gone into banking. This new source of wealth allowed him to spare no expense in building the house and he soon moved in with his wife, Luise. Over the next few years, Luise gave birth to a son, August, and a daughter, Emma but life in the mansion was never really happy. By 1881, it had become tragic.

On January 16, 15 year old Emma died from diabetes. In those days, death from the disease came as a horrible, lingering starvation for which there was no cure. A short time later, Tiedemann's elderly mother, Wiebeka, also died in the house. Over the next three years, the Tiedemann's buried three children, one of them just eleven days old. Rumors began to spread that there may have been more to these deaths than was first apparent.

To take his wife's mind off the family tragedies, Tiedemann enlisted the services of a prominent architectural firm to design some additions to the mansion. It was during this expansion that the secret passages, concealed rooms and hidden doors were added to the house. Gas lighting was also installed throughout the building and many of the fixtures are still visible today. A large ballroom was also added that ran the length of the entire house and turrets and gargoyles were also incorporated into the design, making it appear even more like a castle.

The hidden passages in the house also hide many legends. At the rear of the house is a trap door that leads to a tunnel that goes nowhere. Another hidden room once contained a liquor still, left over from the Prohibition era. During the 1920's, the house was allegedly used as a speakeasy and warehouse for illegal liquor. The most gruesome secret uncovered in the house came from another of the hidden rooms. Here, an occupant found literally dozens of human baby skeletons. It was suggested that they may have been the victims of a doctor's botched experiments or even medical specimens, but no one knew for sure. The medical examiner simply stated that they were "old bones".

On March 24, 1895, Luise died at the age of 57 from what was said to be "liver trouble". Rumors continued to spread about the many untimely deaths in the Tiedemann family, especially when Hannes married again a few years later. By that time, he had sold the castle to a brewing family named Mullhauser and had moved to a grander home on Lake Road. The following summer, Tiedemann decided to vacation at a German resort and there he met (or some have suggested became re-acquainted with) a young waitress named Henriette. He quickly married the woman and lived just long enough to regret it. He divorced her and left her with nothing.

By 1908, Tiedemann's entire family, including his son, August and his children, had passed away. There was no one left to inherit his fortune or to comfort him in his old age. Tiedemann died later that same year, suddenly stricken while walking in the park one day. It is believed that he suffered a massive stroke.

Tiedemann's death did not end the speculation about strange events in the house however. Legend had it that Tiedemann had not been the faithful husband that he appeared to be. There were stories of affairs and sexual encounters within the vast confines of the house that were only whispered about. Tangled in the distasteful stories were also rumors of murder.

One of the bloody tales was told about a hidden passage that extended beyond the castle's ballroom. It was here that Tiedemann allegedly killed his niece by hanging her from one of the exposed rafters. The stories say that she was insane and that he killed her to put her out of her misery. But it's possible this was not the truth because others maintain that he killed her because of her promiscuity. He discovered her in bed with his grandson, it is said, and she paid the ultimate price for this transgression.

Tiedemann is also said to have murdered a young servant girl on her wedding day because she rejected his advances. Another version of the story says that the woman who was killed was Tiedemann's mistress, a woman named Rachel. She accidentally strangled to death in the house after Tiedemann tied her up and gagged her after learning that she wanted to marry another man. It's possible that Rachel's spirit is the resident "woman in black" who has been seen lurking around the old tower. Former residents say that they have heard the sound of a woman choking in this room.

More blood was spilled in the house a few years later, after the Mullhauser family sold the castle to the German Socialist Party in 1913. They used the house for meetings and parties, or so it was said. However, the legends of the house maintain that the Socialists were actually Nazi spies and that twenty of their members were machine-gunned to death in one of the castle's secret rooms. They sold the house fifty-five years later, and during the time of their residence, the house was mainly unoccupied.

It is believed that they may have rented out a portion of the house however, as a Cleveland nurse recalled several years ago that she had cared for an ailing attorney in the castle in the early 1930's. She remembered being terrified at night by the sound of a small child crying. More than forty years later, she told a reporter that she "would never set foot in that house again."

In January of 1968, James Romano, his wife, and six children moved into the house. Mrs. Romano had always been fascinated with the mansion and planned to open a restaurant there, but she quickly changed her mind. On the very day that the family moved in, she sent her children upstairs to play. A little while later, they came back downstairs and asked if they could have a cookie for their new friend, a little girl who was upstairs crying. Mrs. Romano followed the children back upstairs, but found no little girl. This happened a number of times, leading many to wonder if the "ghost children" might be the spirits of the Tiedemann children who died in the early 1880's.

Mrs. Romano also reported hearing organ music in the house, even though no organ was there and sounds of footsteps tramping up and down the hallways. She also heard voices and the sound of glass clinking on the third floor, even though no one else was in the house. The Romano's finally consulted a Catholic priest about the house. He declined to do an exorcism of the place, but told them that he sensed an evil presence in the house and that they should leave.

The family then turned to the Northeast Ohio Psychical Research Society, a now defunct ghost-hunting group, and they sent out a team to investigate Franklin Castle. In the middle of the investigation, one of the team members fled the building in terror.

By September of 1974, the Romano's had finally had enough. They sold the castle to Sam Muscatello, who planned to turn the place into a church, but instead, after learning of the building's shady past, started offering guided tours of the house. He also had problems with ghostly visitors in the mansion encountering strange sounds, vanishing objects and the eerie woman in black.

He invited Cleveland radio executive John Webster to the house for an on-air special about hauntings and Franklin Castle. Webster claimed that while walking up a staircase, something tore a tape recorder from a strap over his shoulder and flung it down the stairs. "I was climbing the stairs with a large tape recorder strapped over my shoulder," Webster later recalled and then told how the device was pulled away from him. "I just stood there holding the microphone as I watched the tape recorder go flying down to the bottom of the stairs, where it broke into pieces."

A television reporter named Ted Ocepec, who also came to visit the castle, witnessed a hanging ceiling light that suddenly began turning in circular motions. He was also convinced that something supernatural lurked in the house. Someone suggested that perhaps traffic vibrations on the street outside had caused the movement of the light. Ocepec didn't think so. "I just don't know," he said, "but there's something in that house."

Muscatello's interest in the history of the house led him to start searching for the secret panels and passages installed by the Tiedemann's. It was he who made the gruesome discovery of the skeleton behind the panel in the tower room. This discovery apparently had a strange effect on Muscatello as he started becoming sick and lost over thirty pounds in a few weeks. He was never very successful at turning the place into a tourist attraction and eventually sold the place to a doctor, who in turn sold the house for the same amount to Cleveland Police Chief Richard Hongisto.

The police chief and his wife declared that the spacious mansion would make the perfect place in which to live but then, less than one year later, abruptly sold the house to George Mirceta, who was unaware of the house's haunted reputation. He had bought the castle merely for its solid construction and Gothic architecture. He lived alone in the house and also conducted tours of the place, asking visitors to record any of their strange experiences in a guest book before leaving. Some reported seeing a woman in white, babies crying and lights swinging back and forth. One women even complained of feeling like she was being choked in the tower room. Strangely, she had no idea of the legend concerning that room and the death of Tiedemann's mistress.

Even though he had a number of strange experiences while living there, Mirceta maintained that the castle was not haunted. If it was, he told reporters, he would be too scared to live there. "There has to be a logical explanation for everything," he told an interviewer.

In 1984, the house was sold once again, this time to Michael De Vinko, who attempted to restore the place. He claimed to have no problems with ghosts in the house but surmised that it may have been because he was taking care of the old place again. He spent huge sums of money in restoration efforts. He successfully tracked down the original blueprints to the house, some of the Tiedemann furniture, and even the original key to the front door, which still worked. Even after spending all of the money though, the house was put back on the real-estate market in 1994.

The castle was sold again in 1999 and the current owner is once again attempting to restore the place, even after an arson fire damaged it badly in November of that same year. As of this writing, work is still being completed on the structure. The owner plans to document the repairs and restoration on-line. Once it is completed, he hopes to open the house for tours once again.

But has the blood-soaked past of the house left a mark that is still being felt in the present? When asked if the castle is really haunted, the owner admits that he's not sure that it is, or if he even believes in ghosts at all. However, he does say that many of his friends and family have had had odd experiences here. "Most of them involve either unexplained sounds, or difficult-to-describe feelings."

He adds that the castle is not a scary place, but it is a little creepy, especially in the middle of the night. "I've heard strange sounds and hoped to see something or hear something that would prove to me that ghosts exist, but so far it hasn't happened," he said. "So far it's been no spookier than sleeping alone in any old house that creaks in the wind or has rattling pipes."

Keep your fingers crossed for him that it stays this way!

## THE HOUSE ON RIDGE AVENUE

*The Original "Most Haunted House in America"*

For many years, stories circulated about what was called the "most haunted house in America". To look at the place, where it was located on the north side of Pittsburgh, one might never suspect what dark secrets lingered inside. There were tales of bizarre murder, human experimentation and gruesome death told about the house and visits to the residence inspired horror stories and even a great inventor's fascination with death and the afterworld.

And if any building deserved the reputation for being America's most haunted house, it was this one!

The house on Ridge Avenue was located in a quiet residential neighborhood in Manchester, on the north edge of Pittsburgh. A man named Charles Wright Congelier built it in the 1860's. He had made a fortune for himself in Texas following the Civil War and such men were commonly referred to in the south as "Carpetbaggers". They made a lot of money preying on the broken economy in the former Confederacy, and they made a lot of enemies too. It was said that Congelier made it out of Texas "just in time", as his enemies soon began to outnumber his friends. He departed for the north by river steamer, taking with him his Mexican wife, Lyda, and a servant girl named Essie. When the steamer docked in Pittsburgh for coal, Congelier decided that the Pennsylvania town looked like a good place to settle. The three of them left the ship and Congelier purchased a lot and began construction of the house.

A few months later, the new brick and mortar mansion was completed. It was located at 1129 Ridge Avenue and was considered one of the finest houses in the area. From the expansive lawn, Congelier could look out and see where the Allegheny and Monongahela Rivers met to form the Ohio, offering a breathtaking view. The former Carpetbagger soon became a respected member of the local business community and his new home became a frequent site for parties and social gatherings.

Then, during the winter of 1871, an event took place that would bloody the location for decades to come.

That winter, as cold and snow settled over the region, Congelier became embroiled in an affair with his servant girl, Essie. Whether she was a willing participant or not, Essie soon became a constant bed partner for her employer. For several months, Lyda Congelier was unaware of the affair, but when three people reside in the same house, it's only a matter of time before secrets are revealed.

One afternoon, when Essie did not respond to her call, Lyda went to the girl's room looking for her. As she came down the hallway, she could hear heavy breathing and moaning coming from behind the door. Knowing that her husband was the only man in the house, Lyda became enraged. She hurried to the kitchen and snatched up both a butcher knife and a meat cleaver. As she began climbing the stairs back to the servant's room, Lyda became screaming with rage, which naturally provoked a panic inside of Essie's bedroom. Before Congelier and the girl could dress themselves and exit the room, Lyda had already taken up a post outside. When the door opened, she brought the meat cleaver down on the head of the first person to open it. Charles Congelier fell to the floor, a cry on his lips and blood streaming from the wound on his head. As Essie reared back, bellowing in terror, Lyda proceeded to stab her husband thirty times.

Several days later, a family friend called at the house and when no one responded to his knock, he opened the door and peered inside. He called out, but there was no answer in the darkened house. However, as he entered the foyer, he could hear a faint creaking noise in the parlor. He called out again, but as there was no answer, he walked further into the house. Following the odd sound, he entered the parlor and saw Lyda Congelier rocking back and forth in front of a large bay window. The wooden chair that she rested in creaked with each backward and forward motion that she made.

"Lyda? Is everything all right?" he spoke to her.

There was no reply. Lyda continued to rock back and forth in the chair. As her friend drew closer, he could hear her softly crooning a lullaby under her breath. It was a child's nursery song, he realized, and he saw a bundle that was wrapped in a blanket in Lyda's arms. She held it close, as she would hold a baby, rocking it gently. The man felt a sudden chill course through him. He knew that the Congelier's had no children.

He spoke to her once again, but there was still no answer. Lyda stared straight ahead at the snow outside, her eyes glazed and unfocused. He gently leaned over and eased the bundle out of her hands. He carefully opened the pink blanket and then recoiled with horror, dropping the bloody bundle onto the floor! It landed on the wooden floorboards with a solid thud and the contents of the blanket rolled away.

The friend fell backwards on the couch as Essie's bloody head came to halt a short distance away from his feet!

For more than two decades, the house on Ridge Avenue remained empty. Local folks considered the place "tainted" and avoided it at all costs. Few dared to even trespass on the grounds, although sometimes small children threw stones at the windows and sang about the "old battle-ax and her meat-ax".

Then in 1892, the house was renovated into an apartment building to house railroad workers. Most refused to stay in the place for long. They constantly complained of hearing screams and the sobbing of a woman that came from empty rooms. Others spoke of the ominous sounds of a rocking chair and of a woman mumbling old nursery rhymes and lullabies. Within two years, the house was abandoned once again.

It remained vacant until 1901, when Dr. Adolph C. Brunrichter purchased the house. The doctor became something of an enigma in the neighborhood. Although he had been warned of the past history of the house, he chose to purchase the place anyway and after moving in, had little to do with the nearby residents. He kept to himself and was rarely seen by those who lived close to him. Everyone in the neighborhood watched and held their breath, waiting for something terrible to happen. They didn't have to wait very long.

On August 12, 1901, the family who lived next door to the Brunrichter mansion heard a terrified scream coming from the house. When they ran outside to see what was going on, they saw a bright red flash illuminate the interior of the mansion. The windows of the house shattered and glass shot out onto the lawn! The air was filled with the smell of ozone and the earth under the neighborhood trembled, cracking the sidewalks and knocking over furniture in the surrounding homes.

By the time the police and the fire department arrived, a crowd had gathered outside of Brunrichter's house. It was assumed that the doctor was still inside as no one had seen him leave, but none of the neighbors were brave enough to go in and check. Finally, a contingent of fire fighters entered the house in search of Brunrichter. They were unable to find him, but what they did discover was enough to send even the bravest among them running for the street outside!

In one of the upstairs bedrooms, a gut-wrenching scene awaited police investigators. Lying spread-eagled on the blood-soaked bed was the decomposed, naked body of a young woman. Her head was missing and was later found in a makeshift laboratory that the doctor had set up in another room. From what the detectives could determine, Brunrichter had apparently been experimenting with severed heads. Using electrical equipment, he had been trying to keep them alive after decapitation. A fault in his equipment had evidently caused the explosion. The young girl's head was found with several others and the graves of five women were discovered in the cellar. Each of the bodies could be matched with one of the heads from the laboratory.

As for Dr. Brunrichter, there was no sign of him. He had apparently escaped during the confusion following the explosion and had vanished. A manhunt produced no clues. He had disappeared without leaving a trace.


Once again, the house on Ridge Avenue was abandoned. It stood empty again for many years, gaining an even more fearsome reputation. Those with an interest in psychic phenomena made occasional visits to the place and it came to be believed that the house was inhabited by a "fearsome presence". One medium who probed the house, Julia Murray, detected a horrible spirit there and witnesses who accompanied her to the mansion stated that "objects hurled by unseen hands barely missed striking her". Murray predicted that the entity would kill and would eventually extend out beyond the confines of the house.

In 1920, the stories about the mansion caught the attention of another man, one of the greatest inventors that America has ever known. His name was Thomas Alva Edison and in addition to creating the light bulb, he went to his grave in search of a device that would be able to communicate with the dead.

Edison was a self-taught genius who began experimenting with scientific theories as a child. Throughout his life, he maintained that it was possible to build anything if the right components were available. This would later include the already mentioned machine. Edison was not a believer in the supernatural however, nor a proponent of the popular Spiritualist movement. He had always been an agnostic and although he did not dispute the philosophies of religion, he didn't necessarily believe in their truth either. He believed that when a person died, the body decayed but the intelligence the man possessed lived on. He thought that the so-called "spirit world" was simply a limbo where disembodied intelligence waited to move on.

He took these paranormal theories one step further by announcing that he intended to devise a machine that could communicate with this "limbo". In the October 1920 issue of "American" Magazine, an article appeared that was entitled "Edison Working to Communicate with the Next World". This was just one of the many magazines attempting to confirm Edison's strange plans. Edison's announcement appeared in newspapers after his visit to the house on Ridge Avenue. What happened during his visit to the house is unknown, but whatever it was, it certainly inspired him to go to great lengths to create the machine.

The news of the invention made headlines around the world. This period was at the height of the Spiritualist movement's popularity and a number of the world's eminent scientists were involved in paranormal studies. Edison began corresponding with Sir William Crooke, the British scientist from whose vacuum tube Edison was able to develop the light bulb. Crooke was also involved in paranormal research, especially in spirit photography. Crooke's collection of photographs, allegedly showing the spirits of the dead, prompted Edison to surmise that if ghosts could be captured on film, then his device might actually work.

According to journals and papers, Edison began working on the apparatus. The famous magician and friend of Edison's, Joseph Dunninger, claimed that he was shown a prototype of the machine but few others ever say they saw it. Edison reportedly continued working on the machine until his death in October 1931. At the precise moment that he died, three of his workers noted that clocks all over his house and workshop suddenly stopped working.

Did Edison's machine actually exist? And if so, would it have worked? In the years following his death, curators at both of the Edison museums in Florida and New Jersey have searched extensively for the components, the prototype or even the plans for the machine to communicate with the dead. So far, they have found nothing, making Edison's device the greatest mystery of his complex and intriguing life.

In the middle 1920's, Julia Murray's premonitions of "evil" connected to the house on Ridge Avenue remained in the back of many minds. During this period, the Equitable Gas Company, which was located just a few blocks away, was nearing the completion of a huge natural gas storage complex. To cut costs, many of the regular workers were laid off and were replaced by Italian immigrants, who would work for a much lower wage. A number of vacant buildings in the neighborhood were converted into apartments, including the house at 1129 Ridge Avenue.

The Italian workers who took up residence in the house quickly realized that something was not right in the old mansion. Their complaints and reports were met with quick explanations from the supervisors at the gas company. They told the immigrants that the strange occurrences were the work of the American workers who had been replaced. The former employees were playing tricks on the new workers, hoping they would abandon their jobs. The men soon dismissed the strange sounds and ghostly footsteps as practical jokes... until an incident occurred a few months after they moved in.

One evening, fourteen men were seated around the table in the common dining room. They had just finished consuming large quantities of pasta and were now laughing and talking over glasses of homemade wine. One of the men got up and carried a stack of dirty dishes into the kitchen. He joked to his brother as he left the room, calling out a humorous insult over his shoulder with a smile. The remark was answered with laughter and his brother tossed a crust of bread at his sibling's retreating back. The conversation continued for several minutes before the remaining man realized that his brother had not returned from the kitchen. He got up and walked into the other room to find the door to the basement standing open.

Suddenly, the festive mood in the dining room was shattered by a chilling scream! Rushing into the kitchen, the men saw the basement door as it yawned open. Taking a lantern from atop the icebox, several of the men descended the steps into the cellar. Before they reached the bottom of the steps, they froze, staring at the macabre scene that was illuminated by the glow of the lantern. In the dim light, they saw the man who had left the dining room just moments earlier, now hanging from a floor beam that crossed the ceiling above!

On the floor, directly beneath his feet, was the man's brother. He was lying face down in a spreading pool of blood. A splintered board had been driven through his chest and now exited out through his back.

The leader of the group on the steps crossed himself religiously and a gasp escaped from his lips. His friends repeated the gesture before all of them found themselves slammed backward by a force that they could not see! The feeling of a cold wind pushed against them and then rushed past up the stairs. The men later said that they could hear the pounding of footsteps on the wooden treads, but could see nothing at all. The door at the top of the stairs slammed shut, startling the men in the kitchen, who didn't hear anything. However, they did report other doors mysteriously slamming throughout the house.

When the police arrived, they attributed both deaths to a bizarre accident. The first man, the detectives stated, tripped on a loose step and fell down, impaling himself on the propped-up board. The other brother's death was the result of the same loose stair step. When he fell though, his head was somehow tangled on an electric wire that was hanging down above the staircase. Accident or not, the other men quickly moved out of the house, wanting nothing more to do with the place.

A short time later, another incident occurred. While it took place hundreds of miles away in New York City, some believe that it would have terrifying consequences and would supernaturally influence an event that would occur just two months later.

In September 1927, an old man was arrested in New York's Bowery district. He was found wandering in a drunken stupor, living among the homeless and the street people. He was arrested and booked for public drunkenness and was taken to the local police station house. Standing in line with the other dirty and disheveled men, this particular vagrant seemed to give off what the officers would later recall as a "bad feeling". As the drunks shuffled along, the policemen entered their names into record one at a time. When the old man reached the head of the line, the officer asked him his name.

He replied in a harsh voice, slightly slurred with a foreign accent. "My name is Adolph Brunrichter," the man said. And soon, he began to tell stories to the officers at the police station and they were tales even the most hardened officers would not soon forget!

Brunrichter began by explaining to the officers that he was once an eminent doctor, a physician who worked diligently to prolong life. Unfortunately, he could only succeed with his experiments by ending the lives of certain test subjects. He told of how many years earlier, he had bought a house in Pittsburgh to which he enticed young women as guests. Anticipating romance, the women were instead beheaded and then used in experiments to keep their severed heads alive. Brunrichter told of sex orgies, torture and murder and then gave the locations of graves for other women who were not discovered in the cellar of the house. Authorities later checked the sites, but no bodies were ever found.

Brunrichter was kept behind bars for one month at Blackwell's Island. Despite newspaper stories that called him the "Pittsburgh Spook Man", the mad doctor was deemed "harmless" and was released. On the wall of his cell, scrawled in his own blood, were the words "What Satan hath wrought, let man beware." After those fateful words, nothing was ever heard from the man who claimed to be Dr. Adolph Brunrichter again.

Two weeks after the "Spook Man's" release, catastrophe occurred in Pittsburgh. On Monday, November 14, 1927, a crew of sixteen workers climbed to the top of the Equitable Gas Company's huge, 5,000,000-cubic-foot natural gas storage tank to find and repair a leak.

At 8:43 that morning, a great sheet of flame erupted from the tank and the huge container shot impossibly upwards into the air. Steel, stone and human bodies were sent hurling into the sky. Two of the men who had been working on top of the tank were thrown against a brick building more than one hundred feet away and their silhouettes were outlined there in blood. Seconds later, another tank exploded, creating another gigantic ball of fire. Then a third tank, this one only partially full, was wrenched apart and added to the inferno. Smoke and flames were visible for miles. The force was so awesome that it blew out windows and shook buildings for a twenty-mile radius. Locomotives were knocked over and homes and structures damaged as far away as East Liberty.

Across the street, the Union Paint Company was flattened and dozens of workers were buried under the rubble of the building. Bloody men, women and children ran frantically about in the streets.

The Battalion Chief of Engine Company No. 47, Dan Jones, was part of the first fire unit to arrive on the scene. He described the holocaust saying "great waves of black smoke swept through the streets and there was a whining noise in the air." According to a book compiled by the Writer's Project of America, the destruction stunned the city. "As houses collapsed and chimneys toppled," they wrote, "brick, broken glass, twisted pieces of steel and other debris rained on the heads of the dazed and shaken residents who had rushed into the streets from their wrecked homes, believing that an earthquake had visited the city."

Even the rescue workers and fire fighters who arrived on the scene were injured and killed when weakened structures collapsed on top of them. Entire neighborhoods were flooded by broken water mains while huge sections of the city lay in ruins. Sections of the giant gas storage tanks were later found more than a thousand feet away. Rough estimates from the following day listed at least twenty-eight killed and more than six hundred people injured from the explosion. Rescue crews dynamited the ruins in a search for the bodies of the dozens of others who were still missing. Thousands were left homeless by the destruction.

Mounds of rubble and debris marked the spots where buildings had once stood. At one place though, not even bricks and stone remained. At 1129 Ridge Avenue, just two blocks away from the blast site, there was nothing but a smoldering crater. Although homes on both sides, and across the street, from where the Congelier mansion had stood were heavily damaged, they were still standing. Yet where the "most haunted house in America' had stood, and where Julia Murray's proclaimed "evil presence" had lingered, there was nothing. A hole that nearly eighty-five feet deep was all that remained. It was the only house in the vicinity of which no trace could be found.

Today, the Carnegie Science Center occupies the site of the Equitable Gas Company tanks and the terrible explosion is only a faint memory from the past. The house on Ridge Avenue is all but forgotten. Its location is the present-day site of the Route 65 and Interstate 279 interchange. Nothing from the days of Dr. Brunrichter, the Congelier's, or the luckless Italian immigrants still lingers, or does it? If it is possible for the spirits of the past to still wander restlessly along a busy highway, then it would be at this place where such spirits would dwell.... the place where one of the most evil houses in the country could be found.

## FAREWELL TO THE GRIMES SISTERS
### The End of Innocence in Chicago

Many readers may remember being a child and taking a trip to the corner drug store for a soda and a comic book, although few of us would allow our children to do that today. But things weren't always that way. I have friends, much older than myself, who grew up in the 1930's and 1940's, when people didn't have to worry so much about what was going when their kids were out of sight. Sure, the "good old days" were not always good, but it just seemed to be a more innocent time in the hearts of all Americans. I was a child in the late 1960's and early 1970's and even then, people were not as cautious as they are today about letting kids do things on their own. Even now though, I can remember the words that I'll probably never forget. "Never talk to strangers", we were always told.

Well, in Chicago of 1956, two young girls did talk to strangers and became the focus of one of the region's most puzzling unsolved crimes. Not only did this event shatter the innocence of the people of Chicagoland forever, but it gave rise to mysterious events and a chilling haunting as well.

It was December 30, 1956 and Patricia Grimes, 15, and Barbara Grimes, 13, left their home at 3624 South Damon Avenue and headed for the Brighton Theater, only a mile away. The girls were both avid fans of Elvis Presley and had gone to see his film "Love Me Tender". The girls were recognized in the popcorn line at 9:30 PM and then seen on an eastbound Archer Avenue bus at 11:00 PM. After that, things are less certain but this may have been the last time they were ever seen alive. The two sisters were missing for the next twenty-five horrific days, before their naked and frozen bodies were found along the banks of Devil's Creek in the southwest part of Cook County. Autopsies were performed and the coroner reported that the girls had died from exposure and shock but were otherwise unharmed. Or were they? This finding became hotly disputed between rival investigators and has become just one of the many unanswered questions in the case.

The last reported sightings of the two girls came from classmates who spotted them at Angelo's Restaurant at 3551 South Archer Avenue, more than twenty-four hours after their reported disappearance. How accurate this sighting was is unknown, as a railroad conductor also reported them on a train near the Great Lakes Naval Training Center in north suburban Glenview.

The police theorized the girls were chasing after two Navy men they had met downtown but this was only supposition. The girl's mother, Loretta Grimes, refused to believe it and while she was sure the girls were not missing voluntarily, the authorities were still not convinced. Regardless, it became the greatest missing persons hunt in Chicago police history. Even Elvis Presley, in a statement issued from Graceland, asked the girls to come home and ease their mother's worries. The plea went unanswered.

Finally, the vigil for the Grimes Sisters ended on January 22, 1957 when construction worker Leonard Prescott was driving south on German Church Road near Willow Springs. He spotted what appeared to be two discarded clothing store mannequins lying next to a guard rail, about five feet from the road. A few feet away, the ground dropped off to Devil's Creek below. Unsure of what he had seen, Prescott nervously brought his wife to the spot, then they drove to the local police station.

Once investigators realized the "mannequins" were actually bodies, they soon discovered they were the Grimes Sisters. A short time later, more than 162 officers from Chicago, Cook County, the Forest Preserves and five south suburban police departments began combing the woods.... and tramping all over whatever evidence may have been there! Between the officers, the reporters, the medical examiners and everyone else, the investigation was already botched.

As mentioned, the coroner ruled the deaths as homicides, but could not provide an actual cause of death. He also stated that the bodies had been exposed to the elements for nearly a month before their discovery. If this was the case, why hadn't anyone else seen them lying there?

Needless to say, the citizens of Chicagoland were stunned. The authorities questioned an unbelievable 300,000 persons, searching for information about the girls, and 2000 of these people were seriously interrogated, which in those days could be brutal. The police named a 17-year-old named Max Fleig as the chief suspect but the current law did not allow juveniles to be tested with a polygraph, or lie detector. Police Captain Ralph Petaque persuaded the boy to take the test anyway and in the midst of it, he confessed to taking the girls. Because the test was illegal and inadmissible, the police were forced to let Fleig go free. Was he the killer? No one will ever know.

Some time later, the police investigated another confession. This one came from a transient who was believed to have been involved in some other murders around the same time period. His confession later unraveled and he admitted that he had lied.

Eager to crack the floundering case, Cook County Sheriff Joseph Lohman then arrested a Tennessee drifter named Benny Bedwell. The suspect related a lurid and sexually explicit tale of drunken debauchery with two young girls that he had picked up at the restaurant where he worked as a dishwasher. But were these girls actually the Grimes Sisters? Everyone doubted the story but Lohman. He booked Bedwell on murder charges, but the drifter's testimony was both vague and contradictory and (most likely) his confession had been beaten out of him.

One of the chief investigators in the case, Harry Glos, believed that Bedwell might have been implicated in the murders in some way but that he was a dubious suspect. State's Attorney Benjamin Adamowski agreed and ordered the drifter released. This set off another round of bickering between police departments and various jurisdictions and the case became even more mired in red tape and inactivity.

Regardless, Glos believed the girls had been beaten and tortured by a sexual predator who lured them into the kidnap car under seemingly innocent pretense. Today, veteran detectives believe that Glos' theory may have been right. According to Richard Lindberg's book, "Return to the Scene of the Crime", they are convinced that Barbara and Patricia were abducted by a front man for a "white slavery" ring and taken to a remote location in the woods surrounding Willow Springs. They are convinced that the girls were strangled after refusing to become prostitutes.

For the next several years, the investigation continued and more suspects were interviewed. A $100,000 reward was posted but the trail went cold and after that, only nuts and cranks who recounted prophetic dreams and psychic visions came forward with information.

Now, more than 40 years later, the mystery of who killed the Grimes sisters remains unsolved. There are many who remember the case and as discussed earlier, remember a time when children did not have to be afraid to walk the streets in their own neighborhood. The impact of this tragedy is still being felt today, as is the impression of what may have been the girl's final moments.

Along German Church Road in the southern suburb of Willow Springs, is a low point in the roadway that played a part in the 1956 murders. It was here where the bodies of the Grimes sisters were discovered and the location where the police claim to have had numerous strange reports over the years. Since the discovery of the bodies, the police have received reports from those who say they have heard a car pulling up to the location with its motor running. They also say they have heard the door open, followed by the sound of something being dumped alongside the road. The door slams shut and the car drives away. They have heard these things...... and yet there is no car in sight!

Another woman claimed that in addition to the sounds, she saw what appeared to be the naked bodies of two young girls lying on the edge of the roadway. When police investigated, there was no sign of the bodies.

Many researchers believe in "residual hauntings", which means that an event may cause an impression to be left behind on the atmosphere of a place. It is highly likely that the traumatic final moments of the Grimes sisters may have left such an impression on this small stretch of German Church Road. It may have also been an impression caused by the anxiety and madness of the killer as he left the bodies of the young women behind.

Regardless, it seems to be very real and I defy anyone to travel and stop along this stretch of road and to say that they are not moved by the tragedy that took place here.... a tragedy that is the destruction of innocence in Chicagoland.

## GOAT CASTLE
### The Legendary History of the Most Haunted Place in Natchez

The Ruins of Legendary Goat Castle

Located in the southern city of Natchez, Mississippi is a charming subdivision of elegant homes called Glenwood. It is a quiet neighborhood, nestled close to an antebellum home called Glenburnie, the only remaining structure from a time now since past. Years ago, Glenburnie was separated from the land where the subdivision now stands by the same thick stand of forest that still darkens the nearby landscape. It is in these woods where legends say the spirits of the past still linger.

More than five decades ago, the land now occupied by the neat homes of the Glenwood subdivision was the location of a plantation house from which the neighborhood now takes its name. The main house was surrounded by outbuildings and a sprawling piece of land and as time passed, and bloody events unfolded, it was no longer called Glenwood but known as "Goat Castle" instead. The murderous events that took place here were tinged with insanity, terror, eccentric wealth and wretched squalor. These dark happenings of the past have created a legend at Goat Castle... one that still lingers today.

Jane Surget Merrill and Duncan Minor were only children, living in Natchez, when Reverend Dana came to town in 1866. He came to minister to the Trinity Episcopal Church, having just completed a long position as the rector of the Christ Church in Alexandria, Virginia. Such a distinguished appointment allowed him to enter Natchez society as a celebrated member and when his son Richard was born in 1871, he too was accepted into the most elite company in the city. His father died two years later and Dick was raised comfortably by his mother. When she passed away in 1885, Dick attended Vanderbilt and then returned home to become the master of Glenwood. His dream was to become a concert pianist, as he had always shown a great musical talent.

As a young man, Dick became friends with Jane, or Jennie as she preferred to be called, and Duncan. Jennie Merrill had been born in 1864 and was a beautiful young woman. She was raised by her wealthy father and enjoyed all of the conveniences that money could offer. She was also well-liked in Natchez, despite the fact that her father had been a staunch supporter of the Union during the Civil War. He befriended General Ulysses S. Grant and thanks to this, was able to preserve his vast holdings during the war. When Grant became president, he appointed Merrill to the position of Minster to Belgium. Jennie accompanied her father to Europe and mingled with both aristocrats and royalty, including Queen Victoria. When Jennie's father became ill, he resigned his ministry and the family returned to Natchez.

Duncan Minor was born in 1862 and like Jennie, who was his cousin, he was raised by a wealthy family that somehow also escaped the ravages of the war. He and Jennie were childhood friends whose romance was rekindled after Jennie returned home from Europe.

Romance came for Dick in the form of a young woman named Octavia Dockery. She had been born in Arkansas in 1865 at the Lamartine Plantation but like many other southern families, the Dockery's had suffered greatly as a result of the Civil War. In 1877, Octavia's father moved his entire family to New York, where he did quite well in business. Octavia attended the fashionable Comstock School for Young Ladies and remained in New York until the death of her mother in the 1880's. Shortly after, her older sister, Nydia, married a Mississippi planter and she accompanied the couple to Natchez, where she entered the city's society.

Octavia was remembered as a dashing redhead, who defied local convention. She was the first woman in Natchez to ride astride a horse instead of the proper sidesaddle. She also became a well-known poet and writer, who was widely published, and enjoyed a full and active social life.

During the 1890's, new and renewed friendships blossomed between Dick, Octavia, Jennie and Duncan. They four of them became the best of friends. They were wealthy and attractive members of the new southern aristocracy, admired and envied by many. Jennie and Duncan became the city's most beloved couple, while Dick and Octavia became renowned for their poetry readings and piano recitals. It seemed as though nothing could go wrong, however strange circumstances awaited them.

For reasons unknown, the friendship between the four "golden" members of Natchez society fell apart. The two couples were never seen together again. It also remains a mystery as to when marriage plans dissolved between Jennie and Duncan as well. The stories say that a wedding was forbidden to them by Duncan's mother, who would not approve of the two cousins getting married, but no one knows for sure.

After the death of her father in 1883, Jennie was left with a great inheritance. Her family home, called Elms Court, was burdened with a heavy mortgage however and for some reason, Jennie neglected to make the payments. The house was seized by the bank, even though Jennie had enough money to pay off the debt. She left Elms Court and for an extended period lived at Glenwood with Dick. For years afterward, she moved from house to house in Natchez, before buying Glenburnie in 1904.

Octavia and her now widowed sister were already living in reduced circumstances when Nydia died in 1893. Before she died, Nydia made arrangements with Dick for Octavia to reside at Glenwood and some have wondered if perhaps the visits by the two women may have overlapped. Could they have argued, leading to the destruction of their friendship? Whatever occurred, Jennie soon moved to Glenburnie, but Octavia remained at Glenwood for the rest of her life.

Soon after taking up residence in her new home, Jennie became increasingly odd. She soon developed a taste for seclusion and isolation and her doors were closed to everyone but Duncan. Each night at dusk, he would ride to Glenburnie and stay with Jennie until dawn. Then he would ride back home and have breakfast with his mother, who had objected to his marrying Jennie. Some believed that the couple had secretly married anyway, but there remains no record of it. In time, Duncan began to share Jennie's eccentricities. He became very withdrawn as he grew older, speaking to no one, apparently satisfied with the life that Jennie had chosen for him. As for Jennie, she became odder still, as well as very domineering and aggressive. She forced her way to the front of waiting lines and refused to yield the right of way when driving her carriage and later, her Packard automobile.

A few hundred yards away from Glenburnie was Glenwood, where Dick and Octavia lived. A tragic accident had brought about a premature end to Dick's promising career as a concert pianist. One day, a window sash fell on his fingers, causing a permanent injury. It was now impossible for him to play without missing certain notes. This did not prevent him from playing though and he often sat at the piano until late in the night, tinkering endlessly with melancholy melodies that never sounded quite right.

Like Duncan and Jennie, Dick also began to become quite strange. He began to fall into states of depression that would last for days at a time. His hair and beard began to grow long and tangled and he wandered the woods for hours as Octavia stood by and watched helplessly. He was often the victim of practical jokes by young local boys and one story recalls how they pursued him through the woods until he finally climbed a tall tree to escape. Octavia had to chase them away and spent more than an hour trying to coax him down. Another prank frightened Dick onto the roof of an outbuilding, where he crouched in terror for several days.

The farm at Glenwood began to fall apart and with no income, Dick's inheritance dwindled and then ran out. The house itself crumbled into a state of disrepair. The herd of goats that had been purchased for their milk soon began to wander in and out of the mansion, joined by the chickens and the other animals. A heavy layer of dust coated everything in Glenwood and birds nested in chairs and on the furniture that had not been stripped and devoured by the goats. Curtains and drapes hung in shreds and priceless books became water-stained and ruined. Only

Dick's piano managed to remain untouched by the devastation.

Years passed and the two houses continued to exist both near and far away from one another. Glenwood continued to deteriorate while Glenburnie became a house of secrets. In an age of electric lights and automobiles, the owners of both mansions shunned electricity and the coming of the modern era.

In 1917, Jennie became disgusted with the ruins of Glenwood. She prodded Duncan into buying the property, which was now burdened with delinquent taxes, so that she could evict her former friends. She didn't count on Octavia being clever enough to outwit her though. She managed to convince the local authorities to declare Dick mentally incompetent and had herself appointed as his guardian. This was all that managed to keep Glenwood's leaky roof over their heads, as an insane person could not be deprived of his home because of tax debts. One can imagine that it didn't take much for the authorities to find Dick mentally ill by that time.

By the end of the 1920's, Glenwood remained a shadow of its former self, while Glenburnie had actually started to show improvement. Jennie had invested her money shrewdly over the years and had managed to pull most of her money out of the banks before the great stock market crash in 1929.

Then an incident occurred, which would be considered minor by most, but which had a bizarre impact on Dick Dana's fragile sanity. On afternoon, Jennie shot and killed one of Dick's goats. The animal had been making regular forays into Jennie's yard and eating her rose bushes. Dick pressed charges against her and the case actually went to trial. The charges against Jennie were dropped, much to Dick's dismay, and the entire town learned of the squalid conditions at Glenwood. They began calling the place "Goat Castle". Some believe that Dick swore revenge on the woman who had once been one of his closest friends.

The incident had been largely forgotten by 1932. Duncan continued to ride out to the house each night, even though his mother had died years before. Each morning, he rode back into town, avoiding an automobile in favor of his horse. On August 4, as he was approaching the drive leading to Glenburnie, he had a premonition that something was wrong. When he arrived at the house, a horrific scene awaited him.

The front room was in shambles. Broken glass and overturned furniture covered the floors. Blood was spattered on the walls and a thick trail of gore led out of the house and to the driveway. After searching the house and grounds and finding nothing, Duncan summoned the sheriff. A posse spent the night combing the woods around the house and near dawn, someone discovered Jennie's body hidden behind some bushes. She was barefoot and wore a bloodstained blue dress. She had been shot several times in the chest and in the head by a .32 caliber weapon.

The authorities immediately suspected Dick and Octavia for the murder, believing that perhaps the incident with the goat and Dick's mental instability may have combined as the motive. Octavia was questioned but was eventually released. Dick was held however because a deformed and bloody handprint was found in Jennie's living room. It could not be proven, but it was thought to be a print from the hand that Dick had injured years before.

Newspapers all over the country carried the murder story, thanks to the prominence and the eccentricity of the principals. The nation was shocked by its first real glimpse into the conditions at Glenwood. Numerous photographs portrayed the poverty of the plantation's inhabitants and revealed a once grand home that had been turned into a veritable barn where farm animals freely roamed.

The mansion had fallen into shambles. A column that once supported the verandah across the front of the house had collapsed and now the ceiling sagged dramatically. Broken windows looked out at the lawn like blackened eyes and holes dotted the porch where the wood had rotted through. Inside, the house was hung with dust and cobwebs. Sections of peeling paper dangled from the walls. Chickens and geese nestled in the velvet and rosewood furniture. The upholstery was alive with fleas and mites, while cockroaches and water bugs skittered across the floor. Animal droppings coated the floorboards and filth shrouded expensive antiques that had once belonged to Jefferson Davis and Robert E. Lee. Dick and Octavia slept on water-stained mattresses that had been stretched between wooden chairs. And always present were the home's new namesake, the goats. The dirty animals wandered freely, munching carelessly on the books and damask draperies.

Horrified and fascinated, tourists and curiosity-seekers flocked to Natchez. While Dick and Octavia were still in jail, souvenir hunters picked through the rubbish at Glenwood and carried off relics and antiques. Public sympathy arose for the bizarre pair and after Octavia was released, an unbiased jury could not be found to hear the case against Dick.

Luckily, the case was dropped when the Police Chief of Pine Bluff, Arkansas notified the authorities in Natchez about a man who had been shot down in his city. George Pearls had been killed after pulling a .32 caliber revolver on a Pine Bluff policeman. Papers found on Pearl's body indicated that he had recently been in Natchez. As Jennie Merrill had been killed with a .32, the Chief offered an examination of the weapon.

The papers would lead detectives to an Emily Burns, who owned a boarding house in Natchez. After being questioned, she admitted that she and Pearls had attempted to rob Glenburnie. They were confronted there by Jennie, who attempted to take the gun away from Pearls. In the struggle, Jennie was shot. A ballistics test confirmed most of the story, or at least the part that had Jennie being killed by the gun found on Pearls. In addition, Pearls' fingerprints were found at the crime scene. He also had a deformed hand that matched the bloody print found in the living room. At that point, the case was closed and the charges against Dick were dropped.

But was there more to this story than meets the eye? There were many who questioned the veracity of Emily Burns' story and still wondered what role the residents of Glenwood had played in Jennie's death. Some of those who wondered must have been in positions of authority for the governor of Mississippi pardoned Emily Burns for her role in the crime in 1940.

As for Dick and Octavia, they achieved fame overnight. People continued to come from all over the country to see Goat Castle and so, like a carnival sideshow, Octavia began distributing leaflets and conducting tours of the house and property, charging fifty cents per person. Octavia crept about the property, carrying a goat in her arms, spinning tales of the plantation's heyday. Dick provided accompaniment for the tours, playing off-kilter classical music on his piano.

Each day at dusk, when the last tourist had departed, Dick would return to the piano and play strange melodies that grew louder as the night wore on. The nocturnal music was explosive and powerful and some would remark that it "was loud enough to wake the dead". And perhaps it did, because after nightfall, people in the area began to avoid the thicket of woods between Glenburnie and Glenwood. It was believed that the area was haunted by Jennie Merrill's ghost, still seeking vengeance for her murder. Numerous reports of her apparition stated that she was seen barefoot, wearing a bloody blue dress and darting among the trees. Sometimes her moans and wails could be heard above the sounds of Dick's disturbing music. It was said that his piano grew louder as he tried to drown out the sounds of his former friend's mournful cries.

Dick and Octavia outlived Duncan, who passed away in 1940. The small amount of money earned by Goat Castle tours sustained the owners of Glenwood for the next sixteen years. Finally, in 1948, Dick died from pneumonia and heart disease, leaving Octavia to care for Glenwood alone. She followed her lover to the grave a few months later, dying in 1949. The few belongings that they had left were auctioned off and in 1950, Glenwood was torn down.

After Dick and Octavia died, the sinister tales of the haunted woods intensified. The empty and overgrown plantation fell into even greater decay and those who trespassed there claimed to often see the ghost of Octavia wandering about the place. She was sometimes described as wearing a calico dress and a straw hat and at other times, as a young beauty in a fine Paris gown. The ghostly sightings were sometimes followed by the strains of piano music, clumsy sounds like notes being played by a crippled hand.

As time passed, the stories of the ghosts died with the legends and Goat Castle was all but forgotten. The tales of Jennie's spirit persisted however. In the 1980's, an owner of Glenburnie reported hearing a disembodied voice call to her repeatedly. She also told of unseen hands that continuously undid electrical work that was being performed during the restoration of the house. Some believe that perhaps Jennie's aversion to electricity and modern life manifested itself from beyond the grave!

### THE GIRL IN THE RED VELVET SWING
*The Murder of Stanford White.... Supernatural Influences or Insanity?*

In 1906, the murder of renowned architect Stanford White would be called the "crime of the century". While many other spectacular murders would follow in the annals of Twentieth Century, few would boast participants as famous, or events as strange, as those in the case of Harry K. Thaw.

Harry Thaw was the son of an ambitious Pittsburgh family and heir to a vast fortune that had been earned by cornering the coke market, a product necessary to make steel. The Thaw family connections and wealth had managed to allow the family into the upper crust of New York society. Though well-educated, Harry Thaw was also considered to be rather odd, even by his own family. His school escapades and wild behavior caused his father to limit his allowance to just $2,000 per year. His doting mother supplemented this income with an additional $80,000 and yet Thaw bemoaned the poor state of his finances. He didn't believe that this could possibly support his standard of living and way of life.

One of Thaw's greatest expenses was the apartment that he maintained at a high-priced New York brothel. Here, he would entice young girls with offers of helping them to star in plays and in Broadway shows. Once he had them in his clutches, as the house madam Susan Merrill later testified, he would rape the girls and often beat them badly for his own sexual pleasure. "I could hear the screams coming from his apartment," Merrill later said, "and once I could stand it no longer. I rushed into his rooms. He had tied the girl to the bed, naked, and was whipping her. She was covered with welts."

Despite Thaw's peculiarities, it is unlikely that he would have come to public attention if her had not become involved with a young woman named Evelyn Nesbit. She had come to New York at the age of sixteen and when Thaw met her, she was becoming known as an actress and a model. She became a member of the chorus of the hit show "Floradora" and posed for a Charles

Dana Gibson drawing called "The Eternal Question". She was described by some as the "loveliest looking girl who ever breathed". Writer Irvin S. Cobb described her in print as having "the slim, quick grace of a fawn, a head that sat on her flawless throat as a lily on its stem, eyes that were the color of blue-brown pansies and the size of half-dollars, and a mouth made of rumpled rose petals". She looked innocent but her gentle beauty hid a more sultry side. Soon after arriving in New York, she had become the mistress of millionaire architect Stanford White.

The red-haired, hulking White was considered the most distinguished architect of his day. He had designed more than fifty of New York's most admired buildings, including the Madison Square Gardens and the Washington Square Arch. He was also a spectacular ladies-man, who kept several different mistresses at once, secreted in a number of love nests throughout the city. In one of them, a heavily curtained pleasure palace on the West Side, he was alleged to keep a red velvet swing hanging from the ceiling. In this swing, he would place his young women, dressed like little girls, and would wildly push them back and forth. It was said that he would peer lasciviously up their billowing skirts in prelude to more adult passions.

In one of his apartments, White kept Evelyn Nesbit, who he had despoiled upon her arrival in New York. He had fallen madly in love with her at first sight and gave her large amounts of money, expensive clothing and jewelry. Evelyn remained with White until she was nineteen and at that point she left him and became involved with Harry Thaw.

At the age of 34, Harry Thaw was slowly going insane. For the next three years, Thaw persecuted Evelyn about her former relationship with White. He forced her to never use White's name and only allowed her to refer to him as "the Beast" or "the Bastard". Once, while crossing the ocean on a vacation to Europe, Thaw tied Evelyn (who had amazingly just become his wife) to a bed in their stateroom. He beat her with a belt for hours and made her confess every sexual act in which she had engaged with Stanford White. To stop the whipping, she later confessed that she made things up just to appease her brutal husband.

After they were married, Thaw continued to harass Evelyn about her relationship with the architect. She told her husband that White had made her empty promises of marriage to get her into his apartment and once there had stripped her and raped her, after making her pose naked on the red velvet swing. Later on, during Thaw's murder trial, she testified that on another occasion White had invited her and a girlfriend to the apartment one evening. Here, they took turns being pushed on the swing and engaging in other activities with the unusual architect.

Evelyn's tales only incensed Thaw even further and he vowed revenge. He would sometimes carry a revolver around the house and would mumble to himself about keeping other young girls from sharing Evelyn's fate.

Thaw's revenge came on the night of June 25, 1906. He and Evelyn, accompanied by two friends, attended the opening of a play called "Mam'zelle Champagne" at the dining theater on the roof of Madison Square Gardens. The theater was a frequent gathering place for New York society and the illuminati were all in attendance. For the occasion, Evelyn donned a daring white satin gown and looked spectacular under the stage lights. Soon after taking their seats, she and Thaw noticed Stanford White being ushered to a table in the privileged section near the footlights.

The play turned out to be a dull one and in time, the Thaw's rose to leave. As Harry stepped out into the aisle, he looked down the length of it and saw White framed dramatically at the end. While the girls in the chorus sang a production number, Thaw walked down the aisle and stopped next to White, who pretended not to see him. He then calmly reached into his coat, withdrew a revolver and fired three shots at White. The architect took two of those bullets in the brain and he died immediately. His heavy frame crashed forward on the table and then rolled over onto the floor. Thaw then changed his grip on the pistol, holding it by the muzzle so that it was plain that he didn't intend to shoot anyone else. He was arrested and taken to Center Street Station. Thaw was soon charged with murder and placed in the Tombs to await trial.

While he was in jail, Thaw had all of his meals catered from Delmonico's, one of New York's finest restaurants. He also had whiskey smuggled to him and was allowed to continue playing the stock market, meeting with his broker in jail at all hours of the day and night.

After he was arraigned for murder, Thaw's mother publicly declared that she would spend her entire fortune to keep Harry out of the electric chair. She hired the famous trial lawyer Delphin Delmas from California to defend her son. He would be opposed by the equally famous district attorney, William Travers Jerome, who upon hearing that the Thaw fortune was at stake for Harry's defense said "with all of his millions, Thaw is a fiend! No matter how rich a man is, he cannot get away with murder!"

While the case certainly seemed open and shut, the trial would last for more than seven months. From the start, Thaw's attorney would claim his client to be innocent and that a form of insanity had made him want to kill White. And while Thaw may have been insane, he would state that his urge to kill had come from a mysterious force outside of his body. Namely, that he was possessed by the spirits of the dead!

The claim was supported by a doctor of medicine and a member of the American Association for the Advancement of Science named Dr. Carl Wickland. The Chicago doctor's wife was a proponent of Spiritualism

Evelyn Nesbit's testimony was said to be so scandalous that she whispered to the District Attorney.

Three weeks after Thaw's arrest, Mrs. Wickland insisted that a spirit voice came through her during a seance and confessed that it had forced Thaw to kill Stanford White! The spirit told the group gathered in the seance room that "I killed Stanford White. He deserved death. He had trifled too long with our daughters".

According to Mrs. Wickland, the ghost identified himself as a man named Johnson. He had been from a lower social scale when he was among the living and denounced the wealthy, saying that the rich womanizers like Stanford White had no right to live, "stealing our children from us and putting fine clothes on them."

In addition to Johnson's angry spirit, another entity also came through during the seance. He identified himself as Harry Thaw's deceased father. He defended his son and claimed that the young man had been sensitive to spirit influence throughout his life. The spirit added that he never understood Harry's actions when he was alive but in death, realized that his son's depraved activities were the result of having "been a tool in the hands of earthbound spirits, evil spirits that ordered death."

The ghost went on to add explicitly that Harry Thaw was "obsessed by revengeful spirits when he killed Stanford White."

It was certainly a novel defense and one that played well with the jury. Delphin Delmas and the other lawyers representing Thaw used it to muddy the waters while they assassinated the character of Stanford White. It only served to help the case that prosecuting attorney William Travers Jerome was curiously inept during this peak moment in his career. He lost his temper several times in court while Delmas stayed calm and clever. He brought Evelyn to court looking very demure and innocent in sailor blouses and Buster Brown collars. A crowd of over ten thousand milled around outside, hanging on news that filtered from the building. Inside of the courtroom, spectators soaked up the seamy details of Evelyn's seduction and her descriptions of sex with Stanford White.

The jury listening to the evidence came to the conclusion that something had temporarily taken over control of Harry Thaw at the time of the murder. They returned a verdict of "not guilty, on the grounds of insanity at the time of the commission of the act". Thaw had been saved from the electric chair, but he certainly wasn't free. He was imprisoned for life at the New York State Asylum for the Criminally Insane at Mattewan, New York. He spent years as a prisoner here while his mother spent tens of thousands of dollars trying to get him declared sane. In 1913, Thaw escaped from the asylum but was captured in Canada and returned.

Meanwhile, Evelyn went on to become a vaudeville attraction. Her beauty was wasted away before cheap audiences, but not before she became pregnant with a son that she stubbornly insisted was Harry Thaw's. When reporters pointed out that Thaw had been inside of a mental institution for the past seven years, Evelyn swore that Harry had bribed a guard at the hospital and she had been allowed to spend the night with him. The baby, for which she filed for huge support payments for, was a result of that one evening.

In 1915, a New York court pronounced Thaw sane. Shortly after his release, he publicly denounced Evelyn and denied that he had anything to do with fathering her child. Soon after, he divorced her and went on an outrageous spending spree, hoping to burn through whatever inheritance he could.

Unfortunately for Thaw, he was jailed again in 1916. He was arrested for horsewhipping a teenager named Frederick Gump and while Thaw tried to buy off the boy's family with over a half million dollars, he was still sent back to the mental hospital. He was kept there under tight security until his release in 1922.

After that, Thaw continued his interrupted career of high living until his death in 1947. He traveled the world, sporting attractive young girls on his arms and billed himself to reporters as a theatrical and movie producer. Needless to say, Thaw never moved in entertainment circles and most laughed off his pretensions to a vivid imagination.

Or perhaps it was something else? On certain occasions, Thaw's playful gaze would become a wild stare and his mouth would open to emit strange words that seemed to pass incoherently from his lips. Insanity... or influences from beyond this world?

## THE MURDER CASTLE
### The History & Hauntings of America's First Serial Killer

The city of Chicago has seen more than its share of crime over the years, from the bloody excesses of Prohibition to the brutal murders committed by deviants like Richard Speck and John Wayne Gacy. However, one of the most horrific of the murderers to walk the streets of Chicago came along many years before these killers were even born. Many regard him as the first serial killer in America. His name was Herman Webster Mudgett and if this tale is unfamiliar to you, then prepare yourself... the recounting of his dark deeds and ghostly legacy is not for the faint of heart!

Herman Mudgett was born around 1858 in New Hampshire. Early in life, Mudgett dropped his given name and became known as HH Holmes, a name under which he attended medical school and began his career in crime. Even as a student, Holmes began to dabble in debauchery. As he attended school in Michigan, he devised a method of stealing cadavers from the laboratory. He would then disfigure the corpses and plant them in places where it would look as though they had been killed in accidents. Conveniently, Holmes had already taken out insurance policies on these "family members" and he would collect on them as soon as the bodies were discovered.

In 1878, Holmes married Clara Lovering and it is believed that he taught school for a brief period in New York. After that, he sent Clara to New Hampshire and then dropped out of sight for two years. What became of him during this period is unknown, but in 1886, he turned up on the south side of Chicago. Upon his re-appearance, Holmes filed for divorce from Clara, but the proceedings were unsuccessful and the case dragged on until 1891. This did not stop him from marrying another woman however, a Myrtle Belknap, who father, John Belknap, was a wealthy businessman in Wilmette, Illinois. Although the marriage did produce a daughter, it was nevertheless a strange one. Myrtle remained living in Wilmette while Holmes stayed in Chicago. John Belknap would later discover that Holmes had tried to cheat him out of property by forging his name on deeds. He would also claim that Holmes had tried to poison him when he was confronted about the fraudulent papers. Myrtle ended the marriage in 1889.

Stories claim that the house in Wilmette where Myrtle lived is haunted today. One has to wonder if the spirits who walk here are that of John Belknap or Myrtle herself. It's possible that her unhappy marriage, and horror as the later crimes of her husband were revealed, has caused her to linger behind.

Shortly after Holmes married Myrtle, he began working in a drugstore in the Englewood neighborhood at the corner of 63rd and Wallace Street. The store was owned by a Mrs. Holden, an older lady, who was happy to have the young man take over most of the responsibilities of the store. Strangely, in 1887, Mrs. Holden vanished without a trace. A short time before, Holmes announced that he had purchased the store from the widow, just prior to her "moving out west". The unfortunate lady had (not surprisingly) left no forwarding address.

In 1889, Holmes began a new era in his criminal life. After a short trip to Indiana, he returned to Chicago and purchased an empty lot across the street from the drugstore. He had plans to build a huge house on the property and work was started almost immediately. His trip to Indiana had been profitable and he had used the journey to pull off an insurance scheme with the help of an accomplice named Benjamin Pietzel. The confederate later went to jail as a result of the swindle, but Holmes came away unscathed.

Holmes continued to operate the drug store, to which he also added a jewelry counter. In 1890, he hired Ned Connor of Davenport, Iowa as a watchmaker and jeweler. The young man arrived in the city in the company of his wife, Julia, and their daughter, Pearl. The family moved into a small apartment above the store and soon, Julia managed to capture the interest of Holmes. He soon fired his bookkeeper and hired Julia to take the man's place. Not long after, Connor began to suspect that Holmes was carrying on with his wife, and he was right. Luckily for him, he decided to cut his losses, abandoned his family and went to work for another shop downtown.

Now that Holmes had Julia to himself, he took out large insurance polices of the woman and her daughter, naming himself as a beneficiary. Years later, it came to be suspected that Julia became a willing participant in many of Holmes' schemes and swindles. When he incorporated the jewelry business in August 1890, he listed Julia, along with her friend Kate Durkee, as directors.

(Left) H.H. Holmes, aka Herman Mudgett   (Right) A Period Illustration showing the crowd that gathered outside of the Murder Castle after word reached Chicago's of Holmes' crimes
(Illinois State Historical Society)

By this time, much of Holmes' ill-gotten gains had been funneled into the construction of his home across the street. It would later be dubbed the "Murder Castle" and it would certainly earn its nickname. The building was three-stories high and built from brick. It had been designed with turrets, bay windows and several entrances. There were over 60 rooms in the structure and 51 doors that were cut oddly into various walls. Holmes acted as his own architect for the place and he personally supervised the numerous construction crews, all of whom were quickly hired and fired. Most likely, he didn't want anyone to have a clear idea of what he had planned for the place. In addition to the eccentric general design, the house was also fitted with trap doors, hidden staircases, secret passages, rooms without windows, chutes that led into the basement and a staircase that opened out over a steep drop to the alley behind the house.

The first floor of the building contained stores and shops, while the upper floors could be used for spacious living quarters. Holmes also had an office on the second floor, but most of the rooms were to be used for guests... guests who would never be seen again. Evidence would later be found to show that Holmes used some of the rooms as "asphyxiation chambers", where his victims were suffocated with gas. Other chambers were lined with iron plates and had blowtorch-like devices fitted into the walls. In the basement, Holmes installed a dissecting table and maintained his own crematory. There was also an acid vat and pits lined with quicklime, where bodies could be conveniently disposed of. All of his "prison rooms" were fitted with alarms that buzzed in Holmes' quarters if a victim attempted to escape. It has come to be believed that many of his victims were held captive for months before their deaths.

The castle was completed in 1891 and soon after, Holmes announced that he planned to rent out some of the rooms to tourists who would be arriving in mass for the upcoming Columbian Exposition. It is surmised that many of these tourists never returned home after the fair, but no one knows for sure. This was not Holmes' only method for procuring victims however. A large number of his female victims came through false classified ads that he placed in small town newspapers that offered jobs to young ladies. When the ads was answered, he would describe several jobs in detail and explain that the woman would have her choice of positions at the time of the interview. When accepted, she would then be instructed to pack her things and withdraw all of her money from the bank because she would need funds to get started.

The applicants were also instructed to keep the location and the name of his company a closely guarded secret. He told them that he had devious competitors who would use any information possible to steal his clients. When the applicant arrived, and Holmes was convinced that she had told no one of her destination, she would become his prisoner.

Holmes also placed newspaper ads for marriage as well, describing himself as a wealthy businessman who was searching for a suitable wife. Those who answered this ad would get a similar story to the job offer. He would then torture the women to learn the whereabouts of any valuables they might have. The young ladies would then remain his prisoners until he decided to dispose of them.

Amazingly, Holmes was able to keep his murder operation a secret for four years. He slaughtered an unknown number of people, mostly women, in the castle. He would later confess to 28 murders, although the actual number of victims is believed to be much higher. To examine the details of the story, the reader cannot help but be horrified by the amount of planning and devious detail that went into the murders. There is no question that Holmes was one of the most prolific and depraved killers in American history.

In 1893, Homes met a young woman named Minnie Williams. He told her that his name was Harry Gordon and that he was a wealthy inventor. Holmes' interest in her had been piqued when he learned that she was the heir to a Texas real estate fortune. She was in Chicago working as an instructor for a private school. It wasn't long before she and Holmes were engaged to be married. This was a turn of events that did not make Julia Connor happy. She was still involved with Holmes and still working at the store. Not long after his engagement became official, both Julia and Pearl disappeared. When Ned Connor later inquired after them, Holmes explained that they had moved to Michigan. In his confession, he admitted that Julia had died during a bungled abortion that he had performed on her. He had poisoned Pearl.

In April 1893, Minnie's property in Texas was deeded to a man named Benton T. Lyman, who was in reality, Ben Pietzel, the already mentioned accomplice of Holmes. Later that same year, Minnie's brother was killed in a mining accident in Colorado, which is said to have been arranged by Holmes. As with Julia, Holmes also managed to get Minnie to go along with his deadly schemes, although in Minnie's case, it was even easier to manage her complicity. Apparently, in June 1893 (according to Holmes), Minnie had accidentally killed her sister, Nannie, during a heated argument. She had hit the other girl over the head with a chair and she had died. Holmes had "protected" Minnie by dropping the body into Lake Michigan. Some believe that Minnie had not killed her sister at all, but had merely stunned her with the chair. It had been Holmes, they say, who finished the woman off and who gained himself yet another accomplice.

A short time later, Holmes and Minnie traveled to Denver in the company of another young woman, Georgianna Yoke, who had come to Chicago from Indiana with a "tarnished reputation". She had applied for a job at the castle and Holmes told her that his name was Henry Howard and that Minnie was his cousin. On January 17, 1894, Holmes and Georgianna were married at the Vendome Hotel in Denver with Minnie as their witness! After that, the wedding party (which apparently consisted of the three of them) traveled to Texas, where they claimed Minnie's property and arranged a horse swindle. Holmes purchased several railroad cars of horses with counterfeit banknotes and signed the papers as "OC Pratt". The horses were then shipped to St. Louis and sold. Holmes made off with a fortune, but it would be this swindle that would later come back and destroy him.

The threesome returned to Chicago and their return marked the last time that Minnie was ever seen alive. Although her body was never found, it is believed to have joined other victims in the acid vat in the basement. Holmes continued to kill, claiming several victims. One of them was Emmeline Cigrand, who was hired as a secretary. She became homesick after a few weeks in Chicago as she hoped to marry an Indiana man named Robert Phelps. Some time later, Phelps made the mistake of dropping by to see her at the castle and that was the last time that either one of them was ever reported alive. Holmes later confessed to killing them both and he described a "stretching experiment" with which he used to kill Phelps. Always curious about the amount of punishment the human body could withstand (Holmes often used the dissecting table on live victims), he invented a "rack-like" device that would literally stretch a person to the breaking point. He would also put the "stretching device" to use on a young lady named Emily Van Tassel, who lived on Robey Street. She was only 17 and worked at a candy store in the first floor of the castle. There is no indication of what caused her to catch the eye of Holmes.

In July 1894, Holmes was arrested for the first time. It was not for murder but for one of his schemes, this time for selling already mortgaged properties. Georgianna promptly bailed him out, but while in jail, he struck up a conversation with a convicted train robber named Marion Hedgepeth, who was serving a 25-year sentence. Holmes had concocted a plan to bilk an insurance company out of $10,000 by taking out a policy on Ben Pietzel. Holmes promised Hedgepeth a $500 commission in exchange for the name of a lawyer who could be trusted. He was directed to Colonel Jeptha Howe, the brother of a public defender, and Howe found Holmes' plan to be brilliant.

It was soon put into action. Pietzel went to Philadelphia with his wife, Carrie, and opened a shop for buying and selling patents under the name of BF Perry. Holmes then took out an insurance policy on his life. The plan was for Pietzel to drink a potion that would knock him unconscious. Then, Holmes would apply make-up to his face to make it look as though he had been severely burned. A witness would then summon an ambulance and while they were gone, Holmes would place a corpse in place of the "shopkeeper". The insurance company would be told that he had died. Pietzel would then receive a portion of the money in exchange for his role in the swindle but he would soon learn, as some many others already had, that Holmes could not be trusted!

The "accident" took place on the morning of September 4, when neighbors heard a loud explosion from the patent office. A carpenter named Eugene Smith came to the door a short time later and found the door locked and the office dark. For some reason, he became concerned and summoned a police officer to the scene. They broke open the door and found a badly burned man on the floor. The death was quickly ruled an accident and the body was taken to the morgue. After 11 days, no one showed up to claim it and so the corpse was buried in the local potter's field. Within days, attorney Jeptha Howe filed a claim with the insurance company and collected his money.

The claim was paid without hesitation and everyone got their share of the money, except for Ben Pietzel and Marion Hedgepeth. Holmes never bothered to contact the train robber again, a slight that Hedgepeth did not appreciate. He brooded over this awhile and then decided to turn Holmes in. He explained the scheme to a St. Louis policeman named Major Lawrence Harrigan, who in turn notified an insurance investigator, WE Gary. He then passed along the information to Frank P. Geyer, a Pinkerton agent, who immediately began an investigation.

Ben Pietzel never received his share of the money either, but even if he had, he would not have been able to spend it. What Holmes had not told anyone was that the body discovered in the patent office was not a cleverly disguised corpse, but Ben Pietzel himself! Rather than split the money again, Holmes had killed his accomplice then burned him so that he would be difficult to recognize. Holmes kept his part of the plan a secret as he and Georgianna were now traveling with Carrie Pietzel and her three children. She believed that her husband was hiding out in New York. The group was last seen in Cincinnati and then in Indianapolis on October 1. Carrie was then sent east and the children were left in the care of Holmes. Needless to say, this did not turn out well for the children.

First, Holmes murdered Carrie's son, Howard, in a secluded farmhouse. From there, Holmes went to Detroit, where the Pietzel daughters wrote letters to their mother and then disappeared again. By now, it is believed that Holmes was aware of the Pinkerton investigation because he crossed the border into Canada and rented a small house in Toronto. One evening, he told the girls that he wanted to play hide-and-seek with them, locked them in a large trunk, ran a gas pipe into it and suffocated them. He then brazenly borrowed a shovel from a neighbor and buried the trunk beneath the floor of his basement.

At this same time, Pinkterton agent Frank Geyer was in Philadelphia, exhuming the body of Ben Pietzel.

Holmes and Georgianna kept moving, traveling first to Boston, then to New Hampshire, where Holmes called on his former wife. He told Clara that he had been in a terrible accident and had been suffering from amnesia for several years. He explained to her that Georgianna had nursed him back to health and that he had been unable to remember Clara, so he had married the other woman. Recently, he had regained his memory and hoped to reconcile with his real wife. Unbelievably, Clara agreed!

Holmes then returned to Boston and in a strange twist of fate was arrested for the horse swindle that he, Minnie and Georgianna had pulled off in Texas. He was given the choice of being returned to Texas and being hanged as a horse thief or he could confess to the insurance scheme that had led to the death of Ben Pietzel. He chose insurance fraud and was sent to Philadelphia. On the way there, Holmes offered his guard $500 if the man would allow himself to be hypnotized. Wisely, the guard refused.

The entire insurance scheme was now completely unraveling. A short time after Holmes was captured, Agent Geyer also arrested Carrie Pietzel and Jeptha Howe. He was slowly starting to uncover the dark secrets of Henry Howard Holmes, he realized, but even the seasoned Pinkerton man was unprepared for what lay ahead. He was beginning to sift through the many lies and identities of Holmes, hoping to find clues as to the fates of Minnie and of the Pietzel children. At this point, he had no idea about all of the other victims. Holmes swore that Minnie had taken the children with her to London, where she planned to open a massage parlor, but Geyer was sure that he was lying.

In June 1895, Holmes pleaded guilty to a single charge of fraud. This opened the door for Geyer to continue his investigation with a search of Holmes' residence in Chicago. He was sure that the answers he was seeking could be found inside of the "castle". He broke into the house with several police officers... and neither he nor the veteran investigators would ever forget what they found there!

Working from the top, they discovered the third-floor "guest rooms" first, puzzled at first by doors that opened to brick walls and staircases that led nowhere. They soon discovered the sliding doors, the secret panels, hidden passages and a clandestine vault that was only a big enough for a person to stand in. The room was alleged to be a homemade "gas chamber", equipped with a chute that would carry a body directly into the basement. The investigators suddenly realized the implications of the iron-plated chamber when they found the single, scuffed mark of a footprint on the inside of the door... the small print had been made by a woman who had attempted to escape the grim fate of the tiny room.

The "chamber of horrors" in the basement stunned the men even further. Here, they sound Holmes' blood-spattered dissecting table and his macabre "laboratory" of torture devices, sharpened instruments and various jars of poison. They also found the acid vat and the crematorium, which still contained ash and portions of bone that had not burned in the intense heat. A search of the ashes also revealed a watch that had belonged to Minnie Williams, some buttons from a dress and several charred tintype photographs. Under the staircase, Geyer also found a ball made from women's hair that had been carefully wrapped in cloth.

Ned Connor was summoned to the castle and he was able to identify a bloody dress that had belonged to Julia. Later on, a child's bones were found beneath the basement floor and were thought to be those of Pearl. The list of Holmes' victims was beginning to grow.

On July 20, city crews began excavating the cellar. The hazy smell of gas hung in the air as the men tore away one wall and discovered a large tank. One of the workers struck a match to peer inside of it and the tank exploded. The men were buried in piles of debris but no one was seriously injured. The tank was lined with wood and metal and was 14 feet long, although tanks to the explosion, no one will ever know that it was used for.

Following the excavation, and the discovery and cataloguing of Holmes' potential victims, the "Murder Castle" (as it came to be called) sat empty for several months. Not surprisingly, it drew onlookers and curiosity-seekers from all over the city. The newspapers were not yet filled with stories and illustrations about Holmes' devious crimes but rumors had quickly spread about what had been discovered there. The people of Chicago were stunned that such things could take place.... and in their glorious city! The people of the Englewood neighborhood watched the sightseers with a combination of fear and loathing, sickened over the terrible things that brought the crowds to their streets.

Then, on August 19, the castle burned to the ground. Three explosions thundered through the neighborhood just after midnight and minutes later, a blaze erupted from the abandoned structure. In less than an hour, the roof had caved in and the walls began to collapse in onto themselves. A gas can was discovered among the smoldering ruins and rumors argued back and forth between an accomplice of Holmes' burning down the house to hide his role in the horror and the arson being committed by an outraged neighbor. The mystery was never solved, but regardless, the castle was gone for good, although many would claim that its memories would linger!

The lot where the castle was located remained empty for many years until finally, a U.S. Post Office was built on the site in 1938. There would be many in the area who had not forgotten the stories of Holmes' castle... or the tales from people who claimed to hear moaning and crying sounds coming from the grounds. Even after the post office was constructed, local folks often walked on the opposite side of the street rather than pass too close by the site where torture and murder had taken place. Neighbors who walked their dogs pass the new building claimed their animals would often pull away from it, barking and whining at something they could see or sense. It was something that remained invisible to their human masters, but which was terrifyingly real to the animals.

In addition, postal workers in the building had their own encounters in the place, often telling of strange sounds and feelings they could not easily explain. The location was certainly ripe for a haunting and if the stories can be believed, it was, and is, taking place!

The trial of Herman Mudgett, aka Holmes, began in Philadelphia just before Halloween 1895. It only lasted for six days and after deliberating for less than four hours, the jury returned a guilty verdict. On November 30, the judge passed a sentence of death.

By now, the details of the case had been made public and people were angry, horrified and fascinated, especially in Chicago, where most of the evil had occurred. Holmes had provided a lurid confession of torture and murder that appeared in newspapers and magazines, providing a litany of depravity that compares with the most insane killers of all time. Even if his story was embellished, the actual evidence of Holmes' crimes ranks him as one of the country's most active murderers.

He remained unrepentant, even at the end. Just before he execution, he visited with two Catholic priests in his cell and even took communion with them, although refused to ask forgiveness for his crimes. He was led from his cell to the gallows and a black hood was placed over his head. The trap door opened beneath him and Holmes quickly dropped. His head snapped to the side, but his fingers clenched and his feet danced for several minutes afterward, causing many spectators to look away. Although the force of the fall had broken his neck, and the rope had pulled so tight that it had literally imbedded itself in his flesh, his heart continued to beat for nearly 15 minutes. He was finally declared dead at 10:25 am on May 7, 1896.

There were a couple of macabre legends associated with Holmes' execution. One story claimed that a lightning bolt had ripped through the sky at the precise moment the rope had snapped his neck. The most enduring supernatural legend of HH Holmes is that of the "Holmes Curse". The story began shortly after his execution, leading to speculation that his spirit did not rest in peace. Some believed that he was still carrying on his gruesome work from beyond the grave. And, even to the skeptical, some of the events that took place after his death are a bit disconcerting.

A short time after Holmes' body was buried, under two tons of concrete, the first strange death occurred. The first to die was Dr. William K. Matten, a coroner's physician who had been a major witness in the trial. He suddenly dropped dead from blood poisoning.

More deaths followed in rapid order, including that of the head coroner. Dr. Ashbridge, and the trial judge who had sentenced Holmes to death. Both men were diagnosed with sudden, and previously unknown, deadly illnesses. Next, the superintendent of the prison where Holmes had been incarcerated committed suicide. The reason for his taking his own life was never discovered. Then, the father of one of Holmes' victims was horribly burned in a gas explosion and the remarkably healthy Pinkerton agent, Frank Geyer, suddenly became ill.

Not long after, the office of the claims manager for the insurance company that Holmes had cheated, caught fire and burned. Everything in the office was destroyed except for a framed copy of Holmes' arrest warrant and two portraits of the killer. Many of those who were already convinced of a curse saw this as an ominous warning.

Several weeks after the hanging, one of the priests who prayed with Holmes before his execution was found dead in the yard behind his church. The coroner ruled the death as uremic poisoning but according to reports, he had been badly beaten and robbed. A few days later, Linford Biles, who had been jury foreman in the Holmes trial, was electrocuted in a bizarre accident involving the electrical wires above his house.

In the years that followed, others involved with Holmes also met with violent deaths, including the train robber, Marion Hedgepeth. He remained in prison after his informing on Holmes, although he had expected a pardon that never came. On the very day of Holmes' execution, he was transferred to the Missouri State Prison to finish out his sentence. As time passed, Hedgepeth gained many supporters to his cause, including several newspapers that wrote of his role in getting Holmes prosecuted. In 1906, he finally got his pardon and was released.

Despite the claims that he had made about his rehabilitation, including that he spent each day in prison reading his bible, Hedgepeth was arrested in September 1907 for blowing up a safe in Omaha, Nebraska. He was tried, found guilty and sentenced to 10 years in prison. He was released however when it was discovered that he was dying from tuberculosis. In spite of his medical condition, he assembled a new gang and at midnight on New Year's Eve 1910, he attempted to rob a saloon in (of all places) Chicago. As he was placing the money from the till into a burlap bag, a policeman wandered into the place for no reason and shot him. Hedgepeth was dead before he hit the floor.

Holmes had always sworn that he would revenge himself on Hedgepeth, as his information had set the chain of events in motion that led to the capture of Holmes, however he never got the chance. But perhaps, in death, Holmes got his revenge after all....

### THE GATE TO HELL
*History & Horror at Bobby Mackey's Music World*

Wilder, Kentucky is a small town that is located just south of Cincinnati, Ohio. For many years, the town has been subject to visits from curiosity-seekers, tourists, paranormal investigators and media reporters. They come here in search of a place called Bobby Mackey's Music World, a night club and tavern that may be one of the most haunted, and most sinister, locations in America!

The building where the nightclub is now located has a long and bloody history in the area, from its origins as a slaughterhouse to its tangible link to one of the greatest ghost stories of southern Indiana. It was constructed back in the 1850's and was one of the largest packing houses in the region for many years. Only a well that was dug in the basement, where blood and refuse from the animals was drained, remains from the original building. The slaughterhouse closed down in the early 1890's, but legend has it that the building was far from abandoned. According to the lore, the basement of the packing house became a ritual site for occultists. The well was used to hide the remains of small animals that were butchered during their ceremonies.

Apparently, a small satanic group made up of local residents gathered at the empty building, managing to practice their rituals in secret. However, they were exposed in 1896 during one of the most spectacular murder trials ever held in northeast Kentucky. It was so large that tickets were sold to the hearing and more than 5,000 people stood outside the Newport, Kentucky courthouse for information about what was taking place inside. The trial, and the murder that spawned it, has become an integral part of Bobby Mackey's haunted history.

Pearl Bryan, the daughter of a wealthy farmer, was an attractive, young woman who lived in Greencastle, Indiana in 1896. Unknown to her friends and the polite members of Greencastle society, Pearl was pregnant. She had been seduced by her boyfriend, William Wood, who was the son of a local Methodist minister. Confused and unsure of what to do, Pearl let Wood convince her to have an abortion. Wood had made arrangements for the operation with a friend of his named Scott Jackson, who was then attending the Ohio College of Dental Surgery in Cincinnati. Unbeknownst to Wood, Jackson was an alleged member of the occult group that met the former slaughterhouse in Wilder.

Pearl left her parent's home on February 1, 1896 and told them that she was going to Indianapolis. Instead, she made plans to meet with Jackson and his roommate, Alonzo Walling, in Cincinnati. It would be the last time that her parents would ever see her alive. She was at that time five months pregnant.

Jackson's medical skills were apparently much more inept than he had led his friend William Wood to believe. He first tried to induce an abortion using chemicals, apparently cocaine. This substance was later discovered in Pearl's system during an autopsy. After that, he tried to use dental tools, but botched that as well. After an hour or so, Jackson and Walling had a frightened, injured and bleeding young woman on their hands and that's when the story takes an even darker turn.

The three of them left Cincinnati and traveled across the Ohio River and into Kentucky. Jackson took them to a secluded spot near Fort Thomas and here, he and Walling murdered Pearl Bryan. Using dental instruments, they severed her head from her body. It was a "clean cut", according to the testimony of the doctor who examined her.

Pearl Bryan

He also determined that Pearl had been alive at the time because of the presence of blood on the underside of some leaves at the murder scene. Pearl's body was found about two hundred feet off the Alexandria Turnpike and less than two miles from the abandoned slaughterhouse. As her head was nowhere to be found, Pearl was identified by her shoes. They bore the imprint of Louis and Hays, a Greencastle shoe company that was able to confirm that they had been sold to

Pearl Bryan. During the trial that followed, Walling testified that it had been Jackson's idea to cut Pearl up and distribute her body in the Cincinnati sewers. Only the head was taken, for which Jackson apparently had other uses. Pearl's luxurious blond hair was later found in a valise in Jackson's room.

Pearl's head was never found and legend has it that it was used during a satanic ritual at the slaughterhouse. It was then dumped into the well of blood and was lost. Jackson and Walling were brought to trial in 1897 and were quickly found guilty and sentenced to death. William Wood was later arrested and charged as an accomplice. Charges against him were dropped when he agreed to testify against the other two men. According to reports, Jackson and Walling were both offered life sentences instead of execution if they would reveal the location of Pearl's head. Both men refused. They went to the gallows behind the courthouse in Newport on March 21, 1897. It was the last public hanging in Campbell County.

The stories spread that Jackson and Walling were afraid of suffering "Satan's wrath" if they revealed the location of Pearl's head. The slaughterhouse was then a closely guarded secret and other occultists would have been exposed if the two men had talked. One reporter commented later that Walling, as the noose was being slipped over his head, threatened to come back and haunt the area after his death. The writer also stated a few days later, in an article in the Kentucky "Post" newspaper that an "evil eye" had fallen on many of the people connected to the Pearl Bryan case. Legend has it that many of the police officials and attorneys involved in the case later met with bad luck and tragic ends.

After the trial ended, the slaughterhouse fell silent and remained empty for many years. It was eventually torn down and a roadhouse was constructed on the site. During the 1920's, the place became known as a speakeasy and as a popular gambling joint. Local lore has it that during this period, a number of murders took place in the building. None of them were ever solved because the bodies were normally dumped elsewhere to keep attention away from the illegal gambling and liquor operation.

After Prohibition ended in 1933, the building was purchased by E.A. Brady, better known to friends and enemies alike as "Buck". Brady turned the building in a thriving tavern and casino called the Primrose. He enjoyed success for a number of years but eventually the operation came to the attention of syndicate mobsters in Cincinnati. They moved in on Brady, looking for a piece of the action. Brady refused offers for new "partners" and outright bids to buy him out of the Primrose. Soon, the tavern was being vandalized and customers were being threatened and beaten up in the parking lot. The violence escalated until Brady became involved in a shooting in August 1946. He was charged and then released in the attempted murder of small-time hood Albert "Red" Masterson. This was the last straw for Buck and he sold out to the gangsters. It was said that when he left, he swore the place would never thrive again as a casino. Brady committed suicide in September 1965.

After Brady sold out, the building re-opened as another nightclub called the Latin Quarter. Several times during the early 1950's, the new owners of the bar were arrested on gambling charges.. In 1955, Campbell County deputies broke into the building with sledgehammers and confiscated slot machines and gambling tables. Apparently, Brady's promises had come to pass.

It was also during this period that the legends of the building gained another vengeful ghost. According to the stories, the owner of the club's daughter, Johanna, fell in love with one of the singers who was performing here and became pregnant. Her father was furious. Thanks to his criminal connections, he had the singer killed. Johanna became so distraught that she attempted to poison her father and then succeeded in taking her own life. Her body was later discovered in the now infamous basement... and according to the autopsy report, she was five months pregnant at the time.

Bad luck continued to plague the owners of the tavern. In the 1970's, it became known as the Hard Rock Cafe, but authorities closed it down in 1978 because of some fatal shootings on the premises.

Finally, the building was turned into the popular bar and dance club that it is today. Bobby and Janet Mackey purchased the building in the spring of 1978 with the intention of turning it into a country bar. Mackey was a well-known as a singer in northern Kentucky and had recorded several albums. He actually scrapped his plans to record in Nashville in order to renovate the old tavern. Once the bar was opened up, it immediately began to attract a crowd.

Despite a number of years success with the place though, the good times have never been able to erase the "taint" caused by the history of murder and death. The hauntings at Bobby Mackey's Music World remain stained with blood.

Carl Lawson was the first employee hired by Bobby Mackey. He was a loner who worked as a caretaker and handyman at the tavern. He lived alone in an apartment in the upstairs of the building and spent a lot of time in the sprawling building after hours. When he began reporting that he was seeing and hearing bizarre things in the club, people around town first assumed that he was simply crazy. Later on though, when others started to see and hear the same things, Lawson didn't seem so strange after all.

"I'd double check at the end of the night and make sure that everything was turned off. Then I'd come back down hours later and the bar lights would be on. The front doors would be unlocked, when I knew that I'd locked them. The jukebox would be playing the 'Anniversary Waltz' even though I'd unplugged it and the power was turned off," Lawson told author Doug Hensley, who has written extensively about the haunted tavern.

Soon, the strange events went from strange to downright frightening! The first ghost that Lawson spotted in the place was that of a dark, very angry man that he saw behind the bar. Even though others were present at the time of the sighting, they saw nothing. A short time later, Lawson began to experience visions of a spirit who called herself "Johanna". She would often speak to Lawson and he was able to answer her and carry on conversations. The rumors quickly started that Lawson was "talking to himself". Lawson claimed that Johanna was a tangible presence though, often leaving the scent of roses in her wake.

Odd sounds and noises often accompanied the sightings and Lawson soon realized that the spirits seemed to be the strongest in the basement, near an old-sealed up well that had been left from the days when there was a slaughterhouse at the location. The lore of the area, Carl knew, stated that the well had once been used for satanic rituals. Some of the local folks referred to it as "Hell's Gate". Although he wasn't a particularly religious man, Lawson decided to sprinkle some holy water on the old well one night, thinking that it might bring some relief from the spirits. Instead, it seemed to provoke them and the activity in the building began to escalate.

Soon, other employees and patrons of the place began to have their own weird experiences. They began to tell of objects that moved around on their own, lights that turned on an off, disembodied voices and laughter and more. Bobby Mackey was not happy about the ghostly rumors that were starting to spread around town. "Carl starting telling stories and I told him to keep quiet about it. I didn't want it getting around, because I had everything I own stuck in this place. I had to make a success of it," he said. He was not one to believe in ghosts or the supernatural and he didn't want his customers believing in it either. But when Janet Mackey revealed that she too had encountered the resident spirits, Mackey was no longer sure what to think!

Janet told him that she too had experienced the strange activity. She had seen the ghosts, had felt the overwhelming presences and had even smelled Johanna's signature rose scent. She also had a very frightening encounter in the basement. While she was there, she was suddenly overcome by the scent of roses and felt something unseen swirl around her. "Something grabbed me by the waist," Janet later recalled. "It picked me up and threw me back down. I got away from it, and when I got to the top of the stairs there was pressure behind me, pushing me down the steps. I looked back up and a voice was screaming 'Get Out! Get Out!'"

At the time of this terrifying encounter, Janet was, like Johanna and Pearl Bryan before her, five months pregnant. A coincidence?

Once Janet admitted that she had seen the ghosts in the building, other people began to come forward. Roger Heath, who often worked odd jobs in the club, remembered a summer morning when he and Carl Lawson were working alone in the building. Heath was removing some light fixtures from the dance floor and Lawson was carrying them down to the basement. Just before lunch, Lawson came up the stairs and Heath noticed that he had small handprints on the back of his shirt. It looked just like a woman had been hugging him!

Erin Fey, a hostess at the club, also confessed to encountering Johanna. She had laughed one day at Lawson when he was talking to the ghost. She stopped laughing when she also got a strong whiff of the rose perfume.

Once the stories starting making the rounds, they caught the attention of a writer named Doug Hensley. He decided to investigate the stories and started hanging around the club, striking up conversations with the regular customers. No one was anxious at first to talk about ghosts. "When I first talked to these people, almost every one of them refused to be interviewed," Hensley said. After he talked to Janet Mackey though, many other people came forward. Soon, Hensley had thirty sworn affidavits from people who experienced supernatural events at the club.

He continued to collect stories and sightings, intrigued by the various spirits who had been seen, including a headless ghost who was dressed in turn-of-the-century clothing. Strangely, independent witnesses provided matching descriptions of the phantom, never knowing that others had seen her. That was when Hensley turned to historic records to shed some light on the building's past. He was stunned to discover that events of the past were closely connected to the hauntings of the present. In old newspaper accounts, he found the story of Pearl Bryan and photos of Buck Brady that matched the description of an often seen ghost. None of the witnesses to the present-day paranormal activity were even vaguely aware of who these people had been or what connections they had to the building!

Hensley has since compiled his stories into a book and has been a part of many of the investigations at the club, including a 1994 exorcism of the place that failed miserably. The activity continues to occur and several individuals have even been physically assaulted by spirits. One customer even tried to sue Bobby Mackey in 1994, claiming that a ghost wearing a cowboy hat attacked him in the restroom! The case was later dismissed.

Bobby Mackey's Music World remains perhaps one of the strangest haunted sites in the Midwest and one that has proven to be a major attraction for ghost hunters and enthusiasts alike. Few go away disappointed from a tavern where "spirits served" has another meaning altogether!

## THE GREENBRIER GHOST
*A Killer is Convicted by Testimony from the Other Side!*

The history of the Greenbrier Ghost may be one of the most unique stories in the annals of ghostlore. This strange tale from rural West Virginia is not only a part of supernatural history, but of the history of the American judicial system as well. It remains a one of a kind event.. the only case in which the word of a ghost helped to solve a crime and convict a murderer!

Elva Zona Heaster was born in Greenbrier County, West Virginia some time around 1873. Little is known about her early life or about her growing up years in the Richlands section of the county, other than she gave birth to an illegitimate child in 1895. One year later, in October 1896, she met a man named Erasmus (also called Edward) Stribbling Trout Shue. He was a drifter who moved to Greenbrier to work as a blacksmith and to start a new life for himself. He went to work in the shop of James Crookshanks, which was located just off of the old Midland Trail. All of the public roads were unpaved in those days and with the county being given over to rolling hills, it was the perfect place to find plenty of horses and cattle. A blacksmith would find plenty of work in Greenbrier County and Trout Shue did just that.

Zona became acquainted with Shue a short time after he arrived in town. The two of them were attracted to each other and soon were married, despite the animosity felt towards Shue by Zona's mother, Mary Jane Robinson Heaster. She had taken an instant dislike to him and always felt there was something the amiable man was hiding.

The two lived together as man and wife for the next several months. Then, on January 23, 1897, Zona's body was discovered inside of her house by a young boy that Shue had sent to the house on a contrived errand. He had asked him to run to the house from the blacksmith shop and see if there was anything that Zona needed from the store. The boy, Andy Jones, found Zona lying on the floor at the bottom of the stairs. She was stretched out, with her feet together and one hand on her abdomen and the other lying next to her. Her head was turned slightly to one side. Her eyes were wide open and staring. Even to this small boy, Zona Shue was obviously dead. Andy, not surprisingly, ran home to tell his mother. The local doctor and coroner, Dr. George W. Knapp, was summoned to the house, although he didn't arrive for nearly an hour.

By this time, Shue had carried his wife's body upstairs and had laid her out on the bed. Contrary to local custom, he dressed the corpse himself. Normally, it was the proper thing for ladies of the community to wash and dress a body in preparation for burial. However, Shue took it upon himself to dress Zona in her best clothing. A high-necked, stiff-collared dress covered her neck and a veil had been placed over her face. While Dr. Knapp examined her and tried to determine a cause of death, Shue stayed by his wife's side, cradling her head and sobbing. Because of Shue's obvious grief, Knapp gave the body only a cursory examination, although he did notice some bruising on her neck. When he tried to look closer, Shue reacted so violently that the physician ended the examination and he left. Initially, he listed her cause of death as "everlasting faint" and then as "childbirth". It is unknown whether Zona was pregnant or not, but for two weeks prior to her death, Knapp had been treating her for "female trouble".

Dr. Knapp sent someone out to notify Zona's parents but word of the young woman's death quickly spread through the community. By late afternoon, two young men who were friends of

Zona's, volunteered to ride out an area called Meadow Bluff and tell the Heaster's family what had happened. The farm was located about fifteen miles west of the Richlands, in an area near Livesay's Mill and the town of Rainelle. They lived in an isolated area where a small scattering of homes and farms were nestled against the side of Little Sewell Mountain.

When she was informed of the news of her daughter's death Mary Heaster's face grew dark. "The devil has killed her!", she reportedly said.

On Saturday, January 24, Zona's body was taken by carriage to her parent's home in an unfinished coffin provided by the Handley Undertaking Establishment. Mrs. Shue's husband and a handful of neighbors presided over the move and they brought Trout Shue along with them to the mountain farm. He showed extraordinary devotion toward the body, keeping a vigil at the head of the open coffin during the move. The body was then "laid out" in the Heaster's house for the wake. This event lasted all day Sunday, throughout the night and up until the time for burial on Monday. It gave neighbors and friends an opportunity to pay their last respects to the dead, give solace to the bereaved, bring food for the family and also to visit with one another.

Those who came to pay their respects during the wake pointed out some fairly bizarre behavior on the part of Trout Shue. His grief changed back and forth between overwhelming sadness and manic energy. He allowed no one to get close to the coffin, especially while he was placing a pillow on one side of her head and a rolled-up cloth on the other. He explained that they were to help Zona "rest easier". In addition, he tied a large scarf around her neck and explained tearfully that it "had been Zona's favorite". When it came time to move the corpse to the cemetery though, several people noticed that there seemed to be a strange looseness to Zona's head.

Needless to say, people started to talk.

There was one person who did not have to be convinced any further that Shue was acting suspiciously about Zona's death. This person was Mary Jane Heaster. She hated Shue from the start and had never wanted her daughter to marry the stranger. She was even more against the marriage when Zona revealed to her that Shue had been married two times before! There was something wrong in all of this, she knew, but there seemed to be no way to prove it.

After the wake, Mary Jane took the sheet from inside of the coffin and later tried to return it to Shue, but he refused it. Folding it back up to put it away, she noticed that it had a peculiar odor, so she washed it out. When she dropped the sheet into a basin, the water inside turned red. Strangely, the sheet then turned pink and the color in the water vanished. Mary Jane then boiled the sheet and hung it outside for several days but the stain could not be removed. She interpreted the eerie "bloodstains" as a sign that Zona had been murdered. That was when she began to pray.

Every night for the next four weeks, Mary Jane prayed fervently that her daughter would return to her and reveal the truth about how she had died. According to legend, a few weeks later, her prayers were answered.

Over the course of four dark nights, the spirit of Zona Shue appeared at her mother's bedside. She would come as a bright light at first and then the apparition would take form, chilling the air in the entire room. She would awaken her mother from her sleep and explain over and over again how her husband had murdered her. Trout Shue had been abusive and cruel, she said and had attacked her in a fit of rage because he thought she had not cooked any meat for supper. He had then savagely broken her neck and to show this, the ghost turned her head completely around until she was facing backwards.

Mary Jane had been right. Shue had killed her daughter and the word of her spirit proved it!

A short time later, Mary Jane went to the local prosecutor, John Alfred Preston, so that she could convince him to re-open the investigation into Zona's death. She offered the visitations from her daughter's spirit as evidence that a miscarriage of justice was taking place. By all accounts, Preston was both polite and sympathetic to Mrs. Heaster. The two of them spoke together for "several hours" and at the end of the meeting, Preston agreed to dispatch deputies to speak with Dr. Knapp and a few others involved in the case. While it seems unlikely that he was willing to take another look at the case because of the statement of a ghost, the investigation did get re-opened. Local newspapers reported that Mrs. Heaster was not the only one in the community who was suspicious about Zona's death. There were also "certain citizens" who had started to ask questions, as well as the growing "rumors in the community".

Preston himself went out to Richlands to see Dr. Knapp, who admitted that his examination of the dead woman had been incomplete. The two of them agreed that an autopsy would clear things up and would confirm or deny the lingering suspicions. It would also give them a better idea of how Zona Shue died and lift suspicions from Trout, if indeed he was innocent.

Days later, an exhumation was ordered and an inquest jury was assembled. The autopsy was performed in the Nickell School House, which was just a short distance away from the Soule Methodist Church graveyard. The schoolchildren were dismissed on the day of February 22, 1897, when the body of Zona Shue was exhumed. It was reported in the local newspaper that Trout Shue "vigorously complained" about the exhumation but it was made clear to him that he would be forced to attend the inquest if he did not go willing. In rebuttal he replied that he knew that he would be arrested, "but they will not be able to prove I did it". This careless statement indicated that he at least had knowledge that his wife had been murdered.

The autopsy lasted for three hours with the doctors working under the uncertain light of kerosene lanterns. The body of the dead woman was "in a near state of perfect preservation" though, thanks to the cold temperatures of February, making their work that much easier. A jury of five men had been assembled to watch the proceedings and they huddled together in the barely warm building with officers of the court, Trout Shue, Andy Jones (the boy who had found the body) and other witnesses and spectators.

The autopsy was carried out by the standard methods, which meant that an examination of the vital organs came first. After that, the doctors cut an incision along the back of the skull so that the brain could be removed. This step was not taken in the case of Zona Shue however, as the doctors quickly found what they were looking for. "We have found your wife's neck to have been broken," one of the physicians spoke to Trout Shue. His head dropped and an expression of despair crossed over his face.

"They cannot prove that I did it," he whispered.

It may seem odd that the broken neck was not found immediately and or that it was not more evident on the skin's surface, but doctors will tell you that this is one of the most difficult injuries to detect. It makes it harder to tell in a corpse because the human head is naturally heavy in comparison to the body. When the muscles of the dead person are relaxed, the head tends to flop about. In addition, the first vertebra is located deep inside of the neck, directly under the skull. This makes it hard to find and it would have been that much harder for rural physicians in the late 1800's.

The autopsy findings were quite damning to Shue. A report on March 9 said that "the discovery was made that the neck was broken and the windpipe mashed. On the throat were the marks of fingers indicating that she had been choken [sic]..... the neck was dislocated between the first and second vertebrae. The ligaments were torn and ruptured. The windpipe had been crushed at a point in front of the neck."

The findings were made public at once, upsetting many in the community. Shue was arrested and charged with murder. He was locked up in small stone jail on Washington Street in Lewisburg. Despite the fact that (outside of spirit communications) the evidence against Shue was circumstantial at best, he was indicted by a grand jury and was formally arraigned for murder. He immediately entered a plea of "not guilty".

While he awaited trial, information about Shue's unsavory past began to surface, leading many to believe that Mary Jane Heaster had been right about him all along. Zona had been his third wife. His first marriage, to Allie Estelline Cutlip, had produced one child but had ended in divorce in 1889 while Shue was in prison for horse stealing. She alleged in the divorce decree that her husband had frequently beaten her. In 1894, Shue had married again, this time to Lucy Ann Tritt. Strangely, Lucy died just eight months later under circumstances that were described as "mysterious". Shue claimed that Lucy had fallen and had hit her head on a rock, but few believed him. Wisely, he packed up and left the area and in the autumn of 1896, moved to Greenbrier.

In jail, Shue remained in good spirits, and reported that his grieving for Zona had ended. In fact, he announced that he had a lifelong goal of having seven wives. Since Zona had only been his third, and he was still a young man, he had a good chance of realizing such a worthwhile ambition. He repeatedly told reporters that his guilt in the matter could not be proved.

The trial began on June 22, 1897 and numerous people from the community testified against Shue. The highlight of the trial, of course, came with the appearance of Mary Jane Heaster. Preston put her on the stand both as the mother of the dead woman and also as the first person to notice the unusual circumstances of her death. He wanted to make sure that she appeared both sane and reliable. For this reason, he skirted the issue of the ghost story because it was bound to make her appear irrational and also because it was inadmissible evidence. The teller of the story, in this case Zona Shue, could obviously not be cross-examined by the defense and so her testimony would be hearsay under the law.

Unfortunately for Shue, his attorney decided to ask Mrs. Heaster about her ghostly sighting. It seemed obvious that he was doing it to try and make Mary Jane look ridiculous to the jury. He characterized her "visions" as a mother's ravings and worked hard to admit that she might have been mistaken about what she allegedly saw. He continued to badger her for quite some time, but Mary Jane never wavered from what she had seen. When the defense counsel realized that the testimony was not going the way that he wanted, he dismissed her.

By that time though, the damage was done. Because the defense and not the prosecution had introduced the testimony about the ghost, the judge had a hard time telling the jury to exclude it. It was apparent that most of the people in the community believed that Mary Jane had seen her daughter's ghost. Despite Shue's eloquent testimony in his own defense, the jury quickly found him guilty. Ten of them even voted that he be hanged, which spoke volumes about Mrs. Heaster's believability as a witness. Without a unanimous verdict of death though, Shue was sentenced to life in prison.

The sentence did not satisfy everyone in Greenbrier County. On July 11, 1897, a citizen's group of anywhere from fifteen to thirty men assembled eight miles west of Lewisburg to form a lynching party. They had purchased a new rope and were well armed with "Winchesters and revolvers" when they started towards the jail. If not for a man named George M. Harrah, who contacted the sheriff, Shue would have surely have been lynched.

Harrah contacted Deputy Sheriff Dwyer at the jail. It was said that when Shue was informed of this threat against his life, he became "greatly agitated" and was unable to tie his own shoes. Dwyer took him to a "place of refuge in the woods" a mile or so from town and then was able to disband the mob and return them to their homes.

Shue was moved to the West Virginia State Penitentiary in Moundsville on July 14, where he lived for the next three years. He died on March 13, 1900 from one of the epidemics of measles, mumps or pnuemonia that swept through the prison that spring. At that time, the prison commonly buried unclaimed remains in the nearby Tom's Run Cemetery, for which no records were kept until the 1930's. No trace of Trout Shue can be found today.

Mary Jane Robinson Heaster lived to tell her tale to all who would listen. She died in September 1916 without ever recanting her story about her daughter's ghost.

And as for Zona, her ghost was never seen again, but she has left a haunting and a historical mark on Greenbrier County. It is one that is still being felt today. In fact, a roadside marker along Route 60 still commemorates the case today. It reads:

Interred in nearby cemetery is Zona Heaster Shue. Her death in 1897 was presumed natural until her spirit appeared to her mother to describe how she was killed by her husband Edward. Autopsy on the exhumed body verified the apparition's account. Edward, found guilty of murder, was sentenced to the state prison. Only known case in which testimony from ghost helped convict a murderer.

## THE BLOODY BENDERS
Murderous Spiritualists on the Kansas Frontier

The eerie sound of a jingling tambourine filled the room and the man seated at the table shuddered a little, as if in immediate response. He shuddered because the ringing of the musical instrument came from a place beyond this world!

Restlessly, he placed his hands on the table in front of him, as he had been instructed to do by the woman who was across from him. She told him to close his eyes again. They had jerked open when the tingling sound came from behind him. As his eyelids fluttered closed, he leaned back slightly and his head brushed the canvas curtain behind him. It moved a little and the fine hairs on the back of his neck stood on end.

"We are going to try and contact the spirit of your dead sister," the woman spoke. "She is attempting to come through."

The man nodded slightly. He felt a rush of warmth at the woman's soft voice. He fought the urge to open his eyes and look at her. She was a stunning creature with long legs and a sturdy form beneath the faded gingham of her dress. He remembered how the front of her blouse curved outward, just below where her thick, golden-blond hair hung past her shoulders. His lips twisted into a smile.

"We are speaking to the spirit of Eliza," the woman's voice intoned in the dimly lit great room of the inn. "Please communicate with us."

The tambourine shook and rattled once more and the man's eyes jerked open. A few feet away, he saw the fluttering movement of something white as it whipped past him. Was it a ghost? Suddenly, the table in front of him began to quiver, and then it lurched back toward him. Was the spirit of his poor dead sister trying to come through?

"Close your eyes!" the medium ordered him. "We must concentrate!"

His eyes snapped shut as the table shook and jerked back and forth. Although he was not aware of it, a slit appeared in the curtain behind him and a dirty, thick-wristed hand emerged from behind the canvas. Gripped in the hand was a heavy, wooden hammer that lifted once and then swung downwards in a fierce, arcing motion. The hammer split the head of the man sitting at the table with a sickening crunch! A fine spray of blood misted the curtain and the man slumped forward onto the table. His face connected with the top of it, making a solid thumping sound, and another blow from the hammer insured that he knew no more.

And he joined his sister forever.

The Bender family appeared quietly in southeastern Kansas in the spring of 1872. They didn't appear to be anything special, just another immigrant family that had escaped the confines of the eastern cities to try their hand out west. Like so many others, they merely wanted to make new lives and fortunes in the untamed west. However, their methods for obtaining such fortunes differed greatly from most of the other homesteaders.

The Bender's constructed a home between the towns of Thayer and Galesburg in Neosho County. It was not a fancy place, but was a general store and a wayside inn that could provide both food and a bed for travelers. The house was made up of one large room that was divided by a canvas curtain. This separated the grocery store and inn from the family's living quarters in the back. Old man Bender, his wife and their dull-witted son spoke little to the strangers who passed through, save for an occasional greeting along the local roads or to sell them canned goods and coffee.

On the other hand, their beautiful daughter Kate was outgoing and aggressive. Men were immediately attracted to the tall, fair-haired beauty and she became quite a draw for the Bender's establishment. She also became well-known in the region as a psychic medium, who could contact the spirits of the dead and even cure sickness and maladies for a generous donation. Kate appeared in a number of small Kansas towns with her spiritualistic show. As "Professor Miss Kate Bender", she gave public seances and entertained crowds. She was very popular with the male members of the audience and some of these men traveled to the Bender's hotel to see her again.

They, like many luckless travelers who passed through, were never seen again.

The danger of dining with the Bender's came when seated with your back to the canvas wall. Some travelers complained of hearing strange sounds from behind the curtain while they ate. They didn't realize what might be coming their way for dessert!

Kate would also place her spiritualist clients with their backs to the curtain. In the darkened room, she made all sorts of strange manifestations appear, usually with her family's earthly assistance, and managed to keep the sitter transfixed in place for an extended period of time.

However, some of the sitters became unnerved with their backs against the canvas wall. One man was so scared that he insisted on being moved to another seat. Kate became so angry with him that he stayed put. Finally though, after hearing what he believed were otherworldly whispers on the other side of the sheet, he jumped up and ran from the inn.

Many travelers were not so discerning though. If a diner, overnight guest or seance participant appeared to be wealthy, he was given a seat of honor with his back to the curtain. While Kate distracted him, Old Man Bender or his son would sneak up to the curtain with a sledgehammer. They would then strike a savage blow to the top of the man's head, killing him instantly. The body was then dragged back beneath the canvas and stripped. A trap door that led to an earthen cellar was opened and the body was dumped below until it could be buried somewhere on the prairie. A favorite burying ground was apparently an orchard that was located on the property.

This system of murder worked well for more than eighteen months. Kate drew a number of victims to their door with her offers of spirit communication and her brother often accosted travelers on nearby roads. He would strike up a conversation with them and convince them that spending the night at the inn was preferable to journeying on.

One victim who was persuaded to enjoy the Bender's hospitality (on a permanent basis) was Dr. William York. He was actually returning to visit the inn, and most likely to see Kate again, in the spring of 1873. He had stayed there once before on his trip west and informed his brother, Colonel York of Fort Scott, that he would be staying with the Bender's again on his return journey. Not surprisingly, Dr. York never returned home.

A short time after his brother's disappearance, on May 4, 1873, Colonel York arrived at the Bender home. York explained that his brother had disappeared and he asked the family about whether or not he had passed through the area. He thought that the doctor had planned to stay with them. Had they seen him?

They answered that they hadn't and suggested that perhaps he was delayed, or had run into trouble with Indians. York agreed that all of this was possible and ate a hearty dinner. Later on that night, while sitting alone in the front room, he happened to notice something glittering underneath one of the beds. He pulled the object out and saw that it was a locket on a gold chain. He opened it and was startled to see the faces of his brother's wife and daughter inside! He recognized the locket then as a trinket that his brother wore on his watch chain. He quickly realized that the inn might have been the last place that his brother had ever been seen alive!

York was in the front part of the inn by himself and so quietly, he slipped out the front door. He would ride to the nearest town and notify the authorities, he decided. Using his clout as a military officer, they would get to the bottom of what was going on at the Bender house. He walked across the dirt yard to the stable and out of the corner of his eye, spotted a lantern swinging back and forth in the dark orchard. York walked in the direction of the light and as he got closer, he crept up on it. In the trees, he saw Old Man Bender and his son digging a hole in the ground. Nearby was a large object wrapped in canvas that looked suspiciously like a body!

York returned to the Bender property the next morning, shortly after sunrise. He did not come alone though. He had convinced the sheriff to send a contingent of deputies and local men from town. The posse planned to investigate the inn and the surrounding area, especially the orchard. When they arrived however, they found that the house was empty. The Bender's, apparently aware that York had disappeared the night before, had packed up and left the place. The men searched the building but almost everything was gone. York inspected the cellar and noted with alarm that the dirt floor was coated with dried blood. The stench of the place was overpowering.

The men set to work searching the fields and the orchard around the house. Among the trees, they found eleven mounds of oddly shaped earth. Several of them appeared to be fresh. The posse began to dig and tragically, the body of Colonel York's brother was found in the first grave that was opened. More graves were found by walking about the edge of the prairie and taking end gate rods from wagons and sticking them in the ground. Here and there, they would strike a soft place and in every instance, these places proved to be graves. More than two dozen bodies were allegedly found but how many went undiscovered remains unknown.

The news soon spread about the "Bloody Benders" deadly deeds and curiosity-seekers flocked to the house. Vengeful groups of riders were formed and began searching throughout Kansas for any trace of the family. They had vanished completely but authorities would go on searching for more than fifty years without success. Officially, the Bender's were gone forever.

But of course, there were the legends.

Some claimed that a small band of riders did catch up with the bloodthirsty family and killed them. The Bender's were all shot down and their bodies burned to obliterate their existence. Only Kate was spared being shot and instead she was burned alive for her crimes. The killers swore each other to silence and because of this, the story has never been confirmed.

By 1886, the house in which the Bender's had lived was reduced to nothing more than an empty hole that had once been the cellar. Relic seekers carried away every last remnant of the building, even taking the stones that lined the cellar walls. Only memories of the dark deeds of the Bender family remained to provide evidence that they had ever existed. Memories... and the ghosts.

The stories claimed that the ghosts of the Bender's victims haunted the ruins of the house and later, the earthen hole that remained. Those who wandered out to the site of the house, hoping to bring back some gruesome souvenir, were often frightened off by the strange, glowing apparitions and the moaning and keening sounds that came from the darkness. Some of these spirits still reportedly wander the area today.

And if they do, they may not walk alone. Some legends say that Kate Bender has returned to haunt the lonely land where she took so many lives. She is, perhaps, doomed to roam the earth in some sort of black penance for her horrific crimes. Of course, this may be only the grim folklore of the region, but few dare to walk these roadways at night to find out!

## SHE WALKS THESE HILLS
### The Murder of Mamie Thurman

Although nearly seventy years have passed, the spirit of a woman named Mamie Thurman lives on in the mountains of West Virginia. The legends say that when the winds wail in the dark of the night, Mamie's ghost still walks the hills of Logan County. There are stories of an apparition that has been seen, while others claim to have picked up a lonely young woman near Trace Mountain, only to find later that the seat beside them in the car is mysteriously empty.

But why does she still walk? Many say that her spirit still cries out for justice, having died under circumstances that combined murder, mystery, a missing grave and sexual depravity. It is a story of dark hearts and minds and one that touched the homes of the area's most prominent citizens in 1932. The legends say that Mamie's ghost still touches them even now!

On June 22, 1932, the lifeless body of a dark-eyed brunette named Mamie Thurman was found dumped along a roadside near Trace Mountain (now referred to as 22 Mountain)in Logan County, West Virginia. The gruesome discovery was made by a deaf-mute named Garland Davis, who stumbled over the body while picking blackberries. The murder would make startling news in the region, galvanizing a community that had just begun to feel the pain of the Great Depression. At a time when many families could barely afford to put food on their tables, the strange death of Mamie Thurman would provide an unwelcome, but desirable, distraction.

R. L. Harris, the undertaker from the Harris Funeral Home and who acted in the position of a coroner, arrived on the murder scene the same afternoon. He later stated that Mamie's corpse found was found facing downhill and that she might have never been discovered if some bushes had not kept the body from sliding down the mountainside. She was found wearing a dark blue dress with white polka dots and one shoe. The other shoe was found near the body. Also nearby was her purse, which contained a pack of cigarettes and about ten dollars. She wore a watch, a diamond ring and her white-gold wedding ring, which seemed to rule out the idea of robbery as a motive in her death. Upon examination, Harris learned that her neck had been broken and that she had been shot twice in the left side of the head with a .38 caliber weapon. Both bullets had passed through her brain and had been fired at close range, leaving severe powder burns on her face. To make matters worse, her throat had also been cut from ear to ear. Harris commented that she had been dead for several hours, matching later investigation notes that reported her last being seen the previous night around 9:00 pm.

Harris removed the body to the morgue on Main Street and embalmed her later that afternoon. He believed that Mamie had already been dead when her throat was cut and that she had not been killed at the scene. Most likely, the killer did not expect the corpse to be found for some time, if ever. In such a rural area, where paved roads were virtually non-existent, it was more likely that animals would carry away the remains long before they would be found.

On the same day that Mamie's body was found, an arrest warrant was issued by Magistrate Elba Hatfield. That evening, a local man named Harry Robertson and his black handyman, Clarence Stephenson, were both arrested.

Robertson was a local politician and was well-known in the community. He worked at the National Bank of Logan and served as the treasurer for the local public library. He was also a prominent sportsman and was liked by nearly everyone who knew him. In addition, his wife was also known in society circles. She was the treasurer of the local Women's Club and both of them were active in their church.

Stephenson, on the other hand, was a native of Chattanooga who had been in Logan County for the past nine years. He had worked in several mines before going to work for Robertson. Prior to his being arrested for Mamie's murder, he had never been in trouble with the law. He mainly worked around the Robertson house, acting as caretaker and doing odd jobs. His primary responsibilities were to feed and care for Robertson's hunting dogs.

What led the police to Robertson's door is unknown, but when questioned, he admitted to the authorities that he had been having an affair with Mamie Thurman. He explained that he had arranged to rendezvous with her with the help of his handyman, Stephenson. He would tell his wife that he was going out hunting and they would take his guns and drive off in Robertson's Ford. Stephenson would then drive him to one of the places where he had arranged to meet Mamie. Both of them men were then taken into custody.

News of the arrests quickly spread through Logan County. Rumors flew and many formed their own theories about who killed Mamie. The stories varied as to what the dead woman had actually been like. Most considered Mamie an active church worker, a perfect lady, a young woman of quiet demeanor and "a very nice lady who minded her own business". Unfortunately though, Mamie was said to have a darker side. It was one that was not so well-known to her friends and neighbors and apparently was closer to the truth. She was sometimes referred to as the "Vixen of Stratton Street" in the days following her death and tongues wagged about her encounters with married men, sexual escapades and about the fact that she was a "temptress". More facts, equally as unseemly, would be revealed in the days to come.

Mamie Thurman had been born in Kentucky on September 12, 1900. Her husband, Jack, was also from Kentucky and was sixteen years older than his wife. The Thurman's had lived in the city of Logan for eight years and they rented a two-room garage apartment behind Harry Robertson's house on Stratton Street. Jack Thurman had a job as a city police officer and had landed the position just fifteen months before his wife's murder. The job came about thanks to the efforts of Harry Robertson, who was the president of the city commission. This would not be the only item in the case to show that the families, friends and political positions of the town were hopelessly entangled. It would also not be the only odd "coincidence" that still has local conspiracy buffs talking all these years later.

Mamie's funeral took place just two days later, on June 24. Without a doubt, it is probably one of the most bizarre services ever held in Logan County. Strangely, the cost of the funeral was more than $7,200, a staggering amount in 1932. The services were paid for in cash by her husband, who as mentioned, was employed as a city patrolman. At that time, he would not have earned a fraction of that amount in a year!

The funeral was attended by 550 women and about 30 men and was conducted at the Nighbert Methodist Church, where Mamie was said to be a member. The pastor of the church, Rev. B. C. Gamble, and the Rev. Robert F. Caverlee of the First Baptist Church both officiated. Oddly, Rev. Gamble did not deliver a sermon. Instead, he read a scripture from the Book of John. The verses told of a woman that was brought before Jesus, having been caught in the act of adultery. It was the intention of her captors to stone her to death. Jesus replied that the one of them without sin should cast the first stone and the once angry crowd left the woman alone. In the moments that followed, Jesus didn't condemn the woman for her actions, but simply told her to go and sin no more.

"This is the text," Rev. Gamble said and then he paused for a few moments before he added, "develop your own sermon on that basis." His words were met with silence from the congregation. Only the sound of weeping could be heard. After that shocking moment, Mamie's obituary was read aloud and the service was concluded. What happened next remains a mystery to this day!

Mamie's death certificate was filed at the courthouse and states that she was buried at Logan Memorial Park in McConnell. It listed her cause of death as "unknown". According to records and a search of the cemetery though, Mamie was never buried there. To make matters more confusing, records at the Harris Funeral Home show a charge of $35 for moving Mamie's body to Bradfordsville, Kentucky. However, the cemetery in Kentucky has no record of the internment of her body either. So, where is Mamie Thurman buried? No one knows, marking yet another unsolved mystery in this perplexing case.

On the day of the funeral, West Virginia State troopers searched the home of Harry Robertson. They made a number of disconcerting discoveries. In the basement, they found several bloodstained rags and found a number of places on the floor where it looked as though someone had attempted to clean something up. That "something" was believed to be blood, a belief that was later confirmed by a Charleston chemist named T. A. Borradaile. He also confirmed that it was human blood but the courts refused to admit his tests into evidence during the trial that followed. The troopers also found a razor hidden in the basement and they discovered a hole in the wall that appeared to have been made by a bullet.

They also discovered blood stains on the window, fender and seat of Robertson's Ford sedan. The car was mostly used to transport hunting dogs when Robertson made the trip up to Trace Mountain, where he owned a hunting cabin. The back seat of the vehicle had been removed and a tarp had been placed over the back of the front seat and on the rear portion of the vehicle. This was supposed to protect the car from the dogs when they were in the back, but investigators also believed it made a perfect transport vehicle for Mamie's body. It should be noted that her corpse had been found about one mile from Robertson's cabin.

On June 27, Harry Robertson was released from jail on a $10,000 bond that was guaranteed by Robertson's defense attorney, C. C. Chambers, Bruce McDonald of the McDonald Land Company, T. G. Moore and C. L. Estep. He would be back in court on July 29 for the hearing into the case.

Somehow, during all of the investigations, Jack Thurman was never suspected in Mamie's death. In fact, the Logan Police Department had granted him a furlough after his wife's funeral. Before the hearing and trial, he traveled to Louisville, Kentucky where he visited Mamie's two sisters at an orphanage. The children had been placed there after Mamie's father was killed in a gun battle with police in Ashland, Kentucky. It is assumed that he broke the news to them about Mamie's death and gave each of them $2, a considerable amount in 1932. After the visit, Thurman returned to Logan for the hearing.

On July 5, the Logan "Banner" newspaper announced that Judge James Damron of Huntington would aid in the Thurman investigation without pay. He was one of the state's most distinguished criminal lawyers and judges and offered to serve as a prosecutor in the case. In a letter to the county's prosecuting attorneys, L. P. Hager and Emmett F. Scaggs, he wrote that "Mamie Thurman's brutal murder was a drastic deed and the handiwork of a well-laid out conspiracy". He also said that he believed the perpetrators of such a "foul and damnable murder" should be apprehended and brought to justice. The district attorneys readily agreed to his sentiments and gave him a seat at the prosecutor's table.

In the meantime, the investigation into the murder continued and detectives were making some rather unsavory discoveries about some of the county's more prominent citizens. One allegation even stated that there was a "club" in Logan where men would meet with the girlfriends and carry on affairs in secret. Mamie was said to be a member of this "club" and had been involved with many of the area's politicians and businessmen. The case was getting heated and the pressure was being felt at the district attorney's office from all sides.

In a press statement on July 26, Assistant D.A. Emmett Scaggs announced that his office had no intention of dragging the names of anyone into the case merely for the purpose of satisfying the curiosity-seekers. He knew that many people were more interested in scandal than in finding out who killed Mamie Thurman, but his office was not. In addition, he assured the public that just because some "prominent people" were involved, they were proceeding forward on the case as quickly as possible. "Murder carries an extreme penalty", Scaggs said, "while adultery is only a misdemeanor." They would, he promised, get to the bottom of the case.

Then, he made another startling announcement. Believing that many honest people in the county could shed some light on the case, but were afraid to get involved, he had asked the court to offer a $1,000 reward for new evidence that would lead to a conviction. This crime, Scaggs stated, was the "most brutish crime in Logan County history" and he was determined to see it solved.

Not surprisingly, a number of people came forward with information. One of them was Oscar Townsend, who rented a room from Harry Robertson and had worked with him at the bank. He said that there had been "ill feelings" between Mamie Thurman and Mrs. Robertson and that they had not been "going around together" for some time. He also informed the police that he had traded a .38 caliber gun to Harry Robertson in exchange for a .32 pistol some time back.

Shortly after receiving the information, another search was carried out of the Robertson home. Police found the .38 caliber pistol under Robertson's pillow, where he kept it at night. They also found a knife and a bloodstained piece of canvas that led them back to the car. Here, a more thorough search revealed a blood clot underneath the rubber floor mat. It appeared that an attempt had been made to wash of the car, but the blood clot was missed because it was attached to the underside of the mat.

Things looked bad for Harry Robertson but it was not because of information given to the police by Clarence Stephenson. Even though he had been named as a co-defendant in the case, and had the same attorney as Robertson, Stephenson was not released on bail prior to the hearing. However, he didn't seem to hold this against his employer. From his cell, he sent a letter to his sister, Josie Carpenter, who was a maid at the Pioneer Hotel. He wrote that he "would die before he would lie on" Robertson and his wife. He asked that Josie get a message to Mrs. Robertson and tell her that he had been moved to the Williamson jail to keep anyone from seeing him. He also wanted her to know he "will not do anything to hurt Mr. Harry or her." He wanted Josie to tell Robertson's wife to stand up and help him and Mr. Harry. He knew that things would go hard for he and his employer, but he said that the police didn't know anything to hurt them.

On July 29, huge crowds of people, many carrying their own chairs, began gathering in front of the Logan County courthouse. Some came as early as 6:00 am, all hoping to gain admittance to the hearing. The hearing attracted more than 1,000 people to the courthouse that morning.

Magistrate Elba Hatfield was in charge of the proceedings. He was already in place when Jack Thurman arrived and when Harry Robertson and Clarence Stephenson were brought in under guard. Stephenson had his hands cuffed in front of him, but Robertson's were free. Both men sat calmly at the witness table and while Stephenson stared straight ahead, Robertson constantly wet his lips and looked around the room.

A few minutes later, Mrs. Robertson was escorted into the grand jury room by Robertson's boarder and police witness, Oscar Townsend. She walked to her husband's side and kissed him lightly on the cheek. She sat down next to him and placed an arm around his shoulders. Huddled close, they proceeded to whisper back and forth to one another for about ten minutes. They were then joined by Judge Estep and C. C. Chambers, attorneys for Robertson and Stephenson. Prosecutors Hager and Scaggs sat down at the other end of the long table. The hearing was about to begin.

The Grand Jury panel was made up of many of the county's most prominent citizens and many of them were associated with Harry Robertson. Instructions were given to the jury and it was added that the murder of Mamie Thurman was one of the most gruesome in the county's history. "If there is enough evidence to indict the parties responsible, the court expects you to do so", the Grand Jury was told.

The news of Mamie Thurman's death made headlines and lengthy articles in the local newspaper in 1932. Unfortunately. the only photos of Mamie (and many other principals in the case) that are available today are grainy illustrations used by newspapers of the period.

(Left) Mamie Thurman as she looked at the time of her death.

A Newspaper Photo of Harry Robertson

Testimony was then given concerning the discovery and autopsy of Mamie's body and the collection of the physical evidence in Robertson's house and car. Later, Harry Robertson himself was called to the stand. His testimony was definitely the most shocking of the day!

On the stand, Robertson recalled an almost two-year affair between himself and Mamie Thurman. He testified that he and Mamie often met at the "Key Club", located in the heart of Logan. According to his story, the club was frequented by a number of well-known and wealthy businessmen and their "lady friends". Both male and female members had pass-keys to the place and it was here where they enjoyed parties, illicit affairs and drunken orgies. Robertson also said that Mamie gave him a list of sixteen different men with whom she had engaged in sex. She had given it to him about a year before, when they had worked together at the Guyan Valley Bank. "One of the men is dead, all except three live in the city of Logan and all are married but one," he added.

Robertson went on to say that he continued to see Mamie, even though she refused to stop sleeping with other men. He testified that Clarence Stephenson was often the "go between" for his trysts with Mamie and Stephenson later corroborated this. He admitted having had "improper relations" with Mamie on many occasions but he had last seen her at around 8:00 pm on the night she had been killed. He did not see her again after that, he said, and apparently the jury believed him. Stephenson was apparently not so convincing.

During Stephenson's testimony, the handyman told of being moved from the jail in Logan to Williamson. He was driven by state trooper along an isolated road over Trace Mountain. At a bend in the road, they came upon two cars that were parked off to the side and surrounded by several men. Shots were fired in their direction and one of the troopers told Stephenson that it was a mob and asked if he was afraid. They urged him to tell all that he knew, or it was likely that he would be "taken off". Stephenson told them that "if I was making a dying statement it would be, I don't know anymore than I've told.

One odd incident took place during Stephenson's testimony that has never been explained. At one point, he suddenly stopped talking and pointed out into the courtroom as though he were deathly afraid. However, he would not tell what he saw. Strangely, the prosecutor asked, "What do you see . . . Mrs. Thurman?" But ghost or not, Stephenson refused to answer.

At the end of the session, Magistrate Hatfield told the Grand Jury that all the evidence was circumstantial, but claimed it very damaging against both defendants. The jury ended a four-day inquiry on September 15 and the next day, a newspaper headline blared "Harry Robertson Not Indicted!" Clarence Stephenson, it was decided by the jury, would stand trial alone for the murder of Mamie Thurman.

The community was stunned and angered and although it's doubtful that any mob violence was actually planned during the incident with Stephenson and the state troopers, there was talk of vigilante action after the hearing. There were a number of Ku Klux Klan members in the community who not only wanted revenge on the black handyman for his killing of Mamie Thurman, but also because they believed that he was having sex with her. This was contrary to Harry Robertson's statement that Mamie had not been sleeping with Stephenson. Rumors and whispers of violence continued to spread, but nothing ever came of them. For the time being, Clarence Stephenson was safe.

Stephenson's murder trial began on Monday, September 10 at the Logan County courthouse. Hundreds of spectators packed into the building, the balcony, and the public gallery and even lined the hallways. Many others waited outside and hoped to get a seat inside at some point during the proceedings. A person who left his seat in the gallery found it immediately filled.

The first witnesses were R. L. Harris and a Dr. Rowan, who had examined Mamie's body. They described the location where the corpse was found and the condition of the body. They again pointed out that Mamie had been killed by the two bullets to the head before her throat had been cut.

They were followed by Jack Thurman, the husband of the deceased, who stated that he had worked his regular shift from 6:00 pm until 6:00 am on June 21. He had last seen his wife at 5:30 in the evening. "I was working my beat with Hibbard Hatfield," he testified, "and I telephoned my wife shortly before one in the morning. When she didn't answer, I went home and found that her bed had not been slept in." Thurman would not see his wife again until the next day, when he identified her body at the Harris Funeral Home.

Throughout his testimony, Thurman had to constantly be told to speak up, as his voice constantly rose and fell in volume. Even when he was cross-examined by the defense, who tried to portray his relationship with his wife as rocky, Thurman remained quiet. He stated that he and Mamie did not argue on the afternoon of her death and that they were on good terms. He had also believed, prior to her death, that his wife had been faithful to him and had been at home while he was on duty. In fact, he praised her many times during the course of his testimony and said that "Mamie was the perfect wife to me, and I cannot realize why she would do the things that she had been accused of". A newspaper writer described his comments as "pitiful".

The next witness was Fannette Jones, a black woman who lived on High Street. According to her testimony, Robertson and Mamie often met at her house for their rendezvous. It was never explained as to why because the woman vigorously denied that she had ever rented a room to them. Jones testified that Mamie had come to her house about 8:00 on the evening that she was killed. "She stayed for about ten minutes and she brought her own linens. She was nicely dressed and wore a yellow, linen dress," she told the prosecutor. Upon cross-examination, she again denied that she had rented a room to Mamie

## INVESTIGATION CONTINUES TO WIDEN IN LOGAN MURDER CASE

*Figures in Logan County Murder Case*

### WIFE IS QUIZZED

Mrs. Robertson Queried by Police in Slaying of Mrs. Thurman

### NEGRO TAKEN AWAY

Stephenson Is Secretly Removed to Jail at Williamson

LOGAN, June 11—Ever widening in its scope, the investigation into the murder of Mrs. Mamie Thurman, 32 years old, wife of a city policeman, today had brought to light three outstanding developments.

She said that Mrs. Thurman had given her a "couple of sheets" and that she had done some work for her to earn the sheets.

Other witnesses included Mattie Bell, a black laundry woman who worked for Mrs. Robertson. There was also Nadine Mabney, a drugstore employee who sold Mamie a pack of cigarettes about 8:30 pm; Jack White, a teenager who said that he saw Mamie shortly before dark and Clyde White, who testified to seeing Mamie enter the house of Fannette Jones and stay there "several minutes". All of these witnesses were used to create the prosecution's timeline of events on the night of the murder, as was the testimony of W. L. Brand who saw Mamie about

9:00 on the night of her death.

The next witnesses were much more damaging to Stephenson. The first was E. F. Murphy, a local businessman who lived close to the Robertson's. He testified that he saw Stephenson alone when he came home from work on the day Mamie was killed. He also stated that he saw Stephenson and Mamie together around 6:00 or 7:00 that evening. Another witness, Sherman Ferguson, also claimed to see Mamie with Stephenson that same night. He spotted the handyman driving a Ford sedan while he was downtown that evening.

The most stunning testimony of the entire trial was provided by Harry Robertson, Stephenson's employer and Mamie Thurman's admitted lover. The newspapers reported that Robertson's testimony "almost brought the crowded courtroom to its feet on several occasions when he revealed the sordid details of his relationship with Mamie Thurman." Robertson slowly began to reveal the inside story of his "hunting expeditions" with Mamie Thurman and the two-year deception that he and Mamie had perpetrated on his wife and Jack Thurman.

He began by testifying that he had known the Thurman's for seven or eight years and that he and Mamie began their affair while working at the Guyan Valley Bank. His relationship with Stephenson had been as a friend and an employer. The defendant maintained an apartment in the attic of the Robertson home and they often went hunting together at the cabin on Trace Mountain. Stephenson usually accompanied him to the cabin, bringing along the dogs in the back of the sedan. Stephenson had always been welcome to use the automobile when it was not being taken to the cabin.

Robertson testified that the last time he saw Mamie around 8:00 pm on the day she was killed. He left his house shortly after that to take his children to a swimming pool at Stollings. "That was the last time that I saw her," he said and added that Stephenson was in the house at that time. After returning to town, he said that he was at the Smokehouse Restaurant until 9:00 pm with his son, where they had listened to a prize fight. The Ford was gone when he returned home. His wife later confirmed his whereabouts on that evening.

Robertson explained that he and Mamie would often meet at the mountain cabin and that sometimes she would take a taxi to meet him (incidentally, all of the taxi bills were found to be charged to Jack Thurman). Mamie always returned home around 11:00 in the evening. After leaving the cabin, Stephenson would meet her at 21 Holden Store and take her back to Logan. He said that Mrs. Robertson didn't know about the routine but probably "suspicioned".

He also said that he went hunting at Crooked Creek the Saturday before the murder and that Mamie was with him at the time. He said that he had no "engagement" with her at that time but later went to Fannette Jones' house and was with Mamie for about an hour. Stephenson then took her home. He testified that this was the last time that he had sex with her before her death and while he and Mamie had planned to go on another "hunting trip" the following Tuesday, but that he had called it off on the afternoon of her death.

On October 13, Mrs. Harry Robertson took the stand. The newspaper reported that the crowd anxiously awaited her testimony and that "they strained to hear every word". She stated her name to be Louise Robertson, who lived at 510 Stratton Street. She said she had been married to Harry Robertson for 18 years, and they had a 14 year-old daughter and an 8 year-old son.

When questioned by the prosecution, she admitted that she knew Mamie Thurman. "We knew each other and frequently she was in my home and I was out there," she said. After that, the relationship between the two women had cooled off. "I stopped going around with Mrs.

Thurman last January... I had reasons to believe that she and my husband were intimate and I wouldn't be around with a woman that was intimate with my husband."

When questioned about where her husband was on the day Mamie was murdered she explained that her husband had left for work that morning, returning home for lunch and then coming home in the evening at the usual time. She then added that he the children to the swimming pool in Stollings that evening. After their return, all of them had dinner together and then Robertson drive his Packard "around the block", as he had recently had some work done on it. After that, he and his son left to go listen to a prize fight and promised to be back around 9:00.

She went on to say that her husband uncharacteristically washed the dishes after dinner. This was a job that was usually done by Stephenson but her husband told her that the handyman was ill. She also noted that she saw Stephenson in the dining room after her husband left and that he "was in the kitchen a time or two." She said that she heard him leave the house later on and that he returned a little while after the family went to bed. "I heard him come upstairs and close his door," she told the prosecutor. "I never heard Clarence anymore that night after 11:00."

The defense, still trying to throw suspicion onto Robertson, questioned Louise about the guns that her husband kept in the house and she simply answered that she didn't know anything about guns, other than that they were kept put away and out of the reach of the children. "My husband had a gun," she said, "but I don't know what kind, as I don't know anything about pistols."

Mrs. Robertson's response when questioned about her husband's alleged affairs with Mamie was described as "very unusual". She replied to the questioning with "I learned they were intimate with each other because I had cause to believe they were. A woman doesn't have to be told these things." She claimed that no one told her about the affair, but it was her "woman's intuition" that caused her to become suspicious.

She was then asked if she had ever spoken to Mamie about the affair. "No, but I was talking to Mrs. Thurman once and she told me that someone had told her that she had better watch her husband," Louise replied. "I told her that if her husband is ever untrue to you, you won't have to be told, you'll know it."

She then went on to add, "I had an enmity toward Mrs. Thurman. Of course, I cared and was hurt... but what was the use to be mad about it?"

While there was nothing really very damaging in Mrs. Robertson's testimony for Clarence Stephenson, the same could not be said for the police officers that testified. Of course, it should be pointed out that these men were friends and co-workers of Jack Thurman and undoubtedly wanted to see the man they believed to be the killer properly punished. That's not to say that they lied about the investigation, but things certainly became heated during the examinations. One intense moment came when defense attorney Chambers began baiting Logan patrolman Bill Bruce about the bloody rags found in Harry Robertson's basement. He suggested that the police had planted them there and Bruce became angry. "If it wasn't for paying a fine, I'd slap your face!" he shouted at Chambers.

"Oh, no . . . you wouldn't slap my face here or any other place!" Chambers snapped back.

The judge banged his gavel and shouted down to both of them. "If you men don't hush, I'll have you both sent to jail!" he yelled.

In addition to Bruce's testimony, Police Chief Smeltzer testified that he saw Stephenson cleaning out the inside of Robertson's Ford Sedan at about 8:00 am on Wednesday, the day that Mamie's body was discovered. Patrolman Bruce was with him when they drove by the house.

After both the defense and the prosecution rested in the trial, the judge began his final instructions to the jury. A rather strange event occurred in the last few minutes of the case. Several women discovered two envelopes in the gallery that were addressed to one of the prosecutors, John Chafin. The notes were signed by "A Voter" and "A Citizen" and each claimed that the writer had seen the murder of Mamie Thurman committed. They also went on to state that they believed the crime would be "white washed" and would go the way that other crimes had gone in Logan County. "We believe there are people here who saw that woman get in the car and go to her death," the notes stated. "We believe there are those who saw her get into the car and go up Trace Mountain." The prosecutors later announced that they didn't think there was anything to the letters.

And at that point, it wouldn't have mattered anyway. The jury was only out for fifty minutes before returning with a guilty verdict against Clarence Stephenson. They did pass on a recommendation of mercy however, charging against the death penalty and opting for life in prison instead.

Stephenson made a statement to the court before his sentence was passed. "I am not guilty," he insisted. "I have no knowledge of the crime that I am accused of. I tried to tell the truth.... I hope the law won't stop until they find the guilty parties."

Unfortunately though, no one was looking for any other guilty parties. The sentence of life imprisonment was handed down on October 13 and Stephenson was given ninety days to appeal to the Supreme Court.

On November 15, pleas from the Logan County Branch of the National Association for the Advancement of Colored People (NAACP) went across the county to raise the $600 needed for Stephenson's appeal. Many churches in Logan began accepting donations and more than 3,000 people attended a meeting in Stephenson's support. The money was raised, but despite all of the efforts on his behalf, the Supreme Court turned down his appeal in 1933.

Stephenson remained in the Logan County jail for some time and then was later transferred to the West Virginia State Penitentiary at Moundsville. The state prison was a horrible place in those years but Stephenson strangely never served "hard time". One Logan resident, Normal Sloan, who served time with Stephenson both in the Logan County jail and at Moundsville, said that Stephenson actually received catered meals while incarcerated in Logan County. "Everything was carried to him three times a day from the New Eagle Restaurant," Sloan said.

After being transferred to Moundsville, Stephenson served as Warden Oral Skeens' chauffeur and in this way, was excused from the often brutal conditions of the prison. According to Sloan, Stephenson continued to deny that he committed the murder, but he did admit that he played a hand in Mamie Thurman's demise. "He told me he was hired to take the body to 22 Mountain, and that he didn't do anything to Mamie Thurman. He never did say who killed her, but he said that he didn't do it. Stephenson told me it was all politics," Sloan stated many years later.

On June 11, 1939, Stephenson was transferred out of Moundsville and was sent to the Huttonsville Prison Farm, where he died of stomach cancer on April 24, 1942. He never spoke of the things that he knew about Mamie's death and he carried the secrets of the crime to his grave. As time has passed, most have realized that Stephenson was little more than a scapegoat in the case.... and that Mamie Thurman's real killer was never punished.

A number of strange events, mysteries and unanswered questions have followed Mamie to the grave. Investigations into her death have continued for years and still continue today. There are dozens of questions that still linger over what took place in 1932. Many of these questions will never be answered, thanks to the fact that many of the details were so conveniently erased from history shortly after the trial occurred. Even the courtroom transcripts and seventeen deposition copies have disappeared!

Many believe that Stephenson took the blame for events that were set into motion by prominent citizens of the area, working to cover up their own illicit activities. Who killed her and why so brutally? Was her death caused because of something she knew, or something she had done? Was her broken neck a key to her death? Was her slashed throat, so unnecessary after two bullets to the head, intended as a warning to others about talking too much? Why was the list of sixteen men that Mamie had slept with suppressed at the trial? What was Harry Robertson's real role in her death? Why didn't Louise Robertson divorce her husband after learning of his affair with Mamie? Why wasn't Louise Robertson ever suspected for the murder of the woman who was sleeping with her husband? And the list goes on and on....

Later inquiries, while not answering any of these questions, have discovered a number of rather unusual things that took place and were learned after the trial of Clarence Stephenson. Regrettably, many of these strange facts have triggered even more unanswered questions.

After the trial was over, Prosecutor Chafin appeared before a board of city commissioners on behalf of Jack Thurman, who had been refused bond to return to work as a police officer. After a closed-door session, Thurman was returned to duty as a Logan patrolman. It was reported that he died a number of years later in an insane asylum in Louisville, Kentucky.

Although Mamie's funeral services were conducted at the Nighbert Memorial Church and then described as "the most unusual ever in Logan County", a check of the records at the church showed no listing of Mamie Thurman ever having been a member, baptized there or married there. Defense attorney C. C. Chambers was placed in charge of these records. Shortly after the murder case, Rev. Gamble of the Methodist Church left Logan and was not heard from again. R. F. Caverlee, pastor of the First Baptist Church, who also officiated at Mamie's funeral, transferred to a church in Fredericksburg, Virginia soon after the trial.

On Friday, December 30, 1932 a road crew discovered several bloodstained garments and a long bladed hunting knife near the spot where Mamie Thurman's body was discovered. The knife was covered with what was thought to be blood. "It is only a miracle," said foreman Joe Buskirk "that my men discovered the rags and knife." Whatever became of these items is unknown. Could they have cleared Clarence Stephenson? We will never know.

And things got even stranger in 1985. In that year, a man named George Morrison, who was a half-brother of Mamie's, came to Logan looking for his sister's grave. Morrison lived in New Mexico and had only just learned about his half-sister and her violent death. He wanted to erect a proper headstone on her grave and it was at this point that many in the public began to learn that her correct burial records were missing. Some said that she was buried in the Logan Memorial Park in McConnell and others claimed that she had been moved to Kentucky. No cemetery records existed to prove this and no markers could be located to show where she had been interred.

Morrison placed a legal advertisement in the Logan "Banner" newspaper, searching for information. He received several calls from the ad, all of them strange. One of the callers claimed that he had been paid by a prominent doctor to exhume Mamie's body back in 1962. He refused to identify himself. A woman called and said that she had once owned a cemetery map that marked the location of Mamie's grave. She no longer had it because someone had purchased it from her for $1000. The man who bought it did not give his name.

Another man wrote in reply to the advertisement and asked Morrison to phone his home. He gave his name simply as "George". Morrison said that the man sounded elderly and he claimed to be a retired Logan businessman. He also claimed to know everyone involved in the original case, including Mamie, the Robertson's, Stephenson and others. "George" told Morrison that a woman had killed Mamie and that the deed had been covered-up. Morrison was skeptical about all of the calls and began to realize that Mamie's death was a mystery that would probably never be solved.

In his search for answers, Morrison approached a reporter named Dwight Williamson, who worked for the "Banner". Morrison offered to show Morrison around the area and in so doing, became intrigued by the story. He wrote a number of articles about the murder and the mystery for the newspaper and spent days of his own time personally searching the local graveyards for Mamie's resting place.

He never found it, although he too received some unusual leads and odd calls. One call came from a man in Omar who said that a county vehicle brought a casket to Chauncey Cemetery for burial in 1932. According to the man, there were no mourners and when some of the residents got curious, they were told that the body was the "blankety-blank" who was killed on 22 Mountain. Another dead end... or merely another piece in the overwhelming puzzle? Who knows?

What really happened to Mamie Thurman? How did she spend her last terrifying moments? We will never know for sure and perhaps for this reason, her ghost has long been reported to walk the hills around the town of Holden. Some believe that her ghostly appearances are caused because she cries out for justice, while others believe that she wants her final resting place to be found. Perhaps it is both.... but regardless, her crying phantom has long been a part of local lore.

The ghostly tales began not long after the dark events of the murder trial started to fade from immediate memory. Hikers, motorists and even Boy Scouts who had any reason to be near Trace Mountain began to tell of seeing a woman in white wandering in the woods near where Mamie's body had been discovered. The reports claimed that she could be heard crying and that the smell of flowers always accompanied the sightings. The strange scent would even occur in the winter, when no flowers were in bloom.

A man who used to deliver supplies to a coal mine located near the murder site once had a rather startling experience in his truck. One night as he was driving along the old road, he was suddenly overwhelmed by the smell of flowers and an ice-cold chill in his cab. He had never heard the stories of Mamie Thurman's ghost but when he mentioned the incident to a friend, she quickly filled him in on the legend. He decided then and there that he would never travel that road again! And he never has!

According to some, the old bridge near where Mamie was found is also haunted by her ghost. This road leads back to some old coal mines and you must travel down a steep incline before reaching the bridge. The stories say that if you park your car on the bridge and shift into neutral, the car will roll up the hill backwards. So far, no one has been able to explain why this occurs, but local lore has it that it is caused by the spirit of Mamie Thurman.

And these are not the only stories. Perhaps the most famous, and most commonly told, is the account of the spectral woman who has been picked up along the old mine road. She is described as wearing a white dress and having dark hair that falls just above her shoulders. The pale woman is often given a ride, back in the direction of Logan, but then she vanishes from the car long before it reaches its destination.

Could this phantom hitchhiker be Mamie Thurman? Many believe so and ghostlore would say that it most likely is. Of course, what of the tale of Mamie Thurman is truly as it seems? I guess that I'll have to leave that up to the reader to decide.

## THE HANDSOME STRANGER
### Hauntings in the Wake of A Serial Killer

We serial killers are your sons, we are your husbands, we are everywhere.
And there will be more of your children dead tomorrow.
#### THEODORE ROBERT BUNDY

As a charming, handsome and well-educated young man, Ted Bundy was the most unlikely serial killer in the history of America... or so he seemed to be appeared to be on the surface. Inside of him was a raging monster that was capable of terrifying depravity. Over the course of several years, Bundy sent as many as 36 women to an early death, and there may have even been more than that.

But regardless of the tragic number of his victims, not all of them are believed to rest in peace.....

He was born as Theodore Robert Cowell on November 24, 1946. His mother, Eleanor Louise Cowell, was not married at the time and Bundy's natural father, Lloyd Marshall, an Air Force veteran and later salesman, was unknown to him throughout his life. Shortly after her son's birth, Eleanor took the baby to her parent's home in Philadelphia, where he learned to refer to his grandparents as his mother and father. In this way, Eleanor avoided the stigma of being an unwed mother. Of course, her son grew up thinking his mother was his older sister.

At the age of four, Eleanor and Ted moved to Tacoma, Washington to live with relatives. A year after the move, Eleanor (now called simply Louise) married an army cook by the name of Johnnie Culpepper Bundy, whose last name Ted would assume for the rest of his life.

Louise and Johnnie were to have four other siblings who Ted spent much of his time baby-sitting after school. Ted never really took to his new father who tried unsuccessfully to raise him as his own son. When he was young, Bundy was incredibly shy and was often teased in school. In spite of this, he maintained a high grade point average that would last into college. Although backward, he was considered good-looking, well dressed and polite. He rarely dated though and fellow students recalled that he was more interested in skiing and in politics.

In 1965, Bundy finished high school and won a scholarship to the University of Puget Sound. In 1966, he transferred to the University of Washington and began intensive studies in Chinese. He worked his way through school in low-level jobs but never stayed in any position for very long. He was far too focused on his schoolwork and he continued to keep a high grade point average. However, this focus changed in the spring of 1967 when he began a relationship that would completely change his life.

Bundy became involved with a beautiful young woman named Stephanie Brooks. She came from a wealthy California family and shared Bundy's love of skiing. During one of their ski trips together, they began to fall in love. Stephanie became Bundy's first love and the first woman with whom he was sexually involved. They spent a lot of time together, but Stephanie was not as interested in Bundy as he was in her. She believed that he had no real direction in his life and became increasingly disinterested in him. Finally, in 1968, shortly after graduating from the University of Washington, she broke things off with him.

Bundy never recovered from the break-up and he lost all interest in school and work and became very depressed. He continued writing to Stephanie after she returned to California and although she answered him, she expressed no interest in them getting back together. Bundy was obsessed with her though and couldn't get her out of his mind. His obsession would trigger a series of brutal and bloody events that would stun the entire world.

On December 6, 1973, a young couple discovered the body of a teenaged girl in McKenny Park, Washington. The girl's name was Kathy Devine and she was last seen about two weeks before when friends said she was running away from home. She set off to hitchhike to Oregon and was never seen alive again. She had been strangled, sodomized and her throat had been cut. An investigation was immediately started, but there was little evidence to discover.

On January 4, 1974 the roommates of a young woman named Joni Lenz found her lying in her bed with blood seeping from her head and face. A metal rod had been removed from her bed and she had been beaten repeatedly with it. Then, the rod had been shoved into her vagina. Joni was taken to the hospital in a coma, suffering from brain damage that would affect her for the rest of her life. She was unable to identify her attacker.

On January 31, Lynda Ann Healy vanished from her home near the University of Washington. When she didn't show up for work or for dinner, her friends and family became worried and contacted the police. Investigators found a blood-soaked mattress in her apartment and a bloody nightgown, but there was no trace of Lynda Ann. She had disappeared without a trace.

During the spring and summer of 1974, seven other female students mysteriously vanished in Oregon and Washington. In all of the cases, the girls were white, thin, single, had long hair that was parted in the middle and all of them disappeared during the evening hours. The only leads came from college students who were interviewed by the police. A number of them spoke of a stranger who was seen on campus wearing a cast on his arm. He appeared to be struggling with an armload of books and asking nearby young women for help. Others stated that the same man, or one with a similar description, also had a cast on his arm and was asking for help getting his Volkswagen Bug started. The independent sightings were certainly unusual, but didn't offer the police much to go on.

In August 1974, the remains of some of the missing girls were found in Lake Sammamish State Park in Washington. Two of the women, Janice Ott and Denise Naslund were identified, having vanished on July 14. The police had only had pieces of various colors of hair, five thigh bones, a jaw bone and a few skulls to work with. It was an amazing piece of forensic detection for that time period.

Police officers began scouring the state of Washington, finally realizing that they were looking for a devastating serial killer. More reports came in about the handsome stranger with the arm sling or cast. One woman who was approached told the man that she would not get into his car, so he nonchalantly removed the cast, got into his car and drove away using both hands. The car was identified as a VW Bug.

A short time later, the remains of Carol Valenzuela, who had disappeared nine months before, were discovered in northern Washington, along with the body of an unidentified woman. Thousands of leads were followed and several suspects were arrested and released. Investigators were baffled and then the disappearances in Washington ceased.

Soon after, young women in Utah began to disappear. On October 2, Nancy Wilcox vanished. On October 18, Melissa Smith, the daughter of Midvale's police chief went missing. She was found nine days later, having been strangled, raped and sodomized. Thirteen days later, on Halloween night, Laura Aimee of Orem went to a party and was never seen again. Her body was discovered on Thanksgiving Day. She was lying facedown in a river in the Wasatch Mountains. She had been beaten about the face and head with a crowbar, raped and sodomized.

The similarities between the Washington State and Oregon murders caught the attention of investigators in Utah, who were trying to track down any leads at all in the cases. Utah police quickly consulted with Oregon and Washington investigators. Almost all agreed that it was highly likely that the same man who had committed the earlier crimes was also responsible for the Utah murders. Using eyewitness accounts of the man in the cast, the authorities came up with a composite drawing of their suspect. Apparently, he called himself "Ted".

Sadly, the police almost nabbed Bundy before he could kill again. A woman named Lynn Banks read the account of Melissa Smith's murder in the newspaper and believed that the composite drawing closely resembled Ted Bundy, the boyfriend of her close friend Meg Anders. She disliked and mistrusted Ted and couldn't miss his resemblance to the drawing. Meg also agreed the picture resembled Ted, but refused to believe that he could be a killer. Although hesitant, she contacted the police on the advice of her friend in the fall of 1974. As it later turned out, she was one of five people who gave Bundy's name to the police. All of the reports were forgotten until a few years later. In 1974, the police were so inundated with tips that reports about Bundy (a respectable citizen) were filed away so that the authorities could investigate more likely suspects.

On November 8, 1974, the police finally got the break they were waiting for. Carol DeRonch was leaving a bookstore in a Salt Lake City shopping mall when she was approached by a young man who explained to her that he was a police detective. He told her that someone had broken into her car and he wanted to her to check and see if anything was missing. When they arrived at the car, she checked it and informed the "officer" that everything was fine. The man, who identified himself as "Officer Roseland", insisted that he accompany her to the police station anyway. He wanted her to file a complaint in person. DeRonch reluctantly agreed and allowed him to escort her to his car. When she saw that it was a VW Bug, and not an official vehicle, she became suspicious and asked him for identification. He quickly flashed her a gold badge and she climbed into the car.

Moments later, after they drove off into the opposite direction of the police station, DeRonch became more nervous. Suddenly, the driver stopped the car, grabbed Carol's wrists and tried to put handcuffs on her. She screamed loudly but stopped when the "officer" pulled out a handgun and threatened to kill her if she didn't shut up. He pulled her out of the car and shoved her up against the side of it. A crowbar had appeared in his hands and he raised it to strike her with it. Thinking fast, Carol kicked him solidly between the legs! As the man reeled in pain, DeRonch slipped away from him and began running towards the road. She flagged down a couple driving by and they stopped. Carol frantically jumped into their car, crying and weeping hysterically that a man had tried to kill her. The couple drove her directly to the police.

At the station, with handcuffs still dangling from her wrists, Carol told the officers what one of their own men had done. She was still convinced that her abductor had been an actual policeman. The officers on duty quickly assured her that no one named "Roseland" worked for the department and they dispatched officers to the place where Carol and the man had struggled. He had vanished but this time, the authorities were able to get a good description of the man and his car and even his blood type from spattering on Carol's coat. They were getting closer but the not yet close enough for more of Bundy's victims.

Young women in Utah continued to vanish and then the killer moved into Colorado. On January 12, 1975, Caryn Campbell, her fiancee, Dr. Raymond Gadowski, and his two children took a trip to Colorado. While relaxing one evening in the lounge of their hotel with Gadowski and his son, Caryn decided to retrieve a magazine that she had left in their room. She never came back. Gadowski waited to look for her, knowing that she had not been feeling well that night, but he soon became worried. By the following morning, he had contacted the police. Detectives searched every room in the hotel but found no trace of Caryn.

Almost a month later, and a few miles from where she disappeared, recreation workers discovered Caryn's nude body lying a few feet from the road. Like the most of the other victims, she had been killed by repeated blows to the head. She had died just hours after she vanished.

Police continued unsuccessfully to look for the killer. Five more women were found dead in Colorado under similar circumstances. All of them had been raped before they were killed. Then, on August 16, 1975, they found Ted Bundy.

On that afternoon, Bundy was driving along a street just outside of Salt Lake City, inspecting the houses very carefully. A Utah Highway Patrolman named Bob Hayward was on duty at the time and spotted a suspicious tan VW Bug drive past him. There had been a rash of residential burglaries in the area lately and Hayward suspected that the driver of the Volkswagen might be casing the neighborhood for his next score. When Hayward signaled for the driver to pull over, Bundy sped up and a chase ensued. Finally, other officers arrived on the scene and Bundy was pulled over.

Hayward asked for the young man's registration and license and found his name was Theodore Robert Bundy. As the patrolman walked around the car, he noticed that Bundy's passenger seat was missing. Suspicious, he and two other officers searched the car with Bundy's permission. They found a crowbar, a ski mask, rope, handcuffs, wire and an ice pick. Bundy was then placed under arrest for suspicion of burglary.

At the station, Bundy explained that he was studying law in Salt Lake City and lived in Seattle. A search of his apartment found nothing incriminating except maps of Colorado, but soon the detectives connected the car to the abduction of Carol DeRonch. Not only did Bundy match "Officer Roseland's" general description, but the handcuffs found in his car were the same type as the ones latched to Carol's wrists. In addition, his car was the same make and model as the abductor's and the crowbar found in his vehicle was the same as the one used to threaten DeRonch. They also suspected that Bundy might be the same man responsible for the murders of Melissa Smith and the other Utah women.

On October 2, 1975, Carol DeRonch was asked to try and pick her attacker from a line-up of seven men, one of whom was Bundy. Investigators were not surprised when she quickly picked Ted as the man who had abducted her. Although Bundy claimed to be a victim of circumstance and that he happened to be in the areas where the women were killed, the police were sure they had the right man. Soon after he was picked out of the line-up, investigators launched an investigation into the man they knew as Theodore Robert Bundy.

During the fall of 1975, police investigators discovered the earlier tips that had been passed along about Bundy and they approached Meg Anders for whatever information she could give them concerning her boyfriend and the mysterious "Ted". On September 16th, 1975, she was called into the King County Police Major Crime Unit building in Washington and was interviewed by Detectives Jerry Thompson, Dennis Couch and Ira Beal. Although nervous, she offered what information that she had, stating that she was unable to account for Bundy's whereabouts on the nights of the murders. She also told them that he often slept during the day and went out at night, although she didn't know where. Over the last year, she told them, Ted had become disinterested in having sex with her (she was still dating and living with Bundy at this time). When he did seem interested in sex, he insisted that she be tied up. Meg sometimes objected to the bondage and Bundy would become upset with her. Meg was also able to link Bundy to Lake Sammamish State Park, where bodies had been found. Shortly after a weekend that Ted spent there, Janice Ott and Denise Naslund had been reported missing.

Further investigation yielded more evidence into Bundy's dark side. Earlier victim Lynda Ann Healy was linked to Bundy through a cousin. More eyewitnesses came forward to say that they recognized him from locations where women disappeared and police investigators were able to find credit card receipts from gas stations in towns were victims were taken. An old friend of Bundy's also reported seeing him with his arm in a cast when there were no records of him ever being treated for a broken limb. The evidence against Ted Bundy continued to mount.

On February 23, 1976, Bundy went on trial for the kidnapping of Carol DeRonch. He remained confident that he would be found innocent of the charges, convinced that the police had no hard evidence against him. However, when DeRonch took the stand and told of her ordeal, she began to cry as she pointed out the man who had called himself "Officer Roseland". The spectators in the courtroom stared at Bundy but he remained emotionless and looked coldly at Carol as she wept on the witness stand. He later took the stand and denied ever having seen DeRonch before, although he could offer no alibi for the time of the abduction.

The judge reviewed the case over the following weekend and then handed down a verdict on Monday morning. He found Ted Bundy guilty of aggravated kidnapping and in June, he was sentenced to 1-15 years in prison.

While Bundy was safely locked up in the Utah State Prison, investigators began a search for evidence that would link him to the murders of Caryn Campbell and Melissa Smith. Another search of Bundy's car by detectives found hair that was examined by the FBI. They were able to match to the strands to victims Campbell and Smith. Further examination of Caryn's skull showed impressions made by a blunt instrument, possibly the crowbar found in Bundy's car. With that, Colorado police filed charges against Bundy for Caryn's murder.

In April 1977, Bundy was transferred to the Garfield County, Colorado jail to await trial for Campbell's murder. During preparation for the case, Bundy claimed to be unhappy with his legal counsel and fired him. He stated that he would represent himself and would act as his own attorney. Bundy was granted permission to leave the confines of the jail and use the courthouse library in Aspen when conducting research. What the police didn't realize was that this fit perfectly into Bundy's plan.

On June 7, during a trip to the courthouse, Bundy managed to obtain a hacksaw and he cut his way out of a window. He jumped the ground below and escaped. He was not wearing leg irons or handcuffs at the time. Aspen police quickly set up roadblocks around town but Bundy stayed within the city limits and hid, blending in easily. A search was launched, using 150 men and dogs to track his scent, but Bundy easily eluded them for days. Finally, he discovered a car with the keys still in it and tried to escape from town. Officers spotted the stolen vehicle however and he was captured again, six days after the escape.

From that point on, he was ordered to wear handcuffs and leg irons while conducting his research at the library in Aspen. However, almost seven months later, Bundy again attempted an escape and this time he was successful. On December 30th, he crawled up into the ceiling of the Garfield County Jail managed to get to another part of the building. An opening led down into the janitor's apartment, where he hid until it was safe. After that, he simply strolled out of the building. His escape would go unnoticed until the following afternoon.

On the run, he moved to Chicago, Ann Arbor and then Atlanta, finally ending up in Tallahassee, Florida in mid-January 1978. Using the name Chris Hagen, he settled comfortably into a one-room apartment in an old rooming house called the Oak, in honor of the ancient tree that graced the front yard of the house.

Bundy enjoyed his new found freedom in a place that knew nothing of his past. He planned to start over again and find a new life but the temptation of the Florida State University campus being so nearby was probably more than he could stand.

On January 14, 1978 broke into the Chi Omega Sorority house on campus. Returning from a party around 3:00 am, sorority sister Nita Neary discovered that the door to the house was wide open. She entered the building and heard the sound of someone running upstairs. As the footsteps came down the staircase, she ducked out of sight. She then watched as a man with a knit blue cap pulled over his eyes, and holding a log with a cloth wrapped around it, ran down the steps and out the door. Thinking that the house had been burglarized, she ran upstairs to awaken her roommate, Nancy Dowdy.

She told her friend of the strange man that she had seen in the building and so they decided to wake up their housemother. Before they were able to get to her room though, a sister named Karen Chandler staggered into the hallway. Her head was bleeding and her nightgown was stained with blood. While Nancy tried to help Karen, Nita roused their housemother and the two of them went to check on another girl whose room was nearby. They found Kathy Klein in her room, also covered with blood from a gash in her head. She was alive, but badly injured. Nancy, by this time hysterical, ran to the phone and called the police.

The police who investigated found two of the girls had been killed in their rooms. They had apparently been attacked while sleeping. Lisa Levy was discovered first. She had been beaten on the head with the cloth-wrapped log, raped and then strangled. They also discovered bite marks on her buttocks and on one of her nipples. The nipple had been so ravaged that it was nearly bitten off the rest of her breast. Lisa had also been sexually assaulted with a hair spray bottle.

An autopsy report on Margaret Bowman revealed that she had suffered similar injuries, although there were no bite marks and she had not been raped. She had been strangled with a pair of pantyhose that had been left at the scene and then had been beaten on the head so severely that her skull was splintered and a portion of her brain exposed. Neither she nor Lisa had ever had a chance to struggle with their attacker.

The investigators learned nothing from the crime scene. Little in the way of clues had been left behind and only Nita Neary had seen the killer at all and she was unable to describe his face.

But Bundy was not quite finished that night.

Less than one mile from the Chi Omega house, a woman named Debbie Ciccarelli was awakened by loud noises coming from the apartment next to hers. She awakened her roommate and they listened to hear next-door neighbor Cheryl Thompson begin moaning, apparently in pain. Frightened, they telephoned her to make sure that she was okay and when no one answered, they called the police.

Officers came quickly from the Chi Omega House and entered Cheryl's apartment. They found her in the bedroom, injured, only partially conscious, half-nude, but alive. Her face was beginning to swell from blows that she had sustained to the head. A mask was found at the foot of her bed that was later be found to be identical to the one found in Bundy's car when he was arrested in Utah.

Forensic investigators worked hard on the evidence from both scenes. They were able to get a blood type from the assailant, a sperm sample, hair from inside the mask, teeth impressions from the bite marks on the victims and a few fingerprint smudges. The problem was that the investigators had no one to compare the evidence to. There were no suspects and Ted Bundy didn't even exist in Florida, except as Chris Hagen.

On February 8, 1978, the Lake City Police Department received a phone call from the worried parents of a twelve-year-old girl named Kimberly Leach. They were frantic and claimed that their daughter had vanished. An investigation began immediately and officers went to the Lake City Middle School, where the girl had last been seen. The last person to see Kimberly had been her friend, Priscilla Blakney. She had spotted Kimberly getting into a car with a man she didn't recognize. Priscilla then saw the man drive away but she was unable to accurately identify the make or even the color of the car. Tragically, Kimberly's body was discovered in a state park in Suwannee County, Florida eight weeks later. Because the body was in such an advanced state of decay, it offered no clues to the investigators.

While the police didn't connect the disappearance of Kimberly Leach to the Chi Omega house murders, they did link it to an attempted abduction that took place a few days before Kimberly disappeared. One afternoon in early February, a man in a white van approached a 14 year-old named Leslie Parmenter as she waited for her brother to pick her up. The man told her that he worked for the fire department and asked if she attended school nearby. Leslie was immediately suspicious, wondering why a fireman would be wearing plaid pants and a navy jacket. Thanks to the fact that her father was the Chief of Detectives for the Jacksonville Police Department, she knew not to trust the stranger. Luckily, her brother, Danny, drove up moments later and perhaps sensing trouble from the man in the van told Leslie to get into the car. Danny then followed the van and wrote down the license plate number so that he could give it to his father. The young man's quick thinking would be instrumental in catching the killer.

After Detective James Parmenter heard his children's account of the white van, he ran the license plate though the system and learned that it belonged to a Randall Ragen. On a hunch, he decided to pay him a visit, only to learn from Ragen that the plates had been stolen. In fact, Ragen had already been issued new ones. Parmenter also learned that the van had also been reported stolen so he brought his children down the station to look through some mug shots. Both of them picked out a photograph of Ted Bundy.

Bundy had obviously started to deteriorate after the Chi Omega slaughter and was now on the move. He had long since discarded the van and now was on his way to Pensacola in a new stolen car, ironically, an orange VW Bug. An officer named David Lee was patrolling West Pensacola when he spotted the car on February 15. He knew the area well and did not recognize the vehicle, so he decided to do a routine check on it. He was startled to discover that the plates belonged to a stolen car. He flipped on his lights and began to follow the Bug.

Once again, just as he had done in Utah, Bundy tried to elude the officer. Then, he suddenly stopped and pulled over. Lee ordered him out of the car and to lay facedown on the pavement with his hands beneath him. As the officer approached and started to handcuff him, the man on the ground quickly turned and started to fight. He broke free and began to run. Lee ordered him to halt and then fired his weapon at him. Bundy crashed to the ground and went sprawling onto the pavement, apparently clipped by the bullet from Lee's gun. The policeman ran to where Bundy lay and was again attacked by him, having faked an injury. This time, Lee wrestled him into submission and got the cuffs on him. Ted Bundy had been captured once again.

Following his arrest, investigators began to collect damning evidence against him in the Kimberly Leach case. The white van that Bundy had ditched was found, along with three eyewitnesses who had seen him driving it on the day that Kimberly disappeared. Tests also revealed Kimberly's blood type on the van's carpet and semen that matched Bundy's blood type on the underwear found near her body. They also found shoes impressions that matched Bundy at the site where her body was left. The police were confident that they could tie him to the murder and on July 31, 1978 he was officially charged. Soon after, he was also charged with the Chi Omega murders as well.

Through it all, Bundy maintained his innocence and again served as his own defense in the three separate trials that awaited him. His first trial date was for the Chi Omega house murders in February 1978 and three months later, he would be tried for the attacks on the girls who survived. In January 1980, he would go on trial for the murder of Kimberly Leach.

During the Chi Omega trial, Bundy acted arrogant and insisted that he was innocent. He was sure that he would be acquitted of all charges, refusing to admit that he was fighting a losing battle. The first bad moment came from Bundy when Nita Neary took the stand and pointed him out as the man she had seen fleeing from the Chi Omega house on the night of the murders. The last devastating blow to the defense came with the testimony of Dr. Richard Souviron, who was able to match the bite marks on Lisa Levy to Ted Bundy's teeth.

Dr. Souviron described the bite marks and then showed the jury full-scale photographs that had been taken on the night of the murder. He pointed out the uniqueness of the indentations on Lisa's buttocks and compared them with impressions that had been made from Bundy's teeth. They matched perfectly. This became one of the strangest, but most convincing, pieces of evidence ever introduced in a murder trial. There was no question that Bundy had left the bites on the young woman's body.

On July 23, the jury returned with a "guilty" verdict after seven hours of deliberation. Bundy showed no emotion as the verdict was read and he was taken away. Later, he would also be found guilty at his second trial for the attacks against Kathy Klein and Karen Chandler. On July 31, he was sentenced to die in Florida's electric chair.

In January 1980, Bundy went on trial for the last time in the murder case of Kimberly Leach. He was once again found guilty and once again, he was sentenced to death. He later confessed to the murders of 28 women, although many law enforcement officials believe the number was higher than that. No one will ever know though, for Bundy took the actual number to his grave.

In an effort to fend off his inevitable death, Bundy began appealing his convictions and also began giving interviews and cooperating with authorities. He was interviewed by the FBI's Behavioral Science Unit and gave insight into the psychology of serial killers. Eventually though he exhausted his appeals and Ted Bundy went to the electric chair on January 24, 1989. Outside of the prison walls, hundreds of people toasted his death and applauded and cheered when the final sentence was carried out.

But the legacy of Ted Bundy was not yet at an end....

A few weeks after his execution, two women were walking past the Oaks in Tallahassee, where Bundy had kept a room under the name of Chris Hagen. As they passed by, one of the women glanced up and noticed a young man standing on the edge of the porch. He was looking out toward the street, seemingly unaware of anything around him. Something about the man was startlingly familiar and she pointed it out to her friend. Whoever he was, she said, he bore a remarkable resemblance to Ted Bundy!

Both of the women looked again, but the man was gone. Whoever he was, he had vanished without a trace. Was he the ghost of Ted Bundy? Or perhaps an impression left behind by the brutal killer? No one knows for sure but the house has since been renovated into the Phi Delta Theta Fraternity house and the spectral young man has been seen no more.

Bitter remnants of Bundy's final crime spree have also been reported at the Chi Omega house. It comes as no surprise that the terrifying events of that night in 1978 have left a mark on the building. Even on the night of the murders, one of the sorority girls confided to crime author Ann Rule that she got out of bed to get a drink of water but for some reason could not bring herself to open the door of her room. She sensed that a horrible evil was waiting for her outside, so she locked it and returned to bed.

According to author Dennis William Hauck, many of the sorority sisters admitted being "uneasy" in the house and over the years, it has come to be accepted that the house is haunted by the two young women who were murdered here. One student, who stated that she did not believe in ghosts, could not shake the "peculiar feeling" that she had in the place and confessed that she had never had such a feeling anywhere else.

But the most heartbreakingly tragic hauntings that has been linked to the horrendous crimes of Ted Bundy is the one said to occur at the Columbia Board of Education building in Lake City, Florida. This building was once the Lake City Middle School and was attended by young Bundy victim Kimberly Leach. On February 9, Kimberly was abducted and murdered but just a few days prior to that, she had been the runner-up in the schools' Valentine Queen contest.

The following year, students reportedly saw the ghost of a young girl who resembled Kimberly roaming the hallways of the school in a red party dress. According to the stories, the girl still returns to the building each year around Valentine's Day, perhaps hoping to re-live her last moments here on earth... or to perhaps experience the ones that were taken away from her.

# LIZZIE BORDEN TOOK AN AX.......
## History & Hauntings in Fall River

*Lizzie Borden took an axe*
*And gave her mother forty whacks.*
*And when she saw what she had done,*
*She gave her father forty-one.*

The August afternoon is unbearably hot, especially for Massachusetts. The temperature has climbed to well over 100 degrees, even though it is not yet noon. The old man, still in his heavy morning coat, is not feeling well and he lies down on a mohair-covered sofa. He sighs as he leans back against the arm of the sofa and he carefully turns so that his boots are on the floor and not soiling the couch's uphostelry. In a short time, he drifts off to sleep, never suspecting that he will not awaken.

The old man also does not suspect that above his head, his wife lays bleeding on the floor of the upstairs guestroom. She had been dead now for nearly two hours and in moments, the same hand that took her life will take the life of the old man's as well.

And even if he knew these things by way of some macabre premonition, he might never guess that his murderer would never be brought to justice!

The case of Lizzie Borden has fascinated those with an interest in American crime for well over a century. There have been few cases that have attracted as much attention as the hatchet murders of Andrew Borden and his wife, Abby. This is partly because of the gruesomeness of the crime but also because of the unexpected character of the accused. Lizzie Borden was not a slavering maniac but a demure, respectable, spinster Sunday School teacher. Because of this, the entire town was shocked when she was charged with the murder of her parents. The fact that she was found to be not guilty of the murders, leaving the case to be forever unresolved, only adds to the mystique and fans the flames of our continuing obsession with the mystery.

Andrew Jackson Borden was one of the leading citizens of Fall River, Massachusetts, a prosperous mill town and seaport. The Borden family had strong roots to the community and had been among the most influential citizens of the region for decades. At the age of 70, Borden was certainly one of the richest men in the city. He was a director on the board of several banks and a commercial landlord with considerable holdings. He was a tall, thin and dour man and while he was known for this thrift and admired for his business abilities, he was not well-known for his humor nor was he particularly likable.

Borden lived with his second wife, Abby Durfee Gray and his daughters from his first marriage, Emma and Lizzie, in a two-and-a-half story frame house. It was located in an unfashionable part of town, but was close to his business interests. Both daughters felt the house was beneath their station in life and begged their father to move to a nicer place. Borden's frugal nature never even allowed him to consider this. In spite of this, and his conservative daily life, Borden was said to be moderately generous with both of his daughters.

The events that would lead to tragedy began on Thursday, August 4, 1892. The Borden household was up early that morning as usual. Emma was not at home, having gone to visit friends in the nearby town of Fairhaven, but the girl's Uncle John had arrived the day before for an unannounced visit. John Vinnicum Morse, the brother of Andrew Borden's first wife, was a regular guest in the Borden home. He traveled from Dartmouth, Massachusetts several times each year to visit the family and conduct business in town.

The first person awake in the house that morning was Bridget Sullivan, the maid. Bridget was a respectable Irish girl who Emma and Lizzie both rudely insisted on calling "Maggie", which was the name of a previous servant. At the time of the murders, Bridget was 26 years old and had been in the Borden household since 1889. There is nothing to say that she was anything but an exemplary young woman, who had come to America from Ireland in 1886. She did not stay in the house during the night following the murders, but did come back on Friday night to her third-floor room. On Saturday, she left the house, never to return.

Lizzie Borden
(Courtesy of Fall River Historical Society)

Bridget came downstairs from her attic room around 6:00 to build a fire in the kitchen and begin cooking breakfast. An hour later, John Morse and Mr. and Mrs. Borden came down to eat and they lingered in conversation around the table for nearly an hour. Lizzie slept late and did not join them for the meal.

At a little before eight, Morse left the house to go and visit a niece and nephew and Borden locked the screen door after him. It was a peculiar custom in the house to always keep doors locked. Even the doors between certain rooms upstairs were usually locked. A few minutes after Morse left, Lizzie came downstairs but said that she wasn't hungry. She had coffee and a cookie but nothing else. It's possible that she had a touch of the stomach disorder that was going around the household. Bridget later stated that she felt the need to go outside and throw up some time after breakfast. Two days before, Mr. and Mrs. Borden had been ill during the night and had both vomited several times. It has been assumed that this may have been food poisoning as no one else in the family was affected. It may have been the onset of the flu.... or something far more sinister.

At a quarter past nine, Andrew Borden left the house and went downtown. Abby Borden went upstairs to make the bed in the guestroom that Morse was staying in. She asked Bridget to wash the windows. At 9:30, she came downstairs for a few moments and then went back up again, commenting that she needed fresh pillowcases. Bridget went about her daily chores and started on the window washing, retrieving pails and water from the barn. She also paused for a few minutes to chat over the fence with the hired girl next door. She finished the outside of the windows at about 10:30 and then started inside.

Fifteen minutes later, Mr. Borden returned home. Bridget let him in and Lizzie came downstairs. She told her father that "Mrs. Borden has gone out - she had a note from someone who was sick." Lizzie and Emma always called their step-mother "Mrs. Borden" and recently, the relationship between them, especially with Lizzie, was strained.

Borden took the key to his bedroom off a shelf and went up the back stairs. The room could only be reached by these stairs, as there was no hallway, and the front stairs only gave access to Lizzie's room (from which Emma's could be reached) and the guest room. There were connecting doors between the elder Borden's rooms and Lizzie's room, but they were usually kept locked.

Borden stayed upstairs for only a few minutes before coming back down and settling onto the sofa in the sitting room. Lizzie began to heat up an iron to press some handkerchiefs.

"Are you going out this afternoon, Maggie?" she asked Bridget. "There is a cheap sale of dress goods at Sargent's this afternoon, at eight cents a yard."

Bridget replied that she was not. The heat of the morning, combined with the window washing and her touch of stomach ailment, had left her feeling poorly and she went up the back stairs to her attic room for a nap. This was a few minutes before 11:00.

"Maggie, Come down!" Lizzie shouted from the bottom of the back stairs and Bridget's eyes fluttered open. She had drifted off into a restless sleep but the urgency of Lizzie's cries startled her awake.

"What is the matter?" Bridget cried. She smoothed out her dress, slipped into her shoes and scurried to the doorway. As he feet tapped down the staircase, she was horrified by what she heard next!

"Come down quick!" Lizzie wailed, "Father's dead! Somebody's come in and killed him!"

As Bridget hurried from the staircase, she found Lizzie standing at the back door. Her face was pale and taut. She stopped the young maid from going into the sitting room, saying "Don't go in there. Go and get the doctor. Run!"

Dr. Bowen, a family friend, lived across the street from the Borden's and Bridget ran directly to the house. The doctor was out, but Bridget told Mrs. Bowen that Mr. Borden had been killed. She ran directly back to the house. "Where were you when this thing happened?" she asked Lizzie.

"I was out in the yard, and I heard a groan and came in. The screen door was wide open." Lizzie replied, and then sent Bridget to summon the Borden sisters' friend, Miss Alice Russell, who lived a few blocks away.

By now, the neighbors were starting to gather on the lawn and someone had called for the police. Mrs. Adelaide Churchill, the next door neighbor, came over to Lizzie, who was at the back entrance to the house and asked if anything was wrong. Lizzie responded by saying, "Oh, Mrs. Churchill, someone has killed Father!"

"Where is your father?" she asked.

"In the sitting room."

"Where were you when it happened?"

" I went to the barn to get a piece of iron."

Mrs. Churchill then asked, "Where is your mother?"

Lizzie said that she didn't know and that Abby Borden, her stepmother, had received a note asking her to respond to someone who was sick. She also added "but I don't know but that she is killed too, for I thought I heard her come in... Father must have an enemy, for we have all been sick, and we think the milk has been poisoned."

By this time, Dr. Bowen had returned, along with Bridget, who had hurried back from informing Miss Russell of the day's dire events. Dr. Bowen examined the body and asked for a sheet to cover it. Borden had been attacked with a sharp object, probably an ax, and so much damage had been done to his head and face that Bowen, a close friend, could not at first positively identify him. Borden's head was turned slightly to the right and eleven blows had gashed his face. One eye had been cut in half and his nose had been severed. The majority of the blows had been struck within the area that extended from the eyes and nose to the ears. Blood was still seeping from the wounds and had been splashed onto the wall above the sofa, the floor and on a picture hanging on the wall. It looked as though Borden had been attacked from above and behind as he slept.

Several minutes passed before anyone thought of going upstairs to see if Abby Borden had come home. "Maggie, I am almost positive I heard her coming in," Lizzie spoke. "Go upstairs and see." Bridget refused to go upstairs by herself, so Mrs. Churchill went with her. They went up the staircase together but Mrs. Churchill was the first to see Abby lying on the floor of the guestroom. She had fallen in a pool of blood and Mrs. Churchill later said that she only "looked like the form of a person."

Bridget saw Mrs. Borden's body. Mrs. Churchill rushed by her, viewed the obviously dead body, and rushed downstairs. "Is there another?" a neighbor asked her.

"Yes," the woman replied. "She is up there."

Dr. Bowen found that Mrs. Borden had been struck more than a dozen times, from the back. The autopsy later revealed that there had been nineteen blows to her head, probably from the same hatchet that had killed Mr. Borden. The blood on Mrs. Borden's body was dark and congealed, leading him to believe that she had been killed before her husband.

Dr. Bowen was heavily involved in the activities of the Borden house on the day of the murder. He was the first to examine the bodies, sent a telegram to Emma to summon her home, assisted Dr. Dolan with the autopsies and even prescribed a calming tranquilizer for Lizzie. He was a constant presence in the house and his involvement with them, especially on August 4, has led to him being considered a major figure in some of the conspiracies developed around the murders.

A call reached the Fall River police station at 11:15 but as things would happen, that day marked the annual picnic of the Fall River Police Department and most of them were off enjoying an outing at Rocky Point. The only officer dispatched to the house was Officer George W. Allen. He ran the 400 yards to the house, saw that Andrew Borden was dead and ran back to the station house to inform the city marshal of the events. He left no one in charge of the crime scene. While he was gone, neighbors overran the house, comforting Lizzie and peering in at the gruesome state of Andrew Borden's body. The constant traffic trampled and destroyed any clues that might have been left behind.

During the 30 minutes or so that no authorities were on the scene, a county medical examiner named Dolan passed by the house by chance. He looked in and was pressed into service by Dr. Bowen. Dolan examined the bodies as well and after hearing that the family had been sick and that the milk was suspected, he took samples of it. Later that afternoon, he had the bodies photographed and then removed the stomachs and sent them, along with the milk, to the Harvard Medical School for analysis. No poison was ever found.

The murder investigation that followed was chaotic. The police were reluctant to suspect Lizzie of the murder as it was against the perceived social understanding of the era that a woman such as she was could have possibly committed such a heinous crime. Other solutions were advanced but were discarded as even more impossible.

A map of the crime scene area appeared in the Boston "Globe" on August 11, 1892.

1. 92 Second Street (The Borden Home)
2. The barn where Lizzie claimed to be when her father was killed.
3. The side entrance with the screen door through which Bridget admitted Mr. Borden
4. Mrs. Churchill's Home
5. Dr. Bowen's Residence
6. The Chagnon House (neighbors)
7. Home of Dr. Kelly

A profusion of clues were discovered over the next few days, all of which went nowhere. A boy reported seeing a man jump over the back fence of the Borden property and while a man was found matching the boy's description, he had an unbreakable alibi. A bloody hatchet was found on the Sylvia Farm in South Somerset but it proved to be covered in chicken blood. While Bridget was also seen as a suspect for a short time, the investigation finally began to center on Lizzie. A circumstantial case began to be developed against her with no incriminating physical evidence, like bloody clothes, a real motive for the killings, or even a convincing demonstration of how and when she committed the murders.

Over the course of several weeks though, investigators managed to compile a sequence of events that certainly cast suspicion on the spinster Sunday School teacher. The timeline ran from August 3, the day before the murders to August 7, the day that Alice Russell saw her friend burning a dress that may (or many not) have had blood on it.

## August 3

There were several incidents that police believed related to the murders that occurred on Wednesday. The first was in the early morning hours when Abby Borden went across the street to Dr. Bowen and told him that she and her husband had been violently ill throughout the night. He told her that he didn't think the vomiting was serious and he sent her home. Later, he dropped in to check on Andrew, who told him rather ungratefully that he was not ill and would not pay for an unsolicited house call. There would be no evidence of poisoning found in the Borden autopsies.

Another incident took place when Lizzie tried to buy ten cents worth of prussic acid from Eli Bence, a clerk at Smith's Drug Store. She explained to him that she wanted the poison to "kill moths in a sealskin cape" but he refused to sell it to her without a prescription. A customer and another clerk also identified Lizzie as being in the store that morning, but she denied it. She testified at the inquest that she had not attempted to purchase the poison and had not been at Smith's that day.

The third incident was the arrival of John Morse in the early afternoon. He came without luggage but intended to stay the night. Both he and Lizzie testified that they did not see each other until after the murders the next day, although Lizzie knew that he was there.

Finally, that evening Lizzie visited her friend, Miss Alice Russell. According to Miss Russell, Lizzie was agitated, worried over some threat to her father, and concerned that something was about to happen. "I feel as if something were hanging over me and I cannot throw it off," she told her. She added that her father had enemies and that she was frightened that something was going to happen to the family.

An eerie foreshadowing of the future? Or laying the groundwork for an alibi?

## August 4

On the day of the murders, there were several parts of the story that did not make sense to the investigators, or could not have happened the way that Lizzie expressed them.

Abby was killed, according to the autopsy, at around 9:30 in the morning. The killer, if it was anyone but Lizzie or Bridget, would have had to have concealed himself (or herself) in the house for well over an hour, waiting for Andrew Borden's return. Abby could have been discovered at any moment.

Abby's time of death also posed another problem for investigators. According to Lizzie, she had gone out but she obviously hadn't. The note that Lizzie said that Abby had received, asking her to visit a sick friend, was never found. Lizzie later said that she might have inadvertently burned it.

When Andrew Borden returned to the house, Bridget had to let him in as the screen door was fastened on the inside with three locks. This would have made it extremely difficult for the killer to get inside. Only a small window of opportunity would have existed while Bridget was fetching a pail and water from the barn. In addition, Bridget later testified that while she was unlocking the door for Mr. Borden, she head Lizzie laugh from upstairs. However, Lizzie swore that she had been in the kitchen when her father came home.

Borden also had to retrieve the key to his bedroom from the shelf in the kitchen to get into his room. This was done as a precaution because of a burglary the year before. In June 1891, a police captain inspected the house after Andrew Borden reported that it had been broken into. He found that Borden's desk had been rummaged through and over $100, along with Andrew's watch and chain, several small items and some streetcar tickets, had been taken. There was no clue as to how anyone could have gotten into the house, although Lizzie offered the fact that the cellar door had been open. The neighborhood was canvassed but no one reported seeing a stranger in the vicinity. According to the police captain, Borden said several times to him, "I'm afraid the police will not be able to find the real thief." It is unknown what he may have meant by this but various conspiracy theorists have their own ideas.

On the afternoon of the murder, an officer asked Lizzie if there were any hatchets in the house and she told Bridget to show him where they could be found. Four of them were discovered in the basement, including one with dried blood and hair on it (later determined to be from a cow). Another of the hatchets was rusted and the others were covered with dust. One of these was without a handle and was covered in ashes. The broken handle appeared to be recent, so it was taken into evidence.

A Sergeant Harrington and another officer asked Lizzie where she had been that morning and she said that she had been in the barn loft looking for iron for fishing sinkers. The two men examined the barn and found the loft floor to be thick with dust, with no evidence that anyone had been up there.

Deputy Marshal John Fleet questioned Lizzie and asked her who might have committed the murders. Other than an unknown man with whom her father had gotten into an argument with a few weeks before, she could think of no one. When asked directly if Uncle John Morse or Bridget could have killed her father and mother, she said that they couldn't have. Morse had left the house before 9:00, and Bridget had been sleeping when Andrew had been killed... then she pointedly reminded Fleet that Abby was not her mother, but her stepmother.

## August 5

On the following day, the investigation continued. By now, the story had appeared in the newspapers and the entire town was in an uproar. Sergeant Harrington found Eli Bence at Smith's Drug Store and interviewed him about the attempt to buy poison. Emma engaged Mr. Andrew Jennings as he and Lizzie's attorney. The police continued to investigate, but nothing of significance was found.

## August 6

Saturday was the day of the funerals for Andrew and Abby Borden. The service was conducted by the Reverends Buck and Judd, from the two Congregational Churches. The burial however, did not take place. At the gravesite, the police informed the ministers that another autopsy needed to be conducted. This time, the heads of the Borden's were removed from the body, the skin removed and plaster casts were made of the skulls. For some reason, Mr. Borden's head was not returned to his coffin.

## August 7

On Sunday morning, Alice Russell observed Lizzie burning a dress in the kitchen stove. She told her friend that, "If I were you, I wouldn't let anybody see me do that, Lizzie." Lizzie said it was a dress stained with paint, and was of no use.

It was this testimony at the inquest that prompted Judge Blaisdell of the Second District Court to charge Lizzie with the murders. The inquest itself was kept secret but at its conclusion, Lizzie was charged with the murder of her father and was taken into custody. The only testimony that Lizzie ever gave during all of the legal proceedings was at the inquest and we will never know for sure what she said. She was arraigned the following day and replied that she was "not guilty" of the charge. She was then taken to the Taunton Jail, which had facilities for female prisoners.

After that, a preliminary hearing was held, again before Judge Blaisdell. Lizzie did not testify but the record of her testimony at the inquest was entered into evidence by her attorney, Andrew Jennings. The judge declared her probable guilt and bound Lizzie over for the Grand Jury, who heard the case during the last week of its session.

The Commonwealth, represented by prosecutor Hosea Knowlton, had the disagreeable task of building the case against Lizzie. When he finished his presentation to the Grand Jury, he surprisingly invited defense attorney Jennings to present a case for the defense. This was something that was simply not done in Massachusetts. In effect, a trial was being conducted before the Grand Jury. Many saw this is as a chance that the charge against Lizzie might be dismissed. Then, on December 1, Alice Russell again testified about the burning of the dress. The next day, Lizzie was charged with three counts of murder. Strangely, she had been charged with the murder of her father, her step-mother and then the murders of both of them. The trial was scheduled to begin on June 5, 1893.

The trial itself lasted fourteen days and news of it filled the front pages of every major newspaper in the country. Between 30 and 40 reporters from the Boston and New York papers and the wire services were in the courtroom every day. The trial began on June 5 and after a day to select the jury, which consisted of twelve middle-aged farmers and tradesmen, the prosecution spent the next seven days putting on its case.

Hosea Knowlton was the reluctant prosecutor in the case. He had been forced into the role by Arthur Pillsbury, Attorney General of Massachusetts, who should have been the principal attorney for the prosecution. However, as Lizzie's trial date approached, Pillsbury felt the pressure building from Lizzie's supporters, particularly women's groups and religious organizations. Worried about the next election, he directed Knowlton, who was the District Attorney in Fall River to lead the prosecution in his place. He also assigned William Moody, District Attorney of Essex County, to assist him.

Moody made the opening statements for the prosecution. He presented three arguments. First, that Lizzie was predisposed to murder her father and stepmother because of their animosity toward one another. Second, that she planned the murder and carried it out and third, that her behavior, and her contradictory testimony, after the fact was not that of an innocent person. Moody did an excellent job and many have regarded him as the most competent attorney involved in the case. At one point, he threw a dress onto the prosecution table that he planned to admit as evidence. As he did so, the tissue paper that was covering the skull of Andrew Borden lifted and then fluttered away. Dramatically, Lizzie slid to the floor in a dead faint.

Crucial to the prosecution in the case was evidence that supplied a motive for Lizzie to commit the murders. This was done by using a number of witnesses who testified to Lizzie's dislike of her step-mother and her complaints about her father's spendthrift ways. The prosecution also tried to establish that Borden was writing a new will that would leave Emma and Lizzie with a pittance and Abby with a huge portion of his half million dollar estate. One of the witnesses called to establish this was John Morse, who first said that Andrew discussed a new will with him and then later said that he never told him anything about it.

The prosecution then turned to Lizzie's predisposition towards murder and her strange behavior before and after the events. They again called Alice Russell to testify about the burning of the dress. The destruction of it seemed a possible answer as to why Lizzie was not covered with blood after killing her parents. It was highly probable that she would have been spattered with it if she did commit the murders. In later years, some have theorized that perhaps she wore a smock over her dress during the murders or that perhaps she was naked when she did it. However, the smock would have been bloody too and would have had to be disposed of. As far as Lizzie being naked, this seems doubtful as well. Ignore the fact that in the Victorian society of Fall River, a young woman would have never appeared nude in front of her father (even to kill him) and focus on the fact that Lizzie never had time to bathe after killing Abby or in the few minutes between the killing of Andrew and her calling for Bridget.

To the prosecution though, the burning of the dress suggested that Lizzie had changed clothing after the murders. But why would she have kept the dress for three days before burning it and what would she have worn for the hours between the two deaths? Someone would have surely noticed a dress covered with blood.

On Saturday, June 10, the prosecution attempted to enter Lizzie's testimony from the inquest into the record. The defense objected, since it was testimony from one who had not been formally charged. The jury was withdrawn so that the lawyers could argue it out and on Monday, when court resumed, the three-judge panel excluded Lizzie's contradictory inquest testimony.

On Wednesday, June 14, the prosecution called Eli Bence, the drug store clerk, to the stand. The defense objected to his testimony as irrelevant and prejudicial. The judges sustained the objection and Lizzie's attempt to buy poison was thrown out of the record.

The prosecution called several medical witnesses, including Dr. Dolan. One of them even produced the skull of Andrew Borden to show how the blows had been struck. Unfortunately for the prosecution, these witnesses had an adverse effect on the case as the defense used their testimonies to strike points in Lizzie's favor. They were forced to state that whoever had committed the murders would have been covered with blood. There was no one to say that Lizzie had been!


Lizzie Borden's defense counsel used only two days to present its case. The two attorneys consisted of Andrew Jennings and George Robinson. Jennings was one of Fall River's most prominent citizens and had been Andrew Borden's private attorney. He was a solemn man who never again spoke about the Borden case after its conclusion. He and his younger associate, Melvin Adams, were instrumental in getting Lizzie's damaging testimony excluded from the case. Jennings was joined by George Robinson, who even with less legal experience was very beneficial to the case.

For the most part, the defense offered witnesses who could either corroborate Lizzie's story, or who could provide alternate possibilities as to who the killer might be. The testimony of the various witnesses was meant to do little but provide "reasonable doubt" about Lizzie's guilt.

For instance, an ice cream peddler testified to seeing a woman (presumably Lizzie) coming out the barn. This bolstered her story that she had actually been there. A passer-by claimed to see a "wild-eyed man" around the time of the murders. Mr. Joseph Lemay claimed that he was walking in the deep woods, some miles from the city, about twelve days after the murders when he heard someone crying "Poor Mrs. Borden! Poor Mrs. Borden! Poor Mrs. Borden!" He looked over a conveniently placed wall and saw a man sitting on the ground. The man, who had bloodstains on his shirt, picked up a hatchet, shook it at him and then disappeared into the woods. Needless to say, Lemay's story has never been given much credibility.

The defense also called witnesses who claimed to see a mysterious young man in the vicinity of the Borden house who was never properly explained. They also called Emma Borden to dispute the suggestion that Lizzie had any motive to want to kill their parents. Emma remained very supportive of her sister during the trial, although there is one witness, a prison matron, who testified that Lizzie and Emma had an argument when she was visiting her sister in jail.

On Monday, June 19, Robinson delivered his closing arguments and Knowlton began his closing arguments for the prosecution. He completed them on the following day. The judges then asked Lizzie if she had anything to say for herself and she spoke for the only time during the trial. "I am innocent", she said. "I leave it to my counsel to speak for me." Instructions were then given to the jury and they left to deliberate over the verdict.

A little over an hour later, the jury returned with its verdict. Lizzie Borden was found "not guilty" on all three charges. Public opinion was, by this time, of the feeling that the police and the courts had persecuted Lizzie long enough.

Five weeks after the trial, Lizzie (who henceforth called herself "Lizbeth") and Emma purchased and moved into a thirteen-room, stone house at 306 French Street in Fall River. It was located on "The Hill", the most fashionable area of the city. Lizzie named the house "Maplecroft" and had the name carved into the top step leading up to the front door.

In 1897, Lizzie was charged with the theft of two paintings, valued at less than one hundred dollars, from the Tilden-Thurber store in Fall River. There were no charges ever filed and it is believed the affair was settled privately.

In 1904, Lizzie met a young actress, Nance O'Neil, and for the next two years, Lizzie and Nance were inseparable. About this time, Emma separated from her sister and moved to Fairhaven. She and Lizzie stopped speaking to one another. Rumors said that sensational revelations about the murders would follow the split, but the revelations never came. Emma stayed with the family of Reverend Buck, and, sometime around 1915, she moved to Newmarket, New Hampshire.

Lizzie died on June 1, 1927, at age 67, after a long illness from complications following gall bladder surgery. Emma died nine days later, as a result of a fall down the back stairs of her house in Newmarket. They were buried together in the family plot, along with a sister who had died in early childhood, their mother, their stepmother, and their headless father. Both Lizzie and Emma left their estates to charitable causes and Lizzie designated $500 for the perpetual care of her father's grave.

Bridget Sullivan, never worked for any of the Borden's again. After the terrible events of the murder and the trial, she left town. She lived in modest circumstances in Butte, Montana until her death in 1948. Those who suggested that she had been "paid off" to keep quiet about the murders could find no evidence of this in what she left behind.

Over 100 years have passed since the murders in Fall River and we still cannot be sure of what we think we know about them. Perhaps because the case remained "unsolved", we still have a fascination for the events surrounding the murders. No single theory has ever been regarded as the correct one and every writer on the case seems to have a favorite culprit.

But how can we explain what draws us to the story? Is it because of the murders themselves, or is Lizzie herself to blame? Who can look at a photo of her, always smiling slightly, and wonder what secrets she carried with her to the grave? We will never know... but that hasn't stopped anyone from trying to guess!

The books and articles that have followed the events have each put their own special spin on the story. They use the same evidence and testimony to argue different suspicions of who really killed Andrew and Abby Borden. During the early days of the investigation, and well into the days of the trial, a number of accusations were made. At times the killer was said to be John Morse, Bridget Sullivan, Emma Borden, Dr. Bowen and even one of Lizzie's Sunday School students. Since that time, there have been other suggested killers. Some of the theories are credible and some are not.

One of the theories remains that Lizzie Borden actually committed the murders of her parents and managed to get away with it. This theory was especially popular in books written prior to 1940 and it still turns up occasionally today. Most of the writers who stand by this solution see the court rulings and poorly executed prosecution case as the reason that Lizzie was never found guilty. They simply refuse to see how an outsider could have committed the crimes.

The main problem with this idea is that it would have taken careful planning for Lizzie to kill Abby Borden and then wait patiently for the time to come to kill Andrew and still interact with Bridget Sullivan. This seems inconsistent with the "blitz" style attacks on the Borden's. The killer was obviously in a frenzy when each murder was committed and during the "cooling down" time between them, it seems unlikely that they would have been able to so easily iron handkerchiefs, attend to household duties and carry on conversations with the maid.

There is also the glaring problem of the blood. If Lizzie did kill her step-mother, where was the blood that would have been on her dress when she called Bridget a short time later? If she did change clothing (twice in the same morning), wouldn't Bridget have noticed this? It has been suggested that Lizzie may have gone to the barn between the murders as she claimed to and washed the blood off (there was running water there), but if she did, how did she wash off the blood after her father's murder?

Some writers believe that Lizzie and Bridget planned the murders together and that Bridget (when she went to Alice Russell's house) spirited away the bloody hatchet and dress so that they were never found. This theory is also used to explain the testimony that each woman gave about the day of the murder, never implicating the other. It seems hard to believe that Abby Borden's fall to the upstairs floor would not have been heard from below, especially since Abby weighed in at close to 200 pounds. However, there is no proof of this either and it still places one or both of the women in the role of a depraved killer.

While it seems hard to believe that Lizzie did commit the murders, it doesn't mean that she was not guilty in other ways. In other words, while she may not have actually handled the hatchet, she may have known who did.

One person who has been accused in this capacity was Emma Borden. It has been noted with some suspicion how she may have arranged an alibi for herself, claiming to be some fifteen miles away in Fairhaven, but actually returned to Fall River, hid upstairs in the Borden house, committed the murders and then returned to Fairhaven, where she received the telegram from Dr. Bowen. Once Lizzie is accused, the two sisters worked together to protect each other. Later, the women had a falling out over their father's estate and Lizzie's alleged affair with Nance O'Neil. However, neither one of them every spoke of the murder again.

Another astonishing theory pins the murders on William Borden, the slightly retarded, illegitimate son of Andrew Borden, who coincidentally (or not) committed suicide a few years after the trial. According to this theory, Lizzie, Emma, John Morse, Dr. Bowen and Andrew Jennings all conspired to keep his involvement a secret because of his illegitimate status and a claim that he might make against the estate if his relationship with the Borden's was found out. Allegedly, William was making demands of his father, who was in the process of writing a new will. Borden rejected the boy and William became enraged. He first killed Mrs. Borden and then after hiding in the house with Lizzie's knowledge, killed his father as well. The conspirators then either paid William off or threatened him, or both, and decided that Lizzie would allow herself to be suspected and tried for the murders, knowing that she could always identify the real killer, should that be necessary. This may be much in the way of speculation, but it's long been a favored theory by many.

So who did kill Andrew and Abby Borden? It's unlikely that we will ever know. It's also unlikely that we will ever discover just what Lizzie, and her defense counsel, really knew about the events in 1892. The papers from Lizzie's defense are still locked up and have never been released. The files remain sealed away in the offices of the Springfield, Massachusetts law firm that descended from the firm that defended Lizzie during the trial. There are no plans to ever release them.....

But the question of who killed Mr. and Mrs. Borden is not the only mysterious riddle that lingers in the wake of this heinous event. Another question might be, who haunts the house at 92 Second Street where the Borden's once lived?
In the years since the murders and the trial, the house has gone on to become the Lizzie Borden Bed and Breakfast Museum, a time capsule of the era when the murders took place and a quaint inn. Guests come from all over the country to be able to sleep in the room where Abby Borden was killed, but not all of them sleep peacefully... and not all of the spirits here rest in peace!
Guests and staff members alike have had their share of strange experiences in the house. Some have reported the sounds of a woman weeping and others claim to have seen a woman in Victorian era clothing dusting the furniture and straightening the covers on the beds. Occasionally, this even happens when the guests are still in the bed! Others have heard the sounds of footsteps going up and down the stairs and crossing back and forth on the floor above, even when they know the house is empty. Doors open and close as well and often, muffled conversation can be heard coming from inside of otherwise vacant rooms.
One man, who had little interest in ghosts, claimed that he accompanied his wife to the inn one night and took their luggage upstairs. The room had been perfectly made up when he entered, the bed smooth and everything put in its place. Over the course of a few minutes of unpacking, he happened to look over to the bed again and saw that it was now rumpled, even though he was in the room alone and had not been near it. With a start, he also noticed that the folds of the comforter had been moved so that they corresponded to the curves of a human body. On the pillow, there was an indentation in the shape of a human head!
His wife found him a few minutes later sitting in the downstairs sitting room. His face was very pale and he seemed quite nervous. When she asked him what was wrong, he took her back upstairs to show her the strange appearance of the bed. However when he opened the door, the pillow had been plumped and the comforter looked just as it did when he first entered the room... the room where Abby Borden had been murdered!

# · CHAPTER TWO ·

# HOLLYWOOD HORRORS!

## MURDER, MYSTERY & THE HAUNTINGS OF TINSELTOWN

Los Angeles... the fabled City of Angels. Home to the rich and famous, palm trees, sandy beaches, orange groves, Disneyland and most of all, to that wonderful place of the American Dream known as Hollywood.

Like many of you, I have always been fascinated by the glamour, the glitter and the decadence of old Hollywood. I have walked the Hollywood streets, searching for the names of favorite celebrities along the Walk of Fame. I have stared in awe at the elaborate facades of the Chinese Theater and have pressed my own palms into the solidified handprints of film greats like Humphrey Bogart. I have always been intrigued by the tales of the movie stars and the secret inner workings of the great film studios.

But like the city of Hollywood itself, the legends of the place have a dark side. About the time that I got interested in ghosts and hauntings, I also got interested in the less glamorous side of Hollywood. I learned that the bright photographs of the sunny streets hid whispers of crime and corruption and that the elaborate homes and architecture hid tales of spirits who did not rest in peace.

There are many unsolved mysteries connected to Hollywood, not the least of which are its ghosts. And not surprisingly, this has never curbed the interest in the place and in fact, has probably enhanced it.

The lure of Tinseltown has been a part of America since the first silent film makers came west to the small town of Los Angeles at the turn of the century. What began as a scheme for movie maker Mack Sennett to make some extra money with a low-cost housing area called "Hollywoodland" became a movie colony for artists, writers and actors who came west to make it big. Today, Hollywood remains not so much a place as a state of mind. In fact, it has not even been incorporated as a city since 1910, when in joined Los Angeles to share its water supply. However, it still retains that strange allure for those of us who have an interest in history and hauntings and for those who have lived their lives against the backdrop of the mythical silver screen.

Of course to understand how Hollywood earned such a starring role in the hearts and minds of America, we have to first look at the history of the city and of the city of Los Angeles... the place which actually invented the Hollywood we all know. The history of the region is a dark journey through tales of crime, corruption, death, murder and of course, Hollywood-style scandal. Nearly every tale of ghosts and hauntings in Hollywood involves some sort of terrible crime or an unsolved murder. Why is this? Well, we don't really know for sure, but perhaps there is something about the region itself that attracts both the brightest lights and the darkest shadows to its streets.

Welcome to the dark side of Hollywood.

Almost from the founding of the city, Los Angeles had a bad reputation. The once sleepy Spanish mission had been stolen from the rightful Mexican owners during the American quest for Manifest Destiny and soon, immigrants from the east were pouring out to the west coast. The Eastern newspapers promised sunshine, warm weather, easy living and, of course, an elusive fortune that could be obtained in the California gold fields. What many of the immigrants found instead was poverty and death. The majority of them returned home with nothing to show for their travels and hard work. Many of them never returned home at all.

By the middle part of the 1800's, Los Angeles (dubbed the City of Angels by the original founders) was literally filled with murderers, thieves and prostitutes. The streets were nothing more than rutted dirt paths where animals roamed and where garbage was dumped. The city gained its first notoriety in 1871 when a massacre of Chinese immigrants was reported in newspapers all over the country. The massacre took place near the old city plaza on the Calle de los Negros, which was commonly mistranslated in those days and called "Nigger Alley". The narrow street was a block of saloons, gambling parlors and dance halls. It was said that three or four men were murdered in the alley every weekend.

It was in 1871 that a huge crowd of white men went on a killing spree in the alley after a drunken Chinese immigrant began firing off his gun and accidentally hit a "white man". Within minutes, an inebriated and enraged mob swarmed through the streets, lynching, burning, stabbing and beating any Chinese man they could get their hands on. Eventually, 19 of them were killed. The Grand Jury indicted 156 men in the affair, with only six of them actually going to jail. Several days later, those six were released for lack of evidence. This would be the first time that charges of corruption would be leveled at local government, but it would not be the last.

Shortly after the turn of the century, a new flock of immigrants arrived, to be welcomed by what would only be rivaled by Chicago as the most corrupt city government and police force in America. Fortunes began to be made in oil and land and, as a matter of course, graft and petty crime became commonplace. The population explosion brought not only the upright citizens but also the scam artists, con men and nut cases who tried to take advantage of the rapid growth.

Like most other cities in the country, corruption and vice came with the territory but Los Angeles was different. It was new and fresh and the geography of the area, the automobile and Hollywood all combined to create a unique combination. Other cities had grown up around horse-drawn carriages, railroad and trolley cars, but Los Angeles was born at the beginning of the automobile age and with over 450 square miles of roads, the city had plenty of room to grow. The car was the principal form of transportation and this created "boomtown" mentality for new arrivals.

Of all of the reasons for the rapid growth, Hollywood was undoubtedly the biggest one. The mere mention of the name guaranteed readers for any newspaper story in the nation. In just a few short years, thanks to huge stars like Mary Pickford, Douglas Fairbanks and many others, Hollywood had managed to set itself apart from the rest of the world, as everything here seemed larger than life.

The rapid growth of Los Angeles was already causing enough problems when Prohibition came about in 1920 and created all new ones. As with just about everywhere else in the country, the demand for illegal liquor was high in Los Angeles and there were dozens of hoods who were happy to bribe the cops to get the kegs and bottles in the right hands. Perhaps the most famous L.A. hotspot for booze was Culver City, known as the "Heart of Screenland". This famous town was home to MGM, Hal Roach and a number of other studios and its main street, Washington Boulevard, played host to dozens of speakeasies, gambling parlors and gin joints. The town's "open" reputation insured gambling and prostitution as well and soon it had added a race track, a boxing arena and a dog racing track to its list of accomplishments. All of them served as a magnet for local gangsters. In addition, the Culver City police department was well known for looking the other way, losing evidence and bungling their investigations (as long as cash landed in the right pockets). Thanks to this, crime operated here undisturbed.

Of course, Culver City was not the only place to find booze, gambling and "broads"... the rest of southern California had a thirst for illegal liquor and vice as well. And Hollywood could always be counted on for corruption and scandal too. The film industry, which was the largest business in the area by the 1920's, provided more than enough money for both excess and debauchery. A series of scandals rocked the film colony in the early 20's including the alleged rape and murder of Virginia Rappe by America's beloved funny man, Fatty Arbuckle; the drug-related death of Wallace Reid, the murder of director William Desmond Taylor and others.

All of this gave America a ringside seat to the scandals of the movie colony and its shining stars. There was no doubt about it... orgies, drugs, illegal hooch, scandals and sex.... Hollywood had it all!

Bathtub gin and prostitutes were not the only forms of vice to hit southern California and by the late 1920's, several sensational crimes had been committed here as well. These would be the first of many to come. In 1927, the case of Edward Hickman and the kidnapping and dismemberment of twelve-year-old Marion Parker would make big headlines as would the 1929 gun battle between Jack Hawkins and Zeke Hayes and the L.A. police within the courthouse elevator. The two men had long records, which included the alleged torture death of a San Francisco cop. When they were discovered in southern California, they found themselves set up for L.A. sheriff-style revenge.

The unsavory reputation of the region became a favorite topic for sermons across America. To those who came west into this "den of iniquity", they found evangelists and preachers like Aimee Semple McPherson and "Fighting Bob" Shuler waiting to save their souls... as long as the collection plates were always full.

Los Angeles also began to earn its reputation as a landing spot for cults and the fringe element as well. According to novelist Nathaniel West, who used the dark side of L.A. for atmosphere in several of his books and stories, some of the local churches included the "Church Invisible", where fortunes were told; the "Tabernacle of the Third Coming", where a woman in male clothing preached the Crusade Against Salt; and the "Temple Moderne", where 'Brain-Breathing, the Secret of the Aztecs' was taught.

One of the most famous cult groups was founded in 1932 by Guy and Edna Ballard, who started the Church of I Am. The "religion" was based on the worship of the questionable deity, St. Germaine, who supposedly gave off a violet ray of supernatural power. The Ballard's accepted "love offerings" at their temple near downtown L.A., which was topped by a glowing neon sign which read "I AM". It was said that they gained tens of thousands of worshippers and they also sold products like "New Age Cold Cream". Their son, Donald, claimed to have the ability to become invisible and said that he possessed a psychic power (derived from ascended spirits) that was so powerful that he sunk several Nazi submarines. The Ballard's were eventually indicted for mail fraud although the charges were later overturned. By this time, however, the cult had collapsed and they vanished into obscurity.

Los Angeles continued to expand in the 1930's. Newcomers arrived on an almost daily basis. There were "Okie's" looking for work, scavengers looking for a quick buck and of course, dream seekers who came to California looking for their big break. Hollywood continued to serve as a beacon for would-be starlets and dreamers, but death and scandal sometimes shadowed even the brightest aspects of Tinseltown.

The year 1938 was a turning point for Los Angeles crime. That same year, a private investigator named Harry Raymond was killed while looking into reports of police corruption. The ensuing investigation revealed proof of bribery and vice throughout the police department and among city officials. L.A.'s mayor Frank Shaw was implicated and he was eventually replaced by Fletcher Bowron. After that, raids increased on nightclubs and gambling spots and as many mobsters lost their political connections, they headed out of town to Las Vegas.

While the heat was undeniably turned up for awhile, it did not bring an end to crime and corruption in the city. As World War II loomed closer, reports of fighting began to replace newspaper headlines about sensational crime. But the war began to expose other problems in L.A., namely the situation with gangsters and the black market. Soon, readers were introduced to the king the Los Angeles underworld, Mickey Cohen.

He was the most recognizable of the city's gangsters and he always dressed and acted the part, hanging out in all the right places and making enemies of all the right people. Connected to almost every type of vice in the city, he was constantly in the newspapers and was trailed by both the LAPD and the Sheriff's department, who busted him for small infractions that inevitably revealed larger crimes. Rival mobsters made several attempts on Cohen's life, but it would be the FBI who would get him in the end. They eventually put him in prison for 15 years on charges of tax evasion.

Los Angeles and Hollywood changed after the war. By this time, the star system and the stranglehold the studios held on their star's lives began to collapse. In L.A., the end of the war saw the collapse of the black market and a falling off of crime. However, the sex trade continued to operate uninhibited. In the late 1940's, Brenda Allen, one of the city's most notorious madams, faced a series of raids on her rented bordello. The case turned into a full-blown scandal when it was learned that a member of the vice squad was in Allen's pocket and that a lot of money had changed hands to keep the house of ill repute open. In the end, Allen was jailed, the police chief resigned and a number of vice cops were demoted.

Several unsolved murders made headlines at the end of the 1940's as well. In June of 1947, a rifle bullet to the head ended the life of Benjamin "Bugsy" Siegel, Hollywood's most notorious gangster celebrity. He had been killed while visiting girlfriend Virginia Hill's Beverly Hills home. There was much speculation as to who had "whacked" Siegel but it was considered to be a mob hit. Apparently, Bugsy had been skimming money from the construction of the Flamingo Hotel, the gambling mecca that would put Las Vegas on the map.

Even more mysterious, and much more gruesome, was the January 1947 murder of Elizabeth Short. Her severed and bloodless body was discovered in a vacant lot in L.A. and would go on to become one of the most famous murders in the city's history. Dubbed the "Black Dahlia" by the local press, Short was the epitome of the girl who came to Hollywood to seek stardom. Her final months were traced back through the darker side of Hollywood and her mysterious life and death has inspired a number of fictional accounts. Today, the case still remains unsolved.

Also that same year came the murder of former aviatrix Jeanne French, whose battered nude body was found in a vacant lot in the Mar Vista section of L.A. The case was quickly coined the "Red Lipstick" murder when her torso was discovered to be inscribed with an obscene message and signed with the words "B.D. - Tex Andy". Police guessed that the words might have been a mysterious reference to the Black Dahlia case that had taken place about a month before. The search for the killer ended with no solutions and remains unsolved.

By the 1950's, the noir reputation which L.A. has earned thanks to books and films was starting to come to an end and by the 1960's was gone altogether. Still, the darker element of society still rears its ugly head here on occasion, as witnessed by the brutal Manson family murders in the late 1960's.

There is no doubt that the culture of Hollywood virtually created the climate of Los Angeles in the early part of the century, and thus has created the region's large collection of ghostly tales and hauntings.

### HOORAY FOR HOLLYWOOD!

The Hollywood movie colony came into existence thanks to a group of eastern film makers and businessmen who saw a good thing in the nickelodeons that were springing up all over America. They were lured to the west coast by the promise of that fabled southern California sunshine (which was said to appear 355 days a year); low cost land; and by the opportunity to elude the process servers of Thomas Edison (who was filing lawsuits against anyone who copied his design of the early movie cameras). They settled into the city of Los Angeles and began building open-air stages and makeshift studios. It would be here where the early movie makers

Began cranking out primitive two-reelers, which would win over the hearts and minds of the American people.

Soon, word trickled back to Hollywood that audiences across the country were flocking to see their favorite performers and at this point, the actors (who prior to this were seen as little more than hired help) suddenly gained importance as the sure way to sell tickets. The rapidly becoming famous faces took on new names and soon earned salaries to match their new status. Almost overnight, the once obscure and disreputable performers suddenly found fame and fortune, becoming America's royalty. Some of them managed to cope with this quite well... while others did not.

Throughout the 1910's, Hollywood re-created itself almost daily as the new art form of movies began to emerge. Money began to roll into studio coffers and then into the pockets of the stars. Cocaine became the drug of choice, or "joy powder" as it was called in those days. It is reported that the manic silent film comedies actually came about thanks to the drug and became known as the Triangle-Keystone "cokey comedy". In 1916, British drug expert and occultist Aleister Crowley journeyed to Hollywood and noted the locals as being the "cinema crowd of cocaine-crazed sexual lunatics". And that's quite a statement coming from Crowley!

In addition to drugs, sex was always plentiful in Hollywood and gossip mongers in the movie colony always had much to talk about. Was it true that famed director D. W. Griffith had an obsession, onscreen and off, with young girls? Could it be true that Lillian and Dorothy Gish, up and coming young sisters, were actually lovers? Were the tales of Mack Sennett's "casting couch" actually true... and were some of Sennett's Sunshine Girls, like Gloria Swanson and Carole Lombard, really part of his hand-picked harem? And what about Hollywood's sex goddess, Theda Bara, who was allegedly a French-Arab demon of depravity born beneath the Sphinx... was it true that she was in truth Theodosia Goodman, a Jewish tailor's daughter from Ohio? Oh, and there was more... much more!

Within a few years of its founding, Hollywood would be the most maligned place to ever be spoken of from church pulpits across America. Preachers and evangelists would brand Hollywood as a place of legendary depravity and would call for boycotts of films and protests against theaters that would dare to show anything made in such a place. But the general public all but ignored the outcry and they continued to spend their hard-earned money at the movies.

The 1920's have been referred to as Hollywood's Golden Age and they were, in terms of both the numbers of movies made and in the amount of cash these films raked in. Unfortunately though, sometimes the golden ones fall just like the rest of us and when they do fall... they fall very hard.

### THE FALL OF FATTY ARBUCKLE
*The Lingering Spirit of Virginia Rappe*

In the 1920's, the film colony lured young would-be stars from across the land and many warned these hopefuls against the dark allure of drugs and fast living. Suicides and early deaths often made the headlines but eventually the death of one Hollywood hopeful would crowd everyone else out of the newspaper copy for weeks. This new girl was just a minor actress, but she was linked to a man who was known as "America's Funnyman"... Roscoe "Fatty" Arbuckle.

She would also go on to become one of Hollywood's first lingering ghosts. Her spirit still dwells, they say, at the Hollywood Memorial Park Cemetery. But what tragic events have caused the ghost of Virginia Rappe to linger here? To answer that question, we have to look back to the doomed history of the man who was accused of her murder, Fatty Arbuckle.

Roscoe "Fatty" Arbuckle was an overweight plumber in 1913 when Mack Sennett discovered him. He had come to unclog the film producer's drain but Sennett had other plans for him. He took one look at his hefty frame and offered him a job. Arbuckle's large appearance, but bouncing agility, made him the perfect target for Sennett's brand of film comedy, which included mayhem, pratfalls, and pies in the face.

He was soon making dozens of two-reelers as a film buffoon and audiences loved him. He made one film after another, all of them wildly successful, and also made a rather substantial fortune, going from a $3-a-day job in 1913 to over $5000 by 1917, when he signed with Paramount.

Fatty's first brush with scandal came in March 1916 at Mishawn Manor in Boston. The incident occurred at Brownie Kennedy's Roadhouse, where the lavish entertainment in Fatty's honor included twelve "party girls" who were paid just over $1000 for their contribution to the evening's fun. Unfortunately for Fatty, things came to an end just before the party could get started. Someone spotted the girls, and Fatty, stripping on the table in the back room of the roadhouse and called the cops. Also in attendance that evening were movie magnates Adolph Zukor, Jesse Lasky and Joseph Schenck. They paid $100,000 in hush money to Boston's District Attorney and Mayor James Curley to keep the incident quiet.

But it would be another of Fatty's frolics that would get him into trouble and earn him his place in Hollywood infamy.

Virginia Rappe came to Hollywood around 1919. She was a lovely brunette model who caught the eye of Mack Sennett and he offered her a job with his company. She soon went to work on the studio lot, taking minor parts and apparently, sleeping around. This fact became so well known that rumor had it Virginia passed along a rather sensitive infestation to so many of Sennett's crew that he closed down the studio and had the place fumigated. Soon however, she earned a part in the film FANTASY and later met Fatty Arbuckle and appeared with him in JOEY LOSES A SWEETHEART. Soon, Virginia was noticed by William Fox, shortly after winning an award for "Best Dressed Girl in Pictures" and he took her under contract. There was talk of her starring in a new Fox feature called TWILIGHT BABY and Virginia certainly seemed to be on her way.

Fatty had taken a shine to Virginia soon after meeting her and insisted that his friend, Bambina Maude Delmont bring her along to a party celebrating his new $3 million contract with Paramount. Fatty decided to hold the bash in San Francisco, which would give him a chance to try out his new custom-made Pierce-Arrow on the drive up the coast. On Labor Day weekend, two car loads of party-goers headed up the coast highway and included Fatty and his friends Lowell Sherman and Freddy Fishback, who were riding in the flashy Pierce Arrow. Bambina Maude Delmont, Virginia Rappe and other assorted starlets were piled in the other vehicle. They arrived in San Francisco late on Saturday night, checking into the luxurious Hotel St. Francis. Fatty took three adjoining suites on the 12th floor.

Shortly after arriving, Fatty made a call to his bootleg connection and the party was on, lasting all weekend. On Labor Day afternoon, which was Monday, September 5, 1921, the party was still going strong. The crowd had grown to about 50 people, thanks to Fatty's "open house" policy. Virginia and the other girls were downing gin-laced Orange Blossoms, some of the guests had shed their tops to do the "shimmy", guests were vanishing into the back bedrooms for sweaty love sessions and the empty bottles of booze were piling up.

Around three in the afternoon, Fatty, who was wearing only pajamas and a bathrobe, grabbed Virginia and steered the intoxicated actress to the bedroom of suite 1221. Bambina Maude Delmont later testified that the festivities came to a halt when screams were heard in the bedroom. She also said that weird moans were heard from behind the door. A short time later, Fatty emerged with ripped pajamas and he told the girls to "go in and get her dressed...she makes too much noise". When Virginia continued to scream, he yelled for her to shut up, or "I'll throw you out the window".

Bambina and another showgirl, Alice Blake, found Virginia nearly nude and lying on the unmade made. She was moaning and told them that she was dying. Bambina later reported that they tried to dress her, but found that all of her clothing, including her stockings and undergarments were so ripped and torn "that one could hardly recognize what garments they were."

A short time later, Virginia slipped into a coma at the Pine Street Hospital and on September 10, she died. The cause of her death almost went undiscovered. The San Francisco Deputy Coroner, Michael Brown, became suspicious after what he called a "fishy" phone call from the hospital, asking about a post-mortem. He went over personally to see what was going on and walked right into a hasty cover-up. He was just in time to see an orderly emerge from an elevator and head for the hospital's incinerator with a glass jar containing Virginia's female organs. He seized the organs for his own examination and discovered that Virginia's bladder had been ruptured, causing her to die from peritonitis. Brown reported the matter to his boss and both agreed that a police investigation was called for.

The hospital staff was grilled as to what they knew and they reluctantly reported the strange incidents that brought Virginia to the hospital. Soon, the newspapers also carried the story and Fatty Arbuckle was charged with the rape and murder of Virginia Rappe. The authorities blamed her death on "external pressure" from Arbuckle's weight being pressed down on her during sex.

Soon, the newspaper stories spun out of control. It was no longer just sex, they told a nation of stunned fans of the "happy fat man", but "strange and unnatural sex". According to reports, Arbuckle became enraged over the fact that his drunkenness had led to impotence, so he ravaged Virginia with a Coca-Cola Bottle... or was it a champagne bottle... or could it have been a piece of ice? Others claimed that Fatty was so well endowed that he had injured the girl, while others stated that the injury had come when Fatty had landed on the slight actress during a sexual frolic.

Needless to say, a lot of guessing was being done and a lot of insinuations were being made about Fatty Arbuckle and Virginia's tragic death.... and Fatty was beginning to feel the heat. In Hartford, Connecticut, a group of angry women ripped down a screen in a theater showing an Arbuckle comedy, while in Wyoming, a group of men opened fire in a movie house where another Arbuckle short was being shown. A "Lynch Fatty" mood was beginning to sweep the land and angry, and increasing boisterous, voices were calling for Hollywood to clean up its act. Finally, Arbuckle's films were pulled from general release.

Held without bail, Fatty sweated it out in the San Francisco jail while his lawyers sought to have the charges reduced from murder to manslaughter. Film tycoon Adolph Zukor, who had millions at stake with Arbuckle, contacted San Francisco District Attorney Matt Brady in an effort to make the case go away. Brady was enraged and later claimed that Zukor offered him a bribe.

Other friends of Fatty called the D.A.'s office and suggested that Arbuckle was being punished because some starlet drank too much and died. They assumed they were helping Fatty's case, but the result was just the opposite. D.A. Brady grew angrier with each call on Fatty's behalf and by the time the case went to trial, he was livid.

The trial began in November 1921 with Arbuckle taking the stand to deny any wrong-doing, although his attitude toward Virginia was one of indifference. He never bothered to express any remorse or sorrow for her death. His lawyers were even more to the point, making every effort to paint Virginia as "loose", suggesting that she slept around in New York, South America, Paris and of course, in Hollywood. After much conflicting testimony, the jury favored acquitting Fatty by 10-2 after 43 hours of deliberating. The judge declared a mistrial.

A second trial was held and this time, the jury was hung at 10-2 for conviction. Fatty was now out on bail and was forced to sell his Los Angeles home and fleet of luxury cars to pay his lawyer fees.

Despite the hard work of Brady, who wanted to convict Arbuckle very badly, Fatty was finally acquitted in his third trial, which ended on April 22, 1922. Thanks to confusing testimony by 40 drunken witnesses and no physical evidence (like the infamous bottle), Fatty was finally a free man. In fact, the jury issued this statement: "Acquittal is not enough for Roscoe Arbuckle. We feel a grave injustice has been done him and there was not the slightest proof to connect him in any way with the commission of any crime."

Fatty may have been free, but he was hardly forgiven. Paramount soon canceled his $3 million contract and his unreleased films were scrapped, costing the studio over $1 million. Fatty's career was finished. Arbuckle was banned from acting in Hollywood productions. The studios just couldn't afford to have his name connected to their pictures. Only a few friends, like Buster Keaton, remained by his side. In fact, it was Keaton who suggested that Arbuckle change his name to "Will B. Good". Actually, Arbuckle did adopt the name William Goodrich in later years and he was able to gain employment as a gag man and as a comedy director.

Arbuckle would never act in the movies again and the public would never allow him to forget his fall from grace either. People shouted "I'm Coming, Virginia" when they recognized him on the street and laughter often greeted him in restaurants and shops. In his forced retirement, Fatty also took to drinking quite heavily and finally, he died in New York on June 28, 1933.

Innocent or guilty? We'll never really know for sure, but in the state of mind called Hollywood, it didn't really matter. Arbuckle had managed to change the image of Hollywood from one linked to dreams to that of one forever linked to scandal.

And now we return to Hollywood Memorial Park.... and the ghost of Virginia Rappe. I would imagine that there is little doubt in the mind of the reader as to why Virginia's spirit may be a restless one. In addition to losing her life during the horrifying incidents of that fateful Labor Day, Virginia lost her reputation as well. The press was nearly as cruel to her as they were to Fatty Arbuckle.

Many have asked why that was, but the answer may lie with William Randolph Heart. It cannot be denied that the Hearst newspapers were instrumental in turning the affair into a nationwide scandal. As it happens, shortly before Fatty went to trial, Heart's affair with a starlet named Marion Davies hit the news and Marion's film career began to suffer. Rumor had it that Hearst gave the go-ahead to his papers to exploit every Hollywood scandal of the time, including Fatty's, to take the focus off himself and Davies. Thanks to Hearst, Virginia Rappe was "raped" all over again in newspapers across the country.

So, it's not surprising that her spirit still lingers behind. Visitors who come to Hollywood Memorial Park have reported hearing a ghostly voice that weeps and cries out near Virginia's simple grave. It is believed by many to be her ghost, still attached to this world, and still in anguish over her promising career, which was cut short... just like her life.

## THE HAUNTED HOLLYWOOD SIGN
### The Ghost of Peg Entwhistle... Patron Saint of Hollywood Actors

Hollywood is no stranger to suicide. Thousands came to the new "Film Capital of the World" in the early 1900's, hoping to make it big in the moving picture business. When failure came instead of success, many of them chose not to go on, to continue dreaming of wealth and celebrity that would never come. Unfortunately, many of these failed actors and would-be starlets found the fame in death they never achieved in life.

One such actress was Peg Entwhistle, who set a new standard for suicide in Hollywood. Not only would she use a Hollywood landmark as a novel way for ending her life, but she would also become a symbol of Hollywood failure and tragedy. And according to some Peg Entwhistle is no mere symbol. She maintains a powerful presence in the vicinity of the Hollywood sign... a presence that is still being felt today.

The Hollywood sign is perhaps the most famous sign in the world. Resting on Mount Lee in Griffith Park, it looms over the city of Hollywood as a constant reminder of the past. The original sign was built in 1923 as a publicity ploy to encourage the sales of homes in the Hollywoodland subdivision, which was located along Beachwood Canyon. Hollywood was in its infancy in those days and was being deluge by people from the east. They came looking for the fabled orange groves and sunshine and when they got here, they needed a place to live. Promoter Mack Sennett wanted the Hollywoodland subdivision to provide that place but like almost everything else in Tinseltown, the sign was merely a facade. The cheap construction was only designed to last for a year and a half.

It cost $21,000 to build and each of the letters were 30 feet wide and 50 feet high. The entire name was studded with low wattage light bulbs and could be seen for miles. In time, the sign would fall into disrepair and the light bulbs would all burn out, were broken, or were stolen by vandals. Maintenance of the sign was discontinued in 1939. Then, late in 1944, the H. Sherman Company, who became the developers of the old Hollywoodland housing district, quit claimed to the city of Los Angeles about 455 acres of land adjoining Griffith Park. This property included the Hollywoodland sign.

The weather beaten sign was untouched for the next five years, falling further into ruin. Then, in 1949, the Hollywood Chamber of Commerce made plans to repair and rebuild the sign. They also removed "land" from the line of letters so that it merely read "Hollywood". The cost to renovate the sign was around $4,000 but the light bulbs were not replaced. In spite of the work that was done, the sign continued to deteriorate (some would say much like Hollywood itself) until the late 1970's, when a fund-raising campaign was begun to replace the letters. Donors were asked to contribute $27,700 each to buy a replacement letter.

In August 1978, the Pacific Outdoor Advertising Company, along with Hughes Helicopters and the Heath Sign Company, demolished the remains of the original sign and installed new, all-steel letters in its place. The sign now stretches 450 feet along the side of Mount Lee and remains 50 feet tall.

Like the Chinese Theater, whether it be called Graumann's or Mann's, the Hollywood sign is one of the definitive symbols of Hollywood and perhaps the film industry itself. For those who are film buffs, no journey to southern California can be complete without a trip to view the sign.... there is nothing quite like it in the world.

The Hollywood sign got its first taste of death on a dark night in September 1932. It was on this night that Lillian Millicent "Peg" Entwhistle climbed up the slopes of Mount Lee with the glowing sign as her final destination. When she arrived, she scaled the heights of the giant letter "H"... and jumped. Her body plunged down the side of the hill and broke on the ground below. As she had planned, the fall had killed her, leaving her body battered and bloody on the unforgiving earth. Peg Entwhistle, Hollywood actress, was only 24 years old.

Peg had been born in London, England in 1908. She grew up in an acting family, although little is known about her early life, save for the fact that her mother died when Peg was quite young. She left Peg's father to raise a daughter and her two brothers, Robert and Milton, alone. A short time later, Peg's father packed up and moved the family to New York where he started working in local theater. Unfortunately, tragedy struck again and Peg's father was run over by a truck on Park Avenue, ending his life. Robert and Milton were then sent to Los Angeles to live with Harold Entwhistle, their uncle, and Peg turned to the stage for solace.

She made her acting debut in Hamlet when she was just 17 years old. To everyone's surprise, she quickly became a bonafide star, loved by audiences, critics and directors alike. There was no question about it, Peg was a knockout and possessed a gentle quality which won the hearts of just about everyone she ever worked with. She quickly became a Broadway star and a member of the New York Theater Guild.

While working on Broadway, Peg met a fellow actor named Robert Keith. He was also a popular star and despite his being 10 years Peg's senior, the two soon fell in love and got married. But the marriage soured quickly. During a visit to her mother-in-law's house, Peg noticed a photograph of a young boy on the mantel. She asked who he was and was informed that he was Robert's son from his first marriage... something that he had kept hidden from her. Incidentally, that surprise stepson was future actor Brian Keith, star of the television show "Family Affair".

Just weeks later, during a dinner party at their home, a police officer came to the door and demanded nearly $1000 in back child support that Robert owed. Peg got the money together, but when she asked Robert about it, he became violent. The bad debts, lies and fights ended the marriage and they were soon divorced.

Peg went back to the Broadway stage, but this part of her life was also coming to an end. The Great Depression had arrived and the majority of the public could no longer afford the expensive theater tickets. Thanks to this, Peg's last seven New York plays bombed. But all wasn't lost. While Broadway may have been suffering, Hollywood was still in its boom era. During Peg's initial fame in New York, Hollywood was making the transition from silent films to talkies. Unfortunately, many of the silent film stars were just not cut out for talking roles and Hollywood producers looked to the stars of the New York stage to fill the acting rosters. Many other stage actors were making it big in Hollywood, so Peg packed up and took the train to California, sure that greater fame and fortune waited for her on the west coast. When she arrived, Peg moved into a Beachwood Canyon bungalow with her brothers and Uncle Harold. The house was located in the Hollywoodland subdivision, just under the towering sign where Peg would later take her life.

Not long after she arrived in Hollywood, Peg found work in small theater. The first production she did was a play called "Mad Hopes", starring Billie Burke, who would go on to play Glenda the good witch in THE WIZARD OF OZ. Also in the show was another Hollywood newcomer named Humphrey Bogart. The play opened to decent reviews, but only lasted a week and a half. When the curtain fell, Peg saw it as another personal failure. She began to wonder if her New York jinx had followed her to Tinseltown. However, she would go on to appear with Billie Burke in a few more small productions although Bogart returned to New York. His days of fame and fortune were still to come.

Thanks to her good looks and her popularity on Broadway, Peg landed a short-term contract with RKO Studios and within weeks of her arrival, landed a small part in the film THIRTEEN WOMEN. She knew that even though it was a small part, it would lead to other offers. It was only her first movie role, she realized.

Little did she know that it would turn out to be her last.

During filming, Peg discovered the part was actually a supporting role, but a good one. Her hopes began to rise. The movie was released, only to be savaged by the critics. RKO quickly shelved it. It was released quietly a short time later but substantial cuts had been made to the 73-minute running time. Peg's part, despite her good showing, had been reduced to little more than a cameo appearance.

Once more, she was bitterly disappointed, but vowed to not let it get to her. She began answering ads for small parts and going to auditions and casting calls. However, Peg soon found that she was just another pretty face in a town filled with beautiful women. All of them had come to Hollywood for the same reason, to make it into show business.

And things went from bad to worse. Her option with RKO ran out and they declined to renew it. She was cut loose and on her own, now unable to even find work in small theater. Soon, promises of future work quickly vanished. As her career fell apart, her new friends made themselves scarce. No one can afford to be seen with a nobody in Hollywood! Peg Entwhistle, the gorgeous young woman who had shot to fame on Broadway, had now fallen to the bottom of the Hollywood barrel. She became even more depressed when she was unable to even scrape together train fare to go back to New York. She would never act again.

So, on that terrible night in September 1932, Peg announced to her Uncle Harold that she was going to take a walk. She was last seen alive heading down Beachwood Canyon toward Mount Lee. Apparently, Peg scratched her way up the slope to the Hollywood sign where she took off her coat and folded it neatly. She placed it, along with her purse, at the base of the maintenance ladder that led up the letter "H". She climbed to the top and then plunged to her death.

The next day, a woman hiker in Griffith Park discovered the purse and coat near the ladder. She opened the purse and discovered a suicide note inside. It read simply " I am afraid I am a coward. I am sorry for everything. If I had done this a long time ago it would have saved a lot of pain..... P.E." The hiker replaced the note and then, in the early morning hours, placed the purse and coat on the doorstep of the Hollywood police station. Two days later, authorities discovered the body of Peg Entwhistle in the brush at the bottom of Mount Lee.

Unsure of her identity, the police ran a description of the woman, along with the contents of the suicide note, in the newspaper. They were quickly contacted by Uncle Harold, who had been frantically searching for his niece sent she had left for her walk several evenings before. He feared the worst when he saw the initials attached to the end of the note. Not long after, he identified the body as that of Peg Entwhistle.

And here's where the ultimate irony comes in....

Two days later, Uncle Harold was sifting through the afternoon mail and he discovered a letter that had been mailed to Peg the day before she jumped to her death. The letter was from the Beverly Hills Playhouse and it had been written to offer Peg the lead role in their next production.

But wait, it gets even better... the part was that of a beautiful young woman who commits suicide in the final act of the play! Pretty spooky, isn't it?

But death was not the last act for Peg Entwhistle.

In the years following her suicide, hikers and park rangers in Griffith Park have reported some pretty strange happening in the vicinity of the Hollywood sign. Many have reported sightings of a woman dressed in 1930's era clothing who abruptly vanishes when approached. She has been described as a very attractive, blond woman, who seems very sad. Could this be Peg's ghost, still making her presence known? Could she also be linked to the pungent smell of gardenia perfume that has been known to overwhelm sightseers in the park? Perhaps it is, as the gardenia scent was known to be Peg's trademark perfume.

In 1990, a North Hollywood man and his girlfriend were walking on a Beachwood Canyon trail near the Hollywood sign with their dog when the animal suddenly began to act very strange. Instead of running around on the trail and through the brush as he normally did, he began to whine and hang back near the couple. They had never seen him act that way before and could find no cause until they spotted a lady walking nearby. One thing they noticed about her was that she was wearing clothing from the 1930's. However, thinking that you could see anything in Hollywood, they didn't pay much attention.

The lady however, seemed to be walking in a daze. Thinking that perhaps she was drunk or on drugs, they started to steer clear of her when she suddenly just faded away before their eyes. At that time, they had no idea who Peg Entwhistle was, nor that she had committed suicide nearby, or even that her ghost reportedly haunted the area. Imagine their surprise when they found out!

Another eyewitness to this haunting was a Griffith Park ranger named John Arbogast. In an interview, he revealed his own encounters with the ghost of Peg Entwhistle. He stated that she normally made her presence known very late at night, especially when it was foggy, and always in the vicinity of the Hollywood sign. He also claimed to have encountered the scent of gardenias in the area as well.

"I have smelled it several times," he said, "and always when any flowers around have been closed because of cold weather. I don't think I have ever smelled it in the summer time."

Arbogast's duties as a ranger often involved the Hollywood sign itself. He explained that in recent years, alarms systems have been installed near the sign to keep people away from it. There is always a danger of vandals, and of course, of suicides who want to go out the same way that Peg did. The alarm systems incorporate the use of motion detectors and lights to keep intruders away.

Arbogast recalled a number of times when the alarm system stated that someone was close to the sign, even though a check by the ranger revealed no one was there. "There have been times when I have been at the sign," he said, "and the motion detectors say that someone is standing five feet away from me... only there's nobody there."

So, what could have made Peg Entwhistle choose to end her life in such a dramatic and violent way? No one knows, but we have to wonder. The Hollywood slogan states that the sign exists as a symbol of hope, so that those who answer the siren call of Hollywood will know that anything in the city is possible. But did Peg glimpse that sign one evening, after spending the day going from one pointless casting call to another, and see it not as a symbol of hope, but one of despair? Did she feel that sign mocking her, laughing that so many others had made it in the movies... so why couldn't she? Did the glowing lights of the sign remind her of why she had come to Hollywood, chasing the bright lights she would never catch up to? Or perhaps she just wanted to go out in a way that people would remember?

If this was the case, she was right. Who may have ever heard of Peg Entwhistle if not for the fact that she took that fatal plunge from the very symbol of Hollywood itself? It is certain that Peg gained much more fame in death than she ever gained in life. To young actors and would-be stars, Peg has become a sort of a patron saint to failed actors in Hollywood.

### HOT TODDY!
#### The Mysterious Death of Thelma Todd

The ghost of Thelma Todd still walks in Hollywood, or at least that's what the owners of a building on the Pacific Coast Highway have claimed for years. It was in this building where Todd's "Roadside Rest Cafe" was once located and its not far from the house where she met her mysterious end. This is a house where the ghostly elements of her demise are still repeated today. But what strange events have caused this glamorous ghost to linger behind in this world? The reader doesn't have to look far for that answer, for the strange death of Thelma Todd remains one of Hollywood's greatest unsolved mysteries!

Monday - December, 16, 1935

On the hills above the Pacific Coast Highway, between Santa Monica and Malibu, stands a house belonging to movie director Roland West. Inside of the garage, a Packard Convertible idles with its top down. The engine is running, filling the air with deadly exhaust fumes. In the front seat is sprawled a gorgeous blond with tousled, curly hair and infectious smile and a face that could stop a passing train... or at least that's how she had been described. On this Monday morning though, she looks somewhat different.

The woman is facedown in the seat of the Packard. Her blond hair is matted and her skin is pale. A porcelain replacement tooth has been knocked out of her mouth and blood is spattered on her skin, her evening gown and the mink coat that she wears. As the gas drains from the engine of the automobile, it slowly steals away the life of the blond. Finally, her heart stops and her lungs breath no more. Thelma Todd, Hollywood's "Ice Cream Blonde" and the queen of the zany comedies of Hal Roach, is dead.

Thelma's body was discovered later that morning and the police were summoned at once. The coroner on the scene believed that she had died from choking on the exhaust fumes from the car. He also admitted that suicide was a possibility, but no note was discovered. She was found because she was late for her expected arrival at the Roach Studios, where she was starring with Laurel and Hardy in THE BOHEMIAN GIRL. She had been Stan Laurel's choice for the leading lady, but the film would have to be finished without her. Thelma's career ended with her death. At the age of only 30, she was already a part of Hollywood history.

Thelma Todd... "Hot Toddy"

Thelma Todd was born on July 29, 1905 in Lawrence, Massachusetts. She was an exceptional student and did very well in school. She became a teacher after graduation but began entering beauty contests to help pay the rent. After winning a contest at the age of 20, she came to the attention of some Hollywood talent scouts, who encouraged her to try her luck in California. She got lucky with Paramount Studios and in 1925, she was placed under contract and started at the studio's new acting school.

A year later, she was awarded her first small part in the film FASCINATING YOUTH, which starred Charles "Buddy" Rogers.

Throughout 1927, Thelma was given small parts in other feature films, like RUBBER HEELS with Ed Wynn and NEVADA, a western starring Gary Cooper. Then, Al Jolson spoke a few words onscreen in THE JAZZ SINGER and the motion picture was changed forever. The industry went through a terrifying series of changes as the "Talkies" became the new medium of choice. The old silent films were gone for good and with them went some of the biggest stars of the era. The careers of screen legends like John Gilbert, Clara Bow, Norma Talmage and many others were suddenly over. They were forced into retirement when the public did not respond to the sound of their voices.

For Thelma, the coming of sound motion pictures could not have occurred at a better time. She was now able to develop her wise-cracking persona and the demise of many screen veterans made room for newcomers and little-knowns like Thelma. A new generation of screen stars was born.

In 1929, Thelma came to Hal Roach, who featured her and comedy actress Zasu Pitts in a successful series of two-reel comedies. A former director at Essanay, Roach persuaded the Pathe company to sponsor him in his own studios and he soon emerged as a comedic talent, envisioning hilarious situations and translating them to film. Roach concentrated more on story than slapstick and audiences loved him at the box office. His biggest stars became Laurel and

Hardy, Charlie Chase and Thelma Todd. She proved to be a real asset to Roach, not only appearing in her own films but as a female foil to Stan and Ollie and others.

In addition, Thelma also played major roles in films for other studios. They were mostly comedies in which she portrayed the sarcastic and wise-cracking blond that most suited her. She appeared in two different films with the Marx Brothers, MONKEY BUSINESS and the classic HORSE FEATHERS. Stan Laurel always wanted Thelma as the female lead in he and Hardy's films, but her personality didn't always mesh with the two comedians on screen. She and Laurel became close friends and he often found work for her in other films when she wasn't working for Roach. He loved her bawdy sense of humor and when she suffered from boyfriend problems, she always confided in Stan.

By 1930, Zasu Pitts had moved on to other work and Thelma was often joined on screen by Patsy Kelly. They were still going strong in 1935 and her professional career was filled with high spots. Unfortunately, the same could not always be said for her private life. She had been married for a short time to Pat DiCicco and after her divorce became involved in a number of affairs. In 1931, she made a picture called CORSAIR, co-starring Chester Morris. It was directed by Roland West. He was married at that time to an actress named Jewel Carmen, but in true Hollywood fashion, he moved in with Thelma.

Roland West was one of the most respected directors in Hollywood during the 1920's and early 1930's. While his output of films was small, his work was very much appreciated by studios and audiences alike. His greatest success came in 1926 with THE BAT, an atmospheric thriller starring Jack Pickford and West's wife, Jewel Carmen. His visually astounding 1928 film, THE DOVE, won an Academy Award for art direction. In 1931, he created one of the most extraordinary chillers of the time, THE BAT WHISPERS with Chester Morris and then filmed THE CORSAIR. This second film led to the end of his marriage and his taking up with the cute blond leading lady of the film, Thelma Todd.

Together, Thelma and West opened up a business called "Thelma Todd's Roadside Rest Cafe", located under the Palisades along the Pacific Coast Highway. Many of their famous friends began frequenting the place and it became popular with actors and star-struck fans alike. They were also living quarters above the cafe, while West also maintained a grand house on Pasetano Road, nestled behind Sunset Boulevard at the point where it connects with the Pacific Coast Highway. It was only a short climb, via steps, from the restaurant.

One fateful afternoon, Thelma was visited at the cafe by none other than gangster Lucky Luciano. At that time, organized crime was starting to appear in California, moving west from places like New York and Chicago. Bootlegging and drug trafficking had already begun in Hollywood, but by and large, it had remained untouched by the underworld. However, by the mid-1930's, Luciano was making an attempt to penetrate California with his illegal gambling enterprise. He already had casinos all over the country and with so much money flowing in and out of Hollywood, he was looking for a way to get a piece of the action. He was also on the lookout for establishments where he could place gambling parlors and Thelma's Roadside Rest Cafe looked to be the perfect front.

Luciano turned out to be very disappointed by his visit to the Roadside Rest. While he may have been one of the biggest gangsters of the time, Thelma Todd turned out to be as gutsy as the characters she portrayed onscreen. Luciano made her a generous offer and in return, he wanted to transform the upper floor of the cafe into a secret casino. All she had to do was to keep business flowing by escorting her rich and famous friends upstairs to try their luck at the gambling tables. He promised that she would be well rewarded with a cut of the take.

Thelma turned him down flat.

Thelma's career continued to soar. In 1935, she appeared with Bing Crosby in the Paramount musical TWO FOR TONIGHT and in November, she began working with Laurel and Hardy again in the feature-length musical THE BOHEMIAN GIRL. This film was also based on an operetta and Stan found an unusual part for Thelma to play. She appeared as a gypsy's daughter, wearing a black wig to cover her blond curls. She continued to work on the film well into December and by the 14th, when she was one of many guests at a Hollywood party, was still shooting scenes.

The party was thrown by Ida Lupino, a relative newcomer to Hollywood, and had the makings of a blowout Hollywood event. The guest list was vast and unfortunately included Thelma's ex-husband, Pat DiCicco. After a few drinks, Thelma and DiCicco exchanged some heated words, which made Thelma drink even more. By the early morning hours of Sunday, she had downed more than her share of alcohol. Luckily, she a driver to take her home.

As she prepared to leave, Roland West, who was at the apartment over the cafe, received a phone call from theater owner Sid Graumann saying that Thelma was a "bit under the influence" and was on her way home. Graumann suggested that West see her safely into bed. But sometime between the telephone call and Monday morning, Thelma Todd died in the garage of West's house on Pasetano Road.

On the morning that she was found by her maid, Stan and Ruth Laurel received a Christmas card from Thelma. Her death stunned the Laurel's and Hal Roach. Throughout the following week, gifts that Thelma had sent continued to arrive at the homes of friends, including Stan's, further adding to the shock and misery.

One week later, on December 23, Thelma was laid to rest at Forest Lawn Cemetery. A huge crowd gathered to view the open casket in which she lay covered with yellow roses. A short time later, Thelma's body was placed in the ground.. forever silencing both the perky actress and the mystery of her death.

The inquest into her death revealed more questions than answers. Many suggested that Thelma might have committed suicide. It was not an uncommon method for such an act, but then murders had been committed in a similar fashion. In addition, if she had killed herself, where had the blood on her face and clothing come from? To make matters more suspicious, an autopsy had revealed that Thelma had suffered a broken nose, several broken ribs and enough bruises to suggest that she had been roughed up. This, combined with Thelma's successful career, seemed to rule out suicide.

But if she had been murdered, who had killed her? Roland West seemed to be the likely suspect and witnesses from the party, including Id Lupino, testified to her state of mind when she left the event. All agreed that she had been drunker than usual and Sid Graumann appeared to testify about his telephone call to West. Also, witnesses from the neighborhood told the court how they had seen Thelma, still in her evening gown and mink coat, screaming obscenities and kicking at the door of the apartment. So, if she was so drunk, how had she gotten from the apartment to the house on Pasetano Road?

West was called to testify and he admitted that instead of helping Thelma into bed on Sunday morning, he had locked the door to the apartment. He also confessed that they had gotten into a terrible fight over her intoxicated condition. However, he added a strange twist to the testimony. He stated that he had been awakened by his dog barking around 3:30 in the morning and was sure that he heard water running in the apartment. He assumed that Thelma had somehow gotten into the house.

An examination of the door did reveal marks where it was apparently kicked. Police were baffled though as to how Thelma could have gotten inside when it was bolted shut on the other side. This made them even more suspicious of West. Someone raised the incredible theory that West had hired an actress to pretend to be Thelma beating on the door while he was actually beating the real woman to death inside. The idea of the look-alike aside, West had a strong alibi against murder. Although his statement was contradictory, there was no evidence to tie him to the murder scene. He was, by his own admission, the last person to speak with Thelma on Sunday morning, just a short time before she died.

Then came more surprising testimony, this time from West's wife, Jewel Carmen. She claimed that she had seen Thelma on Sunday morning, after the sun was up, driving her Packard past the intersection of Hollywood and Vine. At her side was a handsome stranger. This testimony was very bizarre because the coroner and the police believed that Thelma was already dead by then. They were sure that she had died during the early morning hours of Sunday and was not discovered until the following day.

But how reliable was Jewel Carmen? She was West's wife and he was the prime suspect in the case. If she were lying, why would a jilted wife protect her unfaithful husband? Some suggested that perhaps if West did kill Thelma, perhaps Carmen hoped to get back into his good graces by providing an alternate killer in the form of the "handsome stranger". She could also put Thelma in another place and far from the early morning argument with West.

Whatever the facts behind Jewel's testimony, it threw the jury into total confusion. They spent weeks going over and over the evidence and eventually, they announced their verdict.... "death due to carbon monoxide poisoning". That was all they could agree on and the case was closed.

But Thelma's attorney, who attended the inquest, was sure that the police had been on the wrong track all along. He requested a second inquest, in which he would be able to prove his theory. He believed that he could pin her murder, not accidental death, on Lucky Luciano. He was sure that when Thelma had turned down the gangster's offer to turn the cafe into a gambling parlor, she had signed her own death warrant. The attorney was convinced that Luciano ordered Thelma to be "rubbed out" as a warning to anyone else he approached with such an offer or because she became aware of his secret plans for the casino.

The district attorney agreed to the idea and a second inquest was scheduled. However, when Hal Roach learned of the plans for the second inquest, he begged the D.A. to drop the matter. Terrified at the thought of crossing the mobster, he urged the District Attorney to reconsider. Reluctantly, he agreed and the case was closed for good. As a result, the murder of Thelma Todd was never solved.

Although the case was wrapped up as far as the law was concerned, there were just too many unanswered questions and as usual, involvement in the affair was enough to bring on the Hollywood style of retribution. In the past, Hollywood circles had ruined the careers of popular stars like Roscoe "Fatty" Arbuckle and the death of Thelma Todd would bring on the destruction of Roland West. In fact, he never worked again.

Even so, not everyone believed that West was involved in the murder. Many, like Thelma's lawyer, were sure that Luciano had been involved. However, they had no plans to publicly point fingers at the dangerous mobster. Privately though, the Hollywood stars quickly learned to avoid Luciano and his "colleagues". If he could not be avoided, then he was treated with respect and caution. They knew what would happen to them if they didn't... but unfortunately, this warning came a little too late for Thelma Todd.

The mystery over the unsolved death of Thelma Todd has lingered for more than six decades. Some believe this may be why her spirit is so restless. Her ghost is still frequently seen and encountered at the building where the Roadside Rest Cafe was once located. Staff members at the production company that is now located here say that they have often spotted a filmy apparition that resembles the "Ice Cream Blonde". They have been reported to say that the specter usually appears at the top of a staircase and then floats down the steps toward an outside courtyard area. Perhaps re-playing the events on the night before her death when she found herself locked out of her own apartment?

But the Cafe is not the only spot connected to Thelma Todd's death where ghostly events take place. In the garage of the house on Pasetano Road, people have complained about the sound of a spectral engine running when the space is actually empty. Others say they have smelled, and have been nearly overwhelmed, by noxious exhaust fumes in the garage, even when no car is present. Apparently, the terrible events of that night in December have left an indelible impression on the place.

But will Thelma ever rest in peace? It's not likely. Unless new evidence would somehow come to light, her murder will always remained unsolved. This leads me to believe that her ghost will most likely continue to walk for many years to come.

## THE "CREEPY LITTLE MAN"

*The Strange Death and Ghostly Sightings of Paul Bern*

Jean Harlow's big break in Hollywood came about thanks to Howard Hughes' fascination with Tinseltown. His film productions were well received in the movie colony and when he discovered Harlow, he already had a movie in the works called HELL'S ANGELS, starring Greta Nissen. Then, overnight, talking pictures became all the rage and HELL'S ANGELS had to be re-made as a talkie. Jean Harlow won the lead in the new picture and she quickly skyrocketed as an overnight sensation. The Hollywood publicity machine went into overdrive for Harlow. She soon became known for her signature look of platinum blond hair and her notable, low-cut necklines. The Los Angeles "Times" had one word for her: "Sexquisite".

The gossip columns filled with news of Jean's activities and it soon became apparent that despite her many outings on the town, she never went out with other actors. All of her dates were either directors or producers. It was suggested that she was smart enough to realize this was her ticket to the top. One of the men she dated was an assistant to Irving Thalberg at MGM named Paul Bern. He had been the man responsible for getting Jean's contract purchased from Howard Hughes and for bringing her to MGM. It was apparent that he was attracted to the blond bombshell actress.

It would have been hard to find two people more incompatible that Jean Harlow and Paul Bern. Most of Bern's contemporaries considered him a genius. He had been born in Germany in

1889 as Paul Levy, making him 22 years older than Jean. His formal education ended at age 14, but he went on to become of the most intellectual men in Hollywood. He had come to the movie capital in 1926 after first working in New York as a stage actor. He later took a job in Toronto with a fledging film company and then moved west to California when he realized the potential for movies. After landing in Hollywood, he worked as a film cutter and a script editor before directing a few pictures and ending up as a supervisor at MGM. It was here that Thalberg spotted Bern's ability and made him a general assistant.

While Bern may have been intellectually superior to Harlow, he certainly couldn't measure up in the looks department. According to a writer of the day, Herbert Cruikshank, Bern was described as "a slight man, insignificant in stature, slender of shoulder, only as tall as a girl." Apparently, not much to look at either. Regardless, he gained a reputation in Hollywood as a sensitive and compassionate person (a rare thing in Hollywood) and he began to be called "Hollywood's Father Confessor". Everyone took his troubles to Bern for advice, help and sympathy.

Jean Harlow

Bern was also never much for the public life. He was something of a mystery man, especially to those who craved the spotlight and the lure of Hollywood's legendary nightlife. So when he began appearing in local nightspots with Jean Harlow, no one thought much of it. They assumed that it could never last. Of course, that was what made the announcement of their marriage and even bigger surprise!

Apparently, little planning went into the nuptials. In fact, Jean was not even able to purchase a real wedding gown. She simply went into a dress shop that she frequented and bought an off-the-rack white dress and a shawl. They gathered two days after Bern proposed with about 150 friends and relatives at the home of Jean's mother. They were married on July 2, 1932 but had to postpone their honeymoon because of their shooting schedules. They took one day off and then returned to work. According to Jean's friends, she looked "radiant" in the weeks that followed and the couple seemed very happy.

Paul Bern

But soon, that began to change. As the weeks passed, Bern looked less and less happy, becoming pale, distraught and almost haggard. He told no one what was bothering him, but that didn't stop the rumors from spreading. One of the rumors stated that he and Jean were having money problems. The arguments, it was whispered, concerned the house that Bern had given to Jean as a wedding present. The house was set in the midst of five acres of ground in Beverly Hills' Benedict Canyon. The problem was that Jean didn't like the house and wanted to sell it. Bern refused and argued that he wanted it to be their home together.

On September 5, 1932, just four months after his marriage to Jean Harlow, Paul Bern was found shot to death in the house. Bern's butler found his body in his wife's all-white bedroom. He was nude, sprawled in front of a full-length mirror and drenched in Jean's favorite perfume. He had been shot in the head with a .38 caliber revolver, which was still lying by his side.

After finding Bern's body, the butler went running to find his wife, the cook for the household. Then, instead of calling the police. he called MGM. The studio officer in charge that day immediately called MGM's security chief, W.P. "Whitey" Hendry, who was at home in Santa Monica, enjoying the Labor Day Weekend. Hendry immediately called Louis B. Mayer and Irving Thalberg, who still did not notify the authorities. Instead, they both went straight to the Harlow House.

Mayer arrived on the scene first, followed closely by Hendry and Thalberg. But it was not until two hours later that the Los Angeles police were notified of the death. Just what happened in those two hours will never be known, but we do know that Mayer took a suicide note that Bern had left on a dressing table in the bedroom. He returned it to the police on the advice of Howard Strickling, the Publicity Chief for the studio. He was a neighbor of Bern's and insisted that Mayer give the note back to the detectives on the scene.

The note read: "Dearest Dear... Unfortunately, this is the only way to make good the frightful wrong I have done you and wipe out by abject humility. I love you.... Paul" A postscript had been added at the bottom of the note that said: "You understand that last night was only a comedy."

The detectives looked over the note but failed to understand the meaning of it. The case appeared to be a suicide and after speaking with the butler and the staff, they went to Jean's mother's house to talk with the actress. Her physician told them that she was "too hysterical to undergo questioning at this time". She later spoke to detectives but was not called as a witness at the inquest, which is unusual to say the least.

According to the inquest, the following story was learned about Bern's final hours. Bern had sent Jean over to stay with her mother, who was alone on Saturday night. On Sunday, Jean returned to the house and had dinner with her husband. However, Bern sent her back to mother's, telling her that he would be along to pick her up after reading some scripts. When he didn't show up, Jean assumed that he had fallen asleep while reading and thought nothing more of it. Needless to say, the inquest brought many unanswered questions, such as why did Bern send Jean away again on Sunday night? Was he planning to meet someone later? And what was the motive for the suicide?

The official version of the suicide was that Bern had been suffering from a "physical infirmity" that made it impossible for him to have intercourse with his wife. The "comedy" referred to in the suicide note was Bern's attempt to overcome his impotence and carry out his marital obligations to Jean with a realistic, phony phallus. But why would a man with such an infirmity marry any woman, least of all a bombshell like Jean Harlow?

Surprisingly, this was not the most shocking information to come out of the inquest. It was learned that Bern had previously lived with another woman for many years. And, the day after Bern died, the other woman also died "under mysterious circumstances"!

The woman's name was Dorothy Millette and she was a struggling actress when Bern met her in New York. They lived together in both New York and Toronto for many years and she often referred to herself as "Mrs. Paul Bern." Unfortunately, Dorothy fell victim to mental illness and she was institutionalized. Bern paid for all of her expenses. The love affair ended but Bern continued to provide for Dorothy, even after his marriage to Jean.

After being released from the mental hospital, apparently cured, Dorothy moved into a room at the Algonquin Hotel in New York. She lived quietly, spending most of her time reading and walking in the park. Bern always visited her when he was in New York. His 1920 will, in fact, left everything he owned to Dorothy. However, this was changed in a later will, which bequeathed his estate to Jean.

On March 17, 1932, Paul received a letter from Dorothy stating that she was moving to San Francisco. He suggested to her that she stay at the Plaza Hotel, which offered an "attractive rate" and that if she did decide to stay somewhere else, he would "find some way of supplying you with funds in a manner convenient for you."

Once this new information became public, Jean's stepfather, Marino Bello, issued a press statement saying that Jean knew nothing of Dorothy Millette. This was immediately contradicted by Paul's brother, Henry Bern, who said that Dorothy was common knowledge in Bern's circle of friends and that Paul had specifically discussed Dorothy with Jean prior to their marriage.

On September 6, the day after Bern died, Dorothy checked out of the Plaza Hotel and boarded a Sacramento River steamer that journeyed back and forth between San Francisco and Sacramento. An officer later found a woman's coat and shoes beside the ship's railing. Dorothy Millette was not on board when the shipped docked at Sacramento. Her body was found two weeks later by fishermen. Her death was ruled a suicide.

It was said that Jean Harlow loved Bern so much that when his body was discovered, she too attempted suicide. Even though her attempt was not successful, Harlow's days were numbered. Five years later, she died from kidney damage at the age of only 26.

A strange series of circumstances would shed new (and mysterious) light on the case a year after the inquest. At that time, a grand jury had been impaneled to investigate District Attorney Buron Fitts, who had handled the original Bern inquest. The jury foreman insisted that they were only interested in Fitts' expenditures in the case and yet new revelations came to light because of it.

Important information came from Davis, the gardener and Miss Harrison, Bern's secretary. Davis believed that he "thought it was murder. I thought so from the beginning", he said. He believed that the butler had lied about what happened. He testified that the butler told the police that Bern and Harlow were always hugging and kissing and that he sometimes overheard Bern talking of suicide. The gardener said that the opposite was actually true. He never thought that the couple got along that well and he had never once heard Mr. Bern talk about killing himself! He also said that he didn't believe the suicide note was even in his employer's handwriting.

Irene Harrison, Bern's secretary, confirmed this and she also added that Jean Harlow, not Bern, had been the pursuer in the relationship. She also added that she didn't think that Bern looked "particularly happy" at the reception after the wedding ceremony.

The most exciting testimony came from Winifred Carmichael, Bern's cook. She stated that the household staff had seen a strange woman on Sunday evening. The cook stated that a woman's voice, which was unfamiliar to her, was heard. The woman screamed once. She also said that she later found a wet woman's bathing suit on the edge of the swimming pool and two empty glasses nearby.

There is no record of whether or not the police ever "dusted" the glasses for fingerprints or whether or not they followed up further testimony from Davis the gardener who said that he told detectives of finding a small puddle of blood near Bern's favorite chair by the swimming pool.

Even after all of this, Bern's death was still ruled a suicide. It remained that way until 1960 when writer Ben Hecht published an article that stated Bern's death was actually a murder. "Studio officials decided," Hecht wrote, "sitting in a conference around his dead body, that it was better to have Paul Bern as a suicide than as a murder victim of another woman." He wrote that it would be better for Jean Harlow's career that she not appear as a woman who couldn't hold a husband."

The Los Angeles District Attorney got in touch with Hecht, who told him that director Henry Hathaway had told him about the tragedy. But Hathaway, who was living in New York, claimed to have no first-hand knowledge of the case. He had no information to say that the suicide note was not real or that it had been planted by the studio heads.

Still, many believed that Bern might have been murdered. But if he was, who killed him? Could it have been Dorothy Millette? There seems to be no reason for it and besides that, she vanished (to be found dead) the day after Bern's body was discovered. In those days, the fastest transportation between Los Angeles and San Francisco was the Southern Pacific daylight train or the overnight Lark. Either journey took almost ten hours. For Dorothy to be able to catch the 10:00 pm train, she would have had to have called a cab to pick her up at Bern's home by at least 8:00. No trace of any such call or taxi driver was ever located.

But if Dorothy did kill Bern, was she the woman who was heard in the house and left a wet swimsuit behind? If so, why did she bother to go all the way back to her San Francisco hotel after a ten hour train ride, pack her things, board the river boat and after all of that effort, commit suicide? If this was a crime of passion, why didn't she just kill herself there, next to the body of her dead lover?

And if not Dorothy, who did the wet swimming suit belong to? Whose blood was on the tiles near the swimming pool? Who did the second glass belong to? Why was it never dusted for fingerprints?

These questions remain unanswered and for many crime buffs, the death of Paul Bern remains unsolved. Could this be why his ghost is still reportedly haunting the Harlow House? Perhaps, but many believe that Bern's first otherworldly appearance in the house was actually meant as a warning. It was an advance premonition for another beautiful blond actress that, if she had heeded it, might have saved her life. That woman's name was Sharon Tate.

In 1969, Sharon would fall victim to one of the most savage slayings in Hollywood history. But three years before she was brutally murdered at the hands of the Charles Manson "family", she glimpsed a ghostly image of the horrific fate that awaited her. Could the glimpse into the future have been provided by the phantom of Paul Bern?

Sharon was a struggling actress, hoping to make a name for herself, when she met Jay Sebring, who would soon become known as the premier men's hair stylist in Hollywood. The two dated for three years and even announced their engagement at one point, but Sharon broke it off with him in 1966, when she met her future husband, Roman Polanski. The break-up was not bitter and the two of them stayed very close friends. In fact, it was Jay who was keeping Sharon company at the Cielo Drive house while Roman was away filming. And it was Jay who died trying to protect her from the Manson clan.

Jay lived in Benedict Canyon in the former home of Jean Harlow. He loved the house but was always concerned about the fact that it was supposed to be "jinxed". He knew the stories about Paul Bern's death but he also learned that two people had drowned in the swimming pool as well. He shrugged off the idea that the house was "cursed" though, but perhaps he shouldn't have.

One night in 1966, Sharon stayed alone at Jay's house. Unable to sleep, she lay awake in Jay's room with all the lights on. She was very uncomfortable, although she couldn't explain why. She felt "funny", she later told reporter Dick Kleiner, and was frightened by every little sound that she heard.

Suddenly, a person that she described as a "creepy little man" came into the bedroom! She was sure that this man was Paul Bern. The man ignored her though and wandered about the room, apparently looking for something. Sharon put on her robe and hurried out of the bedroom.

What happened next would be especially chilling in light of events to come. Sharon started down the stairs but halfway down them, froze in shock. There was a figure tied to the staircase posts at the bottom of the steps. She couldn't tell if it was a man or a woman. However, she could clearly see that the figure's throat had been cut. Then, the apparition vanished.

Shaken, Sharon went into the living room to pour herself a drink but she couldn't find where Jay kept the alcohol. She felt an inexplicable urge to press on a section of the bookcase and it opened to reveal a hidden bar. Not thinking, she tore away a piece of wallpaper at the base of the bar as she nervously poured herself a drink.

In the morning, Sharon was convinced the whole episode had been a terrible nightmare.... until she saw the wallpaper that had been torn away from the bar. She had indeed seen Paul Bern and at that time, had unknowingly seen a vision of her fate.

Regrettably, it would not be enough to save her just a few years later.

## THE DEATH OF SUPERMAN
### The Unsolved Mystery of George Reeves

Superman died at 1:59 am on June 16, 1959. Not the comic book character, of course, but the man who personified the "real" Superman for an entire generation of television fans. George Reeves, it was discovered, was not faster than a speeding bullet after all. Even though the initial coroner's report listed Reeves' death as an "indicated suicide", after more than four decades, there are many who do not believe that he killed himself.

The death of Superman remains an unsolved mystery. Could this be why his ghost is still said to haunt his former Benedict Canyon Drive home?

George Reeves grew up as George Besselo. His mother, Helen, became pregnant in her hometown of Galesburg, Illinois, eloped and then moved to Iowa. Shortly after settling in, she divorced her husband, took baby George and moved to Pasadena, California. It would not be until George joined the Army during World War II that he would discover a number of parts of his life that his mother had hidden from him. She had concealed his true birth date, the identity of his father and the fact that his stepfather had committed suicide eight years after Helen divorced him. This so disturbed Reeves that he didn't speak to her through most of the 1940's.

Growing up, Reeves was an accomplished athlete and in 1932, entered the Golden Globes Boxing competition against his mother's wishes. He did well in the competition and went to the Olympics in Los Angeles in 1932. After having his nose broken nine times as a boxer, he hung up his gloves and decided to try his hand at an acting career.

In spite of his time in the ring and rugged good looks, Reeves was not a tough guy. In fact, one writer, James Beaver, discovered that Reeves was a "totally decent person. I honestly never spoke to anyone who didn't like him a lot". He began to take acting lessons at the Pasadena Playhouse, where he met his first and only wife, Eleanora Needles. They married in 1940 and divorced nine years later.

Like most struggling performers, Reeves took a number of small parts. In his very first film, he played a minor role as one of the red-headed twins enamored with Scarlett O'Hara in GONE WITH THE WIND. His other screen credits included SO PROUDLY WE HAIL, FROM HERE TO ETERNITY, BLOOD AND SAND and SAMSON AND DELILAH with Victor Mature and Hedy Lamarr. But of course, Reeves' claim to fame came when he was selected to play the mild-mannered reporter Clark Kent, who was really Superman. His portrayal of the character on television became wildly popular and everywhere he went, children (and adults) clamored to meet him and obtain his autograph.

Reeves loved the public and it was said that he loved the ladies as well. Many who were close to Reeves say that he was a womanizer, breaking the hearts of many of the actresses that he worked with. Rumor also had it that he became involved with a number of prominent married women like the wives of film executives and other actors. It is believed that one of these affairs may have led to his death!

In the three months before his death, Reeves was involved in three mysterious automobile mishaps that almost killed him. The first time, his car was nearly crushed by two trucks on the freeway. Another time, a speeding car nearly killed him, but he survived thanks to his quick, athletic reflexes. The third time, Reeves' brakes failed on a narrow, twisting road. All of the brake fluid, it was discovered, was gone from the hydraulic system, in spite of the fact that an examination by a mechanic found the system was in perfect working order.

"When the mechanic suggested that someone had pumped out the fluid, George dismissed the notion," said Arthur Weissman, Reeves' best friend and business manager. Weissman always remained convinced that his friend had been murdered. He tried to convince Reeves that he needed to be careful but Reeves brushed off the warnings.

About a month later, he began to receive death threats on his unlisted telephone line. Most of them came late at night and there were sometimes 20 or more each day. Often, whoever was calling would simply hang up when he answered. They said nothing, but after a few graphic and detailed threats, Reeves knew it was the same person. Nervous after the near-misses in his car, Reeves filed a report with the Beverly Hills Police Department and a complaint with the Los Angeles District Attorney's Office. He even went so far as to suggest a suspect, a woman named Toni Mannix.

It was never explained why Reeves openly pointed the finger at Toni. The Hollywood gossip columnists had linked the two romantically for some time, but their relationship was never a public one. They were a secret couple, as Reeves was engaged to Lenore Lemmon and Toni was married to a man named Eddie Mannix, the vice president of Loew's Theatres, Inc. and a former studio executive at MGM. According to Reeves' friend Arthur Weissman, it was no secret that Eddie Mannix was disliked by everyone and was an uncouth and despicable man. He also believed that Mannix was responsible for the threats and attempts on Reeves' life.

The D.A.'s office investigated Reeves' complaint and it was soon discovered that both Toni and George were receiving telephone threats and crank calls. When that was disclosed, many people assumed that it was Eddie Mannix who had instigated the calls through employees or hired thuds.

Weissman believed that Mannix was behind Reeve's near-fatal auto crashes as well. In the film and theater business, Mannix had access to a lot of people outside of the general public. For a price, these men could maneuver two trucks close together on the highway, or could drain the brake fluid from someone's car. Furthermore, he was sure that Mannix also had access to someone who could arrange a murder too!

In spite of these personal crises, Reeves was on a professional high. He was not in any way despondent and in fact, had much to live for. Things were certainly going his way and offerings were pouring in to cash in on his Superman celebrity status. Just three days after his death, he was to have returned to the boxing ring with light heavyweight champion, Archie Moore. The exhibition match was to be played on television so that viewers across the country could tune in to see Superman beat the champ! Reeves told reporters that the "Archie Moore fight will be the highlight of my life".

After the fight, he was going to marry his fiancée, Lenore Lemmon, an attractive brunette and former New York socialite. They were to honeymoon in Spain and then go to Australia for six weeks, where Reeves would pick up over $20,000 for public appearances as Superman. The series had just been sold to an Australian television network and local viewers were also demanding to meet the "man of steel".

Reeves then planned to return to Hollywood later in the year and star in a feature film that he would direct. He was then scheduled to shoot more episodes of Superman for syndication and with a hefty salary increase. This was not the sort of future that would cause a man to commit suicide. It could even be said that George Reeves had everything to live for.

But it all came to an end on June 16. Around 6:30 that evening, dinner was served at the Benedict Canyon home. Lenore Lemmon had prepared it for Reeves and guest Robert Condon, a writer who was there to do an article on Reeves and the upcoming exhibition with Archie Moore. After dinner, they settled down in the living room to watch television. About midnight, everyone went to bed.

Around 1:00 or 1:30 am, a friend of Lenore and Reeves, Carol Von Ronkel, came by the house with another friend, William Bliss. Even though the house was the frequent site of parties and entertaining, Reeves had an unspoken rule that he did not want guests after midnight. However, Von Ronkel and Bliss banged on the door until Lenore got up and let them in. George also got up and came downstairs in his bathrobe. He yelled at them for showing up so late at night.

Lenore calmed him down and a few minutes later, he poured a nightcap and then went back upstairs to his room. At that point, the other witnesses present stated that Lenore said something like, "well, he's sulking... he'll probably go up to his room and shoot himself!"

Moments later, a shot rang out in the quiet of the house! George Reeves, television's Superman, was dead.

The Beverly Hills Police report of the incident states that while entertaining his fiancee and three others in his home, Reeves suddenly, and without explanation, left the room and impulsively committed suicide. He went up to his bedroom, they said, placed a pistol in his right ear and pulled the trigger.

Even though he believed his friend was murdered, Arthur Weissman surprisingly did not dispute this sequence of events. He said that this was just how it happened but that Reeves did not intend to kill himself! He explained that Reeves was just playing his favorite game (although a morbid one, in my opinion), a practical joke he enjoyed with a gun that was loaded with a blank. According to Weissman, that was why Lenore said what she did. All of Reeves' friends knew that when he was drinking, he would sometimes fire a blank at his head in a mock suicide attempt, making certain that his arm was far enough away so that he didn't get powder burns on his face!

Weissman claimed that, unknown to Reeves, the blank was replaced by a real bullet by someone hired by Eddie Mannix.

Reeves' clandestine girlfriend, Toni Mannix, was an actress and former model who was 25 years younger than her powerful husband. She was also madly in love with Reeves and according to Weissman, their relationship was an open Hollywood secret. It continued for years and then came to an end when George announced that he was marrying Lenore Lemmon. Friends said that Toni was "enraged" over this new development and began bombarding Reeves with phone calls, making all sorts of threats. It was believed that both she and her husband, who was openly humiliated by Reeves over the affair, both had the perfect opportunity to seek revenge, especially since Toni possessed a key to the Reeves house.

Many were unhappy with the findings of "indicated suicide", including Reeves' mother, Helen Besselo. She retained the Nick Harris Detectives of Los Angeles to look into the case. At that time, a man named Milo Speriglio was a novice investigator at the firm and played a small role in the investigation. "Nearly everyone in Hollywood has always been led to believe that George Reeves' death was a suicide," he said in a later interview. "Not everyone believed it then, nor do they believe it now. I am one of those who does not." And neither did Helen Besselo. She went to her grave in 1964 convinced that her son was murdered.

The Nick Harris Agency, which had been founded in Los Angeles before the FBI was even in existence, quickly came to believe that Reeves death had been a homicide. Even based on the fact that many of the witnesses that night were intoxicated and incoherent, the detectives felt that they could rule out suicide. Unfortunately though, the Beverly Hills Police investigators chose to ignore their findings. A review of the facts seems to indicate the agency's suspicions were well founded.

To make matters more confusing, the detectives even managed to rule out Reeves' macabre "suicide game" as the cause of his death. The agency operatives believed that someone else was in the house at the time!

For one thing, the absence of powder burns on Reeves' face shows that he did not hold the gun to his head, as the police report stated. For the weapon to have not left any facial burns, it had to have been at least a foot and a half away from Reeves' head, which is totally impractical in a suicide attempt. In addition, Reeves was discovered after his death on the bed, lying on his back. The single shell was found under his body. According to experts, self-inflicted gunshot wounds usually propel the victim forward and away from the expended bullet casing.

Detective Speriglio made a careful examination of the police report and noticed that the bullet wound was described as "irregular". So, the agency reconstructed the bullet entry and exit. The slug had exited Reeves' head and was found lodged in the ceiling. His head, at the moment of death, would have had to have been twisted, making a self-inflicted shot improbable. Speriglio suspected that an intruder had entered Reeves' room and that the actor had found his gun. A struggle had followed and Reeves was shot. The intruder then escaped from the house unnoticed.

While interesting, this theory does not explain why the gun (normally loaded with blanks) had a bullet in it and how the intruder escaped from the house with other people inside.

Regardless, there is another discrepancy with the police report. It stated that Reeves had pulled the trigger of the gun with his right hand. Prior to his death, Reeves had been in a terrible auto accident. His Jaguar had hit an oil slick in the Hollywood Hills and had crashed into a brick wall. Reeves later filed a personal injury claim in Los Angeles Superior Court asking for a half million dollars in damages... because his right hand was disabled!

But just how disabled was it? If Reeves could fight Archie Moore in an exhibition match, then surely he could have pulled the trigger on a pistol.

Regardless of whether or not he killed himself, it was obvious that Reeves' death was never properly investigated. Police investigators never even bothered to take fingerprints at the scene and people like Arthur Weissman believed they were pressured to make it an "open and shut" case. George Reeves, according to the official findings, had committed suicide. But did he really?

We will never know for sure. In 1961, Reeves' body was exhumed and cremated, forever destroying whatever evidence was left behind. The death of George Reeves will always remain another unsolved Hollywood mystery.

Could this be why ghostly phenomena has been reported at the former Reeves house ever since? Many believe that the ghostly appearances by the actor lend credence to the idea that he was murdered. Over the years, occupants of the house have been plagued by not only the sound of a single gunshot that echoes in the darkness, but strange lights and even the apparition of George Reeves!

After Reeves' death, realtors attempted to sell the house to settle the actor's estate. Unfortunately though, they had trouble. Occupants would not stay long because they would report inexplicable noises in the upstairs bedroom where George had been killed. When they would go to investigate the sounds, they would find the room was not as they had left it. Often, the bedding would be torn off, clothing would be strewn about and some reported the ominous odor of gunfire in the air. One tenant also reported that his German Shepherd would stand in the doorway of the room and would bark furiously as though he could see something his owner's could not. There is also documentation of an extraordinary occurrence when two Los Angeles sheriffs were assigned to watch the house after neighbors reported hearing screams, gunshots, and lights going on and off during the night.

New occupants moved out quickly, becoming completely unnerved after encountering Reeves' ghost, decked out in his Superman costume! The first couple who spotted him were not the first, nor the last, to see him either. Many later residents saw him too and one couple became so frightened that they moved out of the house the same night. Later, the ghost was even reported on the front lawn by neighboring residents.

In the 1980's, while the house was being used as a set for a television show, the ghost made another startling appearance. He was seen by several of the actors and crew members before abruptly vanishing... creating yet another mystery in this strange and convoluted case!

# WHO KILLED THE BLACK DAHLIA?

## A Tragic Ghost Who Still Haunts the Streets of Hollywood

The lobby of Hollywood's Biltmore Hotel is crowded on a warm and sunny afternoon in early spring. A man crosses the room and taps on the call key for an elevator. As the door opens, he steps inside and presses the number 8 button for his floor. He glances down as he does so and he sees that the number 6 is already illuminated. With a quick glance to his left, he realizes that he is not in the elevator alone. A dark-haired young woman stands in the corner and as he looks at her, she offers a faint smile.

The man smiles back and then looks up as the numerals above the door light up with the passage of each floor. He glances at the reflection of the woman in the polished steel of the doors. Even in this blurred view, she is stunning. Her dark, nearly black hair is swept back and up in the style of the 1940's, although it is very becoming on her. Her skin is pale, perhaps looking even more so against the jet black of her dress. The shiny material clings to her every curve and the man can almost hear it shimmer in the close confines of the elevator. Other than the soft rustle of her dress though, she makes no sound.

Finally, the elevator reaches the sixth floor and with a soft chime, the doors slide open. The man steps aside to let her pass and notices that she is not moving. She continues to stand in the corner, seemingly unaware that the lift has reached her floor. "This is the sixth floor," the man finally speaks up and seems to startle the girl into awareness.

She steps forward and moves past him off the elevator. As she does, the man trembles unconsciously. A wave of chilled, ice cold air seems to brush past him as the girl departs. Gooseflesh appears on his arms as he watches the shapely young woman walk past the doors.

Then, just as she steps out onto the sixth floor, she turns back to look at the man inside of the elevator. She does not speak, but there is no mistaking the look of urgency in her eyes. She is begging him for help, the man realizes, but it's almost too late. The elevator doors have started to close, cutting off the young woman as she tries to re-enter the elevator. The man frantically pushes the button that will open the door again and just before they close completely, they slowly start to slide open again.

But the girl in black is gone!

"What the....?" the man mumbles and he leans out into the lobby of the sixth floor. He looks quickly in both directions, but the small lobby and the hallways in either direction are empty and deserted. Where could she have gone so quickly? He calls out, but his voice echoes in the stillness of the corridor. The young woman had vanished, as if she had never existed at all.

Two days later, the man is browsing in a local bookshop and happens to pick up a book about true, unsolved mysteries. As he flips through it, he is startled by a face that he recognizes.... it's the girl from the elevator! He looks at the photograph and is convinced that it is the same young woman in black. Then, he realizes such a thing is impossible! Scanning through the text, he sees that the girl died years before! How could she have been at the Biltmore Hotel just two days ago?

How indeed? Could this young woman, who the man discovers was killed in 1947, still be lingering at the last place that she was seen alive? Is she still looking for help... from the other side?

The face he, and many others just like him, recognized once belonged to a beautiful, young woman named Elizabeth Short. In death, she would come to be known by a more colorful nickname, the Black Dahlia. Her tragic murder would forever leave a mark on Tinseltown. She came here in a search for stardom and only found it in death, becoming lost in the netherworld that is the dark side of Hollywood.

On January 15, 1947 a housewife named Betty Bersinger left her home on Norton Avenue in the Leimert Park section of Los Angeles, bound for a shoe repair shop. She took her three-year-old daughter with her and as they walked along the street, coming up on the corner of Norton and 39th, they passed by several vacant lots that were overgrown with weeds. She couldn't help but feel a little depressed as she looked out over the deserted area. Development had been halted here, thanks to the war, and the open lots had been left looking abandoned and eerie. Betty felt slightly disconcerted and then shrugged it off, blaming her emotional state on the gray skies and the cold, dreary morning.

As she walked a little further along, she caught a glimpse of something white over in the weeds. She was not surprised. It wasn't uncommon for people to toss their garbage out into the vacant lot and this time, it looked as though someone had left a broken department store mannequin here. The dummy had been shattered and the two halves lay separated from one another, with the bottom half lying twisted into what was admittedly a macabre pose. Who would throw such a thing into an empty lot?

Betty shook her head and walked on, but then found her glance pulled back to the ghostly, white mannequin. She looked again and then realize that this was no department store dummy at all... it was the severed body of a woman! With a sharp intake of breath and a stifled scream, she took her daughter away from the gruesome site and ran to a nearby house. From here, she telephoned the police.

The call was answered by Officers Frank Perkins and Will Fitzgerald, who arrived within minutes. When they found the naked body of a woman who had been cut in half, they immediately called for assistance.

The dead woman, it was noted, seemed to have been posed. She was lying on her back with her arms raised over her shoulders and her legs spread in an obscene imitation of seductiveness. Cuts and abrasions covered her body and her mouth had been slashed so that her smile extended from ear to ear. There were rope marks on her wrists, ankles and neck and investigators later surmised that she had been tied down and tortured for several days. Worst of all was the fact that she had been sliced cleanly in two, just above the waist.

It was clear that she had been killed somewhere else and then dumped in the vacant lot overnight. There was no blood on her body and none of the ground where she had been left. The killer had washed her off before bringing her to the dump site.

The horrible nature of the case made it a top priority for the LAPD. Captain John Donahoe assigned his senior detectives to the case, Detective Sergeant Harry Hansen and his partner, Finis Brown. He also added Herman Willis, a bright young cop from the Metro Division, to help follow up on the leads that were sure to come in.

By the time the detectives were contacted and could get to the scene, it was swarming with reporters, photographers and a crowd of curiosity seekers. Hansen was furious that bystanders and even careless police personnel were trampling the crime scene. Evidence was being destroyed, he knew, and he immediately cleared the scene. Then, while he and his partners examined the scene, the body of the woman was taken to the Los Angeles County Morgue. Her fingerprints were lifted and with the help of the assistant managing editor of the Los Angeles "Examiner" (in exchange for information), the prints were sent to the FBI in Washington using the newspaper's "Soundphoto" equipment.

Meanwhile, an examination of the body was started by the coroner's office. It began to detail an incredible and horrifying variety of wounds to the young woman's body, although the official cause of death was "hemorrhage and shock due to concussion of the brain and lacerations of the face."

An autopsy revealed multiple lacerations to the face and head, along with the severing of the victim's body. It also appeared that the woman had been sodomized and her sexual organs abused but not penetrated. There was no sperm present on the body and most of the damage appeared to have been done after she was dead. The coroner also noted that her stomach contents contained human feces. Even the hardened doctors and detectives were shocked at the state of the girl's corpse.

The doctor also revealed to Detectives Hansen, Brown and Willis an important piece of evidence and one that would have a huge bearing on the case as more of the victim's past was later revealed. "It is impossible to tell you if she was raped," he told the detectives, "because traces of spermatozoa are negative, and she did not have fully developed genitals... The area is shallow indicating that she did not have a completed vaginal canal." According to the coroner, the young woman's vagina was almost child-like and normal sex for her would have been impossible.

This information would have an important impact on what they would learn about the victim and Hansen immediately decided not to make this information public. In fact, only a few detectives working the case would know about it. It is a common police practice to hold back some pieces of information when investigating a case. That way, they can tell real confessions from false ones, especially with a highly publicized crime. Hansen's decision was the right one and he must have known how much newspaper coverage such a bizarre murder would get. Soon, tips, calls and false confessions would come pouring into police headquarters. More than 50 people would eventually confess to the killing!

Shortly after receiving the fingerprints, the FBI had a match for the L.A. detectives. The victim of the brutal murder was Elizabeth Short, a 22 year-old woman who originally came from Massachusetts. During World War II, she had been a clerk at Camp Cooke in California, which explained why her fingerprints were on file.

Once the detectives had this information, they went to work finding out who knew Elizabeth Short, believing that this would lead them to her killer. What they discovered was a complex maze that led them into the shadowy side of the city.... in search of a woman called the "Black Dahlia".

Elizabeth Short was an aspiring actress who usually dressed entirely in black. Thanks to her nice figure and attractive face, men easily noticed her. Her hair was black and her skin pale, providing a striking contrast and a look that got her noticed, even in Hollywood, where good-looking dames were a dime a dozen.

Like all of the other pretty girls before and since, Elizabeth (who preferred the name Beth) came to Hollywood hoping to make it big in the movie business. She was smart enough to know that looks weren't everything and that to break into films, she had to know the right people. So, she spent most her time trying to make new acquaintances that she could use to her advantage and to make sure that she was in the right nightspots and clubs. Here, she was convinced, she would come to the attention of the important people in the business. Beth's pretty face got her noticed. She had done some modeling before coming to Hollywood and men couldn't keep their eyes off of her.

In Hollywood, Beth roomed with a hopeful dancer who introduced her to Barbara Lee, a well-connected actress for Paramount. She took Beth to all of the right places, including the famous Hollywood Canteen, where she met a wealthy socialite her own age named Georgette Bauerdorf. Beth loved to socialize, loved the Hollywood nightlife and loved to meet men. Despite the rumors, Beth was never promiscuous and she did not work as a prostitute. Considering the findings of the coroner, it isn't likely that sex with men involved normal penetration. Beautiful, lively and seductive, Beth was sometimes referred to as a "tease" as her boyfriends never had any idea that romance could only go so far.

One of the men who befriended Beth was Mark Hansen, a nightclub and theater owner who knew many important show business people. He eventually moved her into his house, along with a number of other young actresses who roomed there and who entertained guests at Hansen's clubs. On any given day, a visitor to Hansen's house could find a number of beautiful actresses and models sunning themselves by the swimming pool.

Beth soon became a part of this group, although her prospects for film work remained non-existent. She didn't have much of an income and only seemed to eat and drink when others, usually her dates, were buying. She shared rooms with other people and borrowed money from her friends constantly, never paying it back.

Elizabeth Short (Corbis)

She never seemed to appreciate the hospitality given to her by others either, rarely contributing to where she was living and staying out most of the night and sleeping all day. She became known as a beautiful freeloader.

Around this same time, the film THE BLUE DAHLIA, starring Veronica Lake and Alan Ladd was released. Some friends of Beth's starting calling her the "Black Dahlia", thanks to her dark hair and back lacy clothing. The name stuck and Beth began to immerse herself into the glamorous persona that she had created.... and that may have led to her death!

Although she is remembered today as the "Black Dahlia", Elizabeth Short did not start out as a sexy vamp that "haunted" the nightclubs of Hollywood. She was born on July 29, 1924 in Hyde Park, Massachusetts. Her parents, Cleo and Phoebe Short, moved the family to Medford, a few miles outside of Boston, shortly after Elizabeth was born. Cleo Short was a man ahead of his time, making a prosperous living designing and building miniature golf courses. Unfortunately though, the Depression caught up with him in 1929 and he fell on hard times. Without a second thought, he abandoned his wife and five daughters and faked his suicide. His empty car was discovered near a bridge and the authorities believed that he had jumped into the river below.

Phoebe was left to deal with the bankruptcy and to raise the girls by herself. She worked several jobs, including as a bookkeeper and a clerk in a bakery shop, but most of the money came from public assistance. One day, she received a letter from Cleo, who was now living in California. He apologized for running out on his family and asked to come home. Phoebe refused his apology and would not allow him to come back.

Beth (known as Betty to her family and friends) grew up to be a very pretty girl, always looking older and acting more sophisticated then she really was. Everyone who knew her liked her and although she had serious problems with asthma, she was considered very bright and lively. She was also fascinated by the movies, which was her family's main source of affordable entertainment. She found an escape at the theater that she couldn't find in the day to day drudgery of ordinary life.

While she was growing up, Betty remained in touch with her father (once she knew that he was actually alive). They wrote letters back and forth and when she was older, he offered to have her come out to California and stay with him until she was able to find a job. Betty had worked in restaurants and movie houses in the past but she knew that if she went to California, she wanted to be a star! She packed up and headed out west to her father.

At that time, Cleo was living in Vallejo and working at the Mare Island Naval Base. Betty hadn't been in town for long before the relationship between she and her father became strained. He began to launch into tirades about her laziness, poor housekeeping and dating habits. Eventually, he threw her out and Betty (now Beth) was left to fend for herself.

Undaunted, she went to Camp Cooke and applied for a job as a cashier at the Post Exchange. It didn't take long for the servicemen to notice the new cashier and she won the title of "Camp Cutie of Camp Cooke" in a beauty contest. They didn't realize that the sweet romantic girl was emotionally vulnerable though and desperate to marry a handsome serviceman, preferably a pilot. She made no secret of wanting a permanent relationship with one of the men with whom she constantly flirted. The word soon got around that Beth was not an easy girl and pressure for more than just hand-holding kept Beth at home most nights. Several encounters made her uncomfortable at Camp Cooke and she left to stay with a girlfriend who lived near Santa Barbara.

During this time, Beth had her only run-in with the law. A group of friends that she was out with got rowdy in a restaurant and the owners called the police. Since Beth was underage, she was booked and fingerprinted, but never charged. A kind policewoman felt sorry for her and arranged for a trip back to Massachusetts. After spending some time at home, she came back to California, this time to Hollywood.

At the Hollywood Canteen, Beth met a pilot named Lieutenant Gordon Fickling and fell in love. He was exactly what she was looking for and she began making plans to ensnare him in matrimony. Unfortunately though, her plans were cut short when Fickling was shipped out to Europe.

Beth then took a few modeling jobs but discouraged, she went back east. She spent the holidays in Medford and then went to Miami, where she had relatives off whom she could live for awhile. Beth began dating servicemen, always with marriage as her goal, but fell in love again on New Year's Eve 1945 with a pilot, Major Matt Gordon. A commitment was apparently made between them after he was sent to India.

Beth wrote to him constantly and Gordon remained in touch with her. As a pre-engagement gift, he gave Beth a gold wristwatch that was set with diamonds and spoke about her (and their engagement) to family and friends. Best of all, as far as Beth was concerned, he respected her wishes about waiting until their honeymoon to consummate their love. They would get married and have a proper honeymoon, he promised her, after he returned from overseas. One has to wonder how Beth planned to deal with the physical problems they would encounter once the relationship turned sexual, but perhaps she was too caught up in the moment to worry about it at that time.

Beth went back home to Massachusetts and got a job, dreaming of her October wedding. Her friends often commented on how happy she was and after the war ended in Europe, she became ecstatic about Gordon returning home. Then came the dreaded telegram from Gordon's mother!

As soon as it arrived, Beth tore the message open, believing that it was about plans for the upcoming wedding. Instead, Mrs. Gordon had written: "Received word War Department. Matt killed in plane crash on way home from India. Our deepest sympathy is with you. Pray it isn't true."

Sadly, it was true and we are only left to imagine what Beth's life might have been like if Matt Gordon had returned home alive. The Black Dahlia would have never come to be....

Gordon's death left Beth a little unbalanced. After a period of mourning that she spent telling people that she and Matt had been married and that their baby had died in childbirth, she began to pick up the pieces of her old life and started contacting her Hollywood friends. One of those was former boyfriend Gordon Fickling, who Beth saw as a possible replacement for her dead fiancee. They began to write back and forth to one another and then got together briefly in Chicago when he was in town for a couple of days. Soon, Beth was in love with him again. She agreed to come to Long Beach and be with him, happy and excited once again. A short time later, Beth was back in California.

Her excitement over the new relationship didn't last long. She had to stay in a hotel that was miles from the base where Fickling was stationed and he constantly pressured Beth for sex. She had no intention of giving herself to a man except in marriage, she told a friend, and Fickling had no intention of making such a commitment. She began dating other men and when Fickling found out, he ended their relationship.

In December 1946, Beth took up "temporary" residence in San Diego with a young woman named Dorothy French. She was a counter girl at the Aztec Theater, which stayed open all night, and after an evening show, found Beth sleeping in one of the seats. Beth told her that she had left Hollywood because work was hard to find due to the actor's strikes that were going on. Dorothy felt sorry for her and offered her a place to stay at her mother's home. She meant that Beth could stay for a few days, but she ended up sleeping on the French's couch for more than a month.

As usual, she did nothing to contribute to the household and she continued her late-night partying and dating. One of the men she dated was Robert "Red" Manley, a salesman from L.A. with a pregnant young wife at home. He admitted being attracted to Beth, but never claimed to have slept with her. They saw each other on an off for a few weeks and then Beth asked him for a ride back to Hollywood. He agreed and on January 8 picked her up from the French house and paid for a hotel room for her that night. They went out together to a couple of different nightspots and returned back to the motel. He slept on the bed, while Beth, complaining that she didn't feel well, slept in a chair.

Red had a morning appointment but came back to pick her up around noon. She told him that she was going back home to Boston but first she was going to meet her married sister at the Biltmore Hotel in Hollywood. Manley drove her back to Los Angeles. He had an appointment at the home of his employer that evening at 6:30, so he didn't wait around for Beth's sister to arrive. She was making phone calls in the hotel lobby when he saw her last... becoming, along with the hotel employees, the last person to see Beth Short alive.

As far as the police could discover, only the killer ever saw her after that. She vanished for six days from the Biltmore before her body was found in the empty lot.

The investigation into the Black Dahlia's murder was the highest profile crime in Hollywood of the 1940's. The police were constantly harassed by the newspapers and the public for results. Hundreds of suspects were questioned. Because it was considered a sex crime, the usual suspects and perverts were rounded up and interrogated. Beth's friends and acquaintances were questioned as the detectives tried to reconstruct her final days and hours. Every lead that seemed hopeful ended up leading nowhere and the cops were further hampered by the lunatics and crazed confessions that were still pouring in.

As the investigators traced Beth's activities, they discovered their strongest suspect, Red Manley. He became the chief target of the investigation. The LAPD put him through grueling interrogations and even administered two different polygraph tests, both of which he passed. He was released a couple of days later but the strain on him was so great that he later suffered a nervous breakdown.

While the police worked frantically, Beth's mother made the trip to Los Angeles to claim her daughter's body. Her father, who had not seen her since 1943, refused to identify her. Sadly, Phoebe Short had learned of her daughter's death from a newspaper reporter who had called her, using the pretext that Beth had won a beauty contest and the paper wanted some background information about her. Once he had gleaned as much information as he could, he informed her that Beth had actually been murdered

A few days after Beth's body was found, a mysterious package appeared at the offices of the Los Angeles "Examiner". A note that had been cut and pasted from newspaper lettering said "Here is the Dahlia's Belongings.... Letter to Follow". Inside of the small package was Beth's social security card, birth certificate, photographs with various servicemen, business cards and claim checks for suitcases she had left at the bus depot. Another item was an address book that belonged to club owner Mark Hansen. The address book had several pages torn out.

The police attempted to lift fingerprints off the items but found that all of it had been washed in gasoline to remove any trace of evidence. The detectives then began the overwhelming task of tracking down everyone in the address book and while Mark Hansen and a few others were singled out for interrogation, nothing ever came of it. In addition, the promised "letter to follow" never arrived.

The investigation stalled once again although Aggie Underwood, an aggressive crime reporter for the "Herald-Express", urged the detectives to follow-up on the murder of a young socialite named Georgette Bauerdorf, which had occurred a few years before. Aggie believed the murder was connected to that of Beth Short. The two women had known one another from the Hollywood Canteen and Georgette had been strangled and raped before being dumped into a bathtub facedown. Investigators surmised that Beth had been killed and then washed and severed in half over a bathtub.

The Bauerdorf case had never been solved and was under the jurisdiction of the sheriff's department. The investigation had died when deputies were unable to locate a "tall soldier" who had dated Georgette. She had reportedly been frightened by him and had stopped seeing him.

Investigators suspected that he was involved in her death but the links were never made between her death and that of Beth Short. Jurisdictional problems kept the two departments from working together and Aggie Underwood was ordered off the story by William Randolph Hearst himself, the publisher of the newspaper. As a friend of the wealthy Bauerdorf family, he didn't want the sordid details of the girl's murder stirred up again.

Not surprisingly, the leads in the Black Dahlia case came to dead ends and the investigation fizzled, then came to a halt. The Short murder and the murder of Georgette Bauerdorf remain unsolved today, although it's possible that a suspect did finally emerge. The possible killer first came to the attention of John St. John, a respected investigator for the LAPD who eventually took over the Dahlia case. St. John had worked many of the city's most notorious murders and was the basis of the book and television series "Jigsaw John". He had been in charge of the Dahlia case for about a year when a confidential informant came to him with a tape recording that implicated the suspect in the murder. The suspect had also shown the informant some photos and personal items that he claimed had belonged to the Black Dahlia.

The suspect turned out to be a tall, thin man with a pronounced limp who went by the name of Arnold Smith. On the recording, Smith claimed that a character named "Al Morrison" was the violent sexual deviant who had killed and mutilated Beth Short. St. John suspected that Arnold Smith and Al Morrison were actually the same person!

The tape was a chilling and detailed account of how Beth had come to Al Morrison's Hollywood hotel room because she didn't have anywhere else to stay. According to Smith, Beth refused both liquor and sex with Morrison and became upset when he drove her to a house on East 31st Street near San Pedro and Trinity Streets. Here, he assaulted her and prevented her from escaping by beating her into submission. Even though Beth fought back, he was able to overwhelm her with his strength. While she was on the floor, Morrison stated that he planned to sodomize her and Beth began struggling once again. This time, he hit her so hard that she passed out.

The tape then went on the describe how Morrison had gotten a paring knife, a large butcher knife and some rope and had returned to the room to find Beth conscious again. She tried to scream, but he stuffed her underpants into her mouth and tied her up. While she was naked and bound, he began jabbing her over and over again with the knives, cutting and slashing her. One of the lacerations even extended both sides of her mouth and across her face. By this time, the girl was dead.

Morrison then laid boards across the bathtub and cut Beth in half with the butcher knife, letting the blood drain into the tub. He wrapped the two pieces of the body in a tablecloth and a shower curtain and put it into the trunk of his car. From there, he drove to the vacant lot and left the body to be found later that morning.

St. John discovered that this same suspect, Al Morrison, had also come to the attention of Detective Joel Lesnick of the Sheriff's Department for the murder of Georgette Bauerdorf. He was thought to be the "tall soldier" that she had been dating. Lesnick had learned that both Al Morrison and Arnold Smith were aliases for a man named Jack Anderson Wilson, a tall and lanky alcoholic with a crippled leg and a record for sex offenses and robbery.

Lesnick guessed that "as the years went on, Smith's ego drew him closer, not to confessing, but wanting to tell someone in a roundabout way what he got away with primarily through luck."

After hearing the record of events on the tape recordings, St. John became determined to track down "Arnold Smith". He checked into the story of "Al Morrison", the alleged violent pervert, and could find no proof that he existed, thus confirming the idea that Smith (Jack Wilson) was actually the killer. St. John began to leave no stone unturned in his pursuit to link Jack Wilson to Elizabeth Short.

In the midst of the investigation, word came that the press had gotten wind of the fact that a new suspect had emerged in the Dahlia case. Even after all of the years (at this point the mid-1980's) that had passed, interest in the case was still strong. At this point, St. John realized that it was imperative that he move quickly before Wilson / Smith became spooked. The informant did not know where Smith lived, but left message for him in a café. Several messages were left but Smith never returned them, possibly because he got wind of police surveillance of the restaurant. Finally, the informant received a reply and a meeting was set between he and Smith. It was set for a few days later and at that time, the police planned to pick Smith up for questioning.

Unfortunately, just before the meeting took place, Smith passed out while smoking in his bed at the Holland Hotel, where he was staying. He was burned to death in the flames, destroying the photos and belongings that supposedly belonged to Beth Short.... and all hope that her murder would ever be solved.

A short time after Wilson's body was released to the county for cremation, the Los Angeles District Attorney's office was presented with a file on the matter. The prosecutor's office summed up the case by saying: "The case can not be officially closed due to the death of the individual considered a suspect. While the documentation appears to link this individual with the homicide of Elizabeth Short, his death, however, precludes the opportunity of an interview to obtain from him the corroboration...Therefore, any conclusion as to his criminal involvement is circumstantial, and unfortunately, the suspect cannot be charged or tried, due to his demise. However, despite this inconclusiveness, the circumstantial evidence is of such a nature that were this suspect alive, an intensive inquiry would be recommended.

"And depending upon the outcome of such an inquiry.. it is conceivable that Jack Wilson might have been charged as a suspect in the murder of Elizabeth Short ~also known as the Black Dahlia."

But the truth is, no one was ever charged for the murder of Elizabeth Short and, as far as we know, her death has never been avenged. Perhaps this is why her ghost still walks at the Biltmore Hotel and her specter still looms over the shadowy streets of Hollywood.

Even today, an occasional man who stays at the Biltmore encounters the spectral image of a woman in a black dress, sometimes in the lobby, waiting in the corridors or even riding to the sixth floor on the elevator. What is she trying to tell us? Are there still clues to the identity of her killer that have never been found?

Or does the Black Dahlia simply wish to continue the mystery that was created more that a half-century ago? For tragically, she had found the fame in death that she never achieved in life.

## - CHAPTER THREE -

## THE "SPIRIT" OF THE WILD WEST

## GHOSTLY OUTLAWS & LAWMEN OF THE OLD WEST

Growing up in America, and being fascinated with history, I have had a lifelong interest in the Old West. No one can deny that the mythology of the west has an enduring attraction to many of us. The thought of the region conjures up images of outlaws, lawmen, gunfights, train robberies, wagon trains, cattle drives and more. Although these images have been fictionalized and glorified in movies, books and songs, they continue to provide us with adventure, excitement, romance.... and of course, supernatural mysteries of ghosts and hauntings.

You see, despite what the movies and novels might portray, the Old West was seldom a glamorous place. It was a land of unspeakable hardships, danger and death. The early pioneers were threatened at every turn by weather, disease, hostile Indian attacks and sometimes even each other. It was a land known for range wars, outlaws and indiscriminate killing.

Not surprisingly, many Western events have spawned some of America's most elusive ghosts and mysteries. Many of them were created by the violent events of the western criminals and lawmen. The West was indeed a world where a man generally prospered if he carried and used a gun well. The gunmen who robbed banks and hired out to defend the rights of cattle barons and railroad magnates learned their trade while battling Indians, rustlers and the wild animals of the plains. Most of them had little use for the laws of civilization and only became a "bad man" in the eyes of those who believed his actions to be crimes. They killed mostly from ambush and only rarely fought it out with opponents in head-to-head combat. There were few high noon duels in which gunmen and law officers faced one another and fought bravely to the death. In addition, there were only a few of the honorable lawmen that we know so well from the western myth as well. Many of these men were only one step away from the criminals they were sworn to defend against. However, the smattering of these men, like the noble showdowns, were enough to create legends from men like Bat Masterson and Wyatt Earp.

For the most part, the western gunmen were back-shooters who lurked in the shadows to send unknowing victims to their deaths. There existed however, a special breed of gunfighter who thrived on the gunplay alone, having no ambition other than to face down an opponent and to send as many men as possible to an early grave. These men, like the fabled Billy the Kid, Clay Allison and John Wesley Hardin, were rare though and many of them could have been certified as insane by today's standards.

The western lawmen who faced such individuals are regarded as legends today. They had also learned the art of gunfighting at an early age and were men born with a lack of fear. However, like the killers they faced, many of the legends of the men were greater than the reality. Few are the outlaws who actually killed as many men as they claimed and in the case of men like Wyatt Earp, he was much more apt to simply club a lawbreaker over the head than shoot him!

However, as you will soon see, the legions of dead men who tamed the American West were more than enough to leave a myriad of ghosts behind.

### PAT GARRETT'S GHOST
Did the Lawman Make One Last Appearance at the Moment of his Death?

The murder of Pat Garrett remains one of the great unsolved mysteries of the West. To this day, no one has ever been punished and who his killer might have been has never been proven. These are a part of the mystery but there is another element to it that has an air of the supernatural. According to Garrett's wife, he made one final appearance at their home at the moment of his death. Was he trying to contact his family one last time... or was his spirit crying out for revenge?

Over the course of his life, Patrick Garrett was many things, from lawman to cowhand, rancher, gambler and more. Everything that he did and accomplished was overshadowed by one event though, that as the sheriff of New Mexico's Lincoln County, he shot and killed the outlaw known as Billy the Kid. Whether or not Garrett actually killed Billy has been the subject of much debate over the last century and author's like W. C. Jameson have managed to provide enough evidence to the contrary that Garrett's version of the events have been rightfully called into question. But whether he killed the Kid or not, there is no doubt that his fame came about because of that night in 1881.

If this mystery wasn't enough, Garrett's death has also remained unsolved. The fact that the former sheriff was shot down in the desert a few miles from Las Cruces, New Mexico has never been disputed. To this day though, there has never been a clear answer as to who killed him.

Lawman Pat Garrett

Pat Garrett was born in Chambers County, Alabama on June 5, 1850. He and his family moved to Louisiana when he was still quite young and it was here that he grew up and lived until the death of his father. At that point, unwilling to become involved in family disagreements over property, Garrett simply left town and rode west to Texas. Here, he occasionally worked as a cowhand and buffalo hunter and it was also here that he killed his first man, another hunter named Joe Brisco. The killing was ruled self-defense and Garrett was never charged. In the late 1870's, he moved to New Mexico and went to work as a cowboy for rancher Pete Maxwell.

Following the conflict that has been called the Lincoln County War, Garrett ran for the sheriff's office. One of his campaign promises was to rid the county of the outlaw Billy the Kid. Garrett handily won the election and soon had the Kid locked up. He had been captured at Stinking Springs and arrested for the murder of Sheriff William Brady. He was found guilty and sentenced to hang on April 28 in Lincoln. But to Garrett's embarrassment, Billy escaped from jail, killing two deputies in the process. Eventually, Garrett and his men tracked the Kid to Fort Sumner, where Billy had a girlfriend.

Garrett allegedly killed Billy around midnight on July 14, 1881. According to his story, he was visiting with Pete Maxwell in the rancher's bedroom when a stranger stepped through the doorway. Wearing only a pair of socks and carrying a knife, the stranger whispered "Quien Es?" (who is it?). Garrett, believing the stranger was Billy the Kid, raised his pistol and shot the man in the chest.

A moment later, Garrett ran out the door and shouted to his deputies outside, "Boys, that was the Kid, and I think I have got him!" One of the lawmen, John Poe, leaned in the doorway and looked at the body on the floor and then turned to Garrett. "Pat, the Kid would not come to this place. You have shot the wrong man!"

The word quickly spread through Fort Sumner that the dead man was not Billy. Of the three officers present, only Garrett had ever seen the Kid before but the other two men quickly went along with his identification. With Billy "officially" dead, Garrett could claim the reward as well as the fame and prestige of killing the famous outlaw.

But things would not go smoothly for Garrett after that.

Strangely, two different inquests followed the killing, one of them on that same night and the other the following morning. The inquests only made things more confusing. The first was "lost" and the second appears to have been slanted by Garrett to make himself look good. Some have even claimed the second inquest documents are forgeries. According to one author, only three of the six witnesses who signed the report could even identify the body and one of these later stated that it was not the Kid. Neither document was ever recorded and according to W. C. Jameson, "there exists no legal proof of the death of Billy the Kid at the hands of Pat Garrett."

The burial of the dead man was as controversial as the shooting and the inquest. The body of the man who was buried had dark skin and a beard, in spite of the fact that Billy had been described by newspaper editor J. H. Koogler as "a mere boy... with the traditional silky fuzz on his upper lip" and having "light hair and complexion."

Who Pat Garrett actually killed that night is unknown, but it seems unlikely that it was Billy the Kid.

Following that dark night at Fort Sumner, Garrett's luck began to change for the worse. His claim for the reward for killing the Kid was denied and his future political career began to unravel. He lost his bid to be re-elected as sheriff and began working as a cattle buyer and land speculator. He lost so much money though that he got out of that as well.

Garrett then became involved, along with journalist Arthur Upson, in writing a book called THE AUTHENTIC LIFE OF BILLY THE KID, hoping to cash in on his fame for killing the outlaw. Upson did most of the writing, with Garrett contributing little more than his name and a few stories. The book turned out to be a fanciful tale, filled with untruths, legends and lies about the life and times of the Kid. Ultimately, it was a financial failure for both men.

In 1887, Garrett began promoting the damming of the Rio Hondo River to provide irrigation water for the desert near Roswell, New Mexico. He involved a number of wealthy cattlemen and bankers and formed the Pecos Valley Land and Ditch Company. Unfortunately, the company had to be re-structured after some financial problems and Garrett's position was eliminated. Soon afterward, he moved to Uvalde, Texas.

Another mysterious (and unsolved) mystery would bring Garrett back to New Mexico. In 1896, Colonel Albert Jennings Fountain and his nine-year-old son Henry vanished without a trace. Fountain had apparently secured indictments against a gang of cattle rustlers and was returning home from court when he disappeared. Garrett was summoned to New Mexico by Governor William T. Thornton to investigate the case. Garrett soon came to believe that Fountain and his son had been murdered by Jim Gilliland, Bill McNew, and Oliver Lee. They were cowmen who were politically connected to Albert Bacon Fall, an enemy of Colonel Fountain.

Garrett assembled a posse and went after the three men. He tracked them to a cabin about 45 miles east of Las Cruces and closed in for an arrest. Unknown to the lawman, the suspects were sleeping on the roof of the house when Garrett broke into the cabin to confront the only occupant, a woman. However, one of the posse members became suspicious and decided to check the roof, only to be shot by the men hiding there. Taken by surprise, Garrett and his men were forced to surrender and ride away. Word of his humiliation soon spread throughout the area, causing Garrett great embarrassment.

Gilliland, McNew and Lee later turned themselves in, and with Fall as their lawyer, were acquitted of murder charges. The disappearance of Colonel Fountain remains today as one of the west's greatest mysteries.

In 1901, President Theodore Roosevelt appointed Garrett the Collector of Customs at El Paso. Some time later, Garrett and Tom Powers, the owner of the Coney Island Saloon in El Paso, attended a Rough Riders Convention in San Antonio. Garrett convinced Roosevelt that Powers was the "biggest cattleman in West Texas" and the president asked to pose with Power for a photograph. A short time later, Roosevelt learned that he had been made a fool of and did not appreciate the joke. Garrett was allowed to serve out his term in the office but Roosevelt did not re-appoint him.

By 1906, Garrett and his family had returned to their ranch in Dona Ana County. He was a poor manager and with the money he spent on drinking and gambling, he was soon deeply in debt. He was badly in need of money so when James P. Miller offered Garrett $3,000 for his ranch in 1907, it seemed beneficial. Miller, however, was a curious and dangerous man. As a close neighbor, Garrett had heard the rumors about the man for it was said that "Killin' Jim Miller" had murdered at least 30 men. He told Garrett that he wanted the ranch as a location to hold cattle from Mexico until they were sold, but later evidence suggests that he probably wanted to use the property to hide illegal Chinese immigrants that he had smuggled into the country across the Mexican border. Needing the money though, Garrett agreed to sell.

Unfortunately, just prior to the sale, Garrett's son Poe agreed to lease the land to Wayne Brazel, who planned to raise goats on it. To speed up the sale, Miller decided to purchase Brazel's goats. Brazel told the rancher that his goat herd numbered 1,200 animals and Miller offered him $3.50 a head, which was accepted. However, several days later, Brazel came to Miller and told him that he had miscounted the herd and it actually contained almost 1,800 goats. Miller refused to change the terms of the sale and Brazel was, not surprisingly, very angry with him.

At this point, Garrett agreed to step in and help settle the matter. Garrett, Brazel and Carl Adamson, a representative of Miller, agreed to meet in Las Cruces to negotiate a settlement. Adamson came for Garrett at his ranch on February 29, 1908. They followed a road through the Organ Mountains towards Las Cruces. Garrett left his wife and children behind at the ranch.

The road through the mountains wound past Gold Camp, through the San Augustine Pass and into the mining camp of Organ, before heading down into the valley and to Las Cruces. A man named Willis Walter, who was the son of the livery stable owner in Organ, spoke with Garrett and Adamson when they arrived in the camp. They allowed their horses to drink at the livery while they talked.

"Have you seen Brazel?" Garrett asked Willis and the man later recalled that Garrett asked as if he planned to meet up with Brazel somewhere along the road.

"Yes, he just left," he told the two men.

A short time later, the two men rode out and traveled to a fork in the road, where they saw Brazel a short distance away. He was stopped, taking to a stranger, who galloped away as Garrett and Adamson approached. When they caught up with him, Garrett gave Brazel a curt nod in greeting and then they continued on toward Las Cruces. Within minutes, Garrett and Brazel were arguing about the goats. The arguing continued until the men reached the Alameda Arroyo, where Adamson called a halt and asked for a break. He walked around in front of the horses and undid his pants so that he could urinate.

Garrett apparently heard the call of nature as well and he walked over, removed his left glove, turned his back on the two men, and then unbuttoned his trousers. A moment later, a bullet hit him in the back of the head, probably killing him instantly. His body spun around, his knees faltered and then he collapsed onto the hard ground.

Pat Garrett was dead... a few minutes before noon.

Meanwhile, at the Garrett ranch house, his wife Apolinaria was hoping to cool off the hot house. The heat inside was stifling and she thought that a spring breeze might come long and drive out the warm air. She decided that she would use a long, oak board to prop open the door. According to her daughter Pauline, who told the story in a 1967 interview, the air outside was calm and no wind was blowing.

Shortly after her mother, placed the board against the door, it suddenly, for no apparent reason, "tipped up and over, slamming onto the floor with an ear-shattering noise!" A cold wind then sliced through the house and Mrs. Garrett inexplicably began to scream. Outside of the house, all of the dogs began to howl.

"Something has happened!" she cried. "I don't know what it is, but something has happened!"

Pauline tried in vain to comfort her mother, but she was simply too upset. For the rest of her life, she believed that her father's ghost had tried to contact them. She remembered looking over at the clock as the icy chill pervaded the room.... it was few minutes before noon!

No killer was ever punished for the murder of Pat Garrett. Wayne Brazel confessed to the murder, but claimed self-defense. He was arrested but the trial that followed was a sham. It was incompetently prosecuted and few witnesses were called. Brazel was acquitted. The prosecutor, as it turned out, was a close friend of Brazel's defense attorney, Albert Bacon Fall. Was it coincidence that this man was also connected to the disappearance of Colonel Fountain? Many writers suspect that it was not.

While it seems obvious that Wayne Brazel must have been the killer, many believe that he was not. There are many confusing elements to his story, including his claim of self-defense. As Garrett was facing away from Brazel, and was urinating at the time, it seems unlikely that he was any threat to Brazel's life. Furthermore, an inquest revealed that once Garrett was down on the ground, having been shot in the back of the head, he was shot again, this time in the stomach. But by who?

Some believe that the angle of the bullet that hit Garrett in the head could have only been fired by a man on horseback. Brazel was on the ground at the time. In addition, it is believed that he was shot by two different kinds of bullets, only one of which would have come from Brazel's gun. Because of this, Brazel's role in the murder remains cloudy and it is believed that perhaps he was duped into taking the blame for someone else in the case. Could it have been the mysterious rider that Garrett and Adamson saw on the road with Brazel a few minutes before they joined him?

The only official investigation ever conducted into Garrett's murder was done by Fred Fornoff, who at the time of the murder, was the director of the New Mexico Mounted Police. Fornoff was convinced that there was a conspiracy by several men to kill Garrett and he was also of the mind that Brazel did not pull the trigger. Unfortunately, all of his records have since been destroyed.

Fornoff also believed that Jim Miller was tied into the plot and his investigation of the site revealed the tracks of a shoed horse, a spent rifle shell and several cigarette butts on a sand hill about 50 feet away from the road. It looked like someone had waited here for an ambush, which would have been consistent with Miller's method of killing.

The investigation ended however without revealing the killer.

Almost a century has passed since Pat Garrett met his end on a dusty road in New Mexico and many mysteries remain in his wake. Did he really kill Billy the Kid? Who killed Pat Garrett himself? And strangely, did his ghost really make an appearance to his family at the moment of his death? The Garrett family always believed that he did, dropping in one last time on his journey to the other side!

## THE GHOSTS OF DEADWOOD
### Wild Bill and the Haunted Bullock Hotel

Deadwood, in the Dakota Territory, was sometimes referred to as the "wildest gold town in the West". It came into existence thanks to the Black Hills gold rush of 1874 to 1876.

At that time, the Black Hills belonged to the American Indian tribes and trespassing and prospecting here was forbidden. However, men dubbed the "sooners" were the first to learn that gold could be found in the Hills. Scientific expeditions confirmed the presence of the precious metal and before long, packs of "sooners" were squatting illegally in the Hills area. The prospectors were forcibly removed by the authorities.

It wasn't long though before the military was having a hard time keeping the prospectors out, so the U.S. Government embarked upon another round of land cession from the Native Americans. This was not done without an attempt to uphold treaty obligations though. However, postponing the settlement of the region became impossible because of the onslaught of prospectors who came flocking in. Eventually, the land was seized and the Indians were moved out once again.

The prospectors moved in and slowly the Dakota rush moved northward, finally hitting Deadwood Gulch. Tents and shacks began to sprout up in the area and were quickly serviced by saloons, suppliers, opportunists and "camp girls". Soon, Deadwood was born.

The rich takings of the gold fields brought all manner of people to the area, including those who came to take the wealth from the hands of those who worked for it. Those who offered services came first, but the gamblers, the thieves and the lawbreakers soon followed them. The wide-open atmosphere of the region helped spawn the tales of adventure and the legends that still circulate around this area today. These tales were born in the saloons, the gambling parlors and the bordellos of Deadwood. Such establishments were considered the most legitimate of the town's early businesses.

While most of the prospectors who came here went unremembered, the names of a few of Deadwood's personalities have survived. One of the most famous was Nat Love, better known as "Deadwood Dick". Love was born to slave parents in Tennessee. He was freed after the Civil War and moved west to Dodge City. He found work on a cattle ranch and became known in Texas as an outstanding cowhand.

In 1876, Love's outfit received an order for 2,000 longhorns to be delivered to Deadwood. He was in town over the 4th of July and he entered and won a mustang-roping contest and a shooting match. In addition to the prize money, the excited residents bestowed upon him the title of "Deadwood Dick", a nickname that Love saw as a badge of honor. When he returned to the southwest, a warring tribe of Indians attacked Love's party. He was wounded and later awoke in the camp of Yellow Dog. According to Love, the Indians stated that he was "too brave to die" and plans were made to adopt him. He later stole a pony and escaped back to the Pete Gallinger ranch where he worked.

Meanwhile, In New York, author Edward Lytton Wheeler got wind of the adventures of Nat Love and wrote a dime novel for the publisher Beadle and Adams. Wheeler had never been further west than Pennsylvania but in October 1877, the book DEADEYE DICK, THE PRINCE OF THE ROAD OR THE BLACK RIDER OF THE BLACK HILLS was published. It would be followed by 33 more Deadeye Dick novels over the next eight years. The books were extremely popular and put the city of Deadwood on the map.

In 1907, Nat Love wrote his own memoirs as the "real" Deadeye Dick and he passed away in 1921. Western historian Ramon F. Adams noted, after reading Love's book, that he possessed "either a bad memory or a good imagination"!

But Nat Love's alter ego was not the only legend created by the town of Deadwood for there were two other men whose names have become permanently attached to the town. These men are Wild Bill Hickok and Seth Bullock and while they may have passed on many years ago... it is said that their spirits have never left!

James Butler Hickok was one of the rare breed of gunfighters who never asked for fame and notoriety. All he wanted was a good card game and a steady income. On a good day, he managed both but he also went on to become one of the greatest legends of the Old West...

And some say a restless spirit who still roams the town where he met his end.

"Wild Bill" Hickok

James Hickok was born on a farm in Illinois and was raised with a taste for danger, having been exposed to it throughout his life. His father, a long-time abolitionist, allowed the farm to be used as a station on the Underground Railroad. This meant a constant stream of escaped slaves from the South and a constant danger of being found out by the authorities.

During the Civil War, Hickok joined up with the Union forces and served under General John C. Fremont, a future explorer of the far western states. It was said that Hickok greatly impressed his friends and officers by showing a deadly speed and accuracy with a gun.

At the Battle of Pea Ridge in March 1862, he was said to have picked off 36 Confederate soldiers in a matter of minutes.

After the war was over, Hickok settled in Springfield, Missouri and during his time here, made history. On July 20, 1866, while playing cards, Hickok quarreled with a man named Dave Tutt over a poker game, or over a woman named Susannah Moore, depending on the version of the story told. During the altercation, Tutt took Hickok's prized Waltham pocket watch and refused to give it back. The following day, Tutt strolled down the street, wearing the watch. He stood in the dusty road, about 75 feet away from where Hickok waited, leaning against a porch post.

"Don't come any closer, Dave!" Hickok warned the other man.

Tutt came no closer, but he did reach for his gun. He fired first but the shot never came close. It was said that Hickok's hand moved so fast that it blurred. He cleared leather and fired one shot. The bullet entered Tutt's chest and the man died instantly. He was dead before he hit the street.

The West had just seen the first recorded showdown.

The pistol remained in Hickok's hand. He turned to where several of Tutt's friends stood watching. "Aren't you satisfied, gentlemen?" he reportedly questioned them. "Put up your shooting irons or there will be more dead men here." None of the others dared to face him.

Hickok reclaimed his pocket watch from the dead man's coat and he surrendered himself to the local sheriff. He was cleared of all charges on August 5.

In September of that same year, Hickok ran for marshal of Springfield but lost the election. On that same day, a writer for "Harper's" magazine named Colonel George Ward Nichols arrived in town, looking for material for an article that he was writing about the West. He was introduced to Hickok and told the story of the gunfight. Nichols published the story, now very sensationalized, in February 1867. Later that year, a story called "Wild Bill the Indian Slayer" appeared and caught the attention of the public, whose thirst for Western adventure was beginning to grow. It wasn't long before "Wild Bill Hickok" became a household name.

Unfortunately for Hickok though, fame didn't put food on the table. He ran for the Ellsworth County Sheriff's office in November but was defeated again. After that, he turned to scouting and worked briefly for Custer's Seventh Cavalry. In early 1868, he joined William "Buffalo Bill" Cody to supervise prisoner relocation from Fort Hays to Topeka, Kansas. He put the military behind him in February 1869.

Hickok eventually became a lawman. He was elected sheriff of Ellis County, Kansas and on the day after the election, shot to death a man named Bill Mulvey. He was determined to let the lawless element of the region know that he meant business and a month later, he killed a desperado named Jack Strawhim in Drum's Saloon. His tenure as sheriff ended in July 1870 though when he put down a disturbance of drunken soldiers, killing one and wounding another. General Sheridan was furious with the gunfighter and ordered Hickok arrested. By that time though, Hickok had already drifted out of town.

He ended up in Abilene, Kansas, following the card games and the rich pockets of the inebriated cowboys who ended up in town after months on the trail. Hickok found easy pickings for his card-playing skills. Abilene was a rough town at the time, so it's no surprise that Mayor Joseph McCoy tapped Hickok to serve as the town's sheriff. He was appointed with a salary of $150 a month, which supplemented his poker games. His first act as sheriff was to ban firearms within the city limits.

On the night of October 5, 1871, a group of about 50 cowhands began raising hell in town. A stray dog nipped the ankle of a cowboy named Phil Coe and in his intoxicated state, he shot the dog dead. Hickok, gambling at the Alamo Hotel, heard the shot and came running. He demanded to know who had the gun within the limits of Abilene and he spotted Coe with a pistol in his hand. Hickok attempted to disarm him but a fight ensued. Hickok's hat was shot from his head but Coe died with a fatal wound to the groin.

In the confusion, Hickok's friend Mike Williams rushed to help. Hickok saw only a flash of movement and thought that he was being ambushed by one of the other cowhands. He spun and fired and shot Williams dead by mistake. Hickok was so distraught over the shooting that he got drunk and ran every cowboy out of Abilene, shooting up the town in the process.

At the next election, the citizens of Abilene decided that they were tired of both cattle drives and Wild Bill Hickok. They banned one and got rid of the other.

By 1872, Hickok was both famous and broke. He decided to try and cash in on his image and he launched a theater production in Niagara Falls, New York called "The Daring Buffalo Chase of the Plains". It boasted a number of western characters, Indians and even real buffalo... but no audience. The show soon closed and Hickok sold six of the buffalo to pay train fare home for the Indians who retired from show business.

The following year, Hickok joined up with Buffalo Bill Cody for a stage show called "Scouts of the Prairie". This endeavor proved to be much more successful and Hickok stayed with the show for seven months. Although steadily working, Hickok took to drinking and one night, shot out all of the stage lights in the theater. That night's appearance was his last and Cody kicked him out of the show. As he packed up and left, Cody was heard to mutter, "I wish I had killed that son of a bitch when I had the chance years ago."

Although no one knew it, Hickok's drinking was most likely a result of the fact that he was losing his vision to glaucoma. He was having a tougher time seeing and facing down the young toughs who decided to try their hand at beating Wild Bill Hickok to the draw. He drifted across the West, sometimes narrowly avoiding being killed, playing poker and losing just enough money to stay broke. In 1874, he was in Cheyenne, Wyoming when an old flame named Agnes Lake appeared on the scene. The two of them were married on March 5, 1876 but after a short honeymoon in Cincinnati, they parted ways. Hickok was off to hunt gold in the Dakota Territory and in April 1876, rode into Deadwood.

Legend had it that Hickok had a premonition of death as soon as he arrived at the rough and tumble mining camp. "Those fellows over across the creek have laid it out to kill me," he reportedly said. "And they're going to do it or they ain't. Anyway, I don't stir out of here unless I'm carried out."

Early in the afternoon on August 1, Hickok sat down to a game of poker at Carl Mann's No. 10 Saloon. He took his seat in the corner, with his back to the wall, just as he always did. At some point in the game, a saddle bum named Jack McCall got into the game. The stories vary as to what passed between McCall and Hickok. Some say the gunfighter cursed McCall when he fell short on settling up and others say that he embarrassed the cowboy by giving him breakfast money when he played his last bad poker hand. Regardless, Hickok went about his business, oblivious to trouble, while McCall seethed and swore revenge.

The next day, Hickok returned to the saloon to find a game in progress between Carl Mann, Charles Rich and an ex-riverboat captain named William R. Massie. They invited Hickok to sit in and Wild Bill said that he would if Rich, who had the seat by the wall, would trade him places. Rich made a joke about it and Hickok sheepishly took a seat with his back to the door.

By late afternoon, Hickok was losing badly to Massie. Still, he held a promising hand... two black aces, two black eights and a jack of diamonds. There was a potential here, he knew, but was unaware that danger had entered the saloon behind him. Some time around 4:15, Jack McCall had slipped into the saloon. He inched his way along the bar until he was two or three feet behind Hickok. He suddenly pulled his Colt from its holster and aimed it at Hickok's back. "Damn you, take that!" he yelled and pulled the trigger.

The bullet slammed into the back of Wild Bill's skull, exited just under his right cheekbone and struck Captain Massie's forearm, just above his left wrist. (Massie never had this slug removed and carried it with him until his death in 1910. It is now buried in Bellefontaine Cemetery in St. Louis) Hickok died without knowing what had happened to him. He fell forward onto the table and his cards, known today as the "Dead Man's Hand", slipped out of his fingers and fell to the floor.

McCall turned his pistol on the onlookers and dared them to come after him. He ran out of the rear door and cries of "Wild Bill is dead!" followed him out into the alley. Hickok's friends found the man hiding in a butcher shop less than a half-hour later. A trial was organized by the following morning, only to adjourn in the afternoon for Hickok's funeral. When the hearing when back into session, McCall claimed that Hickok had killed his brother in Hays City in 1869, but could offer no proof of this. Regardless, a jury found him not guilty, to the dismay of Hickok's friends and the prosecutor, a lawyer named May.

McCall remained in Deadwood a free man, but he became nervous thanks to threats from Hickok's friends and angry local residents. May claimed that the jury had been paid off in the trial and he harassed and followed McCall everywhere. He would not rest, he vowed, until justice had been done.

May tracked McCall to Laramie and had him arrested. He had found a loophole in the law that said that since Deadwood wasn't supposed to exist because of the Indian treaties, no court decision made there was actually legal. A new trial was held in Yankton, Dakota Territory on December 4, 1876 and two days later McCall was convicted for Hickok's murder. He was hanged on March 1, 1877.

Hickok was buried in Deadwood's Mount Moriah Cemetery but the local legends say that he does not rest there. Many believe that because he died unaware of what was about to happen to him, his confused and angry spirit still walks in Deadwood.

It has even been suggested that Hickok knew that he might die soon and that if possible, he planned to return to this world. A short time before that fateful day in the No.10 Saloon, Hickok posted a letter to his wife, Agnes. In it he said "Agnes Darling, if such should be we never meet again, while firing my last shot, I will gently breathe the name of my wife--- Agnes---and with wishes even for my enemies I will make the plunge and try to swim to the other shore."

Was he planning to stay behind? Who knows?

Whether he planned it or not, some say that he has remained here. In the years since 1876, a shadowy figure has frequently been reported inside of the old No. 10 Saloon, which remains a landmark in Deadwood. Others claim to have seen this figure in the doorway to the building, as if looking out and perhaps seeking someone. Is this the ghost of Wild Bill?

Almost next door to the old No. 10 Saloon is another haunted Deadwood landmark, the Bullock Hotel. Named in honor of Sheriff Seth Bullock, the grandly restored establishment has played host to generations of western visitors and some say, the ghost of Seth Bullock himself.

For years, guests and staff members say they have seen the ghostly figure walking the streets of Deadwood and the hallways of the hotel. A former hotel manager named Ken Geinger even told about a little boy who went downstairs one night looking for his father, who was gambling in the casino. Later, the boy told his father that when he went back upstairs he became lost and a man helped him to find his room. The next day, the boy pointed out a portrait of Seth Bullock in the hotel lobby as the man who helped him get safely back to his room!

Seth Bullock was born in Ontario, Canada in 1849 to a Scottish woman and a retired British major named George Bullock. At the age of 18, Seth grew tired of his father's military discipline and he headed out for Montana. Here, he quickly became involved in business and local politics, becoming an auctioneer, a commission merchant and Chief Engineer of the Helena Fire Department. After an unsuccessful run for the Territorial Legislature at age 20, he was elected as a Republican member of the Territorial Senate of Montana. During the 1871 and 1872 sessions, he introduced a bill that would later result in getting Yellowstone named as a National Park.

In 1873, Bullock was elected sheriff of Lewis and Clark County in the Montana Territory but three years later, he went east to Deadwood in the Dakota Territory in search of gold. He quickly became concerned over the rough conditions of the mining camp though and he sent his wife, Martha, and their infant daughter to stay with her parents in Michigan. Bullock and his partner, Sol Star, quickly realized that fortunes were not to be made in the gold fields, but in supplying the miners. They opened a hardware store that quickly became a booming business.

Unfortunately, tragedy struck a short time later and the store burned to the ground. Undaunted, Seth built the Bullock Hotel on the same site. They was soon considered the only respectable accommodations in town. The hotel was constructed from native pink and white sandstone with 63 luxurious rooms. It had comfortable beds, a Turkish Bath, a reading parlor, a dining room that seated over 100 people and even red velvet carpets in the lobby. There was no question that, outside of San Francisco, it was the finest establishment in the western states.

It was the murder of Wild Bill Hickok in 1876 that sent out a call for law enforcement in Deadwood. Bullock, who had served already as a peacekeeper, answered that call. He was appointed as Deadwood's first sheriff and along with his deputies, all but eliminated crime in the sprawling and dangerous town.

In fact, the town became so peaceful that Bullock was able to continue his many business interests in addition to serving as a law officer. He continued to run the hotel but he also spent time ranching, raising horses and mining. He served as a United States Marshal for South Dakota and also as a member of the Black Hills Rough Riders during the Spanish-American War in Cuba. He is credited for introducing the first alfalfa crop into South Dakota and as a conservationist, he secured a Federal Fish Hatchery for the Black Hills at Spearfish. In addition, he founded the town of Belle Fourche, which became the seat of Butte County and one of the largest livestock shipping points in America.

During these years, a friendship developed between Bullock and Theodore Roosevelt. The two of them had met years before on the trail near Roosevelt's ranch. At that time, Roosevelt was a deputy sheriff in Medora County in the Dakota Territory and had just apprehended Redhead Finnegan, a horse thief. Later on, as the vice-president under McKinley, he appointed Bullock the first Forest Supervisor of the Black Hills Reserve. In 1905, Bullock and 75 cowboys rode their horses in Roosevelt's inaugural parade.

The two remained friends until the former president's death in January 1919. Saddened, Bullock established a memorial to his friend. A tower was constructed of Black Hills' stone and was erected on Sheep Mountain, which was later named for Roosevelt. The memorial was dedicated on July 4, 1919 and two months later, Seth Bullock himself died at the age of 70.

The lawman was laid to rest in Deadwood, but many claim that he still watches over the frontier town and its unknowing inhabitants.

Strangely, one person who tells of Bullock still haunting his former hotel and the streets of Deadwood is a person who had never been to South Dakota at all! In 1990, a psychic from England claimed to receive messages from someone with the same surname as his own. The spirit said that his name was Seth Bullock from Deadwood. Puzzled, the medium, whose name was Sandy Bullock, went to the library to search for information on the town and the man but could find nothing.

A short time later, he wrote letters to the Deadwood Sheriff's office and to the local chamber of commerce, briefly explaining the eerie messages. He received no reply and simply assumed that they had dismissed his correspondence as the work of a nut case. Finally, in March 1991, he sent a letter to the owner of the Bullock Hotel, Mary Schmit. He assured her that he had a good reputation in England as a psychic and that before receiving the messages, he had no knowledge of Deadwood or of Seth Bullock. And he certainly had no awareness of his ghost!

According to the medium, the old lawman was concerned that Deadwood was turning into another Las Vegas (note: limited stakes gambling was legalized in the city in 1989... just before the spirit messages were first received). He also said that Seth believed Deadwood was heading towards a major crime problem and he urged the local sheriff to get more help, as he would need it in 1993.

"He has been back in spirit to Deadwood many times," the medium continued. "There's one person in particular that he's given the frights to, but the bangings going on now means he can't haunt the same place, but he will be back and they'll know it's Old Seth."

Mary Schmit was startled by the letter. The reference to "bangings going on" made sense to her as the hotel was undergoing restoration at the time. She was also intrigued by the mention of "Old Seth". That was nickname that she and her Aunt Jerri had privately given to the original owner of the building. During the remodeling, when they were the only occupants of the hotel, they had often heard someone calling their names. Jerri often laughed and said that it was "Old Seth up to his tricks again".

Mary Schmit later said that her sister Susan had fallen victim to Old Seth's pranks. She was in the building alone on one occasion when she was spooked by the sound of pots and pans banging together in the kitchen. She locked herself into a vault, although it later proved that she was in the hotel by herself. Could Susan have been the one person that he had "given the frights to" in his message to medium Sandy Bullock?

As word of Sandy Bullock's communications spread, hotel employees began to come forward with their own strange experiences in the place. Two men claimed to see a lanky figure in cowboy clothing one night. Others had heard footsteps or had heard their name being called when no one else was around.

One night, the construction manager on the restoration project, Terry Kranz, came to take photographs of the hotel. He moved lights from room to room, leaving doors open as he went down the hallway. On three different occasions, he opened doors and then walked down the corridor to get his equipment. All three times, the doors banged shut behind him, one by one. There were no windows open, no wind blowing and no one else in the hotel. Kranz left without taking the rest of the photos!

In 1991, a writer for "Deadwood" magazine, Reba Webb, interviewed Sandy Bullock about the mysterious messages from Seth Bullock. She decided to see if he could answer something about which he had no knowledge. "Who was a well-known person who was a close friend of Seth Bullock's, and how is Bullock's grave positioned in regards to that friendship?' she asked him in a telephone conversation.

The psychic passed the question on to Seth before replying. He told Webb that "trees block the view from his old bones but they cannot block the friendship, as Teddy and he still meet." He then asked her if the reply made any sense to her.

Amazingly, it did. Before Bullock had died, he had chosen a burial plot high above Mount Moriah Cemetery. It was a site that offered an unobstructed view of the memorial to the president on Roosevelt Mountain. In the years since Bullock's passing, ponderosa pines had grown up around the cemetery and now blocked the view of the memorial.

Mary Schmit's brother, John, visited the psychic in England and one of the things he asked him was whether or not there was something that could be done for Old Seth. Schmit later said that the medium went into a deep trance, looked at the floor and then spoke in a low voice. "There's no gate on my grave", came the words from Bullock's mouth, although John Schmit always maintained that the words had come from Old Seth himself.

Back home, John asked his sister if she had ever visited Bullock's grave site. She described it to him. "It's high on a hill above the other graves," she said, "and it faces Roosevelt Mountain. There's a bench there and a fence around it."

"Anything else?" he asked her.

"Yes, there's no gate on his grave."

Mary Schmit has always said that there is no way that the psychic could have known such a thing except for the fact that he had heard it from Seth Bullock himself.

## THE GHOSTS OF TOMBSTONE
### Spirits of a Town Too Tough to Die

The town of Tombstone is located in southwestern Arizona and during the 1880's gained infamy as one of the most famous silver boomtowns of the Old West. During this period, the eyes of all Americans were focused on the events that took place here, from the first silver strike to the bloody gunfights in the town's dusty streets. The death toll in Tombstone reached such epic proportions in 1882 that President Chester A. Arthur even threatened to declare martial law in the city! It was a rough and dangerous place and certainly lived up to its reputation as one of the wildest towns in the west.

As seems to be the case with many violent locations, the number of ghosts who still linger in Tombstone may outnumber the permanent living population. Many of them, it is believed, don't even yet realize they are dead and continue looking for the next fight, the next drink, or even the next roll of the dice. Such a present, and such a past, makes Tombstone one of America's most haunted small towns!

Tombstone got its start on April Fool's Day 1877. On that afternoon, a prospector named Ed Schiefflin rode into Fort Huachuca in the San Pedro Valley and announced that he intended to look for silver in the Apache country. The soldiers scoffed at his plans and did all they could to dissuade him from such a dangerous endeavor. All that he would find, they told him, would be his tombstone.

Schiefflin spent the entire next summer staying away from the Apache Indians and seeking ore. By October, he was out of supplies, his clothing was in tatters and he had nothing left. Just as he was about to give up, he discovered the first vein of pure silver. It was only seven inches wide, but more than fifty feet long. He called the strike Schiefflin's Lucky Cuss and he produced $15,000 per ton of rich silver. Partnering with his brother Al and an assayer named Dick Gird, they founded the Tombstone Mining District.

Soon, other miners and prospectors began flocking to the area and Tombstone began to boom. The prospectors attracted the suppliers, the saloonkeepers, the gamblers and the whores. It wasn't long before Tombstone became known as the place to find just about any vice known to man. Saloons such as the Oriental and the Crystal Palace operated 24 hours a day. John Clum, editor of the Tombstone "Epitaph" once wrote that "Tombstone is a city set upon a hill, promising to vie with ancient Rome, in a fame different in character but no less important."

While Tombstone certainly attracted more than its share of sin and vice, there were traces of the kinder, gentler life as well. Churches and schools were supported by a heavy tax on gambling and culture could be found at Schiefflin Hall, which had been erected to attract touring theatrical companies.

But of course, it was not the churches that attracted the real stories to Tombstone, it was the gambling, the violence and the death. It would be here that western legends would be created and it was also here that many of them would come to an end. Tombstone's Boot Hill Cemetery was an unforgiving place.

Perhaps the name most connected to Tombstone is that of Wyatt Earp, one of the most famous lawmen and gunfighters of the Old West. Wyatt was born in 1848 in Monmouth, Illinois and his early years were spent farming with his father and brothers in Illinois and Iowa before an 1864 move to California.

In 1870, Earp returned east and ended up in the town of Lamar, Missouri. He wed Willa Sutherland and he defeated his half-brother Newton in an election for town constable. Less than four months after they were married, Willa died. Wyatt and his brothers, James, Morgan and Virgil got into a street brawl with Willa's brothers. What exactly happened is unknown but we do know that after the bloody incident, the Earp brothers headed west.

In 1871, Earp was arrested in Oklahoma for stealing two horses but he jumped bail and fled the area. By 1872, in violation of the Indian treaties, he was hunting buffalo with Bat Masterson at the Salt Fork of the Arkansas River. He and Masterson would remain friends throughout life.

Earp then drifted on to Wichita, where he made a living as a gambler. He was also a policeman for eight months but didn't fare well. He was accused of pocketing fines and on one occasion was almost killed with his own gun. While playing cards at the Custom House Saloon, his revolver accidentally fell out of his holster and discharged as it struck the floor. The slug passed through Earp's coat, struck the north wall of the saloon and then passed out through the ceiling. He later got into a fistfight with a candidate for the office of town marshal and was fired from his job.

After that, he moved to Dodge City, the most famous cow town of the West. Here, he dealt faro at the Long Branch Saloon and again worked as a police officer. He left in 1877 for an unsuccessful attempt to prospect gold in the Black Hills, then returned to Dodge City. During this time, he killed his first man, a drunken cowpoke named George Hoyt, became a deacon of the Union Church and served as a United States Marshal. He remained in Dodge City until 1879, solidifying his friendships with Bat Masterson and Doc Holliday.

Then, with his common-law wife, Mattie Blaylock, he went to Texas, Las Vegas, New Mexico and ended up in the silver boomtown of Tombstone. Here, his brothers, Virgil, James and Morgan joined him.

Virgil Earp had been born in 1843 and served in the Union Army during the Civil War. After working as a wagon teamster and on the transcontinental railroad, he married Rozilla Draggoo at Lamarr, Missouri in 1870. After the feud with the family of Willa Sutherland, Virgil moved to Council Bluffs, Iowa, leaving Rozilla behind. He married another young woman, Alvira Sullivan, and they moved west to Prescott, Arizona. Here, he served as a deputy marshal before being elected as constable of the district. Virgil also became a partner in a silver mine and wrote glowing reports about Arizona to his brothers, Wyatt, Morgan and James. In his letters, he specifically mentioned Tombstone.

Morgan Earp read these letters with great interest. He had worked as a deputy town marshal in Dodge City and then as a deputy sheriff. In Butte, Montana, he shot and killed a man named Billy Brooks just before deciding to head south to Arizona. He would join his brothers in silver speculating and perhaps in some other line of business besides killing.

James Earp, who had been born in 1841, was the oldest of the four brothers. He had also served in the Federal army during the Civil War but had been badly wounded at Frederickstown, Missouri. Because of his injuries, he did not get involved in either law enforcement or the gunplay that would follow the Earp's arrival in Tombstone. He was always supportive of his family though, however his place in the background makes him the least recalled of the brothers.

On December 1, 1879, Wyatt, James and Virgil arrived in Tombstone and the following month, Morgan and Wyatt's long-time friend, Doc Holliday, joined them.

John Henry Holliday was born in Georgia in 1851. He is best remembered as a tuberculosis-stricken gambler and gunfighter today, but he started out as a dentist. In fact, he graduated from the Pennsylvania College of Dental Surgery in 1872, practicing in both Atlanta and Griffin, Georgia. At the age of 21, he was advised that he had contracted "consumption" and was advised to move to the drier climates of Arizona.

So Doc went west, first stopping to practice his dental skills and his luck at the card tables in Texas. His card-playing led to his first brush with the law when a fellow gambler accused him of cheating. Doc abruptly shot the man. Rather than deal with the local authorities, he simply rode out of town. He was next reported 200 miles to the west in Jacksboro, where he gunned down a soldier in another gambling dispute. After that, Doc disappeared for a time.

He next surfaced in Denver, dealing faro, and then passed through Arizona and New Mexico on his way to Fort Griffin, Texas. He became involved with a prostitute here named Mary Katherine Michael, better known as Katie Elder. It was also at Fort Griffin where he met Wyatt Earp for the first time when the lawman came into town in search of the outlaw Dave Rudabaugh.

By December 1877, Doc was in trouble again. A man named Edward Bailey questioned his honesty in a card game and in return, Doc sliced him open with a Bowie knife. Fort Griffin had no jail and so the sheriff locked him up in a hotel room. When Katie heard that a number of angry townsfolk planned to lynch Doc at dawn, she came up with a plan to stop them. As the mob came to the hotel, she set the rear entrance of the building on fire to distract them. She then managed to get the drop on Doc's guard and the two of them quickly headed out for Dodge City.

Doc was soon back at the gambling table and Katie was practicing her chosen profession.

Holliday also renewed his friendship with Wyatt Earp, who was a U. S. Marshal in Dodge. One night, a killer attempted to ambush Earp from behind and Holliday snuck up on the man and disarmed him. He had saved Earp's life and the incident cemented their friendship.

Eventually, the restless Holliday grew tired of both Katie and Dodge City and he left for Colorado, then drifted to New Mexico, where he joined in a saloon venture. After a confrontation at the saloon, Doc Left town and in January 1880, arrived in Tombstone.

After arriving in the city, Wyatt's first job was as a guard for Wells Fargo. Morgan also hired on to ride shotgun for the Tombstone - Tucson stage while Holliday gambled. Things began to change though and soon Wyatt had purchased a quarter interest in the Oriental Saloon. The Earp's also began to be approached by local officials about law enforcement duties. They refused at first but soon realized that this would not only offer them steady work, but a chance to clean up Tombstone of some of the seamier elements. By this time, the brothers had discovered the town as a place where they hoped to permanently settle.

On July 25, 1880, the first in a series of incidents would occur that would begin a feud between the Earp's and an unruly segment of Tombstone's population. On that day, Wyatt, Morgan and Virgil were asked to accompany Lieutenant J. H. Hurst, and several soldiers, to the McLaury Ranch outside of Tombstone. The McLaury's, Frank and Tom, were suspected in the theft of some government mules. The two factions clashed and two days later, Wyatt was appointed Pima County deputy sheriff. The trouble between the Earp's and the McLaury's had just begun.

**Wyatt Earp**

The Earp's soon became local celebrities and were constantly in the newspaper for their law enforcement exploits. Wyatt's image as a virtuous lawman had been created in Dodge City by dime novel writer Ned Buntline and his adventures in Tombstone only added to his popularity.

But not everyone liked the Earp's. At one point, Virgil was appointed city marshal, but he failed twice in getting elected to the post. As a Pima County deputy, Wyatt hoped for a position in the newly created Cochise County, but he was overlooked in favor of rival John Behan.

The McLaury's were not the only ones who disliked the Earp's either. Their neighbors, the Clanton's, were suspected cattle rustlers who also ran afoul of the Earp's. Ike Clanton and his sons, Joseph, Phineas and Billy often joined the McLaury's in their illegal dealings and because of this, frequently ran afoul of the lawmen in Tombstone.

The Earp's had an extreme dislike for the Clanton's and the McLaury's and this wasn't helped when one of Wyatt's fastest horses was stolen, only to reappear a few days later under the saddle of Billy Clanton. Wyatt felt as if the bunch was blatantly allowed to abuse the law, thanks to their friendship with John Behan. Wyatt believed that the Cochise County sheriff overlooked their dealings and he was determined to prove it. The rivalry would lead to bad blood in the days to come.

The tense situation in Tombstone was further strained on the night of March 15, 1881. The Tombstone stage, carrying $26,000 in silver, was robbed outside of Contention City, Arizona. During the holdup, shotgun rider Budd Philpot was killed, as was one of the bandits, Bill Leonard. Two of the other robbers, believed to be Harry Head and Jim Crane, killed a passenger.

A posse that included Doc Holliday and the Earp's organized the following day. Wells Fargo offered a $3,600 reward for the capture of the thieves. On June 6, Leonard and Harry Head, both implicated in the robbery, were shot and killed in the Hachita Mountains of New Mexico. Wyatt would maintain that Leonard had lived long enough to confess. The Hazlett brothers, who had planned the robbery, killed the Head's and in turn, Jim Crane and some cohorts killed the Hazlett's. It seemed to be a case of the criminals wiping one another out!

Not long after though, things got more confusing. A newspaper that was in competition with the "Epitaph", and against the Earp's, started a rumor that Doc Holliday had also been involved in the stage robbery. On July 5, 1881, Judge Wells Spicer issued a warrant for Doc's arrest. He was captured by John Behan, but was immediately released on bail that was posted by Wyatt Earp. Holliday was enraged over the incident but so were the Earp's, as rumors were being spread that they had planned the robbery and Doc had carried it out.

Things continued to simmer over the next few months but that summer, Tombstone itself literally went up in flames. A major fire destroyed a large portion of the city when the proprietors of the Arcade Saloon tossed a barrel of bad whiskey out into the street. Someone got too close to the spill with either a cigar or a match and it exploded into a blaze. Sixty-six buildings in the business district were destroyed.

On September 10, another stagecoach robbery prompted Sheriff Billy Breakenridge to organize a posse that included Morgan and Wyatt Earp. They were able to trace boot tracks at the scene to Deputy Frank Stilwell and Pete Spencer. They were arrested at Bisbee but Ike Clanton posted their $14,000 bail.

On October 4, Breakenridge and another man found the body of a wood hauler in the Dragoon Mountains. It appeared that he had been slain by Indians. At Tombstone, he rounded up a posse, including Wyatt, Morgan and Virgil, and went searching for the renegade Apache. At the ranch of the McLaury's, the posse was told that the fleeing Indians had stolen 27 horses and had escaped.

The following afternoon, Ike Clanton and Tom McLaury drove a wagon into town. They checked into separate hotels and waited for Frank McLaury and Billy Clanton to arrive. Both men went to eat and to look for an evening's entertainment in Tombstone.

Ike strolled into the Alhambra Saloon a little after midnight, sat down and ordered a meal and a whiskey. He didn't see Wyatt and Morgan in the room but he did see Doc Holliday. Doc strolled over to Clanton's table and began to taunt and provoke him, trying to push him into action. Unarmed, Clanton quickly lost his appetite and he quickly fled from the saloon. Doc and Morgan continued to call out to him in the street. "Go heel yourself", Holliday called after him in the street, urging the man to come back with a gun. Ike wisely kept walking and got involved in an all-night poker game at another saloon.

The powder keg had been ignited in Tombstone and it was just about to explode.

Wyatt woke around 11:30 on the morning of October 26. Oriental Saloon bartender Ned

Boyle had seen Ike Clanton earlier that day and he told Wyatt that he was armed and looking to kill an Earp. Ned's story was confirmed by Deputy Sheriff Harry Jones, who told Wyatt that Ike was "hunting you boys with a Winchester rifle and a six-shooter". Wyatt found Virgil and the two of them went looking for Ike.

They spotted him in an alley and Virgil came up behind him, grabbed his rifle and then clubbed Ike over the head with a revolver. "I asked him if he was hunting me," Virgil later said. "He said he was, and if he had seen me a second sooner, he would have killed me."

Ike never had the chance. He was quickly subdued by Wyatt and Virgil and was taken to Justice of the Peace A. O. Wallace's courtroom. Morgan appeared as they were taking him in and he offered Clanton his pistol back. "If you want to make a fight right bad," he reportedly said, "I will give you this one." Another law officer stepped in between them and Judge Wallace was able to hear the case. He fined Clanton $25.

As he was leaving the courtroom, Wyatt ran into Tom McLaury. The two exchanged words and Wyatt whipped out his pistol and slashed McLaury over the head with it. The two men were pulled apart.

"If you want to make a fight, I will make a fight with you anywhere," McLaury threatened and Wyatt shrugged off the hands that bound his arms.

"Jerk your gun and use it!" he shouted at McLaury but the other man refused to draw on him. He knew that he would be instantly killed.

When McLaury backed down, Wyatt slapped him across the face with his left hand. Then, he hit him again with his revolver, drawing blood. A stunned McLaury slumped to the floor. Disgusted, Wyatt walked away.

Around 2:00, Wyatt was buying a cigar in Hafford's Saloon when he saw Frank McLaury and Billy Clanton ride into town. Frank heard about what had happened that morning while drinking at the Grand Hotel. He met with Tom McLaury, a friend named Billy Claiborne, and the two Clanton's. According to their story, they opted against confronting the Earp's and decided to leave town. The five of them would go over to the O.K. Corral and retrieve their horses.

According to Sheriff John Behan, he was getting a shave in a barber shop a short time after this when he saw Doc Holliday standing with the Earp's. Virgil, he reported, was holding a shotgun that later ended up in the hands of Doc Holliday. The barber spoke up that trouble seemed to be brewing and Behan quickly left the shop. He caught up to Doc and the Earp brothers and told them that he would disarm the Clanton's and McLaury's if the Earp's would give him a few minutes to do so. The Earp's agreed and according to their later testimony, they followed Behan to assist in the disarming.

Morgan, Virgil, Wyatt and Doc walked four abreast through the streets of Tombstone. Wyatt had told Doc that this was not his fight, but Holliday refused to step out and turn his back on his friends. Virgil then deputized Doc on the street. Moments later, Behan returned and tried to disarm Doc and the Earp's, stating that the Clanton's and McLaury's posed no threat. He was ignored by Holliday and the Earp's.

As the four men approached the corral, Claiborne, the Clanton's and the McLaury's backed into an adjacent empty lot next to the corral. They turned to face the approaching men while Behan moved out of the way. Nine men, along with horses, were now forced into the crowded lot. It was a deadly setting for a gunfight.

Reports say that Wyatt addressed the men first, but others claim that Virgil cried out to them, ordering them to "Throw up your hands! I want your guns!" According to some, Wyatt yelled "You sons of bitches, you have been looking for a fight and now you can have it!" Either way, the result was the same... someone pulled a gun and the shooting started.

The Earp's and Holliday opened fire. Billy Clanton aimed at Wyatt as Wyatt shot down Frank McLaury. Morgan shot Billy in the wrist and the chest and he fell, firing as he went down.

Ike Clanton scrambled forward toward the Earp's. "Don't shoot me! I don't want to fight", he yelled and he tried to grab Wyatt's arm. When Earp saw that he was unarmed, he pushed the man away from him. "Go to fighting or get away!" he snarled. Clanton ran, burst through the door of a photographer's studio next to the lot and ran out the back. Doc tried to hit him with a shotgun blast but missed.

Frank McLaury's horse ran out into the street leaving Tom exposed. Doc leveled the shotgun at him and fired. He managed to stagger down the street but then collapsed and died. Frank McLaury, already wounded, fired at Doc. Holliday fired at the same time and so did Morgan. Doc was wounded in the hip and a stray shot from Billy Clanton wounded Morgan in the shoulder. Morgan and Wyatt returned fire, knocking Billy off his feet. Virgil was wounded in the calf, but Wyatt never received a scratch.

The legendary Gunfight at the O. K. Corral was over in minutes but the repercussions from the deadly event lasted for months. Wyatt and Doc were both charged with murder but both made the $10,000 bail. Virgil and Morgan, who were both laid up and recuperating from their wounds, were not charged. The two McLaury's and Billy Clanton were placed in matching coffins and placed on display in the windows of the hardware store. The three were put to rest on Boot Hill amid rumors of murder and conspiracy on the part of the Earp's and local officials. The citizens of Tombstone seemed to be split on whether or not the Earp's were heroes, or cold-blooded killers.

In November, the hearings to decide the innocence of Wyatt and Doc were opened. John Behan was the first to testify and he blatantly accused the Earp faction of planning the murders. They were revenge killings, he said, to cover up the fact that Doc Holliday had been involved in the earlier stage robbery.

Wyatt and Virgil both followed him to the stand and both claimed self-defense in the matter. Based on the statements made by Ike Clanton that morning, it was hard not to believe them. And on November 30, Judge Wells Spicer agreed. "I cannot resist the conclusion that the defendants were fully justified in committing these homicides," he pronounced in open court, "that it is a necessary act, done in the discharge of an official duty... I do not believe that any trial jury that could be got together in this territory, would, on all the evidence taken before me, with the rule of law applicable thereto given to them by the court, find the defendants guilty of any offense".

And thus ended the legal matters in the case... but it was far from over.

Retribution came calling three days after Christmas. Virgil left the Oriental Saloon one night around 11:30. He stepped outside into the cool night air and he paused on the wooden porch to light his cigar. He would enjoy it as he walked home, he thought, and stepped into the street. His soft sigh of contentment was never heard for the sound of a shotgun blast shattered the stillness of the dark. Virgil was struck and the wound left him crippled for life.

Just before 11:00 in the evening on March 18, 1882, Morgan was playing pool at Bob

Hatch's Billiard Parlor. Wyatt stood nearby, smiling as his brother chalked up his cue. He leaned over, one eye carefully lining up his shot. Just before the cue ball cracked against the other balls on the table, two rifle shots rang out from the back door of the room. The first shot barely missed Wyatt, but it struck Morgan in the spine. He died just before midnight, his body stretched out on one of the pool tables and his blood seeping into the cloth covering.

Wyatt demanded revenge. Three men had been spotted running away from the pool hall - an unidentified Indian, John Behan's deputy Frank Stilwell and a friend of the Clanton's named Pete Spence. He would hunt them down, he vowed, but he had other things to attend to first.

Another Earp brother, Warren, had joined his family in Tombstone just before the gunfight at the O. K. Corral. Two days after Morgan's funeral, Wyatt convinced Virgil to leave and travel to Tucson. Wyatt, Warren, Doc Holliday, Sherman McMasters and Turkey Creek Jack Johnson escorted Virgil, his wife, Morgan and Wyatt's wives, and Morgan's coffin to the train. With the rest of the family out of the way, the remaining Earp faction got down to business.

The first to die was Frank Stilwell, who was found trying to board another Tucson bound train. As the conductor called out the "all aboard", six shots mowed Stilwell down. His body was found the next day, after Wyatt and his men were back in Tombstone.

On March 22, the group paid a visit to Pete Spence's camp on the outskirts of town. Spence wasn't there, but Florentino Cruz was. Wyatt and the others decided that he was the "unidentified Indian" and they filled him full of holes and left him for dead.

Two days after the Cruz murder, the Earp and his riders headed to the Whetstone Mountains, where they tracked down Curly Bill Brocius, a dangerous killer and thief who was linked to the vigilante riders known as the "Cowboys". He had been a friend of the Clanton's and a constant source of trouble for the Earp's. After another gunfight, Curly Bill was also killed. Shortly after, Wyatt, Doc and the others vanished.

The last victim of Wyatt and his men may have been a mysterious gunfighter known as Johnny Ringo. Little is know about this man, other than he may have come from New Jersey or Missouri and that he spent time in prison with John Wesley Hardin, the notorious killer. In Tombstone, he was known to drink and quote Shakespeare. He was also fluent in Latin and once reportedly killed a drunk for speaking "disrespectfully" to a lady. He also worked as a deputy for John Behan and was associated with the Clanton's and Curly Bill Brocius. Strangely, in the summer of 1882, he was found on the edge of Tombstone, sitting under an oak tree, scalped and with a bullet in his head. His guns had never been fired and his boots were gone. His death has remained as curious as his life.

After the death of Curly Bill (or perhaps Johnny Ringo), Wyatt and Doc Holliday rode for Denver. Arizona authorities later tried to extradite Doc but Bat Masterson spoke to Colorado Governor Pitkin on his behalf. The request was denied.

After that, Doc gambled in Deadwood for a time and then returned to Leadville, Colorado. In August 1884, he got into a fight with a bartender and Doc shot him in the arm. He was acquitted of the assault, which turned out to be his last gunfight. Within three years, he would be dead.

In May 1887, he checked into a tuberculosis sanitarium in Glenwood Springs, Colorado. He was only 36 years old, but looked much older. He was lying in his bed on November 8 and happened to notice that he was barefoot. "This is funny," he said, realizing that he would not die with his boots on. He took a final sip of whiskey and he slipped away to the next world.

In 1883, Wyatt joined up with lawman Luke Short's Dodge City Peace Commission but headed north to Idaho a year later to look for gold and to run two saloons. Later that year, he was wounded in a gunfight during a poker game.

Wyatt never returned to his wife Mattie and instead remarried and he and Sadie Earp traveled west to California. In 1896, Wyatt refereed a boxing match between Bob Fitzsimmons and Tom Sharkey and he was accused of throwing the decision for Sharkey. He left town in disgrace and he and Sadie ran a saloon in Nome, Alaska for nearly four years during the Klondike gold rush. For the next five years, they ran another bar and gaming establishment in Nevada. In 1906, they returned to California and this time, settled in Los Angeles. Wyatt went to work as a bank guard but in 1911 was charged with vagrancy and running a bunco operation.

By the time, his finances dwindling, Wyatt went to work for the fledging motion picture industry. He worked as an unpaid advisor for several westerns before journalist Stuart Lake discovered him in 1927. Wyatt began dictating his memoirs and when he finished, he took one last nostalgic trip back to Tombstone. Wyatt died in his sleep at the age of 80 on January 13, 1929. Two years later, Lake published the book WYATT EARP, FRONTIER MARSHAL and the deceased gambler and lawman became famous all over the world.

In death, a great legend was born.

As for Tombstone, the lawlessness did not end with the demise of the Clanton's and McLaury's. After the Earp's left town, the violent conditions continued. However, a trend toward law and order was slow... but it was coming. The death knell for the Tombstone outlaw factions sounded in 1886 when tough lawman Texas John Slaughter was elected as the sheriff of Cochise County.

Slaughter was an odd man in his own right. He managed to clean up tombstone for good, but he did so (or so he claimed) with the help of his "guardian angel". According to Slaughter, a woman's voice often warned him of danger and saved his life on several occasions. He said that the voice came from the "spirit world".

By the end of the 1880's, Tombstone had become almost a ghost town. After several of the mines struck water and flooded, a disastrous drop in silver prices closed them down for good. The boom was over and the "wildest town in the west" was now just like any other.

After the violent events of the Earp years and the bloody gunfights and killings that took place both before and after, is it any wonder that Tombstone is considered one of the most haunted towns in the west?

There are a number of places in town that still hold the spirits of yesterday and perhaps the most haunted is the legendary Bird Cage Theatre. The building, now a national historic site, is a long, narrow structure that is one and three-quarters stories high, with a basement. It is fronted with wooden sidewalks and gas lights and looks as though it somehow came from another time in place.

The Bird Cage is preserved in the way that it looked when it (and most of the rest of the town) closed in 1889. Visitors here can see the saloon, the gambling parlor, the wine cellar, the dance hall and the stage where the dancing girls performed for the cowboys, gamblers and miners who frequented the place. In its heyday, the theatre also served as a bordello. Fourteen, bird-cage cribs, where the girls entertained their clients, were suspended from the ceiling. These "bird cages" remain today with their red velvet drapes still intact.

The tourists who come here now don't have to try hard to imagine how the hall looked, smelled and sounded when it was still operation. In fact, according to many, the past is still very much alive and well at the Bird Cage!

A few years ago, author Arthur Myers interviewed Bill Hunley, the owner of the Bird Cage. The theatre had been in his family for generations and had been built by his great-grandfather during Tombstone's glory days in 1881. He maintained that the building was a bastion for ghosts, including the spirit of a boy who died in yellow fever in 1882 and Hunley's own aunt, who passed on in 1958. He was pretty used to the ghosts though. "When you've got a place like the Bird Cage, where something happens everyday, you don't pay much attention to things like this."

According to Hunley, one of the most common incidents reported in the building was the sound of a woman singing. "You can't hear the words but you can hear her real clear," he explained. "Hundreds and hundreds of people have heard this. I have no idea who it might be."

Other people have had their own encounters and their own stories to tell. Some have recalled thumping sounds under the floor, muffled music, voices that sound as if they belong to a large group of people and phantom footsteps.

And stories of these strange sounds have been told for years. After the Bird Cage was closed down, it remained boarded up until 1934, when it was opened again as a tourist attraction. Prior to that, in 1921, a high school had been built across the street. Space had been made for it by tearing down Tombstone's old red light district. Students who attended the school claimed that, while walking past the ruins of the Bird Cage, they would hear music playing and people talking inside.

The theatre also features smells and sights, as well as sounds. It is not uncommon for tourists to report people in the building wearing old-fashioned clothing, even when no actors are present. They assume that the costumes are part of the historical presentation of the place, only to discover later that no one was dressed up on that day. In addition, it is not unheard of for people to be engulfed in clouds of cigar smoke when no one among the living is smoking.

Things often tend to turn up where they don't belong around the theatre. A few years ago, a tourist discovered a $100 poker chip lying on a table in the casino. The problem was, the owners had no idea where it had come from. Hunley took a look at it and found that it was genuine. He locked it in a drawer of his roll-top desk and called a couple of historians that he knew to take a look at it. When they showed up a couple of days later, the chip had vanished, even though Hunley had the only key to the desk!

"They left," Hunley recalled, "and I opened this oak file cabinet, and it's in there."

He then took the chip and placed it in a lock box at the bank across the street. "More historians came to see it, and that son of a gun was gone again!" he laughed. There was no way that it could have been removed from the box and a few have asked Hunley if the chip really exists at all. "My ex-wife has seen it, my fiancee has seen it, and all the employees who were there when the tourist found it saw it.... it just keeps jumping around!"

And the Bird Cage Theatre is not the only haunted place in town. In fact, even the streets of Tombstone lay claim to being infested with ghosts. There is a man in a black frock coat that has been seen by residents and tourists alike, always trying to cross the road. However, he never makes it to the other side. There is also a woman in a white dress that has been reported to stop traffic on one of the roads. The legend states that her child died from a fever in the 1880's and she committed suicide shortly after. She is often seen wandering around the town.

The Aztec House is one historically haunted spot. This antique shop is the scene of many phantom sights and sounds. The owners believe that the ghosts are attracted to the place because of the authentic goods and furniture from their own period. The woman in white (mentioned previously) is also seen most frequently in front of the shop.

Another location where ghosts lurk in downtown Tombstone is Nellie Cashman's Restaurant, where employees and patrons have reported objects that move about, crashing sounds and otherwise playful pranks.

Schiefflin Hall, which was once the center for cultural activity in the rollicking days of early Tombstone, is also reportedly haunted. Ghosts still linger here from days gone by and seem to be most active during the periodic meetings of the Tombstone town council, which occur in this building.

An additional haunted location, linked strongly to Tombstone's past, is the old Wells Fargo stage stop. Here, the apparitions of stage drivers and cowboys have been seen wandering about. Near this spot is where the man in the black frock coat is sometimes seen attempting to cross the street.

One of the most active buildings in town is the former Grand Hotel, now called Big Nose Kate's. This old building was constructed three-stories high, which made it the largest structure between Tombstone and San Francisco during its heyday. It still has the original bar and many of the original walls and floors.... and some believe many of the original guests as well!

The old saloon is said to be haunted by the ghosts of cowboys but these range riders may not be the most famous resident haunts. Just before the Clanton's and McLaury's left for their ill-fated appointment at the O. K. Corral, they were believed to have had their last drink at the Grand Hotel. Apparently, they often frequented the place and some feel that it may be one of their ghosts haunting the bar.

Doc Holliday, while living in Tombstone, also called the hotel "home". He lived in Room 201 with a young woman named Mary Katherine Harmony, also known as Big Nose Kate, after whom the saloon is now called. She was said to be a prostitute who made the mistake of falling in love with the elusive gunfighter. Could it be Kate's ghost, or even Doc's, that still lingers in the old hotel?

It's hard to say, but stranger things have happened in Tombstone... and most likely things will grow stranger still in the years to come!

## HAUNTS OF JESSE JAMES
*Ghosts of the James Family Farm*

Jesse James always maintained that he only became an outlaw because the "government pushed him to it". As a product of the Civil War era, he is remembered today as America's greatest outlaw. In his time, he was glorified as a misunderstood, good man gone bad, thanks to the Carpetbaggers, the greedy bankers and the powerful railroads. He has been called "America's Robin Hood", but he and his brother and their fellow gang members did not steal from the rich and give to the poor... they stole from everyone, kept it for themselves and killed a lot of people along the way!

The Civil War conflicts in Missouri are nearly forgotten today by those more interested in the epic battles of the south and the east. There are many who do not even remember that the issues which first boiled over into violence became so heated in what was then known as the "west".

The western state of Missouri had been in the thick of things almost from the very beginning. The act that made Missouri a state, the Compromise of 1820, had been an effort to balance the pro-slavery and anti-slavery scale more than 40 years before the war actually began. After that, the partisans who "made Kansas bleed" in the 1850's, became the guerilla fighters who burned and murdered across Missouri during the years of the war.

But Missouri was always torn in two directions. The state's early settlers had come from the south, yet her economy was linked directly to the north. The state's elected officials were mainly secessionists and intended to link Missouri to the Confederacy. There were a number of battles that took place in the state. In fact, a total of 1,162 battles and skirmishes were fought in Missouri during the official years of the war, a total exceeded only by Virginia and Tennessee.

More dangerous than the military expeditions and regular army campaigns were the bushwhacking raids of the guerillas. The leading guerilla bands, under William Clarke Quantrill, "Bloody Bill" Anderson, George Todd and William Gregg, were mostly backwoods farm boys. All of them seemed to share on thing in common though... all came from families who had been harassed, intimidated, robbed, burned out, or murdered by Federal soldiers. These men would become the prototype for the outlaws of the post-war west. They attacked, using only light weapons, but with an element of surprise that only small bands of riders can utilize. They were not above sneak attacks, guerilla warfare and shooting their enemies in the back. Thanks to the amount of local support they enjoyed, they found it easy to outmatch detachments of Union troops. Often, they would even dress in blue uniforms and hail the Federal columns as comrades before opening fire on them. It was a brutal and ruthless method of fighting, but dangerously effective.

The campaigns, raid and guerilla actions continued throughout the war and while they alone would not decide the question of the war, they would certainly manage to keep things bloody and violent for nearly four years. They would also serve as a training ground for future violence to come, providing valuable lessons for men like Union scout "Wild Bill" Hickok, a 7th Kansas recruit named William F. Cody and of course, for the James and Younger gangs, who would leave the most lingering mark on the state of Missouri.

One would almost be surprised if the James Farm, near Kearney, Missouri were not haunted!

It was here that Zerelda Cole James Sims Samuel was married to three different husbands and bore eight children. It was also here that she saw her son Archie murdered by Pinkerton detectives in an attack where she lost her own right hand. She also saw one of her husbands tortured and driven insane here and she lived in this house while her two famous, outlaw sons eluded capture, sometimes with her devoted assistance. She also guarded over the property where her son Jesse, after his murder, was buried in a grave that she could see from her bedroom window. Zerelda spent her years of widowhood on the farm, as did her daughter-in-law, Annie Ralston James.

And mostly they remained here alone, bereft of companionship save for the company of their household servants, a family of slaves who remained at the farm long after they were set free.

The James Family Farm has always had a reputation for being haunted... with lights that move about in the house and on the property, sounds of pounding hooves, shots, gun fire and cries that seem to come from nowhere. It has had a long and bloody history, dating back to events of the Civil War.

Robert Sallee James was a farmer and Baptist preacher who graduated from Georgetown College in Kentucky in 1843, just two years after he met Zerelda Cole at a revival meeting and married her. They settled on a farm in Clay County, Missouri and there, Zerelda gave birth to four children named Alexander Franklin (Frank); Robert (who only lived 33 days); Jesse Woodson; and Susan Lavina.

Reverend James was a well-liked and respected man in the community and in 1850, he was asked to serve as chaplain to a wagon train of local men who were going west to California to search for gold. Little is known as to what became of the Reverend, save for the fact that he died in a Placerville mining camp on August 18, 1850 and was buried in an unmarked grave.

Zerelda, faced with raising her children alone, married a neighboring farmer in 1852. He was killed in a horse accident a short time later, and in 1855, she married Dr. Rueben Samuel, a kindly doctor and farmer. She would go on to raise four more children with Dr. Samuel and he became the only father the James children would ever know.

The area where the James family resided was near the turbulent Missouri-Kansas border and it was hard to ignore the violence around them. Zerelda, who is remembered as a formidable frontier woman, had been raised in Kentucky and was a slave owner, so there was no question that at the outbreak of the war, her sympathies were directed toward the south. It came as no surprise in May 1861 that Frank James enlisted in the Confederate Army. He fought under General Sterling Price in the battle of Wilson's Creek in southwest Missouri, then after a brief period at home, joined up with Quantrill and his band of raiders. Frank, and his friend, Thomas Coleman "Cole" Younger, from Lee's Summit, Missouri, were with Quantrill during the 1863 raid on Lawrence, Kansas.

Just three months after the Lawrence raid, a party if Union soldiers invaded the Samuel farm looking for information about the location of Quantrill's camp. Jesse, who was just fifteen at the time, was questioned, then horse-whipped when he refused to answer the soldier's questions. Dr. Samuel, who also denied knowing where the raider's camp was located, was dragged from his house and was repeatedly hanged from a tree in the yard. Somehow, the doctor managed to survive the interrogation, but his mental state was so affected by the ordeal that he was placed in an asylum in St. Joseph. He remained there until his death in 1908.

Jesse, at the age of only 16, but with a hatred for the Union, joined up with the raiders in early 1864. He went to war under the command of "Bloody Bill" Anderson, a comrade of Quantrill with a reputation for being even more ruthless. Jesse would later take part in a battle at Centralia, Missouri where 25 Union prisoners were shot down. He was also credited with the murder of Major A.V.E. Johnson, the Federal officer who led 100 men in pursuit of Anderson's band.

Jesse's Civil War service also included fighting in support of Colonel Jo Shelby's brigade in Northwest Arkansas, at Cane Hill near the Indian Territory and at Big Cabin Creek. He was mustered out in the spring of 1865 when he rode into Lexington, Missouri carrying a white flag. He was shot in the chest when he attempted to surrender.

After the war, he went to Rulo, Nebraska to recuperate from his wound and then returned to Missouri. He was living in Kansas City, with his aunt, when he fell in love with his cousin, Zerelda (named for Jesse's mother) Mimms. He became known as a very likable young man, standing just five feet nine and weighing only 135 pounds. He always dressed well, enjoyed a good practical joke, read his bible and always went to church. It was said that he never swore or took the Lord's name in vain, preferring when he was angry to make up his own swear words. His favorite was "Dingus!", which became his brother Frank's favorite nickname for him.

In 1866, Jesse, Frank and their friends, Cole and Jim Younger, gained a new profession when they engaged in the country's first peacetime bank robbery. On February 13, they robbed the Clay County Savings Association Bank in Liberty, Missouri and made off with around $60,000, a considerable fortune at that time. Several innocent bystanders were caught in the gunfire and killed.

And a new legend was born.

Over the course of the next 16 years, the names of the James-Younger gang would achieve both fame and notoriety. But the outlaws did not continue with their new profession right away. In fact, Frank and Jesse actually went to California for a time and did not return back east until 1868. When they did, meeting up with the Younger's around the Kentucky-Tennessee border, they discovered that the newspapers were blaming them for a number of robberies that had taken place in their absence. To live up to their reputation, they then proceeded to rob a bank in Russellville and made off with about $14,000.

Jesse and Frank spent most of 1868-1869 in the Nashville area, living under assumed names and spending their robbery proceeds at racetracks in Tennessee, Kentucky and southern Illinois.

Jesse James

Then, for the next 12 years, they stayed on the move, sometimes working with the Younger's and sometimes in partnership with other stage, train and bank robbers.

On December 7, 1869, Jesse and Frank robbed a bank in Gallatin, Missouri, which gained them only $700 in cash but ended in the death of a teller named John Sheets. It turned out that Jesse hated Sheets, who was a former Union officer who may have been involved in the death of Bill Anderson. Jesse shot him in the back of the head. The Gallatin robbery resulted in a $3000 reward being posted for the brothers.

Shortly after this, began a public relations campaign, started by Zerelda James, during which the brothers were blamed for pretty much.. none of their crimes. This began the folksy tales of the James gang and their roles as Robin Hood figures, stealing from the rich and giving to the poor.

In 1874, Jesse took a respite from robbery and settled down for a time to marry and live with Zee Mimms, who he took to Texas for a honeymoon. Frank would marry a young lady named Annie Ralston later that year and their lives settled down, at least for a brief time.

In 1871, several bankers and railroad owners had hired Alan Pinkerton's famous national detective agency to track down the James gang. By the early part of 1875, Pinkerton himself had become infuriated by the agency's failure to arrest even a single member of the gang. Desperate times called for desperate measures, he believed.

In January 1875, Pinkerton had an agent posing as a field hand at work on a farm across the road from the Samuel Place. One afternoon, the agent thought he spotted Jesse and Frank at the farm house, although in reality, the brothers were many miles away. On January 26, a force of Pinkerton detectives, brought in by special train, surrounded the Samuel farm house and tossed an incendiary device through the window. The bomb exploded and struck and killed Jesse's young half-brother Archie. The blast also mangled Zerelda's right forearm so badly that it had to be amputated at the elbow.

The Pinkertons later said the device was a flare, but contemporary newspaper reports simply called it "a bomb". It would later be discovered that the device had been a grenade-type explosive, which had been obtained at the Rock Island, Illinois arsenal.

In August of that same year, Zee James gave birth to a son named Jesse Edward on a farm that Jesse had leased near Waverly, Missouri. It would be at this farm where plans for the Northfield, Minnesota Raid would be devised.

Jesse and Frank traveled to Minnesota in the company of the three Younger brothers, two Quantrill veterans named Clell Miller and Charlie Pitts and a local outlaw named Bill Chadwell. The gang had been lured up north by Chadwell's tales of easy pickings in his home state and so they began a tour of the region, gambling and staying in whorehouses in St. Paul, then meeting up in a town called Mankato, which they planned to make their first target.

Before they could act, Jesse was recognized and they left town. Riding in pairs, they headed out for Northfield, located 50 miles to the northeast. They met on the outskirts of town on September 6, cased the First National Bank, and then made plans to rob it the following morning.

At dawn, they rode quietly into Northfield, wearing long, linen dusters over their clothes and pistols. Jesse, Bob Younger and Charlie Pitts rode into town, ate breakfast and then sauntered over to the bank, where they tied their horses out front. At that moment, the other five men suddenly rode into town, firing their six-guns into the air, shouting and hollering and scattering the people who were on the streets. While this was happening, Jesse, Bob and Charlie charged into the bank with their guns drawn. Jesse clobbered a bank teller and Bob Younger forced the other employees and customers to their knees while he cleaned out the drawers of cash. One clerk ran out the back door and was shot down by Charlie Pitts.

Meanwhile, the five outlaws outside of the bank were starting to draw gunfire from the local citizens. Clell Miller was hit by a shotgun blast and was knocked from his horse. He was the first to die.

Inside of the bank, Jesse shot the bank teller that he had clubbed and the men ran outside. A crossfire had erupted from the surrounding buildings and the seven outlaws were caught in the middle of it. Bill Chadwell was shot from his horse and killed. Cole Younger got a bullet in the shoulder. Frank was hit in the leg. A bullet struck Jim Younger in the face and his brother Bob's horse was shot out from under him. Bob was hit in the thigh and in the right arm before his brother Cole could pull him onto his own horse.

The Northfield Raid was over in 20 minutes and the outlaws arranged to meet between the town and Mankato. After that, they scattered to the wind. Jesse and Frank headed out for the Dakota Territory. The Younger's were captured one week later, just east of Mankato. In the shootout that followed, Charlie Pitts was killed and the Younger's, all of them wounded, surrendered. Each was sentenced to a life term in prison.

Jesse and Frank pulled off a few more jobs over the next five years including a train robbery at Glendale, Missouri, a stage hold-up near Mammoth Cave, Kentucky, and a few others... but the Northfield disaster really marked the beginning of the end for the James brothers.

In 1879, Jesse took his family to Nashville and they lived for a time with Frank and Annie. That year, Zee gave birth to a daughter, Mary Susan, and Jesse took her to visit the Mimms family in Kansas City. Shortly after, on Christmas Eve 1881, they moved to St. Joseph, Missouri where he rented a house under the name of Thomas Howard.

Here, Jesse began planning his last great bank robbery. He had decided to call it quits and retire, with enough money to become a gentleman farmer. He planned to purchase some land in Nebraska with the proceeds from this last robbery.

At this point, the Younger's were all in prison and Frank was running from the law himself, so Jesse took on two new gang members, Bob and Charley Ford. They planned to rob the Platte City Bank in Kansas City and on April 3, 1882, Jesse called the Fords to his home in St. Joseph to discuss the job. Jesse was relaxing in the parlor, reading the newspaper and Zee was working in the kitchen. The three men sat down and talked for awhile and then Charley went out into the backyard while Bob made small talk with Jesse.

As he was reading, he glanced up and noticed that a framed needlepoint picture, done by his mother, was hanging crookedly on the wall. He moved a cane chair over to the wall and stepped up to straighten it, his back to the room. When he turned, Bob Ford pulled out a revolver and shot Jesse just below the right ear!

The gunshot resounded throughout the house and Jesse's children were the first to reach him. In seconds, Zee followed and tried desperately to stop the blood that was pouring from her husband's head. Bob Ford ran from the house, jumped the back fence and vanished. Charley spent a few moments trying lamely to explain the shooting as an accident, then he ran off after his brother.

In a few minutes, the authorities arrived and Zee tried to continue the masquerade that Jesse was actually a businessman named Tom Howard. This was shattered when the Fords returned to the house and revealed Jesse's true identity. Zee soon grew to believe that Missouri Governor Thomas T. Crittenden, who had previously offered a reward of $10,000 for Jesse James, dead or alive, had arranged the assassination. And Zee may have been right, as Crittenden quickly pardoned the Fords for previous crimes and awarded them the bounty.

A coroner's inquest was held on April 4 and Zee and others formally identified the body. Jesse was then packed in ice and taken by train to Kearney, where he was displayed and viewed by hundreds of friends and admirers, including many old Quantrill veterans. Jesse was later buried on the family farm with only close family and friends present. His seven-foot deep grave was placed near Zerelda's front door, so that she could keep an eye out for trespassers and souvenir hunters.

Later, when Zerelda could no longer live alone, her son's body was moved, on July 29, 1902, to the Mount Olivet Cemetery in town. Zee had died in 1900 and Jesse was placed next to her.

Frank James was present at the re-burial of his brother. He had surrendered to Governor Crittenden on October 5, 1882 but despite the efforts of the state's attorneys, all cases against Frank were thrown out of court for lack of evidence and dismissed. He worked at various honest jobs for the rest of his life and in 1903, joined with Cole Younger (who had been paroled in 1901) in the James-Younger Wild West Show. Frank died at the James Farm on February 18,

1915.

Bob Ford, who became known as "the dirty little coward who shot Mr. Howard" was forced to leave Missouri after being pardoned by Governor Crittenden. He traveled about the west, spending some time performing in a stage show about (ironically) the James gang. He was shot and killed in Creede, Colorado in 1892, by an ex-policeman named Ed O. Kelly.

Ten years before, Charley Ford had committed suicide in Richmond, Missouri.

Jesse may have been re-buried beside his wife in the Mount Olivet Cemetery in 1902... but the question remains as to whether or not he really rests in peace?

Strange disturbances at the family farm have been commonplace for many years, as have the unusual stories. In 1982, the Kansas City Star newspaper arranged an overnight vigil in the house, which was held on the 100th anniversary of the death of Archie Samuel, the only person to ever die violently in the house. Unfortunately, the three men, two from Chicago and the third a writer for the newspaper, experienced nothing more than cold chills in the house. Milton F. Perry, a curator of the house museum explained that this was typical... of any old unheated house in January.

Despite this less than encouraging "ghost hunt", people who work in the house, who are mostly volunteers and staff members of the museum, claim to have had some interesting experiences. They have been present when doors have slammed closed on their own, when lights have been seen moving about in the locked house and when a presence has been so intense in the house that guides refuse to be there alone.

One staff member also admitted that she has, more than one time, heard the low voices of men in the woods near the house and has heard the sounds of restless horses, when no horses are present. On several occasions, she has even gone into the woods later and has found no sign or tracks that any (living) horses had been there.

Restless phantoms... or the sounds of the violent past simply replaying themselves, like a needle stuck in a record groove on an old Victrola? You be the judge...

## - CHAPTER FOUR -

# GANGLAND GHOSTS

## HAUNTS OF ORGANIZED CRIME, BOOTLEGGERS AND PUBLIC ENEMIES

There are few periods of American history as fascinating as that of the "gangster era" of the 1920's and 1930's. During this period, organized crime gained a foothold in America, especially in the larger cities, where gangsters became celebrities and "graft" being paid to cops and politicians was an everyday happening. During the years of Prohibition, the mob came into its own, "giving the people what they wanted" and then diversifying into other criminal pursuits once the liquor began to legally flow again.

But organized crime had come to America long before the years of Prohibition. Its American roots were born in the city of New Orleans but the "Mafia" was created in Sicily around 1282. At that time, it was a secret brotherhood that was dedicated to freeing the country from the French. For years, the Mafia was a champion of the people, waging guerilla warfare against the French and other invaders. The country's chief city, Palermo, became the hub of Mafia activity and the "dons" of the organization sent recruiters out across the land in search of young and ardent patriots who were skilled in the art of killing.

By the early 1800's, the Mafia had evolved from a benevolent society that fed the hungry and sheltered the homeless to an organization that extorted money and power from landowners and peasants alike. Its leaders, known as "capos", directed the group to infiltrate and threaten business, government and even the military.

By 1889, the Mafia had come to America. At that time, New Orleans was probably the most anti-Italian city in America. The city had recently been flooded with thousands of Italian immigrants and statements from the Mayor's office didn't help matters any. In one letter, Mayor Joseph A. Shakespeare called Southern Italians and Sicilians ".... the most idle, vicious and worthless people among us."

Of course, not all of the blame could be laid at city government's door either. In addition to dirty politicians and cops on the take, late 1800's New Orleans was also filled with Italian criminals. There was no denying that the French Quarter ghetto was turning out productive Italian citizens, but it was also turning out criminals as well. Undoubtedly, many of these criminals were not "Mafia", but it has long been conceded that New Orleans represented one of the main ports of entry for the Mafia into the United States.

Between 1888 and 1890, the New Orleans Mafia, made up of several Sicilian groups, committed an estimated 40 murders without opposition. During this period, Antonio and Carlo Matranga took control of the Mississippi River docks. Tribute had to be paid to them before a freighter could be unloaded. Soon, the Provenzano brothers, leaders of another Mafia group, challenged their operation. War broke out between the two gangs and killings on the docks became regular occurrences.

The police failed to stop the battles until the chief of police, David Hennessey, personally took over the case. Soon, the Matranga's began to find themselves investigated and harassed at every turn, while the Provenzano's were not bothered at all.

The Matranga's sent a warning to the chief, but the pressure continued. At this point, they tried to bribe him, but he turned them down, leading them to believe the Provenzano's were simply paying him more. So they fell back onto an old Sicilian custom of killing a government official that got in the way.

Hennessey became a marked man when police, conducting a routine murder investigation, charged two Provenzano brothers with the murder of a Matranga gangster whose head had been cut off and stuffed in a fireplace. The Matranga's, determined to thwart the Provenzano operations, hired some of the city's best attorneys to aid in the prosecution. Then, Chief Hennessey made a startling statement to the newspapers... he told them that he had uncovered the existence of a criminal society, the Mafia, in New Orleans and he would offer proof during the Provenzano trial.

On October 15, 1890, Hennessey left his office for home but was cut down by a shotgun blast less than a half-block from his house. Hennessey managed to fire a few volleys at his fleeing assailants and when asked who shot him, he whispered "dagos", then died.

The murder outraged the citizens of New Orleans. A grand jury was convened and they announced that the existence of the Mafia in the city had now been established beyond doubt. They chose 19 men who they believed were not only members of the Mafia, but also involved in the murder of Chief Hennessey. A trial was held, but was believed by most to be a farce. Not only were a large number of the 60 witnesses threatened and paid off, but members of the jury were bribed too. Despite what was regarded as overwhelming evidence against at least 11 of the defendants, all but three were acquitted and the jury was unable to reach a verdict on those three.

All of the defendants were returned to the parish prison to await final disposition of their cases and what followed was a blight on the history of New Orleans. During the two nights following the trial, mass meetings and protests were held in the city. Finally, a mob of several thousand, headed by at least 60 leading citizens, marched on the prison. They had a "death list" of the 11 defendants against whom the evidence had been the strongest.

Two of the mafiosi were pulled screaming from their cells and were hanged from lampposts. Seven others were executed by firing squad in the prison yard while two more were shot to death when they ran and hid in the kennel belonging to the jail's guard dog.

While some newspapers denounced the murders, the citizens and especially the business community seemed rather pleased about what had occurred. A new song "Hennessey Avenged" made the rounds and became quite popular.

For a short time, the killings threatened international relations. Italy recalled its ambassador and severed diplomatic relations with the United States. The government demanded reparations and punishment against the leaders of the lynch mob. Eventually, the affair was settled when Washington paid $25,000 to the men's relatives in Italy.

From New Orleans, organized crime and the Mafia spread across America, gaining footholds in Kansas City, New York, St. Louis and Chicago. The organization became involved in gambling, prostitution and extortion but it would be an American law that would actually give organized crime its greatest power.

When the 18th Amendment to the Constitution, which abolished the sale and distribution of alcohol, took effect on January 16, 1920, many believed that it would cure the social ills of America. Little did they know at the time, but it would actually do just the opposite. America's great thirst for the forbidden liquor bred corruption in every corner. Law enforcement officials became open to bribes because the majority of the men just did not believe in the law, but worse yet, Prohibition gave birth to the great days of organized crime. The gangsters of America had previously concerned themselves with acts of violence, racketeering and prostitution but the huge profits that came to be made with the sale of illegal liquor built criminal empires.

Across the country, over 200,000 "speakeasys" opened. These drinking establishments were so named because many of them were located behind, above or below legitimate businesses and patrons often drank in silence. Huge bootlegging operations sprang into operation to supply the speakeasys and those who chose to ignore the new law. In addition, ordinary people began brewing their own beer and distilling their own liquor. Some of them even sold the stuff from home, and the product called "bathtub gin" came into existence. Disrespect for the law became the fashion as people who would have never dreamed of doing anything illegal before now found themselves serving illicit liquor in their homes or drinking in the neighborhood speakeasy.

Prohibition was widely considered to be doomed by 1928, but it hung on for another five years before being repealed in 1933. By then, it had taken its toll, leaving law enforcement in disarray and leaving the mobster organizations so powerful they were able to move onto other pursuits, like legalized gambling, with wide public approval.

Shortly after the end of Prohibition, America was plunged into the Great Depression. This era of national poverty gave birth to another breed of criminal, the bank robber. Bank robberies had been taking place almost since the time that the first Americans entrusted an establishment with their hard-earned money, but the robbers of the 1930's were different. They were no longer the outlaws of the "Wild West" for these bank robbers have the new and novel advantage of motorized transportation. Never before in American crime had outlaws possessed the means to escape so easily from law enforcement officials. Now, they went on the rampage through various states using motor cars.

This new era gave birth to legendary criminals like Ma Barker, Bonnie and Clyde and Dillinger, just to name a few. Many of them not only gained a place on the FBI's new "Most Wanted" list, but they became folk heroes too. There were few Americans who didn't feel a twinge of jealousy as they saw these free-wheeling bank robbers get their revenge on the banks, the wealthy and the government itself. Stories were told that some of these outlaws actually stole from the rich and then gave back part of the money to those who really needed it. And in the 1930's, there were a lot of folks who needed it.

These folk heroes, bank robbers and stone-cold killers certainly left their mark on the American landscape and many of them died just as they lived, fast and hard. It's not surprisingly that many of their stories still linger with us today... or that their ghosts do too!

When I sell liquor, they call it bootlegging. When my patrons serve it on silver trays on Lake Shore Drive, they call it hospitality ...... I'm a businessman, I've made my money supplying a popular demand. If I break the law, my customers are as guilty as I am.
**AL CAPONE**

Nobody shot me.

**FRANK GUSENBERG...**
mortally wounded in the St. Valentines Day Massacre

Never trust a woman or an automatic pistol.
**JOHN DILLINGER**

We only kill each other.
**BENJAMIN "BUGSY" SIEGEL**

# THE CASTLE ROYAL CAFE
## Haunts of the Wabasha Street Caves

The Castle Royal Caves (now called the Wabasha Street Caves) are man-made caverns on the outskirts of St. Paul, Minnesota. For decades, they have been rumored to be haunted by a number of resident ghosts, from a man and woman who appear in the bar of this unique restaurant in the early morning hours... to gangsters who were murdered here long ago.

The caves were dug into pure sandstone many years ago. The rock and sand that was hauled out of them by Minnesota immigrants was used to build the early streets of St. Paul. Once the silica was depleted, seven huge caves were left behind, extending about 150 feet into the bluffs along Wabasha Street.

In the 1840's, local residents used the caves to store food as they stayed at a constant 52 degrees. In the middle 1880's, three French immigrants named Louis Lambert, Charles Etienne and Albert Mouchenott established a mushroom-growing business inside of the caves. The business operated steadily for many years but Mouchenott's daughter, Josie Lehmann, had other plans for the place.

She always dreamed of turning the place into an underground nightclub, so in October of 1933, Josie and her husband, William Lehmann, opened the Castle Royal. They spent over $150,000 turning the rough-hewn caves into a club. They had the rooms carved into curving, dome-shaped chambers and created doorways in the shape of mushrooms as a nostalgic remembrance of the cave's earlier enterprise. They brought in expensive furnishings like Italian chandeliers, Oriental rugs and marble fountains to complete the interior design. A 1,600 square-foot dance floor was added and the nightly floor shows attracted the top talent of the era, from Cab Calloway to Harry James to the Dorsey Brothers. Favored by the St. Paul City Council, the Lehmann's were even given the city's first post-Prohibition liquor license, which was issued six months before Prohibition was even repealed.

The most exciting part of the cave's history took place in the 1930's, when the Castle Royal became a favorite hangout for the Midwest's top gangsters. Patrons reported spotting a number of people like John Dillinger and Ma Barker here, along with a lot of lesser-known mobsters and tough guys. Dillinger came to St. Paul in April or May of 1934 but Ma Barker and her sons, along with Alvin "Creepy" Karpis, joined forces to commit a crime at the same time they were spotted at the Castle Royal.

They kidnapped William Hamm, of Hamm's Beer fame, while in the city and they demanded a $100,000 ransom. It came a week later, but during that time, Hamm got along well with his captors. They spent most of the week killing time and playing poker. Karpis even apologized to Hamm for serving him beer that was made by a competitor and Hamm confessed that he couldn't tell the difference anyway.

As you can see, St. Paul was a frequent hideout for gangsters on the run from the law, even going as far to welcome these outlaws, especially the bootleggers of the Prohibition period.

Prohibition led to enormous profits from bootleg liquor and there was plenty of money to go around, even to the corrupt politicians and crooked cops. St. Paul came to be regarded as the safest hideout town for American criminals and many claimed this was of great benefit to the local residents. They insisted that this policy was responsible for the fact that nearly 30 years passed without any gangland violence or robberies.

Around 1900, Police Chief John J. O'Connor let it be known to out-of-town criminals that they were welcome to "lay over" in St. Paul and spend their money freely. The only stipulation was that no crimes could take place in the city. At a result, the city's crime statistics dropped to almost unbelievable levels and St. Paul became one of the few cities where a lone woman could walk down a dark street at night without fear.

When a criminal from out of town visited the city, he reported to Paddy O'Griffin's lodging house on Wabasha Street. He was then given a place to stay in St. Paul, for a hefty price, of course. O'Griffin kept Chief O'Connor informed about all visitors and the Chief made sure that the recent arrival stayed out of trouble and most importantly, was never subjected to police interference. This operation was made by possible thanks to the political clout of O'Connor's younger brother, Richard, the boss of the city and of the state Democratic Party.

It is believed that the O'Connor's never personally accepted money for this arrangement but rather operated the system for the satisfaction expressed by the public for living in a crime-free community. Their income came from running a string of saloons and from the prostitution industry, which paid large sums to the police for the privilege of operating without harassment. One particularly lavish brothel was even allowed to operate directly behind police headquarters!

The system continued for years, even after Richard O'Connor turned his interest to national politics and had little to do with St. Paul. The layover system was so ingrained that it even continued under a police chief that opposed it. Other police officials supervised the operation and criminals checked in at the Green Lantern saloon on Wabasha Street, within sight of the state capitol.

Eventually, a weakening of official control changed the way the city did business. Outside criminal elements no longer saw any reason to exempt St. Paul from criminal endeavors and in time, crime came to the city. The days of the St. Paul layover passed into history.

One of the strange, and still unexplained, events to occur in the Wabasha Street Caves during this time period took place in 1934. A cleaning woman, who was working alone after closing time, witnessed three men gunned down in front of a fireplace in the club. The police were summoned, but they didn't arrive for almost ninety minutes. By the time they bothered to show up, all trace of the crime had been erased. They found no blood and no bodies! Insiders believe that the three men who were killed may be buried under a cement floor in an unfinished part of the cave. Only a careful examination of the fireplace today reveals machine-gun holes in the rock. The chipped bullet marks can still be seen but the murders remain a mystery.

With the arrival of the Great Depression, operating the club became a financial struggle and the place limped along until closing up in 1940. The Lehmann family returned to growing mushrooms in the unfinished portions of the cave, their dreams of the nightclub all but forgotten. The place stood closed and silent for the next 37 years until it was purchased in 1977 and restored with an art deco design. The place soon closed again and held several short-lived enterprises in the years that followed. The bar was purchased again in the early 1990's by Steve and Donna Bremer, who remain the current owners. They opened the doors to invite back the customers and they aren't chasing away the ghosts either.

With the coming of the late 1930's, federal officers began making stronger efforts to end the glory days of the American gangster and many of the Castle Royal's colorful characters were hunted down, imprisoned and killed. The memories of this violent past can still be found in the caves... along with the restless spirits.

It is in the unfinished portions of the cave that the ghosts seem to reside. Many people claim to have heard noises here at night that cannot easily be explained. This area is thought to be where the murdered men were buried years ago. Could it be their ghosts who still linger here? The employees tell of whispers and voices, doors opening and closing, the sounds of people laughing, music playing, glasses tinkling together and lights that turn off and on for no reason.

Even previous owners did not scoff at the ghostly activity, inviting ghost hunters to come in and try to record the strange sounds. Those present often heard the unexplained noises, but nothing has ever shown up on tape.

In addition to the sounds, staff member and customers alike claim to have seen apparitions of a man and woman in the bar area. They are dressed in period clothing of the 1920's or 1930's and vanish whenever they are approached. One staff member also claimed to see a man in a suit and a fedora vanish by walking into a solid rock wall!

## HOLLYWOOD'S FAVORITE GANGSTER

The Ghost of Bugsy Siegel

One of the most tragic underworld figures of his time has to be Benjamin "Bugsy" Siegel. This mobster has long said to be haunting two places that he knew in life… one of them is a place that he loved and the other is a spot where he left a terrified presence behind.

Siegel was probably the most colorful, and the most charming, of the famous syndicate killers. He was also one of the quickest tempered as well, boasting a manic rage that sometimes boarded on insanity. Regardless, he charmed most everyone that he met, especially in Hollywood, operating as a mob killer at the same time that he was seducing nubile young starlets. Although sent to California to watch over mob interests, many believed that what he really wanted from Hollywood was to be an actor. Some would say that he already was one though, leading a double life that would put many Oscar winners to shame!

Ben Siegel grew up on New York's Lower East Side and by the age of 14, was already running his own criminal gang. He formed an early alliance with a youth named Meyer Lansky, who was already a criminal genius in his teens. By 1920, they had formed a gang that specialized in bootleg liquor, gambling and auto theft. On occasion, Siegel and Lansky hijacked liquor shipments from other operations, before realizing that there was more money to be made by hiring out their gang as protection for the other outfits. Soon they were hooked up with rising Italian mobsters like Lucky Luciano, Frank Costello, Joe Adonis, Albert Anastasia and others.

The emerging national crime syndicate assigned Spiegel to carry out numerous murders that were aimed at gaining control of various criminal operations. He became an excellent killer and was so enthused by it that he was called "Bugsy", but never to his face.

In the 1930's Siegel was sent to California to run the syndicate's West Coast operations, including the lucrative racing wire service for bookmakers. It was here that he found his niche. Just because Siegel was probably a psychopath, it didn't mean that he couldn't be charming. He was suave and entertaining and became friends with Hollywood celebrities like Jean Harlow, George Raft, Clark Gable, Gary Cooper and Cary Grant. Many of them even put money into his enterprises. On one hand, he was the life of the party and on the other, a cold-blooded killer. On occasion, Siegel could be at a party with his "high class friends" and then slip away for a gangland execution, all in the same night.

The mob expected Siegel to arrange to have a killing carried out, not actually do it, but Bugsy couldn't help himself. Los Angeles District Attorney Arthur Veitch would later describe Siegel as a "cowboy". He explained that "this is the way that the boys have of describing a man who is not satisfied to frame a murder, but actually has to be in on the kill in person."

Seigel's main business was running the rackets and directing deliveries on the West Coast but in the 1940's, he dreamed up the idea of turning a little waterhole in the Nevada desert called Las Vegas into a legal gambling paradise. He talked the syndicate into coming up with a couple of million dollars to finance the scheme and the figure soon escalated to almost $6 million.

He dubbed the place the "Flamingo", which was the nickname of his mistress, Virginia Hill. At one brief time after the casino opened, Siegel had four of his favorite girlfriends lodged in separate hotel suites. They were Virginia Hill, Countess Dorothy diFrasso, actress Marie McDonald and actress Wendy Barrie, who frequently announced her engagement to Bugsy and never gave up hoping. Whenever she saw Wendy in the hotel, Virginia Hill would go wild and once she punched the actress so hard in the face that she nearly dislocated her jaw.

Unfortunately, Siegel was a man ahead of his time and dame trouble became the least of his concerns. The syndicate was upset about the $6 million they had invested, as the Flamingo, when it opened, was a financial disaster. Reportedly, the mob demanded that Siegel make good on their losses but what they didn't know was that Bugsy had also been skimming from the construction funds and from the gambling profits. Virginia Hill had been busy hiding the money in Swiss bank accounts.

The syndicate passed a death sentence on Siegel at the famous Havana conference in December 1946. His old friend, Meyer Lansky, cast the deciding vote. "I had no choice," he said later. Siegel knew that he was in big trouble but he thought they had given him an extension to get the Flamingo turned around. By May 1947, the casino was making a profit and Bugsy began to relax.

On June 20, Siegel was sitting in the living room of Virginia Hill's Beverly Hills mansion. She was away in Europe at the time. He was reading the newspaper when two steel-jacketed slugs tore through the front window. One of them shattered the bridge of his nose and exited through his left eye, while the other entered his right cheek and blew out the back of his neck. Authorities later found his right eye on the dining room floor, more than 15 feet from his body. Bugsy Siegel was dead before he hit the floor.

Ironically, Siegel even knew that his fellow mobsters had planned the murder in advance. A few months before, construction magnate Del Webb had told Bugsy that he was nervous because of all of the gangsters that were hanging around the Flamingo. Siegel laughed and told him not to worry. "We only kill each other," he told him. And for Siegel, this was certainly true!

But have we really seen the last of Bugsy Siegel? Virginia Hill's former home, which is a private residence on Linden Drive in Beverly Hills, is reportedly still haunted by the panicked presence of Bugsy Siegel as he scrambles for cover, attempting to hide from the bullets that killed him. His stark fear, as he spotted his killer and knew that the game was up, has left an indelible impression on the house. According to reports, witnesses have been surprised for years by the apparition of a man running and ducking across the living room of the house, only to disappear as suddenly as he came.

A psychic who was brought in to investigate the house claimed that the image was the residual presence of Bugsy Siegel, imprinted on the place in his last desperate moments before death.

As the years have passed, Bugsy's ghostly energy here may have faded somewhat, but it has been suggested that his actual spirit may not rest in peace either...

After Siegel was assassinated, the mob continued to support the Flamingo Hotel and eventually saw it grow and prosper. They poured millions of dollars into Las Vegas and it became the gambling mecca that Siegel envisioned in the early 1940's. And it is at the Flamingo where the spirit of Ben Siegel is said to reside today.

Bugsy is believed to haunt the Presidential Suite of the hotel, where he lived for several years before his death. Guests in this room have reported a number of strange encounters with his ghost, from eerie, moving cold spots to items that vanish and move about the suite. They have also seen his apparition in the bathroom and near the pool table. Those who have encountered him say this spirit does not seem unhappy or distressed and in fact, seems content to still be around. Perhaps he is just happy to see that Las Vegas has turned out the way he had planned after all!

## THE CURSE OF THE GREEN CHAIR

*Crime and Superstition in Chicago*

Crime has always been a part of Chicago.

From even the early days, the city thrived on its reputation for being a "wide-open town". As far back as the 1850's, the city gained notoriety for its promotion of vice in every shape and form. It embraced the arrival of prostitutes, gamblers, grifters and an outright criminal element. A commercialized form of vice flourished during the Civil War era and according to author Richard Lindberg, an estimated 1,300 prostitutes roamed the darkened, evening streets of Chicago. Randolph Street, he wrote, "was awash in bordellos, wine rooms and cheap dance halls in plain view of the courthouse". The area became known as "Gambler's Row", mostly because a man gambled with his very life when braving the streets of this seedy and dangerous district.

The famous cartoon by John T. McCutcheon depicting the collusion between criminals and politicians in Chicago.

The Great Fire in 1871 would sweep away the worst of the city's vice areas, destroying both gin rooms and disease-ridden prostitution cribs, but a desire for illicit activities caused it to rebound quickly. By the 1880's, Chicago had gained its place as a mature city and also as a rail center for the nation. Waves of foreigners and immigrants poured into the city and with the arrival of the World's Fair in 1893, thousands of new citizens followed.

The Custom House vice district sprang from the ashes of the Great Fire. For nearly 30 years, the area would be regarded as a blight on the downtown area. Like most segregated vice areas, where gambling, liquor and prostitution are indulged, the Custom House thrived on not only its proximity to the railroads but to an alliance with the police as well. The closest station could be found at the nearby Armory station and they turned a blind eye to questionable activity in the district, for a price, of course.

The Custom House district existed between Harrison Street on the north and Polk Street and the Dearborn train station to the south. It is an area more popularly known as "Printer's Row" today. The boundaries of the area tended to change and expand with the opening of each new saloon or house of ill repute. It also tended to shrink when any of the owners neglected to make their protection payments. Such absent-mindedness was usually followed by a police raid.

The Dearborn Station became essential to operations in the area as it made a perfect recruiting spot for prostitutes during the gaslight era. Naive young women who stepped off the train were often greeted by one of the army of "pimps" who waited in the station. From that point, they were introduced to immoral acts and lured into the "scarlet patch" originally known as the Cheyenne District and later the Custom House.

The most infamous bordello here was Carrie Watson's place at 441 South Clark Street. Despite the seediness of the area, the beautiful Miss Watson's "house" enjoyed a wide reputation for being a charming place, with sixty women in her employ.

There were other "resorts" along the Custom House that were not so elegant or refined though. Often an unsophisticated visitor would stumble into what was called a "panel house", where he might be drugged and tied up while an accomplice slipped through a hidden panel in the wall and liberated him of his valuables. More often, the secret panels hid thieves with long hooks who could relieve a customer of his wallet, from pants hanging on the bed post, while he was "in the act". Few of these victims would report the robbery to the police, lest they suffer the humiliation of having their names printed in the newspaper.

By the time of the Columbian Exposition in 1893, Chicago had become known as the "Paris of America" for its many illicit attractions. Reformist WT Stead, in his book "If Christ Came to Chicago", counted thirty-seven bordellos, forty-six saloons, eleven pawnbrokers, an opium den and numerous gambling parlors in the Custom House district while writing his expose on Chicago vice.

The official stance on such districts was to leave them alone, as long as the operators, thieves and undesirables stayed in the district and kept to themselves. However, this was rarely the case. Granted a wide berth by city officers, the dealers in vice exploited the situation with prostitutes being arrested in the theater district and posing as sales girls in reputable stores. By 1903, conditions had become intolerable and reformers would no longer stand for it. A wave of criminal indictments, pushed through by church groups and the mayor himself, sent the vice operators reeling. Most of them moved to the South Side Levee District, where they were welcomed with open arms. The Custom House Place Levee had vanished completely by 1910.

After that, the deserted area was slowly taken over by commercial printing houses and bookbinderies, creating the name the district bears today, "Printer's Row". Eventually, the printing houses joined the bordellos and they too faded away. The area finally gained its dignity around 1979 when it converted into the condominium and rental community that exists today. The railroad freight yards have also disappeared, although Dearborn station remains. It has been converted into a small shopping mall, serving the residents of this quiet street. The Custom House Levee is now only a memory.

But after the early days of crime, came the Prohibition era and the time of the Mob. Names like Al Capone and Dion O'Banion were no longer spoken in merely the poor neighborhoods, but among the rich of Lake Shore Drive as well. Newspapers carried accounts of gangland slayings and bootleg wars across the country. In his 1940 book, GEM OF THE PRAIRIE, author Herbert Asbury wrote that "the average tourist felt that his trip to Chicago was a failure unless it included a view of Capone out for a spin. The mere whisper: 'Here comes Al', was sufficient to stop traffic and to set thousands of curious citizens craning their necks along the curbing."

Crime ran rampant during this period and even inspired phrases that are still in use today among law enforcement officials. The term "Chicago Amnesia" is still used to describe the reticence of witnesses to testify against organized crime. In Chicago of the 1920's, law enforcement officials found it almost impossible to prosecute gangsters because of the fear they instilled in possible witnesses. Even eyewitnesses who eagerly came forward after seeing a crime take place suddenly developed a memory loss when they learned the identities of the culprits. And it seemed that the disease was contagious, often contracted through bribes, but usually through threats and even murder attempts.

The Prohibition era also spawned a number of curious legends among Chicago underworld figures. Perhaps one of the strangest was that of the "Green Chair Curse", also referred to as the "Undertaker's Friend." The curse was named after a green leather chair found in the office of William "Shoes" Shoemaker, who became the Chicago chief of detectives in 1924. Several of the city's top gangsters were hauled into Shoemaker's office for questioning and ordered to sit in the green chair. Several of them died violent deaths a short time later.

This could hardly be that surprising, given the death rate during the gang wars in Chicago, but the newspapers quickly seized on the story and a belief in the "curse" of the chair began to grow. Shoemaker, probably delighted with the attention, stated that he was now keeping track of the criminals who sat in the chair and later died violently. When the inevitable later occurred, he would put an X by the gangster's name. These men included the Genna brothers (Angelo, Tony and Mike), Porky Lavenuto, Mop Head Russo, Samoots Amatuna, Antonio "The Scourge" Lombardo, John Scalise, Albert Anselmi, Antonio "the Cavalier" Spano and others. Legend had it that other well-known gangsters, even Al Capone, absolutely refused to sit down in the chair.

When Shoemaker retired in 1934, there were 35 names in his notebook and 34 of them had an X after their name. Only one criminal, Red Holden, was still among the living and he was doing time in Alcatraz for train robbery. "My prediction still stands", Shoes told reporters upon his retirement. "He'll die a violent death. Maybe it'll happen in prison. Maybe he'll have to wait until he gets out. But, mark my words, it'll happen."

But Holden managed to outlive Shoes. The detective died four years later and the green chair was passed on to Captain John Warren, who had been Shoemaker's aide. He continued to seat an occasional hoodlum in it, perhaps hoping to "scare them straight" with the eerie legend. By the time that Warren died in September 1953, the chair's death rate stood at 56 out of 57 men. Only Red Holden was still alive!

Holden had been released from Alcatraz in 1948 and afterwards was involved in several shoot-outs, all of which he survived. Then, he was convicted on murder charges and was sent to prison for a 25-year sentence. He died in the infirmary of Illinois' Statesville Prison on December 18, 1953. According to the newspapers, he was smiling when he passed... because he had beaten the green chair!

Holden's death set off a search for the mysterious green chair. No one knew what had happened to it after Captain Warren had died. Finally, it discovered that the chair had been destroyed. It was traced to the Chicago Avenue police station, where it had been confined to the cellar after the death of Captain Warren. When it was found to be infested with cockroaches, it had been broken apart and burned in the station's furnace. This had happened shortly before Red Holden had died in his hospital bed.

Otherwise, some claimed, he would have never escaped the curse!

## THE ST. VALENTINE'S DAY MASSACRE
### History & Hauntings of Chicago's Most Famous Crime

For a city that is so filled with the history of crime, there has been little preservation of the landmarks that were once so important to the legend of the mob in Chicago. The most tragically destroyed of these landmarks was the warehouse that was located at 2122 North Clark Street. It was here, on Valentine's Day 1929, that the most spectacular mob hit in gangland history took place... the St. Valentine's Day Massacre.

The building was called the S-M-C Cartage Company and was a red, brick structure on Clark Street. The events that led to the massacre began on the morning of the 14th. To understand them however, we have to take a look at the men behind the massacre, Al Capone and George "Bugs" Moran.

Al Capone was the leader of the South Side crime organization and was perhaps the most powerful crime boss of his day. He employed over 1,000 gunmen and claimed that he literally "ran" Chicago. It was said that over half the city's police force and most of its politicians were on his payroll, including state's attorneys, aldermen, mayors and even congressmen. His control over elections in Chicago and in suburban areas like Cicero was absolute. Even today, he remains one of the most recognized names in American and Chicago history.

Capone was born in Brooklyn in 1899 and went to work for gangster Johnny Torrio. When Torrio later moved west to Chicago, Capone followed and went to work for restaurant owner and mobster Big Jim Collisimo. Doing Torrio's dirty work, Capone killed Collisimo so that they could seize control of the city's illegal booze market. The two of them worked together to wipe out their opposition and in 1924, assassinated Dion O'Banion, the head of the Irish mob on the North Side. This resulted in an all-out war and almost got Torrio killed. He returned to Brooklyn and left the business in Capone's hands.

Capone took over a crime empire worth more than $30 million and realized that his secret to success was to limit the mob's activities to the rackets in strongest demand by the public, namely liquor, gambling and prostitution. He gave the people what they wanted and he became a local celebrity. Capone also appeared to be socially responsible, opening up soup kitchens and helping out the poor. What most didn't know is that his generosity didn't cost anything. Local merchants and suppliers were leaned on to provide food for the kitchens and those who didn't keep up with quotas found their trucks wrecked and their tires slashed.

But not everyone loved Capone. There were a number of attempts on his life, like the time in

1926 when the Irish mob sent cars loaded with machine-gunners past his headquarters. They poured over 1,000 rounds into the building but Capone somehow escaped injury. Al Capone, it seemed, was invincible but doom was on the horizon following the horrific massacre on Clark Street.

George "Bugs" Moran was born in Minnesota in 1893 but moved to Chicago with his parents around the turn-of-the-century. Here, he joined up with one of the North Side Irish gangs and was befriended by young tough named Dion O'Bannion. The two began working together, robbing warehouses, but after one fouled-up job, Moran was captured. He kept his silence and served two years in Joliet prison without implicating O'Banion in the crime. He was released at age nineteen and went back to work with his friend. He was soon captured again and once more, kept silent about who he worked with. He stayed in jail this time until 1923.

When Moran, known as "Bugs" because of his quick temper, got out of prison, he joined up with O'Bannion's now formidable North Side mob. They had become a powerful organization, supplying liquor to Chicago's wealthy Gold Coast. Moran became a valuable asset, hijacking Capone's liquor trucks at will. He became known as O'Bannion's right hand man, always impeccably dressed, right down to the two guns that he always wore. When O'Bannion was killed in his flower shop in 1924, Moran swore revenge. The war that followed claimed many lives and almost got Moran killed in 1925 when he was wounded on Congress Street in an ambush.

By 1927, Moran stood alone against the Capone mob, most of his allies having succumbed in the fighting. He continued to taunt his powerful enemy, always looking for ways to destroy him. In early 1929, Moran sided with Joe Aiello in another war against Capone. He and Aiello reportedly gunned down Pasquillano Lolordo, one of Capone's men, and Capone vowed that he would have him wiped out on February 14.

A group of men had gathered at the Clark Street warehouse that morning, because of a tip from a Detroit gangster who told bootlegger Bugs Moran that a truck was on its way to Chicago. It was filled, he claimed, with illegal liquor.

One of the men was Johnny May, an ex-safecracker who had been hired by Moran as an auto mechanic. He was working on a truck that morning, with his dog tied to the bumper, while six other men waited for the truck of hijacked whiskey to arrive. The men were Frank and Pete Gusenberg, who were supposed to meet Moran and pick up two empty trucks to drive to Detroit and pick up smuggled Canadian whiskey; James Clark, Moran's brother-in-law; Adam Heyer; Al Weinshank; and Reinhardt Schwimmer, a young optometrist who had befriended Moran and hung around the liquor warehouse just for the thrill of rubbing shoulders with gangsters.

Bugs Moran was already late for the morning meeting. He was due to arrive at 10:30 but didn't even leave for the rendezvous, in the company of Willie Marks and Ted Newberry, until several minutes after that.

While the seven men waited inside of the warehouse, they had no idea that a police car had pulled up outside, or that Moran had stopped for coffee or had spotted the car and had quickly taken cover (whichever you would like to believe). Five men got out of the police car, three of them in uniforms and two in civilian clothing. They entered the building and a few moments later, the clatter of machine gun fire broke the stillness of the snowy morning. Soon after, five figures emerged and they drove away. May's dog, inside of the warehouse, was barking and howling and when neighbors went to check and see what was going on. They discovered a bloody murder scene and summoned the police.

Moran's men had been lined up against the rear wall of the garage and had been sprayed with machine-guns. They killed all seven of them but had missed Bugs Moran. Some accounts say that he had figured the arrival of the police car to be some sort of shakedown and had hung back. When the machine gunning started, he, Marks and Newberry had fled. The murders broke the power of the North Side gang and Moran correctly blamed Al Capone. There have been many claims as to who the actual shooters were, but one of them was probably "Machine Gun" Jack McGurn, one of Capone's most trusted men.

Surprisingly, while Moran quickly targeted Capone as ordering the hit, the authorities were baffled. Capone had been in Florida at the time of the massacre and when hearing the news, he stated, "the only man who kills like that is Bugs Moran". At the same time, Moran was proclaiming that "only Capone kills guys like that".

Moran was right.... Capone had been behind the killing and this was perhaps the act that finally began the decline of Capone's criminal empire. He had just gone too far and the authorities, and even Capone's adoring public, were ready to put an end to the bootleg wars.

But Capone had not seen the last of the men who were killed on that fateful day. While living at the Lexington Hotel, which has since been torn down, Capone claimed to be haunted by the ghost of James Clark, one of the massacre victims and the brother-in-law of Bugs Moran. Capone believed that the vengeful spirit hounded him from 1929 until the day that he died. There were many times when his men would hear from begging for the ghost to leave him in peace. On several occasions, bodyguards broke into his rooms, fearing that someone had gotten to their boss. Capone would then tell them of Clark's ghost. Did Capone imagine the whole thing, or was he already showing signs of the psychosis that would haunt him after his release from Alcatraz prison? Whether the ghost was real or not, Capone certainly believed that he was. The crime boss even went so far as to contact a psychic named Alice Britt to get rid of Clark's angry spirit. Years later, he would state that Clark followed him to the grave.

After the massacre, the authorities were under great pressure to bring an end to the bootleg wars in Chicago. Washington dispatched a group of treasury agents (Eliot Ness and his "Untouchables") to harass Capone and try to find a way to bring down his operation. In the end though, it would not be murder or illegal liquor that would get Capone, it would be income tax evasion. He was convicted and sentenced to eleven years in federal prison. In 1934, he was transferred to the brutal, "escape proof" prison known as Alcatraz.

The prison was a place of total punishment and few privileges. One of most terrible methods of punishment was the "hole", a dungeon where prisoners were housed naked on stone floors with no blankets, toilets and only bread and water for nourishment. The slightest infraction could earn a beating.

Capone spent three stretches in the "hole", twice for speaking and once for trying to bribe a guard. He returned from the "hole" just a little worse for wear each time. Eventually, it would break him.

Many of the prisoners at Alcatraz went insane from the harsh conditions and Capone was probably one of them. The beatings, attempts on his life and the prison routine took a terrible toll on Capone's mind. After he was nearly stabbed to death in the yard, he was excused from outdoor exercise and usually stayed inside and played a banjo that was given to him by his wife. He later joined the four-man prison band. After five years though, Capone's mind snapped. He would often refuse to leave his cell and would sometimes crouch down in the corner and talk to himself. Another inmate recalled that on some days Capone would simply make and re-make his bunk all day long. He spent the last portion of his stay in the prison hospital ward, being treated for an advanced case of syphilis. He left Alcatraz in 1939.

Jake "Greasy Thumb" Guzik, who ran the South Side mob in Capone's absence, was asked by a reporter if Capone would take control again when he was released. "Al, "Said Guzik, "is nuttier than a fruitcake."

The massacre also began the decline of Bugs Moran as well. With the remnants of his gang, he attempted to take back control of the Gold Coast, but Capone's men were too powerful. Although Moran did drift into oblivion after Capone was sent to prison, he did have one small piece of revenge for the events on Clark Street. According to reports, Bugs and two others caught up to "Machine Gun" Jack McGurn in a bowling alley on February 14, 1936. McGurn was machine-gunned to death with his sleeves rolled up and a bowling ball in his hand. A small paper valentine was found on his bloody corpse.

The once powerful gangster was reduced to petty burglaries by the end of World War II. He first moved to downstate Illinois and then Ohio before a failed robbery got him arrested by the FBI. He was sentenced to serve ten years in 1946 and his release found him quickly re-arrested for another robbery. This time, he was sent to Leavenworth, where he died from lung cancer in February 1957.

Chicago, in its own way, memorialized the warehouse on Clark Street where the massacre took place. It became a tourist attraction and the newspapers even printed the photos of the corpses upside-down so that readers would not have to turn their papers around to identify the bodies.

In 1949, the front portion of the S-M-C Garage was turned into an antique furniture storage business by a couple who had no idea of the building's bloody past. They soon found that the place was visited much more by tourists, curiosity-seekers and crime buffs than by customers and they eventually closed the business.

In 1967, the building was demolished. However, the bricks from the bullet-marked rear wall were purchased and saved by a Canadian businessman. In 1972, he opened a nightclub with a Roaring 20's theme and rebuilt the wall, for some strange reason, in the men's restroom. Three nights each week, women were allowed to peek inside at this macabre attraction.

The club continued to operate for a few years and when it closed the owner placed the 417 bricks into storage. He then offered them for sale with a written account of the massacre. He sold the bricks for $1000 each, but soon found that he was getting back as many as he sold. It seemed that anyone who bought one of the bricks was suddenly stricken with bad luck in the form of illness, financial ruin, divorce and even death. According to the stories, the bricks themselves had somehow been infested with the powerful negative energy of the massacre! Whatever became of the rest of the bricks from the building is unknown. Or that's what the legend says....

According to a Canadian man named Guy Whitford, things may not be just as the legend has them. In fact, he writes "you were correct when you wrote about the bricks being offered for sale in the 1970's, but the fact is, although he had many offers, George never sold a single brick." You see, Whitford claims to be a friend of the Canadian businessman, George Patey, who originally bought the back wall of the warehouse many years ago and later began trying to track down a buyer for the authenticated wall of 417 bullet-marked bricks. "He always had a problem with breaking up the wall," Whitford continued. "The last substantial offer for the entire wall was made by a Las Vegas casino about a decade ago, but George quaffed at the offer... so that "bad luck to those who bought one" concept must be a rumor or a journalistic embellishment".

The two men tried to sell the wall for some time. The original lot came with a diagram that explained how to restore the wall to its original form. The bricks were even numbered for reassembly. They remained on the market for nearly three decades, but there were no buyers. Eventually, he broke up the set and began selling them one brick at a time for $1,000 each. But were these all of the surviving bricks from the warehouse?

In recent years, other bricks have emerged that claim to have come from the wall and from the building itself. These were not bricks purchased from Patey but were smuggled out of the lot by construction workers and curiosity-seekers. It was said that from these bricks come the legends of misfortune and bad luck. Are these bricks authentic? The owners say they are, but you'll have to judge for yourself!

Whatever the legend of the bricks themselves and whether or not they have somehow been "haunted" by what happened, there is little doubt about the site on Clark Street itself. Even today, people walking along the street at night have reported the sounds of screams and machine guns as they pass the site. The building is long gone but the area is marked as a fenced-off lawn that belongs to the nearby nursing home. Five trees are scattered along the place in a line and the one in the middle marks the location where the rear wall once stood.

Passersby often report these strange sounds and the indescribable feeling of fear as they walk past. Those who are accompanied by dogs report their share of strangeness too. Animals appear to be especially bothered by this piece of lawn, sometimes barking and howling, sometimes whining in fear. Their sense of what happened here many years ago seems to be much greater than our own.

There is no question that the deeds of men like Al Capone and Bugs Moran have left an indelible mark on the city of Chicago. There also seems to be no doubt that an event on February 14, 1929 has left one too!

## DILLINGER... DEAD OR ALIVE?

Who is the Ghost that Haunts the Alley Next to the Biograph Theater?

On the evening of July 22, 1934 a dapper-looking man wearing a straw hat and a pin-striped suit stepped out of the Biograph Theater where he and two girlfriends had watched a film called "Manhattan Melodrama" starring Clark Gable. No sooner had they reached the sidewalk than a man appeared and identified himself as Melvin Purvis of the FBI. He ordered the man in the straw hat to surrender. Several shots rang out and the fleeing man in the straw hat fell dead to the pavement, his left eye shredded by one of the shots fired by the other agents who lay in wait.

And so ended the life of John Herbert Dillinger, the most prolific bank robber in modern American history and the general public's favorite Public Enemy No. 1...or did it?

One of the most famous haunted theaters in the history of Chicago is the Biograph Theater, located on North Lincoln Avenue. It was here, in 1934, that John Dillinger supposedly met his end. The theater has gained a reputation for being haunted, but the story of the ghost seen here actually revolves around the alleyway outside. But the theater, and the surrounding businesses, has banked on the criminal's name for many years. On the day after the fatal shots were fired, the bar next door placed a sign in the window that read "Dillinger had his last drink here". Theater patrons can examine a window in the box office that describes the set-up of Dillinger by the FBI. They can sit in the same seat where Dillinger sat nearly 65 years ago and after the film, they can emerge into "Dillinger's Alley. It is here where the ghost is said to appear.

But what really happened in the final moments of Dillinger's life? To answer the strange and perplexing questions surrounding his possible death, we have to first look at his bloody and violent life.

On the evening that he was killed, Dillinger left the theater in the company of Anna Sage (the famed "Lady in Red") and with another girlfriend, Polly Hamilton. He had been hiding out in her North Halstead Street apartment but for months he had been pursued diligently by Melvin Purvis, the head of the Chicago branch of the FBI. Purvis had lived and breathed Dillinger (and would, after the robber's death, commit suicide) and had narrowly missed him several times at a State Street and Austin Cafe, at Dillinger's north woods hideout in Sault St. Marie, and at Wisconsin's Little Bohemia, where FBI agents recklessly killed a civilian and injured two others. It was finally at the Biograph where Purvis caught up with Dillinger and put an end to his career.

The criminal life of John Dillinger started in 1925 when he held up a grocery store in his hometown of Mooresville, Indiana. Pleading guilty, he was sentenced to serve 10-20 years in prison while his accomplice, who claimed not guilty, only received a sentence of two years. Dillinger spent the next eight years in jail but when he was released in May of 1933, he robbed three banks in three months and netted more than $40,000. Thus began Dillinger's wild spree of crime.

Dillinger was captured in September 1933 and imprisoned in Lima, Ohio. In three weeks, his gang sprung him in a dangerous escape and again was back to bank robbing. In January 1934, Dillinger shot and killed a police officer in East Chicago, for which he was arrested in

Arizona and jailed in Crown Point, Indiana to await trial. He escaped a month later, using a fake gun that he had carved from a bar of soap (or a piece of wood) and blackened with shoe polish. He eluded the police for another month, shooting his way out of an ambush in St. Paul and dodging the FBI near Mercer, Wisconsin. Dillinger arrived in Chicago in late June and proceeded to rob a South Bend, Indiana bank and kill a police officer and four civilians. In just over a year, Dillinger has robbed six banks, killed two cops, two FBI agents, escaped from jail twice and had escaped from police and FBI traps six times.

In the process of all of this violence, Dillinger managed to become an American folk hero. It was the time of the Great Depression and here was a man striking back at poverty by taking from those who could afford losing their money the most. Stories began to circulate about Dillinger giving away much of his stolen money to the poor and the needy. Were these stories true? Who knows? But the American public believed it, which was more than the government could stand. Dillinger had to be taken, and soon.

He had become J. Edgar Hoover's "Public Enemy No. 1"... and the heat was on.

Dillinger knew that his luck could only hold out for so long and in May 1934, he contacted a washed-up doctor who had done time for drug charges named Loeser. He paid him $5000 to perform some plastic surgery on his recognizable face, getting rid of three moles and a scar and getting rid of the cleft of his chin and the bridge of his nose. The doctor agreed to the surgery and left Dillinger in the care of his assistant to administer the general anesthetic. An ether-soaked towel was placed over Dillinger's face and the assistant told him to breathe deeply. Suddenly, Dillinger's face turned blue and he swallowed his tongue and died! Dr. Loeser immediately revived the gangster and proceeded to do the surgery. Dillinger would have no idea how close he had come to death. Ironically, just 25 days later, he would catch a bullet in front of the Biograph Theater, or so they say.

When Dillinger walked into the theater that night he had been set up by Anna Sage, who had taken him there at the request of the FBI. She had promised to be wearing a red (actually bright orange) dress for identification purposes. Sixteen cops and FBI agents waited over two hours outside the theater, watching for the unknowing Dillinger to exit. They even walked the aisles of the theater several times to make sure that he was still there. How could the clever gangster have not noticed them?

Finally, Dillinger left the theater and was met by Melvin Purvis. He stepped down from the curb, just passing the alley entrance and tried to run. He reached for his own gun, but it was too late. Four shots were fired and three hit Dillinger. The gangster fell, dead when he hit the pavement.

Purvis ordered Dillinger rushed to nearby Alexian Brothers Hospital. He was turned away at the doors as he was already dead and Purvis and the police waited on the hospital lawn for the coroner to arrive. A mob scene greeted the coroner at the Cook County Morgue where curiosity-seekers filed in long lines past a glass window for a last look at Dillinger. Little did they know that the man they were looking at might not have been the famed gangster at all.

The scene at the Biograph Theater was also chaotic. Tradition tells that passers-by ran to the scene and dipped their handkerchiefs in the blood of the fallen man, hoping for a macabre souvenir of this terrible event.

And it is at this theater where the final moments of John Dillinger have left a lasting impression. It would be many years after before people passing by the Biograph on North Lincoln

Avenue would begin to spot a blue, hazy figure running down the alley next the theater, falling down and then vanishing. Along with the sighting of this strange apparition were reports of cold spots, icy chills, unexplainable cool breezes, and odd feelings of fear and uneasiness. Local business owners began to notice that people had stopped using the alley as a shortcut to Halstead Street.

The place certainly seemed haunted. But is the ghost of the man who has been seen here really that of John Dillinger?

Ever since the night of the shoot-out at the Biograph, eyewitness accounts and the official autopsy have given support to the theory that the dead man may not have been Dillinger. Rumors have persisted that the man killed by the FBI was actually a small-time hood from Wisconsin who had been set up by Dillinger's girlfriend and Anna Sage to take the hit.

There are many striking errors in the autopsy report. The dead man had brown eyes while Dillinger's were blue. The corpse had a rheumatic heart condition since childhood while Dillinger's naval service records said that his heart was in perfect condition. It's also been said that the man who was killed was much shorter and heavier than Dillinger and had none of his

distinguishing marks. Police agencies claimed that Dillinger had plastic surgery to get rid of his scars and moles, but also missing were at least two scars on Dillinger's body!

And there is more conflicting evidence to say that the FBI killed the wrong man. On the night of the shooting, a local man named Jimmy Lawrence disappeared. Lawrence was a small-time criminal who had recently moved from Wisconsin. He lived in the neighborhood and often came to the Biograph Theater. He also bore an uncanny resemblance to John Dillinger!

In addition, a photograph taken from the purse of Dillinger's girlfriend shows her in the company of a man who looks like the man killed at the Biograph It's a photo that was taken before Dillinger ever had plastic surgery! Could Dillinger's girlfriend have made a date with Jimmy Lawrence to go to the Biograph, knowing (thanks to Anna Sage) that the FBI was waiting for him there?

Some writers have suggested this is exactly what happened. Respected crime writer, Jay Robert Nash, an expert on Dillinger, reported in his book THE DILLINGER DOSSIER that Dillinger's girlfriend and Anna Sage rigged the whole affair. According to Nash, Sage was a prostitute from England who was in danger of being deported. To prevent this, she went to the police and told them that she knew Dillinger. In exchange for not being deported, she would arrange to have Dillinger at the Biograph, where they could nab him. She agreed to wear a bright, red dress so she would be easily recognized. While FBI agents waited, "Dillinger" and his girlfriends watched the movie and enjoyed popcorn and soda. When the film ended, the FBI agents made their move. Nash believes however, that they shot Jimmy Lawrence instead of Dillinger. He also believes that when they learned of their mistake, the FBI covered it up, either because they feared the wrath of J. Edgar Hoover, who told them to "get Dillinger or else", or because Hoover himself was too embarrassed to admit the mistake.

So, what happened to the real John Dillinger? Nobody knows for sure, but some claim this American Robin Hood, who supposedly only robbed from banks and gave some of his spoils to the poor, married and moved to Oregon. He disappeared in the late 1940's and was never heard from again.

- CHAPTER FIVE -

# NO ESCAPE... EVEN AFTER DEATH

## HISTORY & HAUNTINGS OF AMERICA'S PRISONS & JAILS

*All but the smallest jails are bedlam. They are permeated with catcalls, mumbling, laughter, crying, swearing and any other noises that humans can make. Only during the wee hours of the morning is there any semblance of tranquility.... Sometimes, when a jail is abandoned or converted to another use, the noises continue...*

**RICHARD WINER** *in* **MORE HAUNTED HOUSES**

When compiling a list of places in America where ghosts are most frequently found, prisons and jails fall quite high on the list. The amount of trauma, pain and terror experienced by men who are incarcerated often leaves a lasting impression behind. The horrible events that occur in some of these places can also perhaps cause the spirits of the men who lived and died here to linger behind. Jails and prisons can be terrifying places... in this world and the next!

One of the first institutions brought to the New World by the early settlers was the jail, a place where lawbreakers could be held while they awaited trial and subsequent punishment. There were more than 150 offenses in those days for which the punishment was death and for the rest, there was whipping, branding, beatings or public humiliation. There was little tolerance for the criminal, even in a place founded in freedom and settled by many who had left their native countries one step ahead of the law.

At that time, the jail was not a place where criminals were kept for punishment. In fact, the idea of a prison was a purely American institution that would have a profound effect on both this country and around the world.

The first state prison was the notorious Newgate, established in Connecticut in 1773. It was actually an abandoned copper mine where prisoners were chained together and forced into hard labor about 50 feet underground. Many of the first prisoners were British sympathizers during the American Revolution. In 1776, prisoners rioted after a man who attempted to escape set fire to a wooden door leading to the outside. Smoke filled the mine, choking a number of the prisoners to death and quelling any rebellion in the rest.

Newgate became the first "hell hole" of American prisons, but it would not be the last. Almost immediately, social reformers appeared, but it has been questioned whether or not their efforts to achieve humane treatment helped or harmed the prisoners. The first reform was attempted in 1790 at Philadelphia's Walnut Street Jail. It was renovated by the Quakers for the jail was described as being a scene of "universal riot and debauchery.. with no separation of those accused but yet untried... from convicts sentenced for the foulest crimes."

The jail was remodeled in 1790 and for the first time, men and women were housed separately in large, clean rooms. Debtors were placed in another part of the jail from those being held for serious offenses and children were removed from the jail entirely. Hardened offenders were placed in solitary confinement in a "penitentiary house" and prisoners were given work and religious instruction. Within a short time though, the Walnut Street jail became overcrowded and a new institution had to be constructed.

Around this same time, two new prisons were built and would soon become models for the rest of the nation. Eastern Penitentiary was built in Philadelphia in 1829 to further the Quaker's idea of prisoner isolation as a form of punishment. Prisoners were confined in windowless rooms with running water and toilets. Each prisoner also had his own exercise yard, about 8 x 20 feet, surrounded by a high brick wall. The walls between the cells were thick and soundproof, so no prisoner ever saw another. They would come into contact with no living persons, save for an occasional guard or a minister who would come to pray with them and offer spiritual advice. This extreme isolation caused many of the prisoners to go insane and it comes as no surprise that the prison is believed to be haunted today.

Also in 1829, a rival system, which gained wider acceptance, was started with the building of a prison in Auburn, New York. The designers believed that the Pennsylvania system would fail because the prisoners spent too much time praying and being in isolation and could not "pay for their keep" through convict labor. At Auburn, the prisoners worked together all day fulfilling labor contracts and then were isolated at night, as they were at the Eastern Penitentiary.

Even though they worked together, inmates were forbidden to talk to one another and were forced to march from place to place in the prison with their eyes always directed downward. The warden of the prison was Elam Lynds, who believed the purpose of the system was to break the spirit of the prisoners. He personally whipped the men and urged the guards to treat the prisoners with brutality and contempt. One standard punishment was the "water cure", which consisted of fastening a prisoner's neck with an iron yoke and then pouring an ice-cold stream of water onto his head. At other times, the man would be chained to a wall and then the water would be turned on him through a high-pressure hose. While the pain was unbearable, it left no marks.

The Auburn system began to be adopted throughout America because it was much cheaper to operate than the Pennsylvania system. The cells were much smaller and money was to be made from the inmate labor. And as the system spread, the treatment of the prisoner became even more imaginative. The striped uniform was first introduced at Sing Sing and floggings, the sweatbox, the straitjackets, the iron yoke, the thumb screws and the stretcher became widely used.

The "stretcher" had a number of variations. A man might be handcuffed to the top of the bars of his cell so that his feet barely touched the floor, then left that way all day... or his feet might be chained the floor and his wrists tied to a pulley on the ceiling. When the rope was pulled, the prisoner was stretched taut.

"Sweatboxes" were metal chambers that were so small that the prisoner literally had to crawl inside. They might be left in such confinement all day and in some cases, the boxes were moved close to a furnace so that the heat inside of them would be intensified.

The Auburn system was based on cruelty and repression, with the idea that such treatment would reform prisoners and make them change their ways. Instead, it was a failure and led to riots, death and the closure of many of the institutions. Unfortunately, many of the practices have been adopted (in some degree) by modern prisons.

After the Civil War, new ideas began to be experimented with. In 1870, men like Enoch Cobbs Wines, and others who formed the American Prison Association, started the reformatory system. The Elmira Reformatory, the first of the new type, opened in New York in 1876. Although the reformatory plan was originally intended for all ages, prisoners at Elmira were limited to between the ages of 16 and 30. The principle of the plan was reformation, rather than punishment and was hailed as a great advance in humane treatment of prisoners.

When a prisoner entered Elmira, he was automatically placed in the second of three grades. When he showed improvement, he was moved to the first grade and upon continued effort was eventually paroled. If he turned out to be a troublemaker, he was sent down to the third grade and had to work his way back up. Many of the prisoners were even sentenced to indeterminate terms so that they could be reformed.

By 1900, 11 states had adopted the reformatory system but by 1910, the plan was considered dead. Most guards and wardens were incapable of administering the grading program and fell back on favoritism rather than reformation. Because of this, many of the men who were paroled, and were allegedly "reformed", went right back out and committed new crimes. Today, many prisons are still called by the name of "reformatory" but are merely a part of the general prison system.

Despite some of the claims, there has been little advance in prisons since the introduction of the system in 1829, although thanks to reform wardens like Thomas Mott Osborne and Lewis E. Lawes, much of the outright cruelty and squalor of the earlier prisons has been considerably reduced. Still, many of the extreme punitive concepts have persisted, as evidenced by the 1930's "super prison" of Alcatraz.

The prison, called by some the "American Devil's Island", was the worst of the federal prisons and was said to be escape proof. According to some estimates, almost 60 percent of the inmates went stir crazy there. Alcatraz left an extreme mark on the prisoners and on the guards and staff members as well. It soon lost its original purpose of confinement for escape artists and troublemakers and became a place to put inmates who it was deemed deserved harsher treatment, like Al Capone. By 1963, Alcatraz was shut down, having proven to be a failure.

And some would consider the entire American prison system a failure as well. Many critics have charged that the prisons have failed to reform criminals or even to act as a deterrent to crime. Eventually, prisoners are simply released, mostly due to a lack of space, and they go right back out and commit new crimes. Many of the prisons themselves have returned to the status of "hell holes" as well. The brutal conditions often lead to permanent injury, insanity, trauma and death.

Is it any wonder that prisons and jails have become known as such haunted places?

## SOLITARY CONFINEMENT
*Do Ghosts of the Past Linger at Philadelphia's Eastern State Penitentiary?*

After the changes at the Walnut Street Jail in 1790, the Quakers of Philadelphia began to search for a new method of incarceration for criminals in which "penitence" would become essential in the punishment of the lawbreaker. (Thus, we have the word "penitentiary"). The Quaker's concept of such incarceration would involve solitary confinement, a method already popular in Europe with members of monastic orders.

It was believed that if monks could achieve peace through solitary confinement and silence, then criminals could eventually be reformed using the same methods.

After years of overcrowding at the Walnut Street jail, a new prison was proposed within the city limits of Philadelphia. It would be designed to hold 250 prisoners in total solitary confinement and would open in 1829. An architect named John Haviland was hired and he set to work creating an institution in the popular "hub and spoke" design. It had been used in prisons throughout Europe and was highly effective, allowing for a constant surveillance of the prison from a central rotunda. The original design called for seven cell blocks to radiate outward from the center house and guard post.

Prisoners were confined in windowless rooms that were small, but were equipped with both running water and toilets. This was an amazing innovation for the time period as very few public or private buildings were equipped with indoor facilities. Of course, the reason for this was not for the comfort of the prisoner but to keep him out of contact with other people. The walls were thick and soundproof, so prisoners never saw each other. Each prisoner was also given his own exercise yard, surrounded by a brick wall, furthering the sense of extreme isolation. They would see no other inmate from the time they entered the prison until the time they were released.

Construction began on the prison in May 1822. The site selected for it was an elevated area that had once been a cherry orchard. Because of this, the prison later acquired the nickname of Cherry Hill. As construction began, changes forced John Haviland to create new designs so that the prison could hold an addition 200 prisoners. At that time, the prison was the most expensive single structure ever built but Haviland's design would become so popular that it would be copied for nearly 300 institutions around the world.

Although the prison would not be completed until 1836, it began accepting prisoners in 1829. The first inmate was Charles Williams, who was sentenced to two years for burglary. Like all of the other prisoners who would be incarcerated here, Williams was stripped of his clothing, measured, weighed and given a physical examination. He was also given a number and was not referred to by his name until the day that he was released. A record was made of his height, weight, age, place of birth, age, complexion, color of hair and eyes, length of feet and if he was able to write, the prisoner placed his name on the record.

After the prisoner was examined, he was given a pair of wool trousers, a jacket with a number sewn on it, two handkerchiefs, two pairs of socks and a pair of shoes. Then, a mask that resembled a burlap bag was placed over his head so that he would not be able to see the prison as he was taken to his cells. It was believed that if an inmate were unable to see which direction to go if he slipped out of his cell, it would be harder for him to escape. The masks were eventually discontinued in 1903.

After that, he was taken to his cell. As he entered it, he would be forced to stoop down (as a penitent would) because the doorways were shortened to remind the prisoners of humility. Above him would be the only lighting in the cell, a narrow window in the ceiling that was called the "Eye of God".

Silence had to be maintained at Eastern State at all times. The guards even wore socks over their shoes while they made their rounds. By doing this, they moved in secret around the prison and while the inmates could not hear them, the officers could hear any sounds coming from inside of the cells. The prisoners were not allowed any sort of books or reading material and could not communicate with anyone in any way. If they were caught whistling, singing or talking (even to themselves), they were deprived of dinner or were taken to one of the punishment cells. Any prisoners who repeatedly broke the rules were taken to a punishment cell and were restricted to a half-ration of bread and water.

Even though communication was forbidden, most of the prisoners attempted it anyway. The easiest way to do this was to attach a note to a small rock and toss it over the wall into the next exercise yard. It was probably the quietest form of communication and the most popular. Other forms of contact ranged from coded tapping on the walls to whistling softly and even muffled speech. Since there were vents for heat in every cell, a limited amount of contact could be made through the ducts. They could also tap on the vents and be heard by several prisoners at once. However, if they were caught, they knew with certainty that they would be punished.

At first, punishment at Eastern State was mild compared to other institutions. Most prisons used the lash, a leather strap that was administered to the back, but officials at Eastern State believed that solitary confinement was punishment enough. However, as the prisoners began to repeatedly break the rules, the punishments became more intense. The most common forms of punishment became the straitjacket, the iron gag and the mad chair.

The straitjacket was commonly used by mental institutions to restrain crazed patients and to keep them from hurting themselves or others. At Eastern State, the jacket was used in a different way. Inmates would be bound into the jacket and soon their face, hands and neck would become numb. Eventually, they would turn black from a lack of blood flow and the inmate would usually pass out. The use of the straitjacket was finally discontinued around 1850.

The mad chair was another form of punishment, or restraint, adapted from mental asylums. Here, the prisoner would be tied to the chair by chains and leather straps and held so firmly that he was unable to move at all. After long periods of time, his limbs would become very painful and swollen. Prisoners who spent any length of time in the chair would find themselves unable to walk for hours (or even days) afterward.

The iron gag was the most commonly used punishment. It was a device that was placed over the prisoner's tongue while his hands were crossed and tied behind his neck. His arms were then pulled taut and the hands secured just behind the man's neck. The gag was then attached to his tongue and his hands and locked in place. Any movement of the hands would tear at the gag and cause intense pain. The inmate's mouth would be bloody and sore by the time he was released from their bonds.

While punishments and seclusion were undoubtedly hard on the health of the prisoners, the diseases within the prison were even worse. During the first few years of the prison, poor planning caused the odor of human waste to constantly invade every part of the building. This was caused by the design of the vents and by the plumbing and heating methods that were used. Water was supplied to every cell for the toilets and for the running water. Since the prisoners were only permitted to bathe every three weeks, they were forced to wash themselves in the basins inside of their cells. To heat the water and the rest of the prison, coal stoves were placed in tunnels underneath the floors. Since the sewer pipes from the toilets ran alongside the pipes for the fresh water, the coal stoves also heated the waste pipes. Because of this, the prison always smelled like human waste. The problem was finally corrected in later years because of the frequency of illnesses among the prisoners and the guards.

But most damaged of all was the mental health of the inmates. The inmates at Eastern State often went insane because of the isolated conditions and so many cases were reported that eventually the prison doctors began to invent other reasons for the outbreaks of mental illness. It was believed at that time that excessive masturbation could cause insanity. Because of this, the doctor's log book of the period listed many cases of insanity, always with masturbation as the cause. It was also noted that many of the men went insane because of their genes and these two diagnoses remained popular throughout the 1800's. It was never documented that the total isolation caused any of the men's breakdowns.

Without question though, being imprisoned at Eastern was mind-numbing. The prisoner was required to remain in his cell all day and all night in solitary confinement, thinking of nothing but their crimes. The system was brutal on the inmates but hard for the warden and guards as well. The first warden at Eastern was Samuel Wood and it was up to him to insure that the punishment of total solitary confinement was carried out. He and his family were required to reside on the premises of the prison and were not allowed to leave for periods of more than 18 hours without permission from the prison commission.

One of the biggest problems in the early days at Eastern was keeping the guards sober. It was so boring making the rounds and maintaining total silence that the guards often drank to combat the monotony. At one point, the guards were even given a ration of alcohol during the workday so that they would not drink too much. However, few of them remained sober so the prison commission eventually passed a rule that threatened anyone found drunk on the job with immediate termination.

Eventually, Eastern State Penitentiary became the most famous prison in America and tourists came from all over the country to see it. Some sightseers traveled from even further abroad. Perhaps the most famous Eastern tourist was the author Charles Dickens. He came to the prison during his five-month tour of America in 1842 and named it as one of his essential destinations, right after Niagara Falls. Although he came to the prison with the best of intentions, he really did not believe the officials knew what damage the isolation was doing to the minds of the prisoners. He later wrote about his trip to the prison in 1845 and stated that "the system here is rigid, strict, and hopeless solitary confinement... I believe it, in its effects, to be cruel and wrong." He went on to write about the inhumane treatment of the inmates and after speaking to many of them, came to believe that the solitary conditions were a "torturing of the mind that is much worse that any physical punishment that can be administered."

Is it any wonder that insanity and escapes continued to be a problem throughout the 1800's?

Although it wasn't easy for a prisoner to escape, there were many that tried. The only way to get out was to scale the wall of the exercise yard and then make to the high wall or the front gate. This had to be done without attracting the attention of the guards.

The first escape came in 1832. Prisoner number 94, a prison baker named William Hamilton, was serving dinner in the warden's apartment. The warden stepped out of the room for a moment and Hamilton managed to tie several sheets together and lower himself out the window. He was not caught until 1837 and when he was, he was returned to his old cell.

There were other escapes as well, but the most memorable came in 1926. Eight prisoners took turns tunneling under cells 24 and 25. They went down about eight feet and then started digging toward the outer wall. The tunnel had been extended nearly 35 feet before they were caught. A similar tunnel actually succeeded in making it out of the prison in April 1945. A group of prisoners, using wood from the prison shop for reinforcement, managed to dig a shaft under the prison and beyond the wall. After it was completed, the men went out at slightly different times to avoid being noticed. By the time they all reached the tunnel's exit, the guards had realized they were missing and the last two were caught climbing out of the tunnel. The others were apprehended a few blocks away.

The method of total solitary confinement was finally abandoned in the 1870's. It was largely considered a failure in that it was too expensive to manage and had showed little in the way of results. It was decided that Eastern State would become a regular prison. From this point on, being sent to solitary confinement was a punishment and no longer the accepted norm at the prison.

The prisoners were no longer confined to their cells only and a dining hall and athletic field were built. Since the prisoners no longer needed the individual exercise yards, the areas were converted into cells to help with the overcrowding that was starting to affect the prison. Between 1900 and 1908, many of the original cells were also renovated and what had once been a small chamber for one man, became close quarters for as many as five. Along with these changes came new cell blocks, a wood shop, a new boiler room and other buildings where the prisoners could labor. There were also art and educational programs added as the prison system began to try and rehabilitate the inmates rather than merely punish them. The work done by the inmates also helped both the prisoners and the prison itself. No work was contracted out and the goods that were made in the shops were sold and the proceeds helped to pay for the prison's expenses for many years.

Eastern State underwent sweeping reforms in 1913 after the structure overflowed with a population of 1,700. But despite the renovations that followed, talk began to circulate in the 1960's about closing the place down. By this time, it was in terrible shape and the only way to keep it in operation was to renovate it again. The buildings were still overcrowded and walls had crumbled in some locations and in others, ceilings were starting to collapse. The cost of repairing the prison was nearly as high as building a new one.

By 1970, Pennsylvania Governor Shafer announced that four new prisons would be built to replace Eastern State. Most of the men from Eastern State would be transferred to Graterford Prison, which would be located about 25 miles from Philadelphia. Construction began immediately on this institution to help relieve the overcrowding and the concern about the conditions at the old prison.

As Graterford was completed in 1971, prisoners began to be sent there. On April 14, 1971, Eastern State was completely empty. The last of the men were transferred out and the prison was shut down until a short time later, when it became the Center City Detention Center.

Prison riots at the New Jersey State Prison at Trenton later that year forced Eastern State to open its doors once again. Because of the overcrowding and the riots at the New Jersey prison, a number of the inmates had to be relocated. Eastern State was the closest available facility and they were temporarily moved here. The place operated with a skeleton crew for eight months and then was shut down again.

Once more, the prison stood empty and silent.

In the middle 1970's, the empty prison was designated as a National Historic Landmark and was eventually purchased by the city of Philadelphia to be used as a tourist attraction. The Pennsylvania Prison Society of Philadelphia was placed in charge of operating and promoting it as a historic site and they continue to conduct tours of the penitentiary today.

And from these tours and forays into the prison, come the tales of ghosts and hauntings. Without question, the prison was designed to be a frightening place and in recent times, it has become even more so. The prison still stands as a ruin of crumbling cellblocks, empty guard towers, rusting doors and vaulted, water-stained ceilings. It is a veritable fortress and an imtimdating place for even the most hardened visitors. But does the spooky atmosphere of the place explain the ghostly tales as merely tricks of the imagination? Those who have experienced the spirits of Eastern State say that it does not!

"The idea of staying in this penitentiary alone is just overwhelming... I would not stay here overnight," stated Greta Galuszka, a program coordinator for the prison.

Over the years, volunteers and visitors alike have had some pretty strange experiences in the prison. In Cell Block 12, several independent witnesses have reported the hollow and distant sound of laughter echoing in certain cells. No source can ever be discovered for the noises.

Others have reported the presence of shadowy apparitions in the cells and the hallways, as though prisoners from the past can find no escape from this inhuman place. Several volunteers believe that they have seen these ghostly figures in the "six block", while others have seen them darting across corridors and vanishing into rooms.

A locksmith named Gary Johnson was performing some routine restoration work one day when he had his own odd encounter. "I had this feeling that I was being watched," he recalled, "but I turned and I'm looking down the block and there's nobody there. A couple of seconds later and I get the same feeling... I'm really being watched! I turn around and I look down the block and shoooom.... this black shadow just leaped across the block!" Johnson still refers to the prison as a "giant haunted house."

Angel Riugra, who has also worked in the prison, agrees. "You feel kinda jittery walking around because you feel something there, but when you turn around, you don't see anything," he said. "It's kinda weird, it's spooky!"

But it's the history and the hauntings of the place that continue to bring people back. Many of the staff members, while unsettled by the strange events that sometimes occur are fiercely protective of the place and are determined to see that it is around for many years to come. Even so, they can't help but feel that forces are at work inside of the prison.

"So much did happen here," Greta Galuszka added, "that there's the potential for a lot of unfinished business to be hanging around. And I think that's my fear... to stumble upon some of that unfinished business."

## WHERE THE DEAD STILL LINGER
### History & Hauntings of the Ohio Penitentiary

The Ohio Penitentiary opened in late October 1834 when 189 prisoners were marched under guard from a small frontier jail to the partially completed building. As they walked along the banks of the Scioto River, they must have been amazed and dismayed by the stone walls of their new place of incarceration, as many other men would be in the years to come. Hundreds of thousands of men were sent to this prison over the next 150 years and thousands of them died, usually violently, behind the high walls.

The prison was first condemned by reformers in the early 1900's but was not closed down until 1979. For years afterward, the prison stood empty and decaying, awaiting the wrecking ball to make room for the sports complex that now stands on the site.

If prisons are truly haunted because of the death and tragedy that takes place in them, then the Ohio Penitentiary, once located on Spring Street in Columbus, must have been one of the most haunted buildings in the region! Even though the prison itself is no more, this has not stopped the stories of murder, brutality and of course, ghosts, from being told.

The prison may be gone, but some say the spirits of the past still linger!

The penitentiary that was located on Spring Street was actually the third state prison in Ohio and the fourth jail in early Columbus. The first jail in the city had been built in 1804 and was a two-story log stockade that was surrounded by 13 whipping posts.

Author Dan Morgan noted that "horrible stories were told about this primitive prison" and said that men, women and children were all brought there. They were stripped of their clothing and then tied to the posts. This was followed by whippings that left their backs resembling "raw beef". Further torture was inflicted with hot ashes and coals that were spread onto their bleeding flesh. It was obviously a horrifying place.

The first state prison was built between 1813-1815 along Scioto Street, which later became 2nd Street. It was a simple structure that housed prisoners in 13 cells on the third floor. The prison was full within a year so the General Assembly commissioned a larger structure, designed for 100 prisoners, that was completed in 1818. This building provided unheated cells, straw mats on the floor, infestations of lice and rats and several cholera epidemics. It also had several subterranean places of punishment, called "holes", where conditions were even worse. It was officially named the "Ohio Penitentiary" in 1822.

The prison remained in use until the new building was constructed on Spring Street, however an odd occurrence took place there in 1930. At that time, a fire of "incendiary origin" destroyed most of the prison workshops. Strangely, a century later in 1930, another fire of "incendiary origin" destroyed an entire cellblock and claimed 322 lives at the new penitentiary. It is still considered the worst fire in the history of American prisons.

As mentioned previously, penitentiaries were for penance in those days and those institutions under the Auburn system had prisoners who "labored in silence during the day and were locked in solitary confinement at night." The men were used in factory shops, located behind the walls, to make leather harnesses, shoes, tailored goods, barrels, brooms, hats and other common goods that were not manufactured by legitimate business in Ohio.

The paltry food the prisoners ate usually consisted of cornbread, bacon and beans and was served on "rust-eaten tin plates" and eaten with crude implements fashioned from broom handles. They slept on hay sacks and although fold-down beds were installed around the time of the Civil War, blankets were only issued in the wintertime. The clothing and the bedding were major carriers of filth and disease as laundry facilities were non-existent in the early days. There was also no medical treatment to speak of and epidemics, dysentery and diarrhea killed many. In 1849, a cholera outbreak killed 116 of 423 prisoners. The guards fled the grounds and the prisoners begged for pardons.

The prisoners were routinely punished for both major and minor infractions. Whipping remained the major form of discipline until 1844, but were replaced by no less cruel methods of causing pain. These included dunking inmates in huge vats of water, hanging them by their wrists in their cells and of course, the always delightful "sweatbox". In 1885, the prison would begin carrying out executions as well.

The "golden age" of the prison came during the tenure of Warden E. G. Coffin, from 1886 through 1900. A number of flattering books were written about the institution during this era and visitors who came to tour the place could even buy picture postcards and souvenir books. "It is to Mr. Coffin's revolutionary methods of inaugurating, perfecting and successfully establishing humane for repressive methods in the management of the prison that the Ohio Penitentiary owes it world-wide celebrity," said the souvenir book.

On Christmas Day 1888, Columbus newspapers reported that Warden Coffin had decided to do away with such punishments as the dunking tub and the stretching rings. "A hard box to sleep on and bread and water to eat will cause them to behave themselves," said Coffin. "It may not be so speedy but it is more humane."

Despite the fact that things at the Ohio Penitentiary seemed to be changed from the outside, the prisoners had a different story to tell. In 1894, a newspaper reporter learned that prisoners were still being locked in sweatboxes as punishment and that the ball and chain were also in use. The newspaper denounced the state of Ohio for "a partial return to the dark ages when the stocks and pillory were used for punishment." In addition, the prisoners were still being given bad food and medical care was still very poor. They also complained of pay-offs and political graft that resulted in some prisoners being blindfolded and tortured with water hoses, while well-connected inmates were given large cells and special privileges.

It was also during this era when the Death House was brought within the walls.

Prior to that, the gallows had been set up on a place called Penitentiary Hill, located in a ravine near the present-day intersection of Mound and 2nd Streets in Columbus. The first execution in the county had been carried out in 1844, when a convict was hanged for murder.

Author Daniel Morgan stated that the day of the hanging was "truly the greatest event in the history of Columbus" and was remembered as a day of "noise, confusion, drunkenness and disorder" during which one bystander, Sullivan Sweet, was reportedly trampled by a horse. And the unruly behavior of the day did not end there.

Two sets of physicians were anxious to obtain the remains of the hanged man. According to Morgan "one set repaired to the grave and after exhuming the body were fired upon by the others. They ran off leaving the body to be taken possession of by the opposing party without the labor of throwing out the dirt." The dead man's foot was, for many years, preserved in alcohol and kept on display by Dr. Jones and Dr. Little, who then had an office on East Town Street.

Then, in 1885, the gallows were moved behind the walls of the Ohio Penitentiary. Starting with Valentine Wagner in 1885, 28 men, including a 16-year-old named Otto Lueth, were hanged at the end of the prison's East Hall. The electric chair (considered a humane form of execution) replaced the gallows in the hall in 1897 and 315 men and women were put to death in it.

This aspect of prison life became hated and feared by guards and prisoners alike. "I tried to block my mind of all of them," Corrections Major Grover Powell, who spent 31 years at the Ohio Penitentiary, told reporter David Lore in 1984. "Nobody ever really wanted to work the executions, nobody ever volunteered." Death House duties, such as staying with the prisoner during the last meal, fastening the straps or flipping the switch, were rotated. The warden would get $75 overtime pay to split among the attending officers, but "some of the brass would say, 'I don't want it - throw it in the river or something,'" Powell recalled.

But nothing in the history of the prison, even the macabre execution devices, matched the carnage and horror of April 21, 1930.

The fire began as a candle flame in a bundle of oily rags on the roof of the West Block of the prison, paralleling Neil Avenue. Authorities later reported that three prisoners had set the blaze to start around 4:30 p.m. as a diversionary incident when prisoners were still in the dining hall. It smoldered too long though and didn't erupt for an hour after that, just after the hundreds of prisoners had been returned to the cell block.

Most of the 322 inmates who died that evening perished because of the poisonous smoke given off by green lumber being used in some construction scaffolding on one part of the cellblock, but others suffered a more gruesome fate. Photographs of the debris from the fire showed evidence of incredible heat, which turned the levels of catwalks and bars into a tangle of blackened and twisted metal. Many of the prisoners were literally cooked alive!

It was the worst fire in Ohio history and the worst in the history of American prisons. The cellblock had been dangerous and overcrowded, critics said, citing concerns about too many men in the prison that dated back to 1908. At that time, over 4,500 men had been jammed into the century-old prison (with room for 1,500) and this had created the volatile conditions that had ended in the fire. The attention on the prison led to a repeal of judicial control over minimum sentences, which was thought to have contributed to the overcrowding. A package of new laws in 1931 established the Ohio Parole Board and established parole procedures, which by 1932, had released 2,346 prisoners from the Ohio Penitentiary alone.

Officially, the fire was blamed on three inmates, two of whom committed suicide in the months following the tragedy. This was the official word anyway, although many suggested that the fire had been accidental and that prison officials had blamed the disaster on the prisoners to cover up their own incompetence in the mess.

Only a handful of people named a more sinister source for the fire, noting with interest that the doomed West Cellblock, which had been added to the original prison in 1875, had been built directly on top of the old prison cemetery. The bodies, the legends say, were never removed! Were some of the former prisoners having their revenge against the prison from the other side?

The 1930's saw more problems at the Ohio Penitentiary. On September 22, 1934, two members of John Dillinger's gang of bank robbers, Charles Makley and Harry Pierpont made a daring escape attempt from the prison. As Dillinger had done at the Crown Point, Indiana jail, the men tried to bluff their way of the cellblock with fake pistols. They made it less than 100 feet from their cells before they were met with gunfire and ripped to shreds. Both men fell bleeding to the floor. Makley was killed instantly but Pierpont survived and was taken back into custody.

Pierpont had been brought to the penitentiary under National Guard escort for his part in the murder of Sheriff Jess Sarber. The killing occurred during Dillinger's 1933 escape from the Allen County Jail. On October 17, sufficiently recovered from his wounds, Pierpont was executed in the electric chair.

Pierpont was just one of the many gangsters and bank robbers who ended up at the Ohio Penitentiary during the 1930's and 1940's. The best known of them was George "Bugs" Moran, Al Capone's lucky rival who arrived too late to be killed at the St. Valentine's Day Massacre. Moran came to the Ohio prison in the 1940's to serve out a sentence for bank burglary.

This era began to see an increase in problems at the prison. Many believe that the growth of the "rackets" and the general disrespect for the law in the 1920's and 1930's resulted in an upsurge of prison terms that had the available prisons filled to overflowing. The one-man cells at the prison were converted to handle three or more inmates and the average daily count swelled to 4,100 inmates by the end of the decade. In 1939, Warden William Amrine once again recommended the construction of a new prison, stating that "conditions at the Ohio Penitentiary are a disgrace to the state of Ohio." His request was turned down, but World War II marked the beginning of a new era for the prison.

The 1930's had been a horrendous time at the prison but changes came about because the inmates were now desperately needed to produce good for the war effort. Warden Ralph "Red" Alvis is credited for the major changes in the prison, eliminating the lock step marching, the strict requirements of silence and old striped prison uniforms. And while many of the restrictions were lifted and the men were kept productive during the war, the food became worse. Wartime restrictions and rationing were hard on the ordinary public, but even worse on the prisoners.

"They would give us butter beans with a piece of fat sowbelly in there with hair on it, big hairs up to an inch long," says Gentry Richardson, a prisoner who began serving time here in 1942. Bad food, in fact, was a reason for the 1952 Ohio Penitentiary riot, the first of three to rock the institution over the next two decades. It would not be until after this incident that the rations would start to improve.

Warden Alvis began to implement recreation programs for the prisoners and began to assume a more humane posture toward the prisoners. His goal was to improve prisoner morale and to encourage a sense of dignity in the men. He believed this was the best way to rehabilitate the inmates and hopefully to release changed men back onto the streets.

Holiday boxing and wrestling matches came about as early as 1940 and a bandstand was built on the O. Henry Athletic Field, the home of the inmate's baseball team, the "Hurricanes". For years after, the Ohio Penitentiary drew celebrities, athletes and performers that the city of Columbus couldn't match, like fighters Joe Lewis and Jack Dempsey and entertainers such as Lionel Hampton. Ohio State University students performed classical music and opera behind the walls and pilots from the Lockbourne Air Force base led literary discussions. Legendary coach Woody Hayes even once offered to help start an inmate football team. The high point of each year was always the inmate Christmas show, which was performed by the prisoners and always played to a full house. A few outsiders were allowed in for each show and the tickets were always in high demand.

Despite all of this, the conditions of the prison building continued to deteriorate and overcrowding became more of an issue, especially as the prison population reached a record high of 5,235 in April 1955. Classrooms and visiting areas had to be used as dormitories and many of the programs fell apart.

With more men came more danger. "I saw a lot of men die behind the walls," one former prisoner stated. "How many? I can't even remember half of them, but there was a lot of killing."

On June 24, 1968, the worst series of riots in the prison's history began in the print shop, forcing a number of political decisions that would end with the prison closing down 16 years later. The initial June riots led to at least $1 million in fire damage and the destruction of nine buildings and damage to six others.

Tensions continued to mount through July and led to more riots on August 20-21, when inmates not only started fires, but also took nine guards hostage. This forced a 28-hour standoff between the leaders of the convicts and the authorities that ended with an assault on the prison on August 21. Officers blew holes in the south wall and the roof and invaded the prison with deadly force. Five of the convicts were killed but the guards managed to make it through alive.

The decision was made that the prison needed to be closed down.

Governor James A. Rhodes ordered a new maximum-security prison to be built in remote Lucasville, Ohio and placed the old prison under the control of Warden Harold Cardwell, who immediately cancelled the Christmas shows, the exhibitions and the team sports. The prison was now under a permanent lock-down and would remain that way for the rest of its existence.

In 1972, most of the prisoners were transferred out and sent to the Southern Ohio Correctional Facility, which had just been completed. The old prison now housed only the sick, the psychotic and the troublemakers. Except for the most secure areas, the place was falling into ruin. The fire-gutted buildings had been left to rot and decay and were slowly crumbling away.

In 1979, the prison was ordered closed down for good as of December 31, 1983. For the first time in more than 150 years, the Ohio Penitentiary was completely silent and empty. Or was it?

Not long after the last of the inmates departed, new stories began to be told about the legendary place. And there were stories of a much darker sort.

While some stated that the only ghosts that remained in the prison were those of the stories, the history and the memories of the place, others soon began to argue that point. They believed that the fires, the executions, the stabbings, the shootings and the quiet, desperate suicides that snuffed out thousands of lives behind the prison walls were not the only horrors to be imprinted on the desolate location. They began to believe that the spirits of many of these angry and sinister men remained behind.

Stories began to spread about the old prison site. Those who wandered too close to the old buildings or who dared to go inside began to believe that the otherwise empty cell blocks were haunted by the spirits of the men who died in the prison. There were those who even claimed to experience the phantoms connected to the horrendous fire of 1930. It was said that by standing out in the prison yard, you could hear the roar of ghostly flames from inside and the horrible screams of the men who burned alive in their cells.

These stories continued for several years until finally, the prison was torn down and the lot where it stood was cleared away. A sports arena was built on the site and in the fall of 2000, the arena became the home of the Columbus NHL hockey team. All traces of the old prison were finally destroyed. Or were they?

According to reports, witnesses have spotted presences and have heard disembodied screams echoing across the arena's parking lot at night. This has led many to believe that the site continues to be haunted today.

Years ago, when it was first proposed that a tourist attraction or development would take the place of the prison, one of the former guards spoke up. "I wouldn't care if they dynamited the place," he said. "It's the entrance to Hell itself... I can't tell you what is there, what is seen and unseen...."

Could the destruction of the prison have erased the ghostly memories and restless souls that once lingered here? Or do they remain, still hoping for some sort of redemption to appease their troubled past?

## THE CARROLLTON JAIL
### A New Orleans Haunting

One of the most startling accounts of ghosts in New Orleans came from the old Carrollton Jail. During the years of 1898 and 1899, there were so many stories told of a haunting in the place that there remains little doubt that something very strange occurred in the building. To make matters even more credible, the majority of the witnesses who experienced these bizarre events were hard-boiled and credible officers of the law. Their realistic testimonies to the events in question make them all the more chilling.

This old structure, built around 1850, was officially known as the Jefferson Parish Prison, but more commonly, was simply called the "Carrollton Jail". Carrollton itself had come into existence around 1833 when a man named Charles Zimple laid out a town about five miles from the boundary of New Orleans. Zimple dubbed the new city "Carrollton" after General William Carroll, a hero of the Battle of New Orleans. He had been encamped on the site of the future town with an army of Tennessee volunteers while awaiting orders from Andrew Jackson.

Two years after, the New Orleans and Carrollton Railroad was constructed to connect the city and the small town. The railroad is still used today as the St. Charles Avenue Streetcar line. It is the oldest, continually operating line of public transportation in America. The town was soon growing rapidly and by 1841, it was officially incorporated. Later, in 1852, it was named the county seat of Jefferson Parish and a handsome city hall and courthouse were built. They remain standing to this day, even though New Orleans eventually annexed the city in 1874.

Another part of the administrative collection of buildings was the parish prison. It stood on the corner of Hampson and Short Streets and after being built around 1852, it served as a jail until it was demolished in 1937. The brick building stood two stories tall and boasted large doorways and heavily barred windows. Most called it a "bleak and hideous place" and it was said that many of the prisoners met their ends here. Suicides were apparently quite frequent and disease and the lack of medical care added to the deaths. Violence, as with any prison, was also common. Still more of the prisoners had their fates decided on the gallows that were located in the square central courtyard. Many convicted thieves, rapists and murderers met justice at the end of the rope after being imprisoned in the narrow, stone cells of the jail. One lynching even took place in the courtyard after outraged citizens captured two men who had raped and butchered a little girl in the area.

These deaths and terrible events were said to have created a haunting at the Carrollton Jail.... a haunting that became a matter of public and official record. More than 50 years after the building was erected, the ghostly happenings at the jail became so persistent that they gained the attention of the newspapers of the day. On October 9, 1899, the first detailed reports about the supernatural in the parish prison appeared in print.

At that time, the prison was under the authority of Sergeant William Clifton, the Police Commander of the District. He had served with distinction for many years with the New Orleans Police Department and had taken over command of the jail in 1898. He was well respected and admired by those who served under him, including his clerk, a deputy, two doormen and eight patrolmen.

One summer evening, two men and a woman stopped by the jail to chat with Clifton. They came in through the great front entrance to the prison, which opened into a wide hallway. On the left side of the entryway was a door that opened into Clifton's office, a sparsely furnished room with a desk, a washstand, a sofa and a number of chairs. Behind Clifton's office, with a narrow passage between them, was the clerk's office. In this room were more desks and chairs and a wooden railing that divided the office.

As the woman that accompanied the men leaned against a wall in the office, she was immediately shoved out of the room as though someone had struck her violently. She spun into the hallway and was sent sprawling onto the floor. "Something pushed me!", she cried, her eyes wide with shock. "It pushed my shoulder away from the wall!"

Clifton and the men laughed and one of them joked about her getting old. A little angry about the fact that they didn't believe her, she leaned against the wall again. In seconds, she was sent reeling into the center of the room. Her body was flung into the cluster of men who were standing there and she was forced to take hold of them to keep from falling. This time, her face was pale with fear! "Something's in that wall!", she shouted at them. "I don't care what you say, somebody is there."

The men then took turns leaning against the wall and to their surprise, each was shoved away from it and toward the middle of the office. They carefully examined both sides of the wall but could find nothing to explain the strange event. What could have caused it?

Sergeant Clifton pondered the puzzle for a few moments and then his mind drifted back to an incident that he had heard about a few years before, prior to when he had come to work at the prison. A murderer, who had been arrested for boiling his wife in lye and making soap from her corpse, was arrested and brought to the jail. The story went that a number of angry police officers beat the man to death in the hallway outside of Clifton's office. His blood had been spattered all over the corridor. The story went that the killer swore he would be back to haunt the place. But had he?

Nonsense, Clifton told himself, there had to be a logical explanation for the wall. Or so he thought at that time. The events that followed would cause him to think differently!

A day or so later, Clifton was in his office with Corporal Perez, one of the patrolmen for the district. Their conversation turned to the portrait of General Beauregard that Clifton had hanging on his wall. He had always expressed an admiration for the general and in the course of his discussion, he turned to the portrait and gave it a quick salute. Immediately, with a great crash, the picture fell to the floor! At the same time, the washstand, with its bowl and pitcher, jumped forward and turned over. Strangely, nothing was broken. Even stranger, the heavy cord by which the portrait was hung was found to be in perfect condition. The nail in the wall was solid as well and even slanted upward. The two men, after close examination, could find no reason for the portrait to have fallen.

The following night, Clifton and Perez were telling some of the other officers about the strange happening. As he demonstrated what had occurred, he saluted the portrait once again. As soon as he did, the mirror that hung just below the general's picture flew from the wall. It also smashed into the wooden washstand, knocking everything to the floor. This time, the wash basin shattered into dozens of pieces but everything else remained intact. Clifton examined the mirror hanger and found that it was as strong as the one holding the portrait.

"It seemed as though invisible ears had been listening," Sergeant Clifton later reported, "and that unseen hands pushed the things from the wall.... I know that the portrait and the mirror could not have fallen unaided."

Several nights later, Clifton was sitting at his desk when he was suddenly held by the shoulders and his chair was spun completely around. At first he thought it was one of his men playing a joke, but when he turned to confront them, he found no one there! The room was fully lit and he could no one in the room or in the hallway. He questioned the doorman, but he replied that no one had come in the door.

And the spectral antics in the office didn't stop there!

The sofa in Clifton's office was frequently used by the patrolmen as a place to catch up on much-needed sleep during long shifts. One night, Officer Dell, who drove the patrol wagon, came in for a short nap. He had no sooner stretched himself out on the sofa before it lurched forward and out away from the wall. The bulky piece of furniture slid out about three feet and then suddenly reversed directions and thudded against the wall again. This was the same wall where the man had been beaten to death and the same one that was said to have flung the woman away and onto the floor.

Not long after that, another officer tried to rest on the couch. This time it not only slid out into the room, but it also tilted sharply and bounced the officer off in such a way that he collided with the corner of Clifton's desk and gashed his head open. Hearing his cry, Clifton rushed to his assistance and arrived just in time to see the couch sliding back against the wall again. The next night, another policeman, who boasted that he did not believe in ghosts, lay down on the couch in the presence of a number of other officers. Suddenly, the couch tipped up and the patrolman fell onto the floor! After that, the men began to stay far away from the couch until someone moved it to another part of the room. While the couch was again considered "safe", the patrolmen avoided that particular wall of the office for some time.

In October of that same year, a mounted officer named Jules Aucoin stepped into Sergeant

Clifton's office to make a report. Clifton had stepped out for a few moments and Aucoin stood waiting for him near the desk. Just then, he saw a flash of movement out of the corner of his eye. He looked up quickly at a large, lithograph portrait of Admiral Dewey (a hero of the time period) that had been pasted on the wall.... the same wall that had been the center of much of the strange activity in the office. Before his eyes, Aucoin saw the portrait begin to spin like a wheel. It was as though someone had placed a nail through the center of the picture and then started rotating it! Keep in mind that such an act was virtually impossible as the portrait had been plastered onto the wall with strong glue.

Aucoin was stunned for a moment and then he ran out into the corridor and began shouting for his fellow officers. Those who were nearby came on the run, including Sergeant Clifton. As the men hurried into the office, they saw that the portrait had stopped moving and was in fact, affixed to the wall just as it had been. Aucoin explained what he had seen and the other men, having already witnessed other events for themselves, had no reason to doubt him.

Apparently though, the spirit of the wife-killer was not the only ghost who haunted the prison. Over time, all of the men who were stationed there reported strange and unexplainable noises, furniture and small objects moving about by themselves and falling without assistance, lights that turned on and off and much more. It's not surprising that these bizarre happenings tended to keep everyone on edge. Requests for transfers to other precincts were sent in frequently by officers who were stationed at the Carrollton Jail.

One night in autumn 1899, Corporal Harry Hyatt heard heavy footsteps in a nearby hallway. He stepped to the door of the Sergeant's office and looked around. Although he could still hear the sound of someone walking, he looked both ways down the corridor and found no one was about. The footfalls continued to sound and Hyatt noticed there was something odd about them. It seemed that each solid step was accompanied by another step that dragged, as though taken by a man who was lame. Hyatt also noticed that the corridor seemed to be filled with the faint smell of cigar smoke.

Finally, he left the doorway and walked out front. He asked the doorman, Officer Foster, if he had seen anyone come in. He shook his head until Hyatt described the sound that he heard in the hall. A faint memory stirred in Foster's mind and he grinned at Hyatt. "Maybe it was Harvey come back," he joked with his friend.

"Harvey" had been a gambler and a gigantic man, who walked with a severe limp. This didn't stop him from killing two racecourse jockeys by breaking their necks with his bare hands though. He also cut the tongues out of their horses. Apparently, he had wagered a small fortune on both of them and he was angry when they lost the races they were entered in. Harvey had been brought to the jail and had last been seen standing in the corridor in handcuffs with the cold stump of a cigar clenched between his teeth. Somehow, the man had vanished and had not been seen since. His escape from the jail left two dead guards, and a mystery, behind.

Hyatt shook his head. "Nope, he won't come back to see the inside of this jail," he laughed.

That evening, Hyatt picked up an evening newspaper and found a story about a gigantic man named Robert Brewer who had been found dead in a Pennsylvania town. He had been blind and lame but made a small living selling newspapers. After his death, they found a packet of papers among his effects that showed he was actually Harvey. The news story stated that he was wanted in New Orleans for four murders and elsewhere for other crimes.

Hyatt realized that Harvey had come back to the old prison after all!

The following night, at the same time, Hyatt again heard the shambling footsteps in the hallway. They plodded back and forth, back and forth. Hyatt went to the doorway, but there was still no one to be seen. "Okay, Harvey," he muttered to the empty space, "you can stop your pacing and smoke your cigar now".

The footsteps suddenly stopped. From out of thin air, a great cloud of tobacco smoke appeared about three feet from where Hyatt stood. It swirled and then slowly lifted off towards the ceiling and disappeared.

On another occasion, iron paperweights were raised from desks and flung at officers. Icy cold chills appeared without explanation and always, there were the ghostly footsteps that sounded throughout the building. They paced the corridors and went up and down the stairs. One of the places especially affected by the sounds was the courtroom that was located on the second floor.

The room had been refurbished from the row of dark "condemned" cells that had once been located there. In these cages were kept the men who would soon die on the gallows. One night, very late, the footsteps became unusually strong and several officers followed them upstairs and into the courtroom. The room was eerie and silent, save for the tapping of the phantom boots. They circled the room as the police officers stood back and listened. Then, the footsteps stopped abruptly and the docket book, which was thick and weighed many pounds, flew from the judge's desk and crashed to the floor with such force that Sergeant Clifton heard it downstairs.

The footsteps were heard no more that night but Clifton had another encounter of his own that must have left him questioning the wisdom of remaining in command of the prison. In the early morning hours, he was seated at his desk when there suddenly came the grip of strong hands around his throat. He could feel the air being crushed out of him and he threw his arms up to ward off the attacker. His hands struck nothing but the attack immediately ceased. Clifton whirled around in his chair.... but there was no one behind him! No living person had entered his office, yet the marks of the hands could clearly be seen on his neck. In fact, mottled bruises remained there for some days after.

One afternoon, two quadroon girls appeared outside of the Sergeant's office and were spotted by Officer Foster. As the Sergeant was not in, he went over to speak to them. As he got close, they vanished before the man's eyes! It was believed that they were the ghosts of two young women who had been imprisoned there for carving out the liver of their mutual lover.

On another occasion, Foster also reported seeing a former prison officer named Sergeant Shoemaker standing alone in Clifton's office. The man stood near the desk for a moment and then bowed his head and walked slowly away. He got to within a foot of the sofa and then he too vanished! This was almost as surprising to Foster as the fact that he saw Shoemaker at all.... the man had been dead for over a year at this time!

Stories and reports would also bear out the fact that the officers were not the only ones to be bothered by the ghosts in the jail. In fact, one cell, Number Three, was infamous for the events that took place in it.

One night, a prisoner named Charles Marquez was brought in. All of the other cells were full, so he was placed in Number Three. The next morning, the guards found him lying on the floor of his cell, unable to stand and scarcely able to speak. His face was a mass of cuts and bruises and he looked as though he had been badly beaten. Clifton first assumed that one of the officers had beaten the poor man, but Marquez, once his wounds were treated, quickly convinced him otherwise. He claimed that he had been beaten by unseen hands... ghosts, he said, and that he had had been punched, kicked and pushed against the wall. Not once did he see his assailants and records did show that none of the prison personnel had been near the man's cell during the night.

Other prisoners soon got their own taste of Cell Number Three. Every criminal that was put into it told the same tale the next day and all of them had bruises and cuts to show that their claims were true. No one outside of the cell ever heard a thing, yet the occupant was always in sorry shape the next morning... and usually babbling about ghosts and monsters.

It was later learned that many years before, on a night when the prison was very crowded, three murderers were placed in Cell Number Three together. According to the story, they had fought all night, each man for himself, punching, biting and kicking the others. In the morning, two of them were dead and the third died before a priest could be called for him.

In 1937, the Carrollton Jail was finally torn down. Through its long life, the prison had been the scene of many ghostly tales and stories. Legend even had it that when the workmen demolished the structure, human shapes writhed in the clouds of dust, as though the creatures that had haunted the place now reveled in its destruction.

For years afterward, people in the area also claimed to hear the spectral sound of the gallows trap as it opened and sent another condemned man to his death. It is said that some older residents of the area claim the sounds of the gallows can still be heard today.

## SPIRITS OF THE CIVIL WAR
*Hauntings at the Old Washington Arsenal Prison and Fort Monroe*

When the Civil War ended in April 1865, it did not end for everyone. There were many in the South who simply refused to believe that the Confederacy had fallen.

One of these men was John Wilkes Booth, an actor who professed and undying devotion to the South. Booth was the son of Junius Brutus Booth, a professional actor. The elder Booth was considered by many to be so eccentric that he was nearly insane, a trait which father and son apparently shared. John Wilkes Booth was also the brother of Edwin Booth, perhaps the most famous stage actor of the period. Edwin often spoke of his brother's strangeness and he would have had an even greater cause for concern had he known the dark secrets that his sibling hid in his heart.

While the war was still raging, Booth had been attempting to organize a paramilitary operation with a small group of conspirators. Their plan was to kidnap President Abraham Lincoln and take him to Richmond. After a number of failed attempts, it was clear that the plan would not work. Booth's hatred of Lincoln forced him to change his plans from kidnapping to murder. Booth did not explain to his confederates about this change until two hours before the event took place.

Booth had been a southern sympathizer throughout the war. He was revered for his acting in the South and during the war had been a spy and a smuggler, working with southern agents in Maryland and Canada. He was also rabid in his pro-slavery views, believing that slavery was a "gift from God". He was convinced that Lincoln was a tyrant and Booth hoped the murder of the president would plunge the North into chaos and allow the Confederacy to rally and seize control of Washington.

On the night of April 14, 1865, President Lincoln and his wife decided to attend a play at Ford's Theater in Washington. The Lincoln party arrived at the theater that night and took a reserved box to the cheers of the crowd and to the musical strains of "Hail to the Chief". A young couple, Major Henry Rathbone and his fiancée, Clara Harris, accompanied the Lincoln's. The play was a production called "Our American Cousin", presented by actress Laura Keene. The play was a comedy, the sort of show that Lincoln liked best.

Booth lurked about the theater all evening and at thirteen minutes after ten, approached Lincoln's box. He showed a card to an attendant and gained access to the outer door. He found the box to be unguarded and slipped inside. Booth jammed the door closed behind him.

During the evening, the Lincoln party had been discussing the Holy Land. The President made a comment about wanting to visit Jerusalem someday as he leaned forward and noticed General Ambrose Burnside in the audience of the theater. At that moment, Booth stepped forward. Major Rathbone stood from his seat to confront the intruder but before he could act, Booth raised a small pistol and fired it into the back of President Lincoln's head.

Rathbone seized the actor but Booth slashed him with a knife. Lincoln fell forward, striking his head on the rail of the box and slumping over. Mary took hold of him, believing him to have simply fallen while Booth jumped from the edge of the balcony. His boot snagged on the bunting across the front of the box and he landed badly, fracturing his leg. As he struggled to his feet, he cried out "Sic Semper tyrannis!" (Thus it shall ever be for tyrants) and he stumbled out of the theater.

A scream went up from the back of the theater, crying "Booth!", and the stunned audience was snapped out of its stupor. Soon, more voices began shouting the actor's name and yet somehow, he managed to easily escape from the close and crowded auditorium. Then, there were more screams, groans and the crashing of seats and above all of it came Mary Lincoln's shrill cry for her dying husband.

John Wilkes Booth escaped from Washington on horseback across the Anacostia Bridge, passing a sentry who had not yet learned of the assassination. He made it to a farm in Virginia with the help of his fellow conspirators, only stopping to rest because of his broken leg.

Soon, the hunt for Lincoln's assassin was on and by morning, more than 2000 soldiers were looking for Booth. On April 26, a detachment of 25 men finally tracked down Booth, and a comrade named David Herold, at a tobacco farm near Port Royal, Virginia. The barn where they were hiding was surrounded and Herold decided to surrender. He was manacled and tied to a tree. Booth decided to die rather than be taken alive, or so we are to believe. The mystery remains even today about whether or not John Wilkes Booth was ever really punished for the assassination of President Lincoln... but that, as they say, is another story.

One by one, the confederates of John Wilkes Booth were hunted down, tried and either hanged or imprisoned. The trial of one of them, Mary Surratt, is still considered today possibly one of the greatest travesties of American justice. Mary Surratt had been the proprietor of a Washington boarding house where Booth has lived while plotting the kidnapping, and then murder, of Abraham Lincoln. At midnight, on the same night that Lincoln had been shot, Mary was roused from her bed by police officers and Federal troops. She was accused of being a conspirator in Lincoln's death and was taken to the prison at the Old Brick Capitol. From that point on, Mary never stopped insisting that she was innocent and that she barely knew Booth, but no one listened.

The testimonies of two people were instrumental in Mary's conviction. One of them was a notorious drunk and the other was a known liar, a former policeman to whom Mary had leased her tavern in Maryland. At the trial's conclusion, she and three other defendants were found guilty and sentenced to death by hanging. Mary Surratt was the last of the four to die on July 7, 1865.

It is true that Mary may not have been as blameless as she claimed to be. Besides Booth, the other residents of the boarding house included her son, John, who was a Confederate courier, and several southern sympathizers. It is possible that she knew more than she claimed to, but it is still doubtful that she was in any way involved in the murder plot. To say that the evidence against her was circumstantial is a gross understatement and in light of that, and other factors, the punishment certainly was much harsher than what was believed to be her crime.

Even though Mary Surratt was sentenced to die, the board that convicted her sent a petition to President Andrew Johnson to ask that her sentence be commuted to life in prison. Whether this is because she was a woman or because they had doubts about her guilt is unknown. The commander of the Federal troops in Washington was so sure that a last minute reprieve would arrive that he stationed messengers on horseback along the shortest route from the White House to the Washington Arsenal Prison, where the execution was to take place.

Until the time the hood was placed over her head, officials in charge of the execution were sure that Mary would be spared, but she was not. And it is possibly just this injustice which keeps her spirit lingering behind.

In time, the Washington Arsenal Prison was converted into Fort Leslie McNair. In the courtyard on the north end of the fort is where the execution took place. It is in this spot where Mary and the other conspirators were cut down from the gallows and buried. They were later moved to permanent graves in other locations. There is an old story that maintains that Mary's spirit caused the sudden appearance of a boxwood tree on the spot where the scaffold once stood. It is claimed that the growth of the tree was her way of continuing to attract attention to her innocence.

The courthouse in which Mary was tried, and found guilty, was turned into an officer's quarters for the army base, while the courtroom itself became a five-room apartment. For years, it was reported that occupants of the apartment would hear the sounds of chains rattling throughout the rooms. According to records, the seven male defendants in the conspiracy trial were shackled together with chains and sat on a bench where the apartment is now located. Tradition holds that the reported sounds are these same chains, still echoing over the decades.

And sounds are not the only things reported....

A number of residents of this apartment, and others which are located close to it, have claimed to see the apparition of a stout, middle-aged woman, dressed in black walking down the hallways of the officer's quarters. They have also heard the unexplainable sound of a woman's voice and have reported the sensation of being touched by an unseen hand.

Could this be the ghost of Mary Surratt?

Another tragic and incarcerated figure from the last days of the Civil War was the president of the Confederacy himself, Jefferson Davis. Many believe that his ghost still lingers at old Fort Monroe, Virginia, even today.

Jefferson Davis had been born in Kentucky in 1808 and ironically had been raised just miles away from the early home of Abraham Lincoln. He attended and graduated from West Point in 1828 and was sent to the infantry. He soon fell in love with Sarah Taylor, the daughter of his commander and future president, Zachary Taylor. He left the military in 1835 and moved to Mississippi.

In 1835, Davis married Sarah Taylor without the blessing of her parents. Five weeks later, both of them fell ill from malaria, a disease, like yellow fever, not uncommon in the swampy regions of the south. A short time later, Sarah died at the age of 21 and became the first of many tragedies to come in Davis' life.

In 1845, Davis entered the political arena and was elected to Congress as a Democrat. That same year, he married Varina Howell, a beautiful young woman who was half his age. Davis served for one year in the House of Representatives before resigning to lead a group of Mississippi volunteers during the Mexican War. Davis was wounded at the Battle of Buena Vista and gained a reputation for bravery, which he used to his advantage during the next Senate election. He handily won the seat and remained in office until 1853, when President Franklin Pierce named him war secretary.

In 1857, Davis reclaimed his Senate seat and became one of the most forceful advocates of southern rights, regularly threatening secession if those rights were challenged. A few years later, Davis would test the waters for a run at the White House as a Democratic candidate in 1860. At the Baltimore nomination convention, his name was placed under consideration, but Davis never pressed the issue, knowing that he would never gain enough northern support to win an election.

Later, when the Democrat vote was split between Stephen Douglas and John Breckinridge, they were defeated. Although cautious and still hoping to compromise, Davis pushed for Mississippi's secession. He made an emotional farewell speech to the Senate on January 21, 1861 and then withdrew from his seat with four other senators. He was soon named the commander of the militia in Mississippi and also a compromise candidate for the presidency of the six states that now made up the Confederacy. He was elected on February 9 and inaugurated nine days later in Montgomery.

The years that would follow Davis' election as the President of the Confederacy would be terrible ones and they weighed heavily on Davis, just as the concerns of the north brutally wore down Abraham Lincoln. And this would not be the only sadness and despair the two men would share during the war....

In April 1864, Davis' son, Joe, was killed in an accident. He and his older brother were playing on a balcony attached the back of the Davis' Richmond house when he lost his balance and fell to the brick pavement below. The fall fractured his skull and he died a short time later.

Varina became hysterical and it was said that passersby could hear her screaming inside of the house throughout the afternoon and into the evening. President Davis was himself crushed. He sat beside his wife for more than three hours, turning away everyone who called, including a courier with an important message from General Lee. Then, he vanished into the upper floors of the house, where his footsteps could be heard, incessantly pacing back and forth.

Over the course of the next few days, cards and letters flooded the Davis home, including a heartfelt message from Abraham Lincoln, who was returning the gesture extended by Davis when his own son had died. The funeral took place a short time later and the Hollywood Cemetery in Richmond offered a free plot for the boy's burial. An immense crowd gathered at the cemetery on the day of the burial and it was reported that children from all over the city, many of them Joe's playmates, covered the grave with flowers and crosses.

The last year that Jefferson Davis spent in Richmond was one of extreme sadness and grief. The house had become a place haunted by the memories of Joe's smiling face, and his horrible death. Davis even had the balcony that the boy fell from removed from the house and destroyed. The only moment of joy the Davis' experienced in the house was the birth of Winnie Davis on June 27, 1864. She would be called the "Daughter of the Confederacy."

On Sunday, April 2, 1865, word reached Davis from General Lee.... the army was evacuating the Petersburg and Richmond lines and soon the city would fall. As the Federal forces neared the city, Davis assembled his cabinet and staff and directed the removal of public archives, the treasury, and all records to Danville. Later that afternoon, Davis himself left the city on a special train.

The next 24 hours in Richmond were chaos as the residents struggled to flee the city and the Union Army moved in. Disorder increased with every hour as the streets filled with people trying to make their way to the railroad depots. Two regiments of militia were supposed to be maintaining order in the city, but the panic was beyond their control. Terror ruled the streets and left destruction in its wake. Eventually, the city fell into Union hands.

But in all of the chaos, Davis and his family somehow escaped. After the fighting ended and after Lee had surrendered at Appomattox, Davis and Varina managed to avoid the soldiers who were looking for them and planned to start out for Texas. Here, Davis would gather his still-loyal soldiers, then would establish a new capital of the Confederacy and continue the war. It was during this time of flight when Abraham Lincoln was assassinated. Patrols were stepped up and the gauntlet was tightened around Davis for most believed that he had somehow been involved in Lincoln's death.

On May 10, 1865, a contingent of Federal cavalry surrounded a group of tents near the town of Irwinville, Georgia. It was here that Davis and his followers were hiding and forced to come out. The Confederate president was quickly arrested. When the commanding officer informed him that he had been implicated in the Lincoln assassination, Davis immediately denied it. "I would rather have dealt with President Lincoln than Andrew Johnson," he said.

Davis and Varina were taken into custody and transported by ship to the country's most escape-proof prison of the day, Fort Monroe. The location of the fort dated back almost to the first settlements on the American continent.

In 1608, Captain John Smith had discovered the area and deemed it a worthy place for a fort. A year later, Governor John Ratcliffe was dispatched from Jamestown to build an earthworks called Fort Algernourne, which by 1611, was well-stockaded and fortified by seven heavy guns and a garrison of 40 men.

The War of 1812 prompted the defense department of the United States to begin a series of forts for coastal defense that would stretch all of the way from Maine to Louisiana. This fort was selected to be a key post in the chain and construction and renovations extended over a period dating from 1819 to 1834. The name of the fort was finally changed too, in honor of President James Monroe, a Virginian.

When it was completed, the fort was fitted with nearly 200 guns that could control the channel into Hampton Roads and also dominated the approach to Washington using the Chesapeake Bay. It was called the "Gibraltar of Chesapeake Bay" and remains today the largest enclosed fortification in the United States and one of only two American forts surrounded by a moat.

pair guarded the casemate door. More sentries were positioned on the ramparts overlooking the area and along with the armed guards on the other side of the moat, Davis had 70 captors in all. They were taking no chances that he might escape, either with or without assistance from still loyal Rebel troops.

As Captain Titlow entered the room, he explained to Davis that he had been given orders to put him in leg irons. Almost apologetically, he insisted that he was just following orders. The instructions to place Davis in chains came from Edwin Stanton, Lincoln's Secretary of War. At that point, most believed that Davis had somehow been involved in the assassination of the northern president. Davis paced about the small cell and then nervously rested his left foot on a chair. Thinking that Davis was submitting to this indignity, he instructed the blacksmith to go about his work.

The blacksmith knelt down to shackle the chains on the president's leg when suddenly Davis attacked the man holding the chains, sending him sprawling onto the floor of the cell. The blacksmith jumped to his feet and raised the hammer above his head to strike Davis, but Titlow pushed between them. It took four men to hold Davis down as the chains were shackled to his legs.

Captain Titlow was the last man to leave Davis' cell. As he walked out the door, he turned and looked back at the Confederate leader. He later remarked that Jefferson Davis was seated on the edge of his prison cot, his head in his hands and tears streaming down his face. Even though Captain Titlow held no sympathies for the Confederate cause, he believed that the utter destruction of Jefferson Davis was one of the saddest things he had ever seen.

The days that followed were filled with humiliation for Davis. The fort's chief medical officer, Lieutenant General John Craven, recommended that Davis' chains be removed. The Confederate president's health was fragile and being chained like an animal was simply cruel. Not surprisingly, his recommendation was ignored. Soon however, word of the shackling leaked out and reached the newspapers. Public disapproval of the punishment, in the south and the north, created so many problems that the War Department finally ordered Davis to be unchained.

After more than four months in solitary confinement, Davis was moved to better quarters, although he remained a prisoner. Soon, the public would also begin to clamor for Davis' release. There was no proof that he had, in any way, been involved in the Lincoln assassination. Even men like Horace Greeley and Senator Thaddeus Stevens got behind the effort and created a stir that was simply too big to ignore.

At last, on May 13, 1867, after two years of confinement, Jefferson Davis was released. He lived on for 24 years after the end of the Civil War, traveling extensively and writing about the "Lost Cause" and its consequences. He died in 1889 of bronchial pneumonia and was buried in New Orleans after three days of ceremonies. However, four years later, his body was exhumed and moved to Richmond, the former capital of the Confederacy. But many do not believe that Davis rests in his honored grave in peace!

Over the years, numerous apparitions have been sighted in and around the cell where Davis was confined at Fort Monroe. Most of the sightings have been of pale, apparitional forms that most feel are associated with Davis as he relives his suffering here.

In 1970, some of the fort's older buildings were being readied for the Officer's Wives Club house tour. In one house, just across from the Casemate Museum (where Davis was imprisoned), some white draperies were taken down and cleaned. They were returned and then laid across a chair so that they could be hung back up. When the workers returned to next day to take care of this, they found that every one of the drapes had been somehow covered in black soot. The rest of the room though, was spotless. There had been no way that anyone could have gotten into the room. Most blamed the occurrence on Davis' ghost.

Or could the spirit of Varina Davis have been to blame?

The room was the same chamber in which she had looked out the window each day toward the prison where her husband was held. The windows in this room have been known to rattle mysteriously on some nights, even when there is no wind. Debunkers have even tried to wedge pieces of wood into the frames to stop the movement, but it does no good. Varina has been seen many times over the years, standing and staring out the second-floor windows.

One night, a female guest at the fort was sleeping in that room. She was awakened in the early morning hours by a cold chill and looked up to see a plumb, middle-aged woman standing by the window. The woman was dressed in white and she stared out at the prison across from the house. She got out of bed and walked to the figure and she cautiously put out her hand to touch the woman in white. The lady simply vanished and left the guest alone, holding onto a white window curtain.

## THE NEWSTEAD AVENUE POLICE STATION
*The Most Haunted Building in St. Louis?*

In 1994, Matt and Denise Piskulic moved into a wonderful old building on Newstead Avenue in St. Louis. The place was perfect for their graphic design business with spacious rooms, hardwood floors, and a central studio with high ceilings. They had heard rumors about the place over the years but they didn't let that stop them from moving in.... little did they realize that just because people said the place was haunted, they never told them that the house was infested with ghosts!

The Newstead Avenue Police Station, which was built in 1904, was located in the Central West End of St. Louis. For years, it operated as a precinct house and jail, becoming well known for its strange and violent past. The first major tragedy struck in July 1945 when a waiter named Edward Melendes was arrested for petty theft. At some point during the night, Melendes was beaten to death in his cell. Three police officers and the victim's cellmate were indicted for manslaughter. There was no evidence to ultimately convict the men and the prosecution's case fell apart. Significantly, the accused officers resigned from the police force just two months after the murder occurred.

Horror returned to the police station in 1953 when it played a key role in the notorious Bobby Greenlease kidnapping case. The crime would shake the city of St. Louis and would have lasting repercussions for years to come.

The case became known as one of the most tragic crimes of the 1950's. The month of September 1953 marked the kidnapping and murder of 6-year-old Bobby Greenlease and also the subsequent disappearance of half the $600,000 ransom his family pointlessly paid for his release. The money disappeared at the Newstead Avenue police station.

Bobby was the son of Robert and Virginia Greenlease, residents of Mission Hills, Kansas, a prominent suburb of Kansas City. Robert Greenlease was one of the largest Cadillac dealers in the nation. In comparison to the wealth of the Greenlease family, Bobby's kidnappers, Carl Austin Hall and Bonnie Heady, were dead broke. However, both had known privilege earlier in their lives. It had been at military school that Hall had met Paul Greenlease, Bobby's older, over the years but they didn't let that stop them from moving in.... little did they realize that just because people said the place was haunted, they never told them that the house was infested with ghosts!

The Newstead Avenue Police Station, which was built in 1904, was located in the Central West End of St. Louis. For years, it operated as a precinct house and jail, becoming well known for its strange and violent past. The first major tragedy struck in July 1945 when a waiter named Edward Melendes was arrested for petty theft. At some point during the night, Melendes was beaten to death in his cell. Three police officers and the victim's cellmate were indicted for manslaughter. There was no evidence to ultimately convict the men and the prosecution's case fell apart. Significantly, the accused officers resigned from the police force just two months after the murder occurred.

Horror returned to the police station in 1953 when it played a key role in the notorious Bobby Greenlease kidnapping case. The crime would shake the city of St. Louis and would have lasting repercussions for years to come.

The case became known as one of the most tragic crimes of the 1950's. The month of September 1953 marked the kidnapping and murder of 6-year-old Bobby Greenlease and also the subsequent disappearance of half the $600,000 ransom his family pointlessly paid for his release. The money disappeared at the Newstead Avenue police station.

Bobby was the son of Robert and Virginia Greenlease, residents of Mission Hills, Kansas, a prominent suburb of Kansas City. Robert Greenlease was one of the largest Cadillac dealers in the nation. In comparison to the wealth of the Greenlease family, Bobby's kidnappers, Carl Austin Hall and Bonnie Heady, were dead broke. However, both had known privilege earlier in their lives. It had been at military school that Hall had met Paul Greenlease, Bobby's older, adopted brother. Hall later inherited a large sum of money from his father, but lost it all in bad business ventures. After that, he turned to crime. He was arrested for robbing cab drivers (his total take was only $38) and he was sent to the Missouri State Penitentiary. In prison, he dreamed of the "big score" and began planning the kidnapping that would help him to retire.

After getting out of prison, Hall moved to St. Joseph, Missouri and he started dating Bonnie Heady. She was no catch, having a reputation for not only sleeping around but also for occasionally dabbling in prostitution. The good news was that she owned her own home and she and Hall often drank themselves into a stupor there, never being bothered by anyone. Hall often knocked her around though and in fact, when she was arrested for kidnapping, she still bore the bruises of her latest beating. Her willingness to put up with Hall's abuse is probably a clue as to why she agreed to go along with his kidnapping scheme.

During the summer months of 1953, Hall and Heady made repeated trips to Kansas City to follow the Greenlease family. After some debate, they decided that Bobby would be the easiest prey. At that time, the boy was enrolled at Notre Dame de Sion, a fashionable Catholic school. In the late morning of September 28, Heady entered the school and told a nun that she was Bobby's aunt. She and Virginia Greenlease had been shopping at the Country Club Plaza, she told the nun, when Virginia had suffered a heart attack. Heady said that she had come to take Bobby to the hospital. When Bobby was brought out of his class, he immediately took Heady's hand in his, as if he knew her. Heady would later say that "he was so trusting."

Heady met Hall a few minutes later at the Katz Drugstore and they drove across town and across the state line into Kansas. The crime, enacting the Lindbergh Statute (named for the famous case) had just become a matter for the Federal authorities. And it was just about to get worse....

In a vacant field in Overland Park, Heady got out of the car and walked a short distance away while Hall killed Bobby. First, he tried to strangle the little boy but the rope he used was too short. Then, he punched him in the face, knocking out one tooth. Finally, he pushed Bobby down and shot him in the head with a .38 caliber pistol. The boy was dead less than 30 minutes after he had been abducted.

After that, they drove back to St. Joseph and buried the body in the back yard of Heady's home. Hall had dug the grave the night before. After the body was covered, he planted flowers in the freshly churned soil, hoping to cover all evidence of the horrific crime.

The Greenlease family got their first inkling of trouble when the nun who had released Bobby from school called to inquire about Virginia's health. Soon after, they got the ransom demands. Hall also mailed them a pin that Bobby had been wearing when he was taken. The killer demanded a ransom of $600,000 in $10 and $20 bills.

Robert Greenlease called several of his closest friends and he began putting together the money. He also called the head of the local bank, Arthur Eisenhower (brother of Dwight D. Eisenhower) and the two men put together a plan to record the serial numbers of all of the ransom bills. While the money was being accumulated, Hall called the Greenlease residence repeatedly. He continually reassured them that Bobby was alive. Finally, a week after the kidnapping, the money was delivered. Actually, it was delivered two times because Hall couldn't find it the first time.

While Robert and Virginia waited for word of where to find Bobby, Hall and Heady drove to St. Louis. As they traveled, word of the kidnapping leaked to the media and it became a nationwide sensation. When they arrived in St. Louis, Hall and Heady were stunned to find themselves at the center of the story. They ditched their car and started using taxicabs. They rented a small apartment in south St. Louis and decided to lay low. Hall quickly got restless though and one afternoon, left a drunken Heady in the apartment with a few thousand dollars and vanished. He departed for the "good life".

Hall then hooked up with an ex-con cab driver and a prostitute. The three of them ended up at the Coral Courts Motel, St. Louis' legendary "no-tell motel" located along old Route 66. It was renowned as a place where a fellow could stay for awhile with no questions asked. The Coral Courts was built in 1941 by John Carr, who was long rumored to be mob-connected after operating a posh brothel in St. Louis for many years.

Hiding out in the motel, Hall began to lavish money on the cab driver and the prostitute. The hooker would later say that Hall stayed so drunk, and was so nervous, that he couldn't perform sexually. As for the cab driver, Hall had turned the man into his own personal valet. He gave the man fistfuls of money and told him to buy new clothes and whatever else he thought he might need. What the cab driver brought him was trouble. The owner of the cab company was a man named Joe Costello, a well-known local gangster. When Costello heard about the big spending customer, he contacted St. Louis police lieutenant Louis Shoulders. Since Costello and Shoulders always denied stealing the ransom money, it is unknown whether Costello figured out that Hall was the Greenlease kidnapper and gave Shoulders a tip for the arrest of a lifetime... or whether they simply conspired to rip Hall off.

However, what is known is that Hall, guided by the cab driver, rented an apartment on the edge of St. Louis. A short time after moving in, he was arrested by Shoulders and a patrolman named Elmer Dolan. Hall was picked up for questioning about the large amount of money that he was flashing around. He was then taken to the Newstead Avenue police station and after that, history becomes quite blurry about the ransom money. Shoulders and Dolan said that they brought a suitcase and a foot locker jammed with more than $550,000 in cash into the station but some later testimony stated otherwise. No one else could remember seeing what turned out to be the elusive suitcase. Regardless of what occurred, only $300, 000 was ever recovered.

Once he was arrested, Hall almost immediately broke down. Heady was quickly arrested at the small apartment where Hall had dumped her. On October 7, police officers and reporters raced for Heady's house in St. Joseph, where they dug up Bobby's body from the backyard.

And once Hall and Heady confessed to the crime, they resigned themselves to being executed for the murder. When a Federal jury in Kansas City returned the verdict, it has been said that Heady smiled. On December 18, only 81 days after the kidnapping, Hall and Heady were executed side-by-side at the Missouri State Penitentiary. The pair had declined to seek mercy at the trial and did not appeal the verdict. Missouri authorities had a second chair installed in the gas chamber so that Heady and Hall could be executed at the same time. Heady was the only woman to ever be put to death in the gas chamber and it's said that she talked cheerfully to the guards and the officials while she was being strapped in. She did not fall silent until Hall finally told her to shut up.

Amidst the widespread anger about the murder of Bobby Greenlease, there was also an immediate investigation into the money that went missing at the Newstead Avenue police station. The glory that should have led to promotions for Shoulders and Dolan became a dirty scandal that highlighted the widespread corruption of the St. Louis police department in the 1950's.

The two officers were later convicted in a Federal court on a charge of perjury, for supposedly lying about the sequence of events from the time they arrested Hall until the time the money was brought to the Newstead station and counted. Various police clerks and officers testified that they never saw the men carrying anything when they entered the station with Hall and they certainly did not see the suitcase or the foot locker. Shoulders stated that the money was outside in the car and that he brought it into the station after bringing Hall inside.

The official theory was that Shoulders and Dolan, who both left the station on personal errands after booking Hall, returned to Hall's apartment and stole half the money. They brought the remaining half (I suppose thinking that no one would notice) to the station through the rear door. Hall's statement, not surprisingly, directly contradicted that of Shoulders and Dolan. Hall maintained that the money had been left in the apartment when he was arrested.

Over time, numerous theories have been floated as to who actually took the money. Most pointed fingers at Shoulders and his connection with Joe Costello, while others blamed the corruption in the police department itself.

However, it is possible that the money vanished somewhere else entirely. It's not a far reach to think that perhaps Hall took his revenge on the two police officers who arrested him and sent him to the gas chamber. If this is true, and Shoulders and Dolan did not take the money, then a tremendous injustice was done to the officers because their careers were destroyed over the incident.

So, where could the money have gone? Some have suggested that the mob-connected hotel owner, John Carr, may have been involved. If Carr knew about the money (and it's possible that he did), he could have entered Hall's room using a pass key and walked out with half the money, believing that Hall would never miss it. And even if he did miss it, what would he be able to do about it? When John Carr died, he was a multi-millionaire. Could any of that remaining fortune have been part of the Greenlease kidnapping money?

Obviously, we will never know. Even the old Coral Courts Motel has been torn down. The land where it was once located has now been turned into a subdivision, erasing that piece of history forever.

Whoever took the money though, it was gone. For many years after, it was news whenever any of the bills linked to the missing Greenlease money turned up. But where was it coming from? No one knew and now, with so many principals in the case long dead, it can only be realized that the vanished money will always remain a mystery.

In 1960, the Newstead Avenue police station closed its doors for good. For the next five years, it sat empty until artist Howard Jones and his wife Helen, converted the place into a private residence. The former drill room was turned into a spacious studio and living quarters. Jones was an art instructor at Washington University and was famous for his "light paintings" and electronic art. The couple would soon find that the old police station was anything but a peaceful place to live.

They began to hear the sound of heavy footsteps in the studio at night, followed by a dragging sound and then more footsteps. The sounds were heard night after night, although nothing in the building was ever disturbed or moved. Stereo and electronic equipment in the place would be turned off and yet sound would still come from the speakers. The Jones' unplugged everything and yet the noises continued. The only thing that seemed to help was when Jones began leaving the light on in the studio all night long. The burning lamp seemed to keep the ghostly intruders away.

The house became one of the first investigation sites for famous psychic investigator Gordon Hoener in the 1960's. Hoener ran a small organization called "Haunt Hunters", which set the standard for many paranormal research groups that followed. Hoener ran newspaper ads and appeared on television and radio shows looking for haunted places to investigate. While he would track down many pointless cases, a few of them did turn out to be interesting. His investigations at 14 Newstead Avenue revealed at least one spirit in the building.... one who seemed to be the waiter who was killed there years before.

Hoener came to the building with a reporter named William Keenan from the "St. Louis" Magazine and a couple of independent witnesses. They say down with a Ouija board and attempted to contact the spirit who was haunting the Jones'. Hoener began to ask the presence a number of questions.

"Was the unknown presence a prisoner in this building when it was a jail?" Jones asked the Ouija board.

"YES", came the reply.

"Did he die here?" YES

"A policeman?" NO

"A prisoner?" YES

"Would the presence manifest itself for the group?" YOU - 4 - NO

The group took this to mean that the ghost wanted nothing to do with the other observers, but that it had no problem manifesting itself for the Jones'. This still left Howard Jones feeling unsettled. The only solution he could devise was to add more lamps to the rest of the house. He left them burning day and night and "for the first time, we slept undisturbed," Jones told reporter Walter Orthwein in a 1975 interview.

Between the Jones' and the Piskulic's, another artist used the building as a studio and an apartment. When he moved out of the place, he assured the Piskulic's that the stories about the house had been just that... simply stories. "About this Newstead ghost thing, I've never had any problems with it," he told Matt Piskulic when he was looking over the building to buy it. Matt didn't think anything about it at the time. He knew that it was no secret that the house had often been featured on many local radio and television specials, but the Piskulic's were determined not to let that worry them.

Unfortunately, they started having trouble shortly after they moved in. Each day, the couple heard footsteps banging up the front stairs in broad daylight. Matt first assumed that it was a delivery person, but no package was ever left behind.

The couple planned to live in the building with their company, V.I.P Graphics, until they could afford to move. They selected a small loft just a short flight of stairs away from the attic for their bedroom. One night, Denise was startled awake in the darkness because she heard a baby crying. She first believed that she imagined it and she lay there for several minutes, waiting for it to happen again. Moments later, the crying began once more. It sounded as though it was coming from inside of the walls. It soon became so loud that it woke up Matt as well. The couple tried to figure out a possible cause for the noise (the wind, an animal or anything) and then the screaming began. The sound of a man shrieking began to sound from the attic. It was a long, piercing cry of pain. The Piskulic's slept no more that night.

The following morning, Denise began calling everyone she knew to tell them of their horrifying experience. She then contacted the former owner of the house, an artist named Corey Fosmire. She told him what had happened and then asked that he tell her honestly if anything strange had occurred while he lived there.

The Fosmire's had also attempted to live in and do business at the old police station. Whatever presence was already there however did not seem to care for Fosmire and his family. Disembodied voices called out at night and they heard the same heavy footsteps that the previous occupants, and the Piskulic's, had reported. Stranger still, handprints and footprints appeared on freshly varnished floors and clean windows.... prints that matched no one in the house. Finally, the family was terrified one night by the sound of screaming that echoed throughout the entire house. It was so intense that it seemed to shake the building! The screaming drove them out into the street and they left the house that night.

Despite the bad experiences of past owners, Matt and Denise were determined to make the house and business work. They started to do some renovations that, of course, accentuated the phenomena.

In the summer of 1992, Denise heard a woman calling "hello" while she was in the bathroom. Assuming that someone had arrived on business, she told the visitor that she would be right out. But when Denise opened the door, she found no one waiting for her. She searched the building but no one was there.

The footsteps were heard all summer with much of the activity being centered around the front staircase. Strangely, the footsteps sounded like hard shoe soles on the concrete staircase, even though the steps are thickly carpeted. Normal footsteps make no sound on the stairs, only the phantom ones do.

The steps continued, becoming louder and more frequent. They were sometimes accompanied by the odor of perfume and then evolved into actual apparitions. The first ghost was seen by Denise. Lars Hamilton, who did sales work for the graphics design company, had an office across the hall from Denise. One day as she happened to look across the hall toward the other office, she saw a man stand by the doorway for a moment and then duck out of sight. Assuming that this was Hamilton, Denise went across the hall to ask him a question. There was no one in the office!

Other employees had their own strange experiences. Mary Adler, a layout design artist, was working on a project one morning when she felt someone blowing on the back of her neck. Startled, she spun around to find no one behind her.

Shortly after, a visitor to the business encountered an apparition and the presence continued to show up regularly after that. Strange reports have become commonplace with the staff ever since.

On September 26, 1992, Matt and Denise invited six psychics to the building. They claimed there were many ghosts in the old station house.... some of them permanent residents and others just passing through from one plane to the next.

Eerily, the psychics had no knowledge of the past history of the building and yet they were able to reveal many hidden aspects of the place, impressing the Piskulic's. They stated that the station was filled with confused energy and most of it was centered in the attic. The basement was believed to be the part of the building where most of the violence in the place had occurred. Unknown to the mediums, this was where the prisoners had once been housed.

They also identified a number of ghosts who stayed on in the building, including police officers, jail inmates, a woman whose husband had worked at the station and even a teenaged girl.

The psychics offered to "sweep the building with light" to get the spirits to move on, but Denise declined the offer. "I told them, no, they weren't hurting anything by being here," she told author Robbi Courtaway. "It's kind of live and let live, and they've been here longer than we have, and I just didn't feel the need to do anything like that. They've never really done anything, as far as I'm concerned."

And so, the haunting continues. The glimpses of the people who aren't there continue to occur as do the ghostly footsteps, the opening and closing doors, the calling voices and the water faucets that turn on and off by themselves. The ghosts, it seems, are here to stay.

But what draws the spirits to the former police station on Newstead Avenue? Is it because of the violence and strange events that took place here in the past? The answer to that is still a mystery... but one thing is sure, it may just be one of the most haunted places in St. Louis.

## THE HAUNTINGS OF ALCATRAZ
### Doing Time for Eternity on the Rock

Alcatraz, which earned the nickname of the "Rock", was the ultimate American prison. Bloodletters and badmen and assorted public enemies like Al Capone, Alvin Karpis and Machine-Gun Kelly and others, called this place the end of the line. For 29 years, the damp, fogged-in prison kept the country's most notorious criminals put away from the rest of the world. The heavy mists, cold wind and water and the foghorns of the bay made Alcatraz the loneliest of the prisons.

From the time it became a federal prison in 1934 until it was closed down in 1963, the steel doors clanged shut behind more than 1,000 hardened convicts, criminals and escape artists. Alcatraz was not conceived as a facility for rehabilitation. It was a place of total punishment and minimum privilege. And those who survived it often did so at the cost of their sanity... and some believe their souls.

Alcatraz Island, located in the mists off of San Francisco, received its name in 1775 when the Spanish explorers charted San Francisco bay. They named the rocky piece of land La Isla de los Alcatraces, or the "Island of Pelicans". The island was totally uninhabited, plagued by barren ground, little vegetation and surrounding water that churned with swift currents.

In 1847, Alcatraz was taken over by the United States military. The Rock had extreme strategic value, especially during these times of tension between the United States and the Mexican government. Topographical engineers began conducting geological surveys and by 1853, a military fortress was started. One year later, a lighthouse was established (the first on the Pacific Coast) to guide ships through the Golden Gate.

A few years later, a military fort was erected on the island and in 1859, Alcatraz saw its first prisoners, a contingent of court-martialed, military convicts. Then in 1861, Alcatraz started to receive Confederate prisoners, thanks to its natural isolation created by the surrounding waters. Until the end of the Civil War, the number of prisoners here numbered from 15 to 50. They consisted of soldiers, Confederate privateers, and southern sympathizers. They were confined in the dark basement of the guardhouse and conditions were fairly grim. The men slept side-by-side, head to toe, lying on the stone floor of the basement. There was no running water, no heat and no latrines. Disease and infestations of lice spread from man to man and not surprisingly, overcrowding was a serious problem. They were often bound by six-foot chains attached to iron balls, fed bread and water and confined in "sweatboxes" as punishment.

After the war ended, the fort was deemed obsolete and was no longer needed. The prison continued to be used though and soon, more buildings and cell houses were added. In the 1870's and 1880's, Indian chiefs and tribal leaders who refused to give into the white man were incarcerated on Alcatraz. They shared quarters with the worst of the military prisoners. The island became a shipping point for incorrigible deserters, thieves, rapists and repeated escapees.

In 1898, the Spanish-American War sent the prisoner population from less than 100 to over 450. The Rock became a holding pen for Spanish prisoners brought over from the Phillipines. Around 1900 though, Alcatraz again became a disciplinary barracks for military prisoners. Ironically, it also served as a health resort for soldiers returning from the Phillipines and Cuba with tropical diseases. The overcrowding caused by a combination of criminals and recovering soldiers resulted in pardons to reduce the number of men housed on the island.

By 1902, the Alcatraz prison population averaged around 500 men per year, with many of the men serving sentences of two years or less. The wooden barracks on the island had fallen into a ramshackle state, thanks to the damp, salt air and so in 1904, work was begun to modernize the facility. Prisoner work crews began extending the stockade wall and constructing a new mess hall, kitchen, shops, a library and a wash house. Work continued on the prison for the next several years and even managed to survive the Great Earthquake of 1906. The disaster left San Francisco in shambles and a large fissure opened up on Alcatraz, but left the buildings untouched. Prisoners from the heavily damaged San Francisco jail were temporarily housed on the island until the city's jail could be rebuilt.

Construction of the new buildings was completed in 1909 and in 1911, the facility was officially named the "United States Disciplinary Barracks". In addition to Army prisoners, the Rock was also used to house seamen captured on German vessels during the First World War. Alcatraz was the Army's first long-term prison and it quickly gained a reputation for being a tough facility. There were strict rules and regulations with punishments ranging from loss of privileges to solitary confinement, restricted diet, hard labor and even a 12-pound ball and ankle chain.

Despite the stringent rules though, Alcatraz was still mainly a minimum-security facility. Inmates were given various work assignments, depending on how responsible they were. Many of them worked as general servants, cooking and cleaning for families of soldiers housed on the island. In many cases, the prisoners were even entrusted to care for the children of officers. However, this lack of strict security worked to the favor to those inmates who tried to escape. Most of those who tried for freedom never made it to the mainland and were forced to turn back and be rescued. Those who were not missed and did not turn back usually drowned in the harsh waters of the bay.

Other escape attempts were made by men who did not go into the water. During the great influenza epidemic of 1918, inmates stole flu masks and officer's uniforms and causally caught a military launch heading for the base at the Presidio. The convicts made it as far as Modesto, California before they were captured.

During the 1920's, Alcatraz gradually fell into disuse. The lighthouse keeper, a few Army personnel and the most hardened of the military prisoners were the only ones who remained on the island. The mostly empty buildings slowly crumbled... but a change was coming.

The social upheaval and the rampant crime of the 1920's and 1930's brought new life to Alcatraz. Attorney General Homer Cummings supported J. Edgar Hoover and the FBI in creating a new, escape-proof prison that would send fear into the hearts of criminals. They decided that Alcatraz would be the perfect location for such a penitentiary. In 1933, the facility was officially turned over to the Federal Bureau of Prisons and the Attorney General asked James A. Johnston of San Francisco to take over as warden of the new prison. He implemented a strict set and rules and regulations for the facility and selected the best available guards and officers from the federal penal system.

Construction was quickly started on the new project and practically the entire cellblock building was built atop the old Army fort. Part of the old Army prison was used but the iron bars were replaced by bars of hardened steel. Gun towers were erected at various points around the island and the cellblocks were equipped with catwalks, gun walks, electric locks, metal detectors, a well-stocked arsenal, barbed and cyclone wire fencing and even tear gas containers that were fitted into the ceiling of the dining hall and elsewhere. Apartments for the guards and their families were built on the old parade grounds and the lighthouse keeper's mansion was taken over for the warden's residence. Alcatraz had been turned into an impregnable fortress.

Wardens from prisons all over the country were polled and were permitted to send their most incorrigible inmates to the Rock. These included inmates with behavioral problems, those with a history of escape attempts and even high-profile inmates who were receiving privileges because of their status or notoriety. Each train that came from the various prisons seemed to have a "celebrity" on board. Among the first groups were inmates Al Capone, Doc Barker (who was the last surviving member of the Ma Barker Gang), George "Machine Gun" Kelly, Robert "Birdman of Alcatraz" Stroud, and Floyd Hamilton (a gang member and driver for Bonnie & Clyde), and Alvin "Creepy" Karpis.

When they arrived on Alcatraz, the inmates were driven in a small transfer van to the top of the hill. They were processed in the basement area and provided with their basic amenities and a quick shower.

Al Capone arrived at the prison in August 1934. Upon his arrival, he quickly learned that while he may have once been famous, on Alcatraz, he was only a number. He made attempts to flaunt the power that he had enjoyed at the Federal prison in Atlanta and was used to the special benefits that he was awarded by guards and wardens alike. He was arrogant and unlike most of the other prisoners, was not a veteran of the penal system. He had only spent a short time in prison and his stay had been much different than for most other cons. Capone had possessed the ability to control his environment through wealth and power, but he was soon to learn that things were much different at Alcatraz.

Warden Johnston had a custom of meeting new prisoners when they arrived and he gave them a brief orientation. Johnston later wrote in his memoirs that he had little trouble recognizing Capone when he saw him. Capone was grinning and making comments to other prisoners as he stood in the lineup. When it became his turn to approach the warden, Johnston ignored him and simply gave him a standard prison number, just like all of the other men. During Capone's time on Alcatraz, he made a number of attempts to convince Johnston that he deserved special consideration. None of them were successful and at one point, Capone finally conceded that "it looks like Alcatraz has got me licked."

And he wouldn't be the only one to feel that way.

Alcatraz was not a recreational prison. It was a place of penitence, just as the Quakers who had devised the American prison system had planned for all prisons to be. There were no trustees here. It was a place where the inmates had but five rights... food, clothing, a private cell, a shower once a week and the right to see a doctor.

Each of the cells in America's "first escape-proof prison" measured 4 x 8 feet, had a single fold-up bunk, a toilet, a desk, a chair and a sink. An inmate's day would begin at 6:30 in the morning, when he was awakened and then given 25 minutes to clean his cell and to stand and be counted. At 6:55, the individual tiers of cells would be opened and prisoners would march in a single file line to the mess hall. They were given 20 minutes to eat and then were marched out to line up for work assignments. The routine never varied and was completely methodical.

The main corridor of the prison was given the name "Broadway" by the inmates and the cells here were considered the least desirable. The ones on the bottom tier were always cold and damp and they were also the least private, since guards, inmates and staff members were always passing through this corridor. New prisoners were generally assigned to the second tier of B Block in a quarantine status for the first three months of their sentence.

The guards at Alcatraz were almost as hardened as the prisoners themselves. They numbered the inmates one to three, which was stunning considering that most prisons were at least one guard to every twelve inmates. Gun galleries had been placed at each end of the cell blocks and as many as 12 counts each day allowed the guards to keep very close tabs on the men on their watch. Because of the small number of total inmates at Alcatraz, the guards generally knew the inmates by name.

While the cells the prisoners lived in were barren at best, they must have seemed like luxury hotel rooms compared to the punishment cells. Here, the men were stripped of all but their basic right to food and even then, what they were served barely sustained the convict's life, let alone his health.

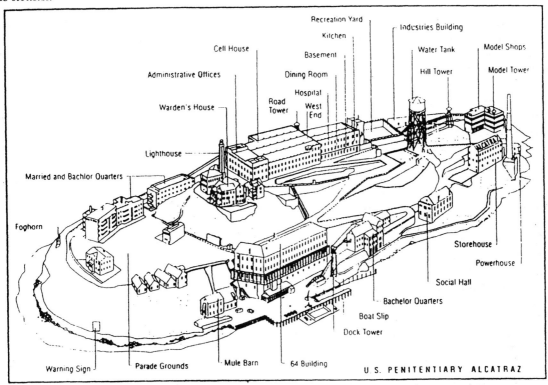

A diagram of the cell house and administrative offices on Alcatraz. Featured in a manuscript called "Alcatraz Screw" by Velma Gregory. Drawing by ArtWorks of San Anselmo, California and commissioned by George H. Gregory (Courtesy of Rob and Anne Wlodarski)

One place of punishment was the single "Strip Cell", which was dubbed the "Oriental". This dark, steel-encased cell had no toilet and no sink. There was only a hole in the floor that could be flushed from the outside. Inmates were placed in the cell with no clothing and were given little food. The cell had a standard set of bars, with an expanded opening to pass food through, but a solid steel door enclosed the prisoner in total darkness. They were usually kept in this cell for 1-2 days. The cell was cold and completely bare, save for a straw sleeping mattress that the guards removed each morning. This cell was used a punishment for the most severe violations and was feared by the prison population.

The "Hole" was a similar type of cell. There were several of them and they were all located on the bottom tier of cells and were considered to be a severe punishment by the inmates. Mattresses were again taken away and prisoners were sustained by meals of bread and water, which was supplemented by a solid meal every third day. Steel doors also closed these cells off from the daylight, although a low wattage bulb was suspended from the ceiling. Inmates could spend up to 19 days here, completely silent and isolated from everyone. Time in the "hole" usually meant psychological and sometimes even physical torture.

Usually, convicts who were thrown into the "hole" for anything other than a minor infraction were beaten by the guards. The screams from the men being beaten in one of the four "holes" located on the bottom tier of D Block echoed throughout the block as though being amplified through a megaphone. When the inmates of D Block (which had been designated at a disciplinary unit by the warden) heard a fellow convict being worked over, they would start making noises that would be picked up in Blocks B and C and would then sound throughout the entire island.

Often when men emerged from the darkness and isolation of the "hole", they would be totally senseless and would end up in the prison's hospital ward, devoid of their sanity. Others came out with pnuemonia and arthritis after spending days or weeks on the cold cement floor with no clothing. Some men never came out of the "hole" at all.

And there were even worse places to be sent than the "hole". Located in front of unused A Block was a staircase that led down to a large steel door. Behind the door were catacomb-like corridors and stone archways that led to the sealed off gun ports from the days when Alcatraz was a fort. Fireplaces located in several of the rooms were never used for warmth, but to heat up cannonballs so that they would start fires after reaching their targets. Two of the other rooms located in this dank, underground area were dungeons.

Prisoners who had the misfortune of being placed in the dungeons were not only locked in, but also chained to the walls. Their screams could not be heard in the main prison. The only toilet they had was a bucket, which was emptied once each week. For food, they received two cups of water and one slice of bread each day. Every third day, they would receive a regular meal. The men were stripped of their clothing and their dignity as guards chained them to the wall in a standing position from six in the morning until six at night. In the darkest hours, they were given a blanket to sleep on.

Thankfully, the dungeons were rarely used, but the dark cells of D Block, known as the "hole, were regularly filled.

Al Capone was in the "hole" three times during his 4 1/2-year stay at Alcatraz. The first years of Alcatraz were known as the "silent years" and during this period, the rules stated that no prisoners were allowed to speak to one another, sing, hum or whistle. Talking was forbidden in the cells, in the mess hall and even in the showers. The inmates were allowed to talk for three minutes during the morning and afternoon recreation yard periods and for two hours on weekends.

Capone, who remained arrogant for some time after his arrival, decided that the rule of silence should not apply to him. He ended up being sent to the "hole" for two, 10-day stretches for talking to other inmates. He also spent a full 19 days on the "hole" for trying to bribe a guard for information about the outside world. Prisoners were not allowed newspapers or magazines that would inform them of current events. Each time that Capone was sent to the "hole", he emerged a little worse for wear. Eventually, the Rock would break him completely.

Many of the prisoners who served time in Alcatraz ended up insane. Capone may have been one of them for time here was not easy on the ex-gangland boss. On one occasion, he got into a fight with another inmate in the recreation yard and was placed in isolation for eight days. Another time, while working in the prison basement, an inmate standing in line for a haircut exchanged words with Capone and then stabbed him with a pair of scissors. Capone was sent to the prison hospital but was released a few days later with a minor wound.

The attempts on his life, the no-talking rule, the beatings and the prison routine itself began to take their toll on Capone. After several fights in the yard, he was excused from his recreation periods and being adept with a banjo, joined a four-man prison band. The drummer in the group was "Machine-Gun" Kelly. Although gifts were not permitted for prisoners on the Rock, musical instruments were and Capone's wife sent him a banjo shortly after he was incarcerated. After band practice, Capone always returned immediately to his cell, hoping to stay away from the other convicts.

Occasionally, guards reported that he would refuse to leave his cell to go to the mess hall and eat. They would often find him crouched down in the corner of his cell like an animal. On other occasions, he would mumble to himself or babble in baby talk or simply sit on his bed and strum little tunes on his banjo. Years later, another inmate recalled that Capone would sometimes stay in his cell and make his bunk over and over again.

After more than three years on the Rock, Capone was on the edge of total insanity. He spent the last year of his sentence in the hospital ward, undergoing treatment for an advanced case of syphilis. Most of the time he spent in the ward, he spent playing his banjo. His last day on Alcatraz was January 6, 1939. He was then transferred to the new Federal prison at Terminal Island near Los Angeles. When he was paroled, he became a recluse at his Palm Island, Florida estate. He died, broken and insane, in 1947.

And Al Capone was far from the only man to surrender his sanity to Alcatraz. In 1937 alone, 14 of the prisoners went rampantly insane and that does not include the men who slowly became "stir crazy" from the brutal conditions of the place. To Warden Johnston, mental illness was nothing more than an excuse to get out of work. As author Richard Winer once wrote, "it would be interesting to know what the warden thought of Rube Persful".

Persful was a former gangster and bank robber who was working in one of the shops, when he picked up a hatchet, placed his left hand on a block of wood and while laughing maniacally, began hacking off the fingers on his hand. Then, he placed his right hand on the block and pleaded with a guard to chop off those fingers as well. Persful was placed in the hospital, but was not declared insane.

An inmate named Joe Bowers slashed his own throat with a pair of broken eyeglasses. He was given first aid and then was thrown into the "hole". After his release, he ran away from his work area and scaled a chain-link fence, fully aware that the guards would shoot him. They opened fire and his body fell 75 feet down to the rocks below the fence.

Ed Wutke, a former sailor who had been sent to Alcatraz on murder charges, managed to fatally slice through his jugular vein with the blade from a pencil sharpener.

These were not the only attempts at suicide and mutilation either. It was believed that more men suffered mental breakdowns at Alcatraz, by percentage, than at any other Federal prisons.

In 1941, inmate Henry Young went on trail for the murder of a fellow prisoner and his accomplice in a failed escape attempt, Rufus McCain. Young's attorney claimed that Alcatraz guards had frequently beaten his client and that he had endured long periods of extreme isolation. While Young was depicted as sympathetic, he was actually a difficult inmate who often provoked fights with other prisoners. He was considered a violent risk and he later murdered two guards during an escape attempt. After that, Young and his eventual victim, McCain, spent nearly 22 months in solitary confinement.

After the two men returned to the normal prison population, McCain was assigned to the tailoring shop and Young to the furniture shop, located directly upstairs. On December 3, 1940 Young waited until just after a prisoner count and then when a guard's attention was diverted, he ran downstairs and stabbed McCain. The other man went into shock and he died five hours later. Young refused to say why he had killed the man.

During his trial, Young's attorney claimed that because Young was held in isolation for so long, he could not be held responsible for his actions. He had been subjected to cruel and unusual punishment and because of this, his responses to hostile situations had become desperately violent.

The attorney subpoenaed Warden Johnston to testify about the prison's conditions and policies and in addition, several inmates were also called to recount the state of Alcatraz. The prisoners told of being locked in the dungeons and of being beaten by the guards. They also testified to knowing several inmates who had gone insane because of such treatment. The jury ended up sympathizing with Young's case and he was convicted of a manslaughter charge that only added a few years on this original sentence.

After the trial, he was transferred to the Medical Center for Federal Prisoners in Springfield, Missouri. After serving his Federal sentence, he was sent to the Washington State Penitentiary and was paroled in 1972. He had spent nearly 40 years in prison. He later disappeared and it is unknown whether he is still alive today.

During the 29 years that Alcatraz was in operation, there were over 14 escape attempts in which 34 different men risked their lives to try and make it off the Rock. Almost all of the men were either killed or recaptured. Only one of the men was known to have made it ashore. John Paul Scott was recaptured when he was found shivering in the rocks near the Golden Gate Bridge. As for the men who vanished, it was believed that most of them succumbed to the cold water and the always churning currents that moved past the island. Although no bodies were ever recovered, the authorities always assumed that the men had drowned and marked the cases as closed.

Of all of the escape attempts though, two of them left a lasting mark on the history of the island. The most traumatic and violent of the two took place in 1946. It was later dubbed the "Battle of Alcatraz" and it began as a well-planned and well-organized breakout from the "escape-proof" prison.

In May 1946, six inmates captured a gun cage, obtained prison keys and took over a cell house in less than an hour. The breakout attempt might have succeeded if not for the fact that a guard, Bill Miller, didn't return one of the keys to the gun cage as soon as he finished using it, as was required by prison regulations. The strange twist of fate completely disrupted the escape attempt. When the cons captured the gun cage, they found all of the keys except for the one that would let them out of the cell building. This was the key that Miller failed to return to the guard cage. The breakout was grounded before it even began.

But the prisoners, Bernard Coy, Joe Cretzer, and Marvin Hubbard, Sam Shockley, Miran Thompson, and Clarence Carnes, would not give up. They took a number of guards hostage and before the escape attempts was over, three of the guards were dead and others were wounded.

Two of them were murdered in cold blood in cells 402 and 403, which were later changed to C-102 and C-104.

Thousands of spectators watched from San Francisco as U.S. Marines invaded the island and barraged the cell block with mortars and grenades. The helpless inmates inside of the building took refuge behind water-soaked mattresses and tried to stay close to the floor and out of the path of the bullets that riddled the cells. But even after realizing that they could not escape, the six would-be escapees decided to fight it out.

Warden Johnston, unable to get a report on how many convicts were actually involved in the battle, came to believe that the safety of San Francisco itself might be at risk. With the entire prison under siege, he called for aid from the Navy, the Coast Guard, as well as the Marines. Before it was all over, two Navy destroyers, two Air Force planes, a Coast Guard cutter, a company of Marines, Army officers, police units, and guards from Leavenworth and San Quentin descended on the island.

The fighting lasted for two days. With no place to hide from the constant gunfire, Cretzer, Coy and Hubbard climbed into a utility corridor for safety. The other three men returned to their cells, hoping they would not be identified as participants in the attempt. In the bloody aftermath, Cretzer, Coy and Hubbard were killed in the corridor from bullets and shrapnel from explosives. Thompson and Shockley were later executed in the gas chamber at San Quentin and Carnes received a sentence of life, plus 99 years. His life was spared because he helped some of the wounded hostages. The cell building was heavily damaged and took months to repair.

While this may be the most violent escape from Alcatraz, it is by all means not the most famous. This attempt was that of Frank Morris and brothers Clarence and John Anglin. In 1962, a fellow prisoner named Allen West helped the trio to devise a clever plan to construct a raft, inflatable life vests and human-like dummies that could be used to fool the guards during head counts. Over a several month period, the men used tools stolen from work sites to chip away at the vent shafts in their cells. They fabricated the life vests, the rafts and the dummies. They also ingeniously created replicated grills that hid the chipped away cement around the small vents. The quality of the human heads and faked grills was remarkable as they used only paint kits and a soap and concrete powder to make them. They also collected hair from the barbershop to make the dummies more lifelike. These painstaking preparations took over six months.

On the night of June 11, 1962, immediately following the head count at 9:30, Morris and the Anglin's scooted through the vents and scaled the utility shafts to the upper levels. Once they reached the roof, they climbed through a ventilator duct and made it to the edge of the building. After descending pipes along the cement wall, all three climbed over a 15-foot fence and made it to the island's shore, where they inflated the rafts and vests. They set out into the cold waters of the bay and were never seen again.

The next morning, when one of the prisoners failed to rise for the morning count, a guard jammed his club through the cell bars at the man. To his shock, a fake head rolled off the bunk and landed on the floor!

Almost 40 years later, it is still unknown whether or not the prisoners made a successful escape. The story has been dramatized in several books and was made into a gripping film starring Clint Eastwood. The FBI actively pursued the case but never found any worthwhile leads.

After this last escape attempt, the days of the prison were numbered. Ironically, the frigid waters around the island, which had long prevented escape, were believed to be the leading ruin of the prison. After the escape of Morris and the Anglin's, the prison was examined because of the deteriorating conditions of the structure, caused mostly by the corrosive effects of the salt water around it. In addition, budget cuts had recently forced security measures at the prison to become more lax. On top of that, the exorbitant cost of running the place continued to increase and over $5 million was going to be needed for renovations. According to U.S. Attorney General Robert Kennedy, the prison was no longer necessary to have open.

On March 23, 1963, Alcatraz closed it doors for good. After that, the island was essentially abandoned while various groups tried to decide what to do with it. Then, in 1969, a large group of American Indians landed on the island and declared that it was Native American property. They had great plans for the island, which included a school and a Native American cultural center. The Indians soon had the attention of the media and the government and a number of meetings were held about the fate of Alcatraz.

The volume of visitors to the island soon became overwhelming. Somehow, during the talks, the island had become a haven for the homeless and the less fortunate. The Indians were soon faced with the problem of no natural resources and the fact that food and water had to be brought over from the mainland. The situation soon became so desperate that island occupants were forced to take drastic measures to survive. In order to raise money for supplies, they began stripping copper wire and pipes from the island buildings to sell as scrap metal. A tragedy occurred around this same time when Yvonne Oakes, the daughter of one of the key Indian activists, fell to her death from the third story window. The Oakes family left Alcatraz and never returned.

Then, during the evening hours of June 1, 1970, a fire was started and raged out of control. It damaged several of the buildings and destroyed the Warden's residence, the lighthouse keeper's home and even badly damaged the historic lighthouse itself.

Tension now developed between Federal officials and the Indians as the government blamed the activists for the fire. The press, which had been previously sympathetic toward the Native Americans, now turned against them and began to publish stories about beatings and assaults that were allegedly occurring on the island. Support for the Indians now disintegrated, especially in light of the fact that the original activists had already left Alcatraz. Those who remained were seen as little more than "squatters". On June 11, 1971, the Coast Guard, along with 20 U.S. Marshals descended on the island and removed the remaining residents.

Alcatraz was empty once more.

In 1972, Congress created the Golden Gate National Recreation Area and Alcatraz Island fell under the purview of the National Park Service. It was opened to the public in the fall of 1973 and has become today one of the most popular of America's park sites.

During the day, the old prison is a bustling place, filled with tour guides and visitors... but at night, the building is filled with the inexplicable. Many believe that the energy of those who came to serve time on the Rock still remains, that Alcatraz is an immense haunted house... a place where strange things can and do happen today!

Every visitor who arrives by boat on Alcatraz follows the same path once walked by the criminals who came to do time on the Rock. The tourists who come here pass through the warden's office and the visiting room and eventually enter the cell house. After passing the double steel doors, a visitor can see that just past C Block. If they look opposite the visiting room, they will find a metal door that looks as though it was once welded shut. Although the tour guides don't usually mention it, behind that door if the utility corridor where Coy, Cretzer and Hubbard were killed by grenades and bullets in 1946.

It was also behind this door where a night watchman heard strange, clanging sounds in 1976. He opened the door and peered down the dark corridor, shining his flashlight on the maze of pipes and conduits. He could see nothing and there were no sounds. When he closed the door, the noises started again. Again, the door was opened up but there was still nothing that could be causing the sounds. The night watchman did not believe in ghosts, so he shut the door again and continued on his way. Some have wondered if the eerie noises may have been the reason why the door was once welded shut? Since that time, this utility corridor has come to be recognized as one of the most haunted spots in the prison.

Other night watchmen who have patrolled this cell house, after the last of the tourist boats have left for the day, say that they have heard the sounds of what appear to be men running coming the from the upper tiers. Thinking that an intruder is inside the prison, the watchmen have investigated the sounds, but always find nothing.

One Park Service employee told author Richard Winer (anonymously, of course) that she had been working one rainy afternoon when the sparse number of tourists were not enough to keep all of the guides busy. She went for a walk in front of A Block and was just past the door that led down to the dungeons when she heard a loud scream from the bottom of the stairs. She ran away without looking to see if anyone was down there.

When Winer asked why she didn't report the incident, she replied "I didn't dare mention it because the day before, everyone was ridiculing another worker who reported hearing men's voices coming from the hospital ward and when he checked the ward, it was empty."

Several of the guides and rangers also expressed to Winer a strangeness about one of the "hole" cells, number 14D. "There's a feeling of sudden intensity that comes from spending more than a few minutes around that cell," one of them said.

Another guide also spoke up about that particular cell. "That cell, 14D, is always cold. It's even colder than the other three dark cells. Sometimes it gets warm out here - so hot that you have to take your jacket off. The temperature inside the cell house can be in the 70's, yet 14D is still cold... so cold that you need a jacket if you spend any time in it."

Oddly, the tour guides were not the only ones to have strange experiences in that particular cell. Authors Rob and Anne Wlodarksi were able to interview several former guards from the prison and one of them told of some pretty terrifying incidents that took place near the "holes" and in particular, Cell 14D.

During the guard's stint in the middle 1940's, an inmate was locked in the cell for some forgotten infraction. According to the officer, the inmate began screaming within seconds of being locked in. He claimed that some creature with "glowing eyes" was locked in with him. As tales of a ghostly presence wandering the nearby corridor were a continual source of practical jokes among the guards, no one took the convict's cries of being "attacked" very seriously.

The man's screaming continued on into the night until finally, there was silence. The following day, guards inspected the cell and they found the convict dead. A horrible expression had been frozen onto the man's face and there were clear marks of hands around his throat! The autopsy revealed that the strangulation could not have been self-inflicted. Some believed that he might have been choked by one of the guards, who had been fed up with the man's screaming, but no one ever admitted it.

A few of the officers blamed something else for the man's death. They believed that the killer had been the spirit of a former inmate. To add to the mystery, on the day following the tragedy, several guards who were performing a head count noticed that there were too many men in the lineup. Then, at the end of the line, they saw the face of the convict who had recently been strangled in the "hole"! As they all looked on in stunned silence, the figure abruptly vanished.

When authors Richard Winer and Nancy Osborn visited Alcatraz, they ventured down to this cell with a park ranger. As Osborn entered the cramped chamber, she immediately felt strong vibrations coming from inside. Winer and the ranger followed her inside and both experienced a tingling sensation in their hands and arms. They were convinced that something else was in the cell with them. According to the writers, the strongest energy seemed to come from the far corner of the cell. Here, naked and frightened prisoners would huddle in the darkness. Osborn stated that she had never felt such energy in one spot.

And that's not all... It may come as no surprise to many readers to learn that this same cell was the one where Henry Young was confined after his attempted jailbreak with Rufus McCain. He was confined here in the darkness for almost two years and when he emerged, he was mad from the horrible isolation that he had endured. Just 11 days later, he killed McCain in the prison shop. Young found sympathy from the jury as it was said that his years of confinement in the "hole" had deprived him of everything spiritual and human.

Did Henry Young leave a piece of his insanity behind in Cell 14D... or did something already there give a piece of itself to Young?

If, as many believe, ghosts return to haunt the places where they suffered traumatic experiences when they were alive, then Alcatraz must be loaded with spirits.

According to Rob and Anne Wlodarksi, a number of guards who served between 1946 and 1963 experienced strange happenings on Alcatraz. From the grounds of the prison to the caverns beneath the buildings, there was often talk of people sobbing and moaning, inexplicable smells, cold spots and spectral apparitions. Even guests and families who lived on the island claimed to occasionally see the ghostly forms of prisoners and even phantom soldiers.

Phantom gunshots were known to send seasoned guards cringing on the ground in the belief that the prisoners had escaped and had obtained weapons. There was never an explanation. A deserted laundry room would sometimes fill with the smell of smoke, even though nothing was burning. The guards would be sent running from the room, only to return later and find that the air was clear.

Even Warden Johnston, who did not believe in ghosts, once encountered the unmistakable sound of a person sobbing while he accompanied some guests on a tour of the prison. He swore that the sounds came from inside of the dungeon walls. The strange sounds were followed by an ice-cold wind that swirled through the entire group. He could offer no explanation for the weird events.

And since the prison has been closed down, the ghostly happenings seem to have intensified. Famous psychic Peter James went to Alcatraz during the taping of a television show in 1992. During the filming, a number of the staff members confirmed the hauntings at the prison. Many of them had experienced the bizarre crashing sounds, cell doors that mysteriously closed and the intense feeling of being watched.

Peter James walked through the prison, hoping to get impressions about various parts of the place. At one point, he began to pick up the voices of souls that had been driven mad and unusual vibrations of abuse and pain. In one particular cell, he sensed that a man had been murdered. Having no idea of the history of that particular cell, he didn't realize that one of the guards who was killed during the 1946 escape attempt was shot down in that room.

Renowned ghost hunter and psychic Richard Senate also spent the night on Alcatraz as part of a radio promotion. He chose to stay in Al Capone's old cell. According to Senate, emotions seemed to drip from every corner of the prison as the night progressed. He and another psychic visited a number of locations where rangers had reported marching feet and other strange sounds but nothing out of the ordinary happened.

Finally, Senate locked himself inside of the one of the "hole" cells, 12D, where there have been reports of an angry ghost being present. As soon as the steel door clanged shut, Senate said that he felt icy fingers creep up the back of his neck. Every hair on his body seemed to stand on end!

And while Senate found no trace of Al Capone in his former cell, there is a possibility that the famous gangster managed to leave a mark on the old prison anyway.

As Richard Winer and Nancy Osborn left Alcatraz on a foggy afternoon in the late 1970's, a Park Service employee approached them and asked if they were the ones writing the book about ghosts at Alcatraz?

"I overheard some of your conversations back on the island," he explained. "I myself heard something in the cell house early one morning. It was down in the shower room. A con killed his homosexual lover in there once - right in front of a guard. I guess it was a broken romance thing."

The man paused in his story as the ferryboat back to San Francisco lurched on the rough water of the bay.

"It's kind of strange what I heard," he continued. "It was like banjo music. The room was empty, but I definitely heard banjo music coming from there. Maybe back in the days when it was a fort or Army stockade, there was some guy here who played that instrument."

As the boat continued on toward San Francisco, Winer said that he looked back at the Rock, which was now completely enshrouded in fog. "I thought of Al Capone during the most traumatic days of his life," he wrote," when, rather than risk going out to the exercise yard with the other inmates, he sat in the shower room strumming on his banjo."

Special Thanks for this section goes to authors Rob and Anne Wlodarksi and their excellent book, HAUNTED ALCATRAZ (1998)

# SELECT BIBLIOGRAPHY &
# RECOMMENDED READING
## For Crime Buffs and Fans of the Supernatural

Adams, Charles J., III - Philadelphia Ghost Stories (1998)
Aiuto, Russell - Lizzie Borden (2000)
Anger, Kenneth - Hollywood Babylon (1975)
Anger, Kenneth - Hollywood Babylon 2 (1984)
Asbury, Herbet - Gem of the Prairie (1940)
Austin, John - Hollywood's Unsolved Mysteries (1970 / 1990)
Bardens, Dennis - Ghosts & Hauntings (1968)
Bardsley, Marilyn - The Black Dahlia (2000)
Bell, Rachel - Ted Bundy (2000)
Bingham, Joan & Dolores Riccio - More Haunted Houses (1991)
Black Dahlia Website (www.bethshort.com) note: excellent!
Brown, Arnold - Lizzie Borden: The Legend, the Truth, the Final Chapter (1991)
Bruce, J. Campbell - Escape from Alcatraz (1963 / 1976)
Bryant, Marley - Jesse James (1998)
Callon, Sim & Carolyn Vance Smith - Goat Castle Murder (1985)
Canning, John - 50 Great Horror Stories (1971)
Christensen, Madonna Dries - The Black Hills Phantom (Ghosts of the Prairie Magazine / 1999)
Churchill, Allen - Pictorial History of American Crime (1964)
Collins, Max Allan - Angel in Black (2001)
Courtaway, Robbi - Spirits of St. Louis (1999)
Culler, Sara Jo - Goat Castle or Ghost Castle? (Ghosts of the Prairie Magazine / 1998)
Deakin, James - A Grave for Bobby (1990)
Edmonds, Andy - Hot Toddy! (1989)
Esslinger, Michael - The Rigid Silence: A Brief History of Alcatraz (2001)
Fate Magazine - October 1995 / Various Issues
Flanagan, Mike - Complete Idiot's Guide to the Old West (1999)
Franklin Castle Website (www.franklincastle.com)
Gilbert, Joan - Missouri Ghosts (1997)
Gilmore, John - Severed (1994)
Graham, D. Douglas - The Most Haunted House in Town (Fate / 1995)
Guiley, Rosemary Ellen - Encyclopedia of Ghosts & Spirits (1992 / 2000)
Heimann, Jim - Sins of the City (1999)
Helmer, William - Public Enemies (1998)
Hensley, Douglas - Hell's Gate (1993)
Jacobson, Laurie - Hollywood haunted (1994)
Jameson, WC - Unsolved Mysteries of the Old West (1999)
Kane, Harnett - Natchez on the Mississippi (1947)
Knowlton, Janice - Daddy was the Black Dahlia Killer (1995)
Hauck, Dennis William - Haunted Places: The National Directory (1996)
Kent, David - Forty Whacks (1992)
Kurland, Michael - Complete Idiot's Guide to Unsolved Mysteries (2000)
L'Aloge, Bob - Ghosts and Mysteries of the Old West (1991)
Lamparski, Richard - Lamparski's Hidden Hollywood (1981)
Lincoln, Victoria - A Private Disgrace: Lizzie Borden by Daylight (1967)
Lindberg, Richard - Chicago by Gaslight (1996)
Lindberg, Richard - Return to the Scene of the Crime (1999)
Lore, Davis - Inside the Pen (Columbus Dispatch Newspaper / 1984)
Lyle, Katie Letcher - The Man who Wanted Seven Wives (1986)
Martinez, Lionel - Murder in North America (1991)

May, Antoinette - Haunted Houses of California (1990)
Mercado, Carol & O.A. - Voice from the Grave (1979)
Michaels, Susan - Sightings (1996)
Munn, Michael - Hollywood Murder Case Book (1987)
Myers, Arthur - Ghost Hunter's Guide to Haunted Landmarks (1993)
Mysteries & Scandals (E! Entertainment Television)
Nash, Jay Robert - Bloodletters and Badmen (1995)
Nash, Jay Robert - Encyclopedia of Western Lawmen and Outlaws (1992)
Night Visitors (Documentary - Impact TV / 2000)
O'Donnell, Eliot - A Casebook of Ghosts (1989)
Phillips, Ben - Eastern State Penitentiary: 140 Years of Reform (1996)
Radin, Edward - Lizzie Borden: The Untold Story (1961)
Reynolds, James - Ghosts in American House (1955)
Roberts, Nancy - Haunted Houses (1998)
Ross, James - I, Jesse James (1988)
Schechter, Harold - Depraved (1994)
Schechter, Harold - A-Z Encyclopedia of Serial Killers (1996)
Scott, Beth & Michael Norman - Haunted Heartland (1985)
Senate, Richard - Ghost Stalker's Guide to Haunted California (1998)
Shelton, Herma - Personal Correspondence & Information
Sifakis, Carl - Encyclopedia of American Crime (1982)
Sifakis, Carl - The Mafia Encyclopedia (1987)
Smith, Barbara - Ghost Stories of Hollywood (2000)
Somerlott, Robert - Here, Mr. Splitfoot (1971)
Spiering, Frank - Lizzie (1984)
Steiger, Brad & Sherrie Steiger - Hollywood and the Supernatural (1990)
Steiger, Brad & Sherrie Steiger - Montezuma's Serpent (1992)
Sullivan, Robert - Goodbye Lizzie Borden (1974)
Taylor, Troy - Haunted Illinois (1999/2001)
Taylor, Troy - Gangland Ghosts (Ghosts of the Prairie Magazine / 1998)
Taylor, Troy - Haunted New Orleans (2000)
Taylor, Troy - Spirits of the Civil War (1999)
Tefertiller, Casey - Wyatt Earp (1997)
Topeka Daily Capital (1886)
Walker, Dale - Legends and Lies (1997)
Winer, Richard & Nancy Osborn- Haunted Houses (1979)
Winer, Richard & Nancy Osborn Ishmael - More Haunted Houses (1981)
Winer, Richard - Houses of Horror (1983)
Williams, Brad & Choral Pepper - Mysterious West (1967)
Williamson, Dwight - Mamie Thurman Story (Logan Banner Newspaper - 1985)
Wlodarksi, Robert & Anne - Haunted Alcatraz (1998)
Wlodarski, Robert & Anne - Southern Fried Spirits (2000)
Woodyard, Chris - Haunted Ohio II (1992)
Woodyard, Chris - Haunted Ohio III (1994)

Personal Interviews and Correspondence

Note: Although Whitechapel Productions Press, Troy Taylor and all affiliated with this book have carefully researched ass sources to insure the accuracy and completeness of all information contained here, we assume no responsibility for errors, inaccuracies or omissions.

# ABOUT THE AUTHOR: TROY TAYLOR

Troy Taylor is the author of 16 previous books about ghosts and hauntings in America, including HAUNTED ILLINOIS, SPIRITS OF THE CIVIL WAR, THE GHOST HUNTER'S GUIDEBOOK. He is also the editor of GHOSTS OF THE PRAIRIE Magazine, a travel guide to haunted places in America. A number of his articles have been published here and in other ghost-related publications.

Taylor is the president of the "American Ghost Society", a network of ghost hunters, which boasts more than 450 active members in the United States and Canada. The group collects stories of ghost sightings and haunted houses and uses investigative techniques to track down evidence of the supernatural. In addition, he also hosts a National Conference each year in conjunction with the group which usually attracts several hundred ghost enthusiasts from around the country.

Along with writing about ghosts, Taylor is also a public speaker on the subject and has spoken to well over 100 private and public groups on a variety of paranormal subjects. He has appeared in literally dozens of newspaper and magazine articles about ghosts and hauntings. He has also been fortunate enough to be interviewed over 300 times for radio and television broadcasts about the supernatural. He has also appeared in a number of documentary films like AMERICA'S MOST HAUNTED, BEYOND HUMAN SENSES, GHOST WATERS, NIGHT VISITORS and in one feature film, THE ST. FRANCISVILLE EXPERIMENT.

Born and raised in Illinois, Taylor has long had an affinity for "things that go bump in the night" and published his first book HAUNTED DECATUR in 1995. For six years, he was also the host of the popular, and award-winning, "Haunted Decatur" ghost tours of the city for which he sometimes still appears as a guest host. He also hosts the "History & Hauntings Tours" of Alton, Illinois.

In 1996, Taylor married Amy Van Lear, the Managing Director of Whitechapel Press, and they currently reside in a restored 1850's bakery in Alton.

# WHITECHAPEL PRODUCTIONS PRESS
# HISTORY & HAUNTINGS BOOK CO.

Whitechapel Productions Press was founded in Decatur, Illinois in 1993 and is a publisher and purveyor of books on ghosts and hauntings. We also produce the "Ghosts of the Prairie" Magazine and the "Ghosts of the Prairie" Internet web page. We are also the distributors of the "Haunted America Catalog", the largest specialty catalog of ghost books in the United States.

## - OTHER CURRENT TITLES INCLUDE -

HAUNTED ILLINOIS by Troy Taylor (2001) The History & Hauntings of Illinois From Little Egypt to the Windy City! Join the author for the second edition of this best-selling title... with even more ghosts, strange history and haunted places than ever before! A chilling trip into the dark side of the state! $19.95

BEYOND THE GRAVE by Troy Taylor (2001) The History of America's Most Haunted Cemeteries! Join the author for a journey that will span the country in search of tales of ghosts, hauntings, vampires and death! Discover the compelling history of the American Graveyard and the hauntings that have plagued out burial grounds for centuries. $18.95

HAUNTED NEW ORLEANS by Troy Taylor (2000) Ghosts & Hauntings of the Crescent City ..... Haunted New Orleans is one of the most complete books ever written about the ghosts and spirits of what is considered one of America's most haunted cities! $14.95

HAUNTED DECATUR REVISITED BY TROY TAYLOR (2000) Journey back in time with author Troy Taylor as he takes you into the dark side of Central Illinois and reveals the "Land of Lincoln" in way that no other book has done before. We dare you to read this book... you'll never look at the Haunted Heart of Illinois in the same way again! $18.95

THE GHOST HUNTER'S GUIDEBOOK BY TROY TAYLOR (2001) The Essential Handbook for Ghost Research! This must-have guide solves not only the mysteries of finding haunted places, but what to do when you discover them!$ 14.95

SEASON OF THE WITCH by TROY TAYLOR (1999) The Haunted History of the Bell Witch of Tennessee! Explore one of the most famous hauntings in American History... the Infamous Bell Witch of Tennessee! One of the most comprehensive volumes ever written about this fascinating case... and one you won't want to miss! $13.95

SPIRITS OF THE CIVIL WAR BY TROY TAYLOR (1999) A GUIDE TO THE GHOSTS & HAUNTINGS OF AMERICA'S BLOODIEST CONFLICT.... Join author Troy Taylor on a spell-binding journey through the horrific events of the Civil War! Meet the lingering spirits of the past and discover the places where the dead still walk today! $17.95

HAUNTED ALTON: HISTORY & HAUNTINGS OF THE RIVERBEND REGION (2000) Take a journey through the dark side of Alton, Illinois with author and Troy Taylor! Discover the hidden past of the Riverbend Region and its haunted history of death, the Civil War, the Underground Railroad, murder, disease and strange deeds... and learn how the events of yesterday have created the hauntings which still linger in the city today. $14.95

WINDY CITY GHOSTS BY DALE KACZMAREK (2000) TRUE TALES FROM AMERICA'S MOST HAUNTED CITY! Windy City Ghosts is a spell-binding journey to the haunted places of Chicago, America's Most Haunted city! Join author and real-life ghost researcher Dale Kaczmarek as he takes you on a personal trip to the Windy City's most haunted sites, including homes, churches, cemeteries and even Chicago landmarks! $16.95

## UPCOMING TITLES INCLUDE
Haunted History
A Series begins with a look at Historical Ghosts & Mysteries By Troy Taylor

Haunted History: Ghosts of the Prairie
Hauntings Across the Midwest by Troy Taylor

Ghost Lights and Grease Paint
History & Hauntings of American Theaters by Troy Taylor

# Call us Toll~Free for More Information at 1~888~Ghostly

Printed in the United States
62849LVS00002B/4

9 781892 523136